S0-FJD-203

JOHN LOCKE'S MORAL PHILOSOPHY

In Memory of H. B. Acton

JOHN LOCKE'S MORAL PHIL-OSOPHY

JOHN COLMAN

EDINBURGH UNIVERSITY
PRESS

Edinburgh University Press
22 George Square, Edinburgh

Printed in Great Britain by
Redwood Burn Ltd
Trowbridge, Wilts

British Library Cataloguing in Publication Data
Colman, John
John Locke's moral philosophy
1. Locke, John, *1632–1704*—Ethics
2. Ethics
I. Title
170'.92'4 B1295

ISBN 0 85224 445 2

CONTENTS

ACKNOWLEDGEMENTS

A draft of some two-thirds of this study was written during 1976–7 when I was Research Fellow in Philosophy at the University of Western Australia, and I wish to thank that University for the award of the Fellowship. Since then it has been completed during the time I have been teaching at the University of New England, Armidale. My main debt is to Professor S. A. Grave of the University of Western Australia who first taught me the history of philosophy and who has read and commented upon most of my work on Locke. I have also been helped by David Wood and Julius Kovesi. In Armidale I have profited in various ways from discussion with Dr Marion Knowles, Deborah Crisp and Heather Penman. The manuscript was typed with unwavering patience by Mrs Cheryl Chant. I would also like to thank Dr John Anglim of Flinders University for allowing me to see his transcriptions from Locke's papers, and the Reader appointed by Edinburgh University Press for his comments on my final text. Quotations from Locke's papers in the Lovelace Collection are by permission of the Librarian, Bodleian Library, Oxford. The errors which no doubt remain are, of course, my own responsibility.

I first studied Locke as a post-graduate student at the University of Edinburgh. Though little, if anything, of my thesis remains in the present work, I would like to take the opportunity of expressing a very considerable debt to Dr John Jenkins who was then my supervisor. Professor Acton had no hand in any of my work on Locke, but I owe a great deal to the friendship he and Mrs Acton showed me during several very agreeable years spent in Edinburgh.

I also acknowledge generous grants from the University of New England, Armidale, and the Australian Academy of the Humanities.

REFERENCES

The references and quotations from Locke's *Essay* given as, e.g., (I.i.2) are from the P.H. Nidditch edition listed in the bibliography under Locke. The abbreviation *Education* refers to *The Educational Writings* edited by James Axtell; *1st Tract* and *2nd Tract* to Abrams' edition of *Two Tracts*; *1st Treatise* and *2nd Treatise* to Laslett's edition of *Two Treatises*. Aaron & Gibb refers to their edition of Draft A of Locke's *Essay*. Quotations from Draft A are taken from a copy of P.H. Nidditch's edition issued prior to general publication. Details can be found in the bibliography under Locke. The works of Porter and King are listed in the bibliography and abbreviated to the author's name in the references.

INTRODUCTION

1. The programme of John Locke's *Essay Concerning Human Understanding* is 'to enquire into the Original, Certainty, and Extent of humane Knowledge; together, with the Grounds and Degrees of Belief, Opinion, and Assent' (I.i.2). This is to be carried through by a detailed examination of the faculty of human understanding. Locke presents himself as *'an Under-Labourer . . . clearing Ground a little, and removing some of the Rubbish, that lies in the way to Knowledge'* (Epistle to the Reader, p.10). The rubbish he has in mind is the terminology and methodology of what he calls 'the schools'. Only when this is cleared can the true master-builders of knowledge, such as Boyle, Sydenham, Huygens and Newton, work on unimpeded. The famous under-labourer self-image, coupled as it is with mention of the leading contemporary scientists, gives the impression that Locke's enquiry is prompted and guided by a concern for the knowledge of natural phenomena. He has been seen as first and foremost a philosopher of science, intent to provide an epistemological foundation for the scientific discoveries and methodology of his contemporaries in the Royal Society. The remarks pertaining to ethics which appear in many places in the *Essay* have consequently been viewed as merely an intellectual by-product of the pursuit of his major scientific interests.

Yet we have the report of Locke's friend James Tyrrell that the *Essay* grew out of a discussion 'about the Principles of morality and reveal'd Religion'.[1] While Tyrell's information cannot be taken as an authoritative pronouncement on the aim of a book composed over a period of almost twenty years, it does indicate some degree of continuity between the *Essay* and two early works which Locke did not publish, the *Two Tracts on Government* and the *Essays on the Law of Nature*. In these works Locke is directly concerned with ethics, and both conspicuously lack a properly worked out epistemology of morals. We know also that the unfinished paper 'Of Ethick in General' was originally intended as the final chapter of the *Essay*.[2] And the final chapter as it now stands lists ethics as one of the three sciences falling within the compass of human understanding. Moreover, it would be a great mistake to suppose that Locke sees in what we would now call natural science the paradigm of knowledge. On the contrary, he believes that it is in this area in particular that we must confess our ignorance.

It does not take any very close reading of the *Essay* to notice the emphasis Locke places on the paucity of human knowledge:

> He that knows any thing, knows this in the first place, that he need not seek long for Instances of his Ignorance. The meanest, and most obvious Things that come in our way, have dark sides, that the quickest Sight cannot penetrate into. The clearest, and most enlarged Understandings of thinking Men find themselves puzzled, and at a loss, in every Particle of Matter. (IV.iii.22)

Man's ignorance is not a matter of chance, nor can it be dispelled by attending to the correct method for the discovery of truth; it is ineluctably part of the human condition. Locke characterises this condition as 'a State of Mediocrity'. As described in a letter to Denis Grenville, it is a state 'which is not capeable of extreams though on one side or other of this mediocrity there might lie great excellency and perfection' (*Correspondence,* I, p.559). At the back of this notion is the doctrine of the Great Chain of Being, a doctrine which Locke accepts unquestioningly. According to this doctrine everything in existence occupies a position in an hierarchical order. The order, or chain, is conceived as both descending from and ascending to God, the source of all existence and perfection. Locke maintains that observation of the world teaches us that the chain has 'no Chasms or Gaps'; for the various species of things can be seen to differ from one another not absolutely but by degrees. As the descent from man, the highest of all earthly creatures, is visibly 'by easy, steps, and a continued series of Things', it is reasonable to suppose an analogous ascent from man towards the infinite perfection of God. The distance between God and man being far and away greater than that between man and even the meanest of earthly things, it follows that the species of creatures superior to man are much more numerous than those which are inferior (III.vi.12). Thus, human intellectual capacities must be lowly indeed in comparison with the capacities which belong to angels and such like beings (IV.iii.5, 17, 23). The view that the compass of human understanding is virtually limitless is, therefore, not merely erroneous, it expresses a kind of *hubris.*[3]

As there are 'no chasms or gaps' in the Great Chain of Being, it would seem to follow that creatures endowed with just those intellectual capacities possessed by human beings must exist. There would otherwise be an unoccupied place in the order of intellectual beings. But Locke does not conceive the compass of human understanding, and the complementary extent of human ignorance, to be dictated solely by this quasi-aesthetic principle of plenitude. Happiness is our 'great end' (II.xxi.68), and our understanding is suitable to 'our Happiness or Misery, beyond which, we have no concernment to know, or to be' (IV.ii.14). That man constantly seeks after happiness is a major thesis in Locke's moral philosophy. Happiness, however, is not to be construed purely in earthly terms. The complete achievement of happiness is not possible here on earth, but only in Heaven.

With respect of our final happiness even our ignorance is, in a sense, providential. Reflection on how little we can know in this life turns our attention to the supernatural aspect of our destiny:

> as God has . . . given us some certain Knowledge . . . probably, as a Taste of what intellectual Creatures are capable of, to excite in us a Desire and Endeavour after a better State: So in the greatest part of our Concernment, he has afforded us only the twilight . . . of *Probability*, suitable . . . to that State of Mediocrity and Probationership, he has been pleased to place us in here; wherein . . . we might by every day's Experience be made sensible of our short-sightedness and liableness to Error; the Sense whereof might be a constant Admonition to us, to spend the days of this our Pilgrimage with Industry and Care, in the search, and following of that way, which might lead us to a State of greater Perfection. It being highly rational to think . . . That as Men employ those Talents, God has given them here, they shall accordingly receive their Rewards at the close of the day. (IV.xiv.2)

This passage exhibits one of the well-known themes of the *Essay*: that probability, rather than knowledge, must be our guide in most of the affairs of life. It exhibits also another theme which, though it has been less frequently noted, is of no less importance: that men are on a pilgrimage and under probation in this world. It is by their actions that they fulfil, or fail to fulfil, the terms of their probationship and so achieve the reward of heavenly happiness; hence, 'Our Business here is not to know all things, but those which concern our Conduct' (I.i.6). Therefore it is practical knowledge which is the truly valuable part of knowledge. This being so, men have no legitimate grounds for complaint respecting the narrowness of their understanding; for God has given them 'Whatsoever is necessary for the Conveniences of Life, and Information of Vertue . . . [and] it yet secures their great Concernments, that they have Light enough to lead them to the Knowledge of their Maker, and the sight of their own Duties' (I.i.5).[4]

The speculative knowledge Locke deems beyond the compass of human understanding comes under the general heading of metaphysics, or as he calls it, the attempt to fathom 'the vast Ocean of *Being*' (I.i.7).[5] He has specifically in mind attempts to explain the ultimate nature and workings of material substances, or bodies: 'This *way* of getting, and *improving our Knowledge in Substances only by Experience* and History, which is all that the weakness of our Faculties in this State of *Mediocrity*, which we are in this World, can attain to, makes me suspect, that natural Philosophy is not capable of being made a Science' (IV.xii.10). Locke's use of 'science' here and elsewhere in the *Essay* echoes scholastic, rather than modern terminology. It is the anglicised form of '*scientia*', which is itself a translation of Aristotle's '*episteme*'. Briefly, the term denotes the knowledge of a thing through the cause or principle which makes it to be what it is. When we have such knowledge we understand that the thing could not be other than it is. Scientific knowledge in any area will, therefore, consist in a system of apodictic truths.[6]

While scientific knowledge is highly unlikely to be attained in the sphere of physical phenomena, there is, in Locke's opinion, good reason to believe that it can be attained in the sphere of morality:

> since our Faculties are not fitted to penetrate into the internal Fabrick and real Essences of Bodies; but yet plainly discover to us the Being of a GOD, and the Knowledge of our selves, enough to lead us into a full and clear discovery of our Duty, and great Concernment . . . 'tis rational to conclude, that our proper Imployment lies in those Enquiries, and in that sort of Knowledge, which is most suited to our natural Capacities, and carries in it our greatest interest, *i.e.* the Condition of our eternal Estate. Hence I think I may conclude that *Morality* is *the proper Science, and Business of Mankind in general.* (IV.xii.11)

The recommendation of the *Essay*, then, is that we should put aside our ambition of constructing a metaphysics of Nature and turn our intellectual efforts instead in the direction in which they are most likely to meet with success, that is, to the study of morality.

There is no doubt that Locke was considerably influenced by contemporary developments in the study of nature, and the *Essay* is obviously not devoted entirely to the problem of moral knowledge. However, from what has been said so far it should be clear that the 'under-labourer' passage is not indicative of the full range of his intentions in writing the *Essay*. The theory of knowledge developed in that work may be usefully examined in the light of his original interest in ethics. Specifically, the main doctrine of the *Essay* may be considered with a view to determining the grounds upon which

Locke concludes that the study of morality may be made an *a priori* science, or, as he usually puts it, that morality is capable of demonstration.

Locke's significance in the history of philosophy is a sufficient reason for a study of the relationship between his general epistemology and the ethical views expressed in the *Essay* and other of his writings; and a major aim of the present work is to show that, contrary to what has often been supposed, he does produce a consistent moral theory. But, granted a consistent moral theory is to be found in Locke, it is a further question as to the worth of that theory: is it merely an historical curiosity, or does it have aspects which are still of interest to the modern moral philosopher?

The theory which is sketched in the *Two Tracts* and expounded in detail in the *Essays* is essentially theological and legalist. Locke holds that, were there no God or had He not promulgated a law to mankind there would be no such things as moral right and wrong, virtue and vice. He also maintains that conclusions about what actions God commands or forbids can be derived from certain facts concerning human nature and the human situation, and that the ultimate reason a person has for living virtuously is that God's law is backed by sanctions, that in the next life virtue will be rewarded and vice punished. All three propositions would be rejected by many modern philosophers; but the fact that the type of theory Locke puts forward is uncongenial to much current moral thought does not prove it untenable or invalidate his arguments.

A theist – as distinct from a deist – is presumably committed to the view that God takes an interest in human conduct and wills that we perform some kinds of actions and refrain from others. Such a view, however, does not entail the thesis that the moral worth of actions is determined by God's will. It is often claimed that the rightness or wrongness, moral good or evil, of actions cannot consist in their having the relational properties 'being commanded' or 'being forbidden' by God. Rather, God's will with respect to actions is itself determined by non-relational properties of those actions. This thesis is, of course, not atheistic, but it does raise problems for the theist. It means that there is a realm of moral distinctions and values which is independent of God's creative power and which determines His will. It appears, therefore, that God's sovereignty and freedom are limited. If, in defence of divine omnipotence, the theist maintains that the moral worth of actions does depend solely upon God's unconditioned will, he would seem to be committed to the paradox that the difference between right and wrong is purely arbitrary. Locke's theory provides a solution to this problem. Although he holds that without a law set by God there can be no moral right or wrong, he does not suppose the distinction between right and wrong actions to be arbitrary. For Locke the concepts of moral right and wrong are inseparable from the concept of moral obligation, and he analyses the latter in terms of law and a sovereign law-maker. His account of obligation is distinct from his account of the content of the obligations human beings are under in virtue of God's law. The question of content is to be settled by a consideration of the facts of human nature. God might have created human nature differently, in which case there would be a different law appropriate to man's being; but this does not mean that the moral worth which now belongs to human actions depends upon God's arbitrary will.

Locke distinguishes between our having moral obligations and our having reasons to fulfil those obligations. In his opinion the only conclusive reason a person can be given for doing something is that that thing will contribute to his happiness, either positively in that it increases his pleasure or negatively in that it lessens his pain. It is because actions in accord with the demands of morality may have consequences contrary to the individual agent's happiness that Locke maintains the necessity that the moral law be backed by rewards and punishments. In this respect his theory might be thought to conflict with the well-entrenched view that anyone doing the right things for some reason other than its rightness is not properly virtuous. However, Locke may be interpreted as distinguishing between a person's having a reason for adopting the moral point of view and his having a reason, once that point of view is adopted, for acting in one way rather than another. A person who has adopted the moral point of view will see the rightness of an action as a reason for performing it. On the other hand, it is legitimate to ask why one should consider the moral worth of actions in deciding what to do, and in the nature of the case it would seem that the reasons given must be non-moral ones. Locke's answer is that, even if conduct in accord with the moral point of view did render the agent unhappy in this life, it would still be rational for him to live virtuously; for he thereby earns the reward God has ordained for virtue and escapes the punishment due for vice.

Locke, then, develops a coherent theological ethic in a way that meets at least some of the difficulties often thought to be fatal to this type of moral theory. There is another aspect of his thought which is worthy of attention quite apart from the theological and legalist framework of his general theory. This is his account of moral notions. Moral philosophers tend to confine themselves largely to a discussion of the highest level moral notions such as 'right' and 'good'. Locke pays most attention to lower level notions such as 'murder' and 'theft'. He conceives these as complex ideas which, for various reasons, we have constructed, and which we apply in classifying human behaviour. As moral notions are made by us we are capable of knowing exactly how they are constructed. For Locke this means we can discover precisely what simple ideas are combined in each notion. However, he may be interpreted as maintaining that we can completely understand moral notions because we know the human needs and interests which prompt their construction. In our ordinary moral judgments we employ these lower level notions; we do not usually declare a particular action to be simply right or wrong, but right or wrong in virtue of being a specific kind of action, or falling under a specific moral notion. An investigation of these notions and their origins is, therefore, important for an understanding of morality. Further, we suppose that there are areas of conduct which are outside the sphere of morality, that what a person does is often not a proper object of moral appraisal. Concentration on the highest level moral notions can blur the distinction between the morally neutral and the morally significant. For example, if it is accepted that the rightness of an action consists in its contribution to the greatest happiness of the greatest number, it would seem that all voluntary actions fall within the sphere of morality quite independently of the notions under which they fall. And it would also seem that most of what we do will be morally deficient; for in most circumstances we do not choose the action that will maximise the general happiness. Locke holds human happiness to be the end of morality, but he does not apply the greatest happiness principle directly to particular actions and he insists on a sphere of conduct which is morally neutral.

That moral notions are of our own making does not conflict with Locke's main thesis that actions are right or wrong in virtue of a law promulgated by God and binding on all men. The content of this objective law is manifest in the way God has created human nature, and valid moral notions are those arising out of human needs and interests which are universal and permanent. Nevertheless, his account of moral notions and their origin is not essentially connected with his legalism and may be considered as a separate contribution to moral philosophy.

Though he continued to believe in its possibility, Locke did not produce a science of morals. From an examination of his writings and some unpublished manuscripts we can arrive at an idea of the kind of projects he had in mind. The most interesting feature of his demonstration of morality is his attempt to trace the origin of certain moral notions. As a moral philosopher Locke does not belong in the front rank. Nonetheless, a study of what he has to say in the area of ethics is worthwhile for reasons other than the desire to establish for the historical record the fact that he did have a moral philosophy.

I

CONSCIENCE AND THE PROBLEM OF MORAL KNOWLEDGE

Locke's first extended essay in the field of moral philosophy consists of two papers, one in English, the other in Latin, dating from the early 1660s. They were not published by their author and, except for a brief extract in Lord King's *Life of Locke,* remained unknown until they were edited by Philip Abrams as *Two Tracts on Government.* The English work is a detailed refutation of a pamphlet entitled *The Great Question Concerning Things Indifferent in Religious Worship* by one of Locke's Oxford contemporaries, Edward Bagshaw the younger. In the Latin work Locke develops the arguments deployed against Bagshaw at a much more theoretical level.[1]

The *Two Tracts* are Locke's contribution to what at the beginning of the Restoration had once again become 'the Great Question': whether the magistrate, or supreme civil legislator, has authority to impose a set form of dress and ceremony in religious worship.[2] The *Two Tracts* present views on toleration and the extent of civil authority markedly different from those Locke chose to publish in later life. It would, however, be a mistake to dismiss them as a false start to Locke's intellectual career. In them he sets forth the leading idea in his moral philosophy: that there exists a law embodying the moral duties of mankind which, although it ultimately derives from God, is accessible to human reason without the aid of revelation. Although Locke does considerably modify his early position on religious toleration and civil authority in his published works, there are no grounds for supposing that this modification represents a denial of the doctrine of a rationally discernible moral law, or that the doctrine ceases to play a dominant role in his thought. There is a further reason why a study of Locke's moral philosophy should begin with the *Two Tracts*: in them he encounters, and fails to solve, a problem which provides the impetus for much of his subsequent thought in ethics. This is the problem of moral knowledge, a problem which is brought to the fore by the Post-Reformation doctrine of conscience.

1. The question of imposition and individual freedom with respect to the form of religious worship was, as Locke was well aware, a manifestation of a complex and many-featured debate concerning the relation of church to state, the nature of government and finally the nature of the moral order itself. The parties to this debate in the mid-seventeenth century may conveniently be labelled 'Puritan' and 'Anglican'. Initially, the Puritan position may be characterised as stressing the individual agent and the dictates of private conscience, the Anglican position as stressing an objective and universal moral order explicated as a system of laws. The difference between these positions is more a matter of emphasis than of direct opposition. Those for whom conscience is of central importance are not committed to the denial of an objective moral order serving as a measure of conscience, nor are the exponents of such an order committed to the rejection of conscience. Nevertheless, the importance accorded conscience does tend to erode the notion of an objective moral order; for the more conscience is exalted the more difficult it becomes to discern a system of moral standards external to conscience. The drift is thus towards moral subjectivism. Once the finality of what the individual's conscience dictates is asserted, it is tempting to see these dictates not simply as opinions concerning the application of a moral law, but as either infallible intuitions of that law or as autonomous personal legislations.

The *Two Tracts* are Anglican documents in that they maintain the demands of an objective moral order against what Locke considers the dangers inherent in individual liberty of conscience. At the beginning of the first tract Locke briefly expounds a legalist ontology of morals: 'were there no law there would be no moral good or evil, but man would be left to a most entire liberty in all his actions, and could meet with nothing which would not be purely indifferent, and consequently, what doth not lie under the obligation of any law is still indifferent' (*1st Tract,* p.124). All laws derive ultimately from God; either as they are the immediate expression of His will or as they are enjoined by some authority derived from His will. Morality is the immediate expression of God's will, and is both revealed in the Bible and discovered by human reason. But not every action falls within the sphere of morality. There is a broad class of 'indifferent things' which, being neither commanded nor forbidden by God, are morally neutral. With respect to actions within this class, men are naturally free. They may, however, consent to give up their freedom in these things. Indeed they must do this in order for there to be civil society; for a government must have authority to introduce laws within the sphere left free by the moral law (*1st Tract.* pp.124–5).

The problem which engages Locke and Bagshaw arises because men are sometimes mistaken about what properly belongs to the class of indifferent things. In the matter of God's worship some believe themselves bound in conscience to practise one form of ceremony, and some to practise another. Locke and Bagshaw both accept that the formal details of religious worship are morally neutral. Bagshaw, while granting the magistrate authority to legislate concerning indifferent things which have to do with civil life, holds that there is a class of religious indifferent things respecting which man's natural freedom is inalienable. It is, he argues, contrary to the liberty Christians enjoy under the Gospel that the individual should be forced to worship in one way rather than another. Any ceremony, so long as it conforms to the general precept enjoining order and decency, is to be allowed by the magistrate. Locke argues that the magistrate's authority extends over *all* indifferent things and that the conscience of the individual citizen must always be subordinate to the positive law of the state.

Locke's first move is to reject any special category of things indifferent in religion: 'there is no action so indifferent which a scrupulous conscience will not fetch in with some consequence from scripture and make of spiritual concernment' (*1st Tract,* p.140, cf. pp.126–7; cf. *2nd Tract,* p.229). Once it is granted (as it is by Bagshaw) that the magistrate has authority over indifferent things, no argument drawn from the nature of those things can set a limit to that authority. Locke admits that legislation concerning indifferent things may on occasion be harsh and oppressive in that it too narrowly confines the citizens in their use of such things. In this case the magistrate may be guilty before the tribunal of God, but he is not, Locke insists, liable to the censures of man. This guilt in the magistrate 'would not discharge our obedience. And I think 'tis no paradox to affirm that subjects may be obliged to obey those laws which it may be sinful for the magistrate to enact' (*1st Tract,* p.152). In the *Second Tract* Locke goes further. Even if a piece of legislation is contrary to the moral law, the citizen is bound to a passive obedience with respect to that legislation. That is, although the immorality of what the law demands forbids the citizen's active compliance with it, he is still under an obligation not to resist the magistrate, but must suffer the penalties imposed upon him: 'the subject is bound to a passive obedience under any decree of the magistrate whatever, whether just or unjust, nor, on any ground whatsoever may a private citizen oppose the magistrate's decrees by force of arms, though indeed if the matter is unlawful the magistrate sins in commanding' (*2nd Tract*, p.220). In the early 1660s, then, Locke was an advocate of non-resistance no matter what the conditions of government. However, it is important to keep in mind the context in which the *Two Tracts* were written. Locke's absolutist argument is directed against a plea for toleration based on a specific premise: that the conscience of the individual is the ultimate authority in matters of conduct.

Locke uses two main arguments against the thesis that the individual has a claim to religious toleration on the grounds of conscience. The first is an appeal to the supposed consequences of toleration; the second may be termed an appeal to the 'order of things'. The appeal to consequences is the more prominent in the *Two Tracts*. Nevertheless, as Locke admits, it is the second argument on which his case finally rests. These two arguments will be considered in turn.

2. A deeply pessimistic view of mankind pervades the *Two Tracts*. Men are, Locke holds, so in love with their own opinions that they will go to any lengths to maintain them. The majority are not concerned with truth but with the defence of beliefs which are more often than not founded upon ignorance and blind passion. The rational, responsible citizens, who constitute the minority within the state, are thus under constant threat from a multitude ever ready to do violence in the cause of arbitrary prejudices. To limit positive civil law out of deference to private conscience is to open the flood gates to anarchy and to the arbitrary tyranny of the mob. It is impossible for civil law to suit the consciences of each and every man. Even a law providing for toleration would as much offend the consciences of some as a law imposing on conscience would offend others (*1st Tract*, p.140). In short, 'If private men's judgments were the moulds wherein laws were to be cast 'tis a question whether we should have any at all' (*1st Tract*, p.137). The authority of the magistrate is the only barrier strong enough to withstand the incursions of the mob, and the kind of absolutism Locke advocates is far from a high price to pay for the security of society: 'Nor will the largeness of the governor's power appear dangerous or more than necessary if we consider that as occasion requires it is employed upon the multitude that are as impatient of restraint as the sea, and whose tempests and overflows cannot be too well provided against' (*1st Tract*, p.158).[3]

To the modern reader it may well seem that Locke's reaction to Bagshaw is excessive. The latter's claims are modest enough: those who, even though mistakenly, believe certain aspects of religious ceremonial – such as the wearing of a surplice, or the sign of the cross in baptism – to be contrary to the proper worship of God, should not have these things imposed by the civil law; they should be left alone to follow their own conscientious devices. There is nothing in Bagshaw's pamphlet to suggest that the judgments of private conscience are the moulds wherein civil laws are to be cast. It may be true that no hard and fast line can be drawn between religious and civil indifferent things, but it is sufficient for Bagshaw's case that he can cite examples of what he means by religious indifferent things. If it could be shown that toleration of differing religious practices leads to civil unrest, Bagshaw would not deny that ceremonies should come under the jurisdiction of the civil magistrate. But it is repression rather than toleration which prompts civil disorder.[4] Further, Bagshaw argues that religion is essentially a matter of free inner conviction, and that no civil law imposing uniformity can either produce or regulate this conviction. It might be thought that in the *Two Tracts* Locke makes the mistake of supposing that a measure of disorder, in the sense of variety in religious practice, inevitably leads to civil disruption. In his later writings on toleration he comes to the realisation that Church and State are distinct institutions serving different human needs, and that a diversity of religious practice is compatible with the regulations which must be enforced on the citizens of a commonwealth.[5]

However, to dismiss Locke's appeal to consequences is to neglect the historical background of the *Two Tracts.* The Civil War and its aftermath, and specifically the political aspirations of the Puritan Sectaries, are clearly the experiences shaping Locke's intellectual attitudes during this period.[6] The notion of conscience is central to Puritan morality, and 'conscience' was a potent word during the Revolution and amongst the Sects.

The word 'conscience' and its derivatives appear in a great variety of locutions. Conscience itself is often thought to be an internal legislator lodged in the breast of each agent informing him of right and wrong. However, this popular conception is at variance with the grammar of 'conscience'. It would be absurd to say that my conscience tells me that what *you* did is right or that it is wrong. The judgments of conscience concern only the particular actions of the owner of that conscience. They are, therefore, not pieces of moral legislation. If they were, then the judgments of my conscience would apply equally to your actions. Nevertheless, the Puritan view does come close to the notion of conscience as an internal legislator. And, as we shall see later, the term 'conscience' does come to be used for what the eighteenth century called 'the moral sense'.

In the scholastic tradition, the distinction between a general knowledge of right and wrong and the knowledge embodied in the judgments of conscience is explicit. The great Puritan theoreticians of conscience, William Perkins and William Ames, are basically scholastic in their approach to the topic. Perkins writes: 'conscience determines of . . . a mans owne actions. . . . To be certen what another man hath said or done; it is commonly called knowledge: but for a man to be certen what he himselfe hath done or said, that is conscience. Againe, conscience meddles not with generals, onely it deales in particular actions'.[7] Although, as it is characterised here, conscience is just the individual's awareness of his own doings, Perkins is concerned with an awareness of the moral quality of actions. The individual comes to this moral awareness when he judges his own actions in the light of general moral principles. Thus, judgments of conscience apply to particular actions and presuppose principles or laws. Such judgments, therefore, cannot be the source of moral principles. However, our moral judgments of the conduct of others equally presuppose general moral principles. Why then cannot my conscience be said to pass judgment upon your actions as well as my own?

The reason there should be this logical restriction on the scope of judgments of conscience becomes clearer when we consider the phenomenon of a conflict between conscience and desire. This conflict consists of our conscience disposing us to act in one way while our desires dispose us to act in a contrary way. But such conflict can occur only because our acceptance of the principles we apply in judgments of conscience is not a mere academic assent, but a conviction which manifests itself in a disposition to act in accord with those principles.[8] A person who pays lip-service to a moral principle does assent to it, but it is only when the principle gains a purchase on his conduct that he can be said to take it over as a moral conviction, or a principle which he holds *conscientiously*. What you do may be contrary to what I, given my moral convictions, judge that you ought to do, but, as my convictions logically cannot have a purchase on your conduct, there can be no conflict between my conscience and your conduct. It is because judgments of conscience are made against the background of conflict, or at least opposition, that they have to do solely with the actions of the person making the judgment. When I follow the prompting of my desires against the disposition which manifests my moral conviction, my conscience condemns me. Of course, my moral convictions may win out in this conflict, in which case my conscience will pass an approving judgment. This is not to say that the moral convictions of others never enter into the conflict which brings conscience into play. The conscientious objector is typically a person whose moral convictions are in opposition to what others endeavour to persuade him he morally ought to do. Such a person acts in accordance with his convictions against forces designed to dispose him to act in a contrary manner. The important point is that in the absence of some conflict of dispositions, conscience has no role.[9] When I act in accord with my moral convictions without having any contrary desires and without meeting opposition from others, conscience can have nothing to say in the matter.

The mistaken view of conscience as an internal legislator arises, at least in part, because we talk of consulting our consciences not only when we make moral assessments of our own past conduct, but also when we are deciding what to do in a given situation. But even in the latter case, I do not require my conscience to inform me of what I ought to do: my moral convictions tell me this. What I am doing is reminding myself that there is a disagreement between certain of my moral convictions and what I desire or am inclined to do in the situation. Further, as they are general principles, my moral convictions are the basis upon which I judge the rectitude of what you do. But I cannot be said to consult my conscience when I pass these judgments. Such consultation is occasioned only by the conflict between a disposition to act which manifests one's moral convictions and a contrary disposition manifesting one's desires; and logically neither my desires nor my moral convictions can be manifested in your dispositions.

A judgment of conscience, then, is private to the individual in that it is a judgment passed by the individual respecting his own conduct. With this the Puritans would agree. However, there is a point at which the Puritan account does enlarge the sphere of conscience: it is maintained that a correctly informed conscience is supreme over the positive enactments of earthly institutions. As Perkins writes: 'the courts of men and their authoritie are under conscience. For God in the heart of every man hath erected a tribunal seate, and in his stead he hath placed neither Saint or Angell, nor any other creature whatsoever, but conscience it selfe, who therefore is the highest judge that is or can be under God'.[10] Perkins is not retracting his dictum that 'conscience meddles not with generals'. The point he wishes to make is that the principles to be applied in judgments of conscience, or the laws which bind conscience, are the laws of God, not the enactments of any civil or ecclesiastical authority. He adds that 'wholesome lawes' made by men for the good of the community do bind the individual. They do not bind of their own force but by virtue of God's commanding men to be subject to civil authority. Nonetheless, the implications of Perkins' doctrine are plain. It is up to the individual to determine whether or not a given positive law is wholesome. How can he do this except by comparison with his own *knowledge* of the moral law? Strictly, conscience does not have a legislative function, but only a judicial one; but if conscience is to perform its function properly it must be informed of what morality demands. However, each individual's moral convictions are what he takes to be the demands of morality. In effect, it is these convictions which Perkins sets above the laws of civil and ecclesiastical institutions.

The revolutionary tenor of the doctrine of the supremacy of conscience is reinforced when it is connected with the doctrine of predestination, or election. Conscience may be a judgment made at the moment of moral decision or it may be a judgment a man passes on his past conduct and his spiritual state. In the latter case it is a judgment not merely of the moral rectitude of what has been done, but of the kind of obedience paid to the moral law. The elect are blessed with a regenerate conscience, and this means they obey God in a specific manner. Those whom God chooses enjoy 'Christian liberty'; for them the law of God becomes an internal principle guiding their conduct, just as it was for Adam in his integrity. That is, obedience is no longer a matter of being coerced contrary to inclination, but is given freely and with alacrity. In Perkins' words, 'As a regenerate conscience gives testimonie of oure newe obedience, so it doth also by certaine sweete motions stirre men forward to performe the same'.[11] For the unregenerate the law remains an alien, coercive force. There are, therefore, two types of human being: the elect serving God in freedom and the unregenerate who are, and must be, under coercion. Political institutions are of their nature coercive, being established by God to curb the havoc in human relations wrought by Adam's Fall. The Church, as the body of the elect, is the realm of freedom. This realm of freedom may be conceived in purely spiritual or other-wordly terms, in which case, the conviction that one is of the elect carries no implications for social action. There is, however, a strong tendency in Puritan thought to view Christian liberty as an embodiment of God's plan for this world. The elect are not simply those who are going to inherit heaven, but God's chosen instruments for reshaping the earth.[12]

Opinions as to the pattern after which God intends society to be reformed did, in the seventeenth century, vary over a wide spectrum, from the Presbyterian ideal of a church-dominated state after the godly and gloomy model of Calvin's Geneva to millennarian hopes for Christ's personal reign upon earth. But, so long as mankind is seen as divided into the elect and the unregenerate, it is inevitable that the reformation of society should involve some kind of dictatorship. Even though the judgments of a man's conscience do not announce what men in general ought to do, those possessed of a regenerate conscience must think of themselves as an elite vis-à-vis the unregenerate. If they conceive their election in terms of a divine mandate to reshape society, their conscience will prompt them to do things which have considerable consequences for others. The general moral convictions of the elect are exact reflections of the moral law of God. But more than this, the elect have received a special command to impose the law of God upon society at large, a task they are in conscience bound to attempt. However, moral convictions may differ from individual to individual. How are the truly elect to be distinguished from those who falsely believe themselves to be elect? Here Puritanism is at its most uncompromisingly individualistic. The individual becomes aware of election in the experience of conversion, a kind of infusion of God's grace. Once this experience is had nothing can shake his assurance, for one cannot lapse from election. The conviction of election is therefore necessarily arrived at privately and is infallible knowledge. To have a regenerate conscience is to be one of the elect.[13] Thus, the easy conformity with one's own moral convictions is a sure sign of spiritual status as one of the elect, and one's spiritual status may in turn be seen as involving a divine call to reshape society in accord with one's moral convictions.

Read against this historical background, Locke's rejection of Bagshaw's distinction between civil and religious indifferent things, and the strength of his reaction against the plea for religious toleration on the grounds of conscience, is at least understandable. His opposition is not dictated by a regard for uniformity, but by a fear of those who see themselves conscientiously bound to impose their beliefs upon others:

> if men would suffer one another to go to heaven every one his one way, and not out of a fond conceit of themselves pretend to greater knowledge and care of another's soul and eternal concernments than he himself... our author's doctrine of toleration might promote a quiet in the world. . . . But it is like to produce far different effects among a people that are ready to conclude God dishonoured upon every small deviation from that way of his worship which either education or interest hath made sacred to them and that therefore they ought to vindicate the cause of God with swords in their hands. (*1st Tract*, p.161)[14]

Yet, in so far as Locke rests his case on the appeal to consequences, his debate with Bagshaw must end in a stalemate. While Locke depicts the danger of mob rule and reminds his readers of the Fifth Monarchy Men, the advocates of toleration depict, with equal force, the danger of a tyrannical magistrate.[15] However, Locke does disclaim any final reliance on the appeal to consequences: 'Principles ought to be of unalterable verity and therefore are not to be established upon our uncertain and commonly partial judgment of their consequences.... The question being of lawful or unlawful we are to be judged by some law' (*1st Tract*, p.155). But it is only in the *Second Tract* that Locke attempts to carry through his argument from the 'order of things'.

3. In the *Second Tract* Locke distinguishes four kinds of law: divine, human, fraternal and private law. This, he says, is not the only division possible, but is the one which best suits his purpose.[16] These laws form a strict hierarchy, each having as its legitimate sphere of influence the area left free by the law immediately above it. Divine law is the rule of morals. As it is made known by revelation it is positive law; as it is discovered by reason it is the law of nature. By human law Locke means the positive law of civil society (though he does include the commands of parents to children under this heading). The divine law and the enactments of human law, then, constitute the objective norms governing man as a moral being and a citizen. The fraternal law, or law of charity, originates in the Pauline injunction against scandalising a 'weak brother'.[17] Private law is twofold: the law of contract and the law of conscience. The former is the law a man places himself under when, by a promise or a vow, he binds himself to the performance of that which is in itself indifferent. The latter Locke defines as 'that fundamental judgment of the practical intellect concerning any possible truth of a moral proposition about things to be done in life' (*2nd Tract*, p.225).

Each of the laws below the divine law has obligatory force only in a derivative sense, for, 'no other law immediately and of itself binds the conscience of men except for the divine, since the others do not bind men by virtue of their own innate force but by virtue of some divine precept on which they are grounded; nor are we bound to obey magistrates for any other reason than that the Lord has commanded it' (*2nd Tract*, p.226). The civil magistrate must be competent to legislate in the sphere of indifferent things for two reasons. First, although the moral law set by God is complete, its precepts are not meant to cover all the contingencies which arise in the life of civil society. Therefore, 'God left many indifferent things untrammelled by his laws and handed them to his deputy the magistrate as fit material for civil government, which, as occasion should demand coud be commanded or prohibited, and by the wise regulation of which the welfare of the commonwealth could be provided for' (*2nd Tract*, p.223). Secondly, if all indifferent things were outside the competence of the magistrate there could be no such thing as civil authority, for the magistrate would be entitled to do nothing more than reiterate the moral law, and this any private citizen may do (*2nd Tract*, p.228). Each law having as its proper province the things left free by the laws above, no law can legitimately claim to abrogate another which is above it in the hierarchy. Conscience, being the bottom-most law, cannot have a claim against human law. To suppose otherwise is to overthrow the 'order of things':

> the subordination of these laws one to another is such that an inferior law cannot in any way remove or repudiate the obligation and authority of a superior. For this would be to overturn the order of things and subject master to servant, to establish not order and government in the world but anarchy, and to own no other legislator than the meanest and most ignorant member of the mob. To appeal from the divine tribunal to man is not lawful, nor can a subject's vow or a private error of conscience nullify the edicts of the magistrate, for, if this is once granted, discipline will be everywhere at an end, all law will collapse, all authority will vanish from the earth and, the seemly order of affairs being convulsed and the frame of government dissolved, each would be his own Lawmaker and his own God. (*2nd Tract*, pp.226–7)

What Locke envisages in this passage is not simply the dissolution of society consequent upon individuals following their own prejudices in defiance of the moral and civil law; it is the dissolution of morality itself. To preach the supremacy of conscience is, Locke holds, to replace the objective moral law and its one universal legislator by a tangle of subjective laws; it is to make each individual 'his own Law-maker and his own God'.

In insisting on the objectivity and universality of the moral law, Locke does not differ from writers such as Perkins and Ames. For them a judgment of conscience is the conclusion of a practical syllogism, the major premise of which is a general moral principle. These principles are known in what is termed *synteresis* (or *synderesis* – both spellings are used), a concept taken over from Scholasticism. According to Ames: 'That *Synteresis* out of which the proposition of this syllogisme or the Law of Conscience is taken, is most properly a habit of the understanding, by which we doe assent unto the principles of *morall actions*, that is, such actions as our duty'.[18]

Synteresis, as Ames points out, is not to be confused with conscience. Rather, it is our grasp of the moral principles, or laws, we apply in judgments of conscience. Nor is there any suggestion that *synteresis* is a form of self-legislation. The principles grasped in *synteresis* are taken over by the individual as moral convictions, and his acceptance of them is therefore manifested in a disposition to act in accordance with them. The principles themselves, however, are quite independent of the individual.[19] As there is no one so desperately wicked as to be void of all inclination towards moral goodness, some traces of *synteresis* are to be found in all men. Nevertheless, Perkins and Ames hold that the Fall not only destroyed man's ability to pay proper obedience to the moral law, but also that it destroyed his ability to know the law properly. The former disability can be rectified only by grace, the latter by revelation.[20] It follows that not all men can acquire complete knowledge of the moral law, but only those acquainted with the Judaeo–Christian scriptures. But it is notorious that accounts of what Scripture demands vary from one interpreter to another, and it is essential to the Protestant rejection of Rome's *magisterium* that there is no instituted authority competent to pronounce upon rival interpretations. The way is then open for the view that the private judgment of the individual decides what the law demands.[21]

The doctrine that conscience – in the sense of the moral convictions consulted in judgments of conscience – has a higher authority than the enactments of the civil magistrate is, of course, not in itself a form of moral subjectivism. In one sense it means only that morality takes precedence over the positive laws of the state, and that the individual may judge the rectitude of those laws. The advocates of the supremacy of conscience do not maintain that civil laws are morally good or evil relative to the moral convictions of the individual citizens. Nevertheless, the doctrine does drift towards subjectivism in so far as it provides no place for a criterion of moral truth external to personal conviction. The metaphor which Perkins and many other writers use, of a tribunal set up by God in the heart of every man, suggests that each of us has been granted, seemingly at least, an infallible grasp of the moral principles to be applied in judgments of conscience.

In the face of conflicting judgments of conscience it may be maintained that only the regenerate conscience is truly informed of the moral law. The problem then becomes one of identifying the regenerate conscience. It may also be maintained that the law is revealed in Scripture for all to read (even if the unregenerate cannot properly obey it). The problem then becomes one of identifying the correct scriptural reading. In both cases there would appear to be no criterion available other than personal conviction.

Locke characterises conscience in two ways: first, it is 'nothing but an opinion of the truth of any practical position, which may concern any actions as well moral as religious, civil as ecclesiastical' (*1st Tract*, p.138). Secondly, it is for the individual the ultimate moral authority, for 'God implanted the light of nature in our hearts and willed that there should be an inner legislator (in effect) constantly present in us whose edicts it should not be lawful for us to transgress even a nail's breadth' (*2nd Tract*, p.225). As an opinion of what ought to be done, conscience may be true or false. In Locke's hierarchy of laws the only law which binds of its own force is the divine law. A person's moral convictions are, therefore, binding only when they are true reflections of the content of the divine law: we cannot be objectively and directly bound in conscience with respect to anything left indifferent by the divine law. However, as it is a precept of the divine law that the civil magistrate is to be obeyed, and as the proper province of human law is that which is left indifferent by divine law, civil legislation does create an objective moral obligation with respect to indifferent things, even though such obligation is indirect or derivative. So long as the enactments of the civil magistrate are not contrary to the precepts of the divine law there can be no objective clash between the subject's moral and civil obligations. There can, however, be a clash between such enactments and the subject's moral convictions, and Locke is forced to admit that an erroneous conscience, or conscientiously held moral opinion which is false, does bind the individual.

Locke's second characterisation of conscience recalls the passage from Perkins quoted earlier, but he is far from suggesting any infallible status for the principles applied in judgments of conscience. He is, as the context makes plain, thinking of an erroneous conscience: that of the individual who believes certain forms of religious ceremony, which are in fact indifferent according to the divine law, to be forbidden by that law. As the individual cannot act contrary to this belief without doing wrong in his own eyes, the indifferent thing becomes wrong for him. That is, by his mistaken belief he restricts the freedom he in actual fact enjoys under the divine law. Now a person can hold an opinion and yet concede that the opinion is open to doubt; he believes it, he does not claim to know it. But a conscientiously held opinion is one concerning which the individual 'digs in his heels'; it is something he claims to be settled and certain.[22] It is because of this that what Locke calls the law of conscience must present itself to the individual as having final authority. It is a tautology that a person cannot act against his conscience without being convinced that he has acted wrongly. In this sense even an erroneous conscience carries an obligation, but the obligation is subjective.

Locke treats the law of conscience as a 'private law' on all fours with the law of contract. The latter is private in that, while the contract creates a new obligation, it is an obligation which applies only to those who are party to the contract. The sphere within which contracts can properly be entered into is limited to those things left indifferent by both divine and human law. If a man contracts to do that which he is already under a moral or civil obligation to do, he merely reiterates and does not create an obligation; if he contracts to do that which is forbidden by either law, the contractual obligation is null and void. Locke holds that an erroneous conscience concerning things indifferent lays a further obligation on the individual. Objectively he is free to do, or not do, the indifferent thing he thinks to be morally forbidden or commanded. Nevertheless, 'our liberty in indifferent things is so insecure and so bound up with the opinion of everyone else that it may be taken as certain that we do indeed lack the liberty which we *think we lack*' (*2nd Tract*, p.225). That is, the individual's error creates a new obligation *for him*.

However, this account of the binding force of the individual's moral convictions clearly will not do, for Locke completely disregards the point of view of the conscientious objector. A person entering into a contract does see himself as imposing a private obligation with respect to something in itself indifferent. Thus, by the act of contracting he knowingly restricts his own freedom. But the conscientious person does not see himself as creating a new obligation: he accepts his moral opinions as reflecting the demands of morality, and he takes it that these demands apply not only to himself but to everyone else. If he subsequently comes to reject some of his moral opinions, he will agree that in conscientiously abiding by them he was placing a private restriction on himself with respect to things really indifferent. But, so long as he holds his opinions conscientiously, he logically cannot see them as erroneous. Therefore, when the individual finds his conscientiously held opinions to be opposed to the law of the state, it is the civil law, and not his own opinions, which he sees as conflicting with the moral law.

Locke does accept the 'fraternal law', in which God (through the mouth of St Paul) commands 'that things indifferent and altogether lawful should be refrained from if there is any fear that a brother may be offended by that liberty' (*2nd Tract*, p.224). But he understands this law as, in practice, demanding very little. In the first place, so far as the magistrate is concerned, the fraternal law forbids him to present his legislation concerning indifferent things as a piece of divine law binding the conscience by its own force. Secondly, the fraternal law enjoins us not to slight or undervalue those brethren who are scrupulous with respect to things which are in fact indifferent. The magistrate, Locke points out, may fully obey this law concerning weak brethren 'whilst he makes laws for their observance, he may pity those whom he punishes, nor in his thoughts condemn them because not so strong in the faith as others' (*1st Tract*, p.139). The only consolation Locke allows the individual who is conscientiously opposed to a civil law derives from the distinction between 'material' and 'formal' obligation. A civil law binds materially when it does no more than reiterate a moral precept. As the subject matter of such a law is a thing in itself demanded by morality, the law's obligatory force is identical with that of the divine law. But a piece of legislation concerning things morally indifferent binds only formally; that is, by virtue of the moral precept that magistrates are to be obeyed. The subject must still conform to the law, but he is free to judge what the law enjoins to be in itself morally neutral. He need not, therefore, think of himself as under a material obligation respecting these demands of human law. It is on the basis of this distinction that Locke provides for liberty of conscience. So long as the magistrate does not present his legislation concerning indifferent things as positive announcements of the divine law, the subject's freedom of judgment (although not his freedom of action) with respect to those things is unimpaired (*2nd Tract*, pp. 238–9).[23] But this is hardly likely to satisfy anyone who firmly believes that what the magistrate demands is not indifferent, but morally forbidden, and that therefore he is under a material obligation to reject it.[24]

In his notion of a hierarchy of laws and his appeal to the order of things manifested in that hierarchy, Locke assumes the ready availability of knowledge of the moral law. He takes it for granted that those whose reason is not clouded by passion or prejudice will see that the magistrate must have supreme authority:

> mankind was by the light of nature and their own conveniences sufficiently instructed in the necessity of laws and government and a magistrate with power over them . . . the light of reason and nature of government itself making evident that in all societies it is unavoidably necessary that the supreme power (wherever seated in one or more) must be still supreme, i.e. have a full and unlimited power over all indifferent things and actions within the bounds of that society. (*1st Tract*, p.172)

That the magistrate's authority extends over all indifferent things is disputed by writers such as Bagshaw. However, even if Locke is granted this, it is beside the real point at issue. The question is what things really are bound by the divine law and what things really are left indifferent? Unless this can be answered, talk of a hierarchy of laws fixed in the order of things is mere rhetoric. Locke would appear to place the magistrate in a privileged epistemological position. We are told that the 'private *error* of conscience' cannot be allowed to nullify the edicts of the magistrate. This may be so, but why should it not be the edicts of the magistrate which are in error when there is a clash between the moral convictions of the individual and the law of the state?

4. As Abrams points out, Locke's arguments throughout the *Two Tracts* assume three things: that there is a universal moral law established by God and accessible to human reason; that there is a class of things left indifferent by that law; and that the relation between conscience and that law can be demonstrated (*Two Tracts*, p.37). For Locke's purposes the assumption of fundamental importance is the first one. With respect to its content the moral law coincides with the morality of the Bible, but it is also the law of nature accessible to reason without the aid of revelation. The controversy concerning indifferent things arose because Scripture was appealed to as the source of moral knowledge. Therefore, if the controversy is to be resolved in the direction Locke proposes, moral knowledge must be founded in something other than revelation, that is, in the law of nature.

That the order of the universe is knowable and explicable in terms of laws informing all of creation, and that among these laws is the law of nature governing the conduct of mankind, is the main axiom of Christian humanism. This humanism found its most complete expression in St Thomas Aquinas' synthesis of faith and reason, a synthesis which was carried over into Anglicanism, pre-eminently by Richard Hooker. In his defence of Christian humanism against Puritan Bibliolatory, Hooker appeals to the 'general and perpetual voice of men [which] is as the sentence of God himself. For that which all men have at all times learned, Nature herself must needs have taught'. Eccentric moral views and practices he ascribes to 'lewd and wicked custom' grown so strong as to 'smother the light of natural understanding'.[25] But Hooker, writing near the end of the sixteenth century, was among the last of those who could with any conviction appeal to a common moral knowledge shared by all mankind. By the 1660s, as the fact of the continuing controversy over indifferent things indicates, the 'general and perpetual voice of men' could no longer be heard. It is significant that in his one major work devoted to moral theory Locke takes pains to demolish the view that the general consent of men is a proper guide to what the moral law demands. In the fifth of the *Essays on the Law of Nature* he writes:

> 'The voice of the people is the voice of God.' Surely, we have been taught by a most unhappy lesson how doubtful, how fallacious this maxim is. . . . Indeed, if we should listen to this voice as if it were the herald of a divine law, we should hardly believe that there was any God at all. (*Essays*, p.161)

The crisis in the epistemology of morals (and indeed the general epistemological crisis) which faced thinkers in the seventeenth century owes its origins in large part to the Reformation. The assumption that an error of conscience is always easy to indicate, and thus to rectify, is understandable, and perhaps psychologically inevitable, when in the background stands an institution accepted as possessing an infallible *magisterium* in faith and morality. St Thomas Aquinas, for example, recognises the binding force of an erroneous conscience even when it dictates something directly contrary to the moral law. He concludes nonetheless that in such a case the agent will be blameworthy whichever way he acts, for ignorance of the moral law is always in some degree voluntary and therefore culpable.[26] But Protestantism, in so far as it shifts authority from the institution of the Church to the written word of the Bible, lacks a reply to the conscientious dissenter. It soon became evident that without an authoritative interpretation, the Bible is more a source of diversity than a unity of belief.

Moral scepticism might be thought the most obvious reaction to a proliferation of conflicting moral beliefs. In the absence of any mark whereby a true conscience can be distinguished from one which is erroneous there can be no moral knowledge, but only varieties of moral opinion each with an equal claim to correctness and an equal liability to error. It is to be noted that this scepticism presupposes the existence of objective moral norms. The sceptic takes it for granted that moral opinions are either true or false, their truth or falsity depending on an external standard; his thesis is that there is no way of telling of any given opinion whether it is true or false.[27] Such scepticism is, however, quite incompatible with the natural law doctrine Locke adopts. This law, being set over men to govern their conduct, must be knowable by men. As Aquinas puts it; 'law is laid on subjects to serve as a rule and measure. This means that it has to be brought to bear on them. Hence to have binding force, which is an essential property of a law, it has to be applied to the people it is meant to direct. This application comes about when their attention is drawn to it by the fact of promulgation'.[28] Strictly speaking, an unknowable law of nature is a contradiction in terms. The problem raised by conscience is, then, not simply a problem in moral epistemology. Here epistemology is bound up with ontology. For, unless knowledge of the law of nature can be established, it is in vain to claim that such a law exists.

There are in fact several possible responses to this crisis in the epistemology of morals. In the first place it might be accepted that conscience is both supreme as a moral arbiter and ineluctably subjective. There being no means of telling a true from an erroneous conscience, the notion of objective truth and falsity in moral matters should be dropped. The individual's moral convictions are 'true' for him. A moral disagreement between two individuals is a clash of conflicting moral 'truths'. As this response denies the existence of any objective realm of moral distinctions it is not a form of moral scepticism, but of moral subjectivism, and as such is vulnerable to a serious objection. The major premise in this argument for subjectivism is the binding force of conscience, for it is because conscience (either in the broad sense of conscientiously held beliefs or in the sense of particular judgments based on those beliefs) is taken as binding that it is considered the final moral guide. However, it may be argued that, unless there is some objective moral truth which can inform a person's conscience, there are no grounds for taking conscience as binding. In other words, if subjectivism is correct, the binding force of conscience is an illusion. Therefore, to accept the subjectivist conclusion is to reject the premise upon which it is based. A second response consists in a downgrading of conscience. To elevate private conscience above civil law is to overthrow the principles of order and authority necessary for the existence of civil society. As the only alternative to civil society is anarchy, any government is better than none. Therefore, the individual must accept the civil law as overriding his private moral convictions. It might seem that Locke approaches this pragmatic solution in his argument from consequences. Nonetheless, he is anxious that government should have not merely a pragmatic justification, but a moral foundation in the divine law. Finally, there remains the attempt to meet the crisis head-on, and to establish moral knowledge in a new, unshakable foundation. This is Locke's response.

5. The opinions maintained in the *Two Tracts* are markedly different from those Locke chose to publish in the *Epistola de Tolerantia* and the *Two Treatises of Government.* In the early work he argues

for the civil magistrate's authority over religious worship and for passive obedience on the citizens' part, even in the face of unjust laws. In the *Epistola* (and in the earlier, unpublished *Essay Concerning Toleration*[29]) he sharply divides the sphere of civil authority from that of religious authority. He agrees with Bagshaw that since what constitutes an acceptable worship of God is a matter of personal conviction no set form of religious ceremony or belief can be legitimately imposed by the state. In the *Second Treatise* he argues the people's right to rebellion should the government betray its trust.

Certainly Locke's thought develops after the *Two Tracts*, but this is not to say that he abandons the basic concepts he deploys in his early work. The conception of morality as a matter of law remains, and the law of nature plays a dominant role in the *Second Treatise*. Other concepts, such as the contract theory of government, which are merely mentioned in the *Two Tracts*, later attain far more importance. Neither does Locke retract his original thesis that no opinion has a claim to toleration merely on the ground that it is conscientiously held, and that the magistrate has a right to legislate concerning indifferent things when such legislation is for the good of the community. There is no need here to examine Locke's mature views on toleration and the extent of civil authority.[30] Perhaps the simplest explanation of the differences between his early and later views is not that he tacitly abandoned his original conceptual apparatus, but that the historical circumstances changed. 'Besides the submission I have for *authority*', Locke writes in the preface to the *First Tract*, 'I have no less a love of *liberty* without which a *man* shall find himself less happy than a *beast*' (*1st Tract*, p.120). At the end of the Commonwealth Locke saw the Sectaries as posing the main threat to liberty. But subsequent to the Restoration the Sects withered away or declined into passive non-conformity. As the 1660s progressed Locke came to see the threat no longer as originating with the people, but with the tyrannical authority of Stuart government. In the *Two Tracts* Locke apologises for the largeness of the power he grants the civil magistrate on the ground that it is necessary to restrain the rebellious multitude, 'that are as impatient of restraint as the sea'. In the *Second Treatise* he writes of the people that they 'are not . . . easily got out of their old Forms. . . . They are hardly to be prevailed with to amend the acknowledg'd Faults, in the Frame they have been accustom'd to. And if there be any Original defects, or adventitious ones introduced by time, or corruption; 'tis not an easie thing to get them changed, even when all the World sees there is an opportunity for it' (*2nd Treatise*, §223). The change is in the times rather than in Locke's basic philosophical position.

In the *Two Tracts* Locke complacently assumes that knowledge of the content of the law of nature is readily available, at least to all those whose understandings are not clouded by totally irrational prejudice. In the *Essays on the Law of Nature,* written some few years later, he begins the task of establishing the foundations of moral knowledge. And the *Essays* serve as an introduction to the much more ambitious epistemological programme of *An Essay Concerning Human Understanding.*

II

LAW AND OBLIGATION

The *Essays on the Law of Nature* were written by Locke in the early 1660s and probably formed the substance of a lecture series given during his term as Censor of Moral Philosophy at Christ Church in 1664. Like the *Two Tracts*, the work remained in manuscript until recently.[1] Each of the eight essays considers a specific question and maintains an affirmative or a negative answer. Locke endeavours to prove 1) that there is a law of nature; 2) that moral obligation under that law extends to all men at all times; 3) that the law is neither innate nor known from the general consent of men, but is discovered by reason working on material supplied by the senses; 4) that the law is not founded on the self-interest of the individual. In short, in the *Essays* Locke argues for, and explicates in detail, the natural law ethic which he deploys without argument in the *Two Tracts*.

1. *Essay I* presents a number of arguments for the existence of the law of nature. Locke explicitly takes over the first from Aristotle: all things are designed to fulfil some function and, as man's distinguishing characteristic is his rationality, it follows that his function is to act in accordance with reason. Moreover, besides positive laws which differ from society to society, we believe there are laws which have validity everywhere; these must constitute the universal law of nature.[2] That many men act as if there were no law of nature or disagree as to what the law demands does not cast doubt on its existence, for there are many factors which can hinder the operation of reason in the individual. In any case, a sincere and rational disagreement as to the content of the law only goes to show that there is some law concerning which men can disagree. The second argument derives from 'the sting of conscience'. Even men who refuse to acknowledge themselves bound by positive laws accuse themselves of wrong-doing. The law they acknowledge in their conscience, as it is not positive, must be the law of nature. Thirdly, each thing in the universe operates according to a law appropriate to its nature. In a passage which strongly echoes Hooker, Locke defines law as 'that which prescribes to every thing the form and manner and measure of

working' (*Essays,* p.117).[3] It would be contrary to God's wisdom for Him to create man alone of all things without some function in the scheme of the universe. Therefore, there must be a law which prescribes man's proper function. Fourthly, were there no law of nature there could be no civil society, for society depends on obedience to a constituted civil authority and on the fulfilment of contracts. Without the law of nature the government of society would be completely arbitrary, the ruler being free to legislate as he pleased. Although he could perhaps compel obedience by brute force, he could not impose any obligation; 'positive civil laws are not binding by their own nature or force or in any other way than in virtue of the law of nature, which orders obedience to superiors and the keeping of public peace' (*Essays,* p.119). As to the fulfilment of contracts, 'it is not to be expected that a man would abide by a compact because he has promised it, when better terms are offered elsewhere, unless the obligation to keep promises was derived from nature, and not from human will' (ibid.). Finally, the law of nature is necessary if terms such as 'virtue', 'vice', 'moral rewards and punishment' are to have meaning:

> there is no fault, no guilt, where there is no law. Everything would have to depend on human will, and, since there would be nothing to demand dutiful action, it seems that men would not be bound to do anything but what utility or pleasure might recommend, or what a blind and lawless impulse might happen perchance to fasten on. The terms 'upright' and 'virtuous' would disappear as meaningless or be nothing at all but empty names. (*Essays,* pp.119–21)

The major difficulty with these arguments is that they assume what they purport to prove. The second and fifth of the arguments are really no more than a statement of Locke's fundamental thesis that morality must be a matter of law. The fourth embodies the view we have already come across in the *Two Tracts,* that civil authority has a moral foundation in the divine law. The first and third assume that the universe has a teleological structure which may be explicated in terms of laws. These 'proofs' are of interest mainly because of the light they throw on Locke's conception of the law of nature.

Seemingly there is an ambiguity to Locke's conception of law. By 'law' he sometimes appears to mean the rules according to which things, including men, actually operate. This conception seems best suited to his teleological view of the universe. At other times, however, the law of nature is resented as binding men to behave in a manner contrary to their natural inclination. Thus Locke supposes that, were it not for the law of nature, no man would keep a promise when breaking it was more to his advantage, and that all men would pursue nothing but their own pleasure. At least since the publication of John Stuart Mill's essay 'Nature', it has been commonplace to dismiss the natural law theory of morality as springing from a naive confusion. The word 'nature' refers to the sum total of properties and capacities which things in fact have. Hence, a law of nature properly so called is nothing more than a description of regularities of behaviour exhibited by things.[4] As such, it is quite different from a law which places men under an obligation to behave in specific ways. No description of how men in fact behave can say anything about how they ought to behave; vice is just as natural as virtue. But Locke, it would appear, wants the law of nature to both describe and prescribe human conduct. He cannot have it both ways. A law which describes carries no obligation; one which prescribes is not a law of nature.

However, it would be over hasty to conclude that, because Locke talks of morality in terms of the law of nature, he has fallen into the confusion to which Mill draws attention. As we shall see, Locke does maintain that the law of nature is rooted in human nature. Yet, when he talks of the law as natural, he is usually not thinking of the facts of human nature as supplying the norms of moral conduct. What he does have in mind is the mode of cognition of moral norms. As stated in the *Two Tracts,* the moral law is the divine law of God. God has made this law known to us in two ways. He has revealed it in the Scriptures, and as it is known by revelation it is a positive law. But He has also created human beings such that the law is accessible to their natural reason, and it is in this sense that it is called the law of nature: 'The two laws differ only in method of promulgation and in the way in which we know them: the [one] we know with certainty by the light of nature and from natural principles, the [other] we apprehend by faith' (*Essays,* p.189). Roughly half the text of the *Essays* is taken up with a discussion of moral epistemology; however, this is only one aspect of Locke's general natural law theory. The theory also provides an account of moral obligation. For Locke, morality must be a matter of law, because it is only within the context of a law that we can talk of a moral 'ought'.

2. In *Essay I* Locke characterises the law of nature as 'the decree of the divine will discernible by the light of nature and indicating what is and what is not in conformity with rational nature, and for this very reason commanding or prohibiting' (*Essays,* p.111). As such it meets the three conditions which must be fulfilled by anything that can be called a law: 'in the first place, it is the decree of a superior will, wherein the formal cause of a law appears to consist. ... Second-

ly, it lays down what is and what is not to be done, which is the proper function of a law. Thirdly, it binds men, for it contains in itself all that is requisite to create an obligation' (*Essays*, pp.111–13).

In *Essay V* Locke adds that laws must have sanctions attached to them 'for there is no law without a law-maker, and law is to no purpose without punishment' (*Essays*, p.173). The necessity of laws having sanctions attached to them will be considered below. For the time being, what is to be noted is the centrality of will in Locke's conception of law. It is this which has led commentators to the conclusion that Locke is an ethical voluntarist: that is, he holds the moral good or evil, rightness or wrongness of things and actions to be determined, not by any characteristics they possess in themselves, but solely by the fact that they have been commanded or forbidden by a superior will.

But while commentators have pinned Locke down as a voluntarist, they have generally added the rider that he is not a voluntarist *simpliciter.* He explicates moral right and wrong in terms of God's law and law itself in terms of will. Yet he is also concerned that what God wills should be just; and he can declare it to be just only if he accepts some standard of justice external to God's will. W. von Leyden has argued that this ambivalence on Locke's part amounts to a fundamental inconsistency in his account of the law of nature. What Locke presents in the *Essays* is not one unified natural law theory, but two alternative theories. He tempers his initial voluntarist position with elements from what von Leyden calls the 'intellectualist' theory. At times Locke 'regards natural law as a set of commands proceeding from the will of God and that it is on this account that this law is righteous and binding. . . . Yet, . . . his position shifts and inclines towards the "intellectualist" theory . . . according to which law has its foundation in a dictate of Right Reason, in the essential nature of things, and is thus independent of the will' (*Essays*, Intro. p.51). It will be argued that von Leyden is mistaken in this assessment of Locke. He does not waver between a voluntarist and an intellectualist theory of law, but consistently maintains the former. Nevertheless, it is true that Locke is not a voluntarist with respect to the content of the moral law. His voluntarism is strictly a theory of moral obligation. But before turning to a criticism of von Leyden's interpretation, something needs to be said about the two stools between which, it is claimed, Locke falls in his account of the law of nature.

The refutation of ethical voluntarism is a conspicuous theme in seventeenth- and early eighteenth-century moral philosophy. The 'atheist' Hobbes was understood as founding morality on nothing but the will of the secular Leviathan, but what came primarily under attack was theological voluntarism.[5] In its widest sense, theological voluntarism may be taken as the thesis that right and wrong, good and evil, depend on the will of God. But this formulation is too broad to be informative. Although they do not always clearly differentiate them, the anti-voluntarists are in fact attacking at least three different positions, or three forms of ethical voluntarism: (1) That the precepts which make up morality have their source in God's unconditioned will. As God's will is unconditioned no reason can be assigned as to why these precepts are as they are, for God might have willed them quite otherwise. Thus the only possible answer to the question why, say, murder is wrong is that it is so because God forbids murder. (2) That God is above all moral norms. Reasons may be given for the moral precepts binding mankind, but God can on particular occasions suspend these precepts. What God Himself does, or what He commands particular men to do, is in no way conditioned by moral norms, but is simply the expression of His supreme power. (3) Although God's will is conditioned by reasons, including moral reasons, these are – at least very often – inscrutable from man's point of view. What God wills, whether it be the general precepts of morality or particular commands, may appear arbitrary and unjust; but this is only an appearance due to the feebleness of human understanding. This third variant of the voluntarist thesis, it should be noted, contradicts both the extreme voluntarism expressed in (1) and the limited voluntarism expressed in (2).

It is no easy task to find unequivocal examples of extreme voluntarism. Even the writers standardly cited often turn out upon examination to be less extreme than they are represented by their seventeenth-century opponents. Descartes, in his *Reply to the Sixth Set of Objections,* comes at least very close to voluntarism of the first form. Not only moral distinctions but all possible objects of knowledge are as they are simply because God wills them so:

> To one who pays attention to God's immensity, it is clear that nothing at all can exist which does not depend on Him. This is true . . . of every law, and of every reason of truth and goodness. . . For if any reason for what is good had preceded His preordination, it would have determined Him towards that which it was best to bring about; but on the contrary because He determined Himself towards those things which ought to be accomplished, for that reason, as it stands in Genesis, *they are very good*; that is to say, the reason for their goodness is the fact that He wishes to create them so.[6]

Whatever may be said of this moral philosophy as a whole, Hobbes does at times endorse voluntarism of the second form. For example, in reply to Bishop Bramhall he writes: 'the power, which is absolutely irresistible, makes him that hath it above all law, so that nothing he doth can be unjust. But this power can be no other than the power divine'.[7] Although utterances which appear to be voluntarist in senses (1) and (2) are plentiful in Calvinist writings, they are not always to be taken at face value. Calvin himself is a voluntarist only in the third sense. The gulf between Almighty God and fallen human nature is so immense that man can never hope to comprehend the ways of God, but it is blasphemous to suppose that God's will is divorced from justice:

> since God claims to himself the right of governing the world, a right unknown to us, let it be our law of modesty and soberness to acquiesce in his supreme authority, regarding his will as our only rule of justice, and the most perfect cause of all things, – not that absolute will, indeed, of which sophists prate, when by a profane and impious divorce, they separate his justice from his power, but the universal overruling Providence from which nothing flows that is not right, though the reasons thereof may be concealed.[8]

But while the opponents of ethical voluntarism tend to neglect ambiguities and qualifications in the authors they criticise, this is of secondary importance, for ethical intellectualism repudiates all three forms of voluntarism.

What then is the intellectualist alternative to voluntarism? It would, of course, be a mistake to suppose all those who attack voluntarism to be expounding an identical moral theory. Still, the intellectualist position vis-à-vis voluntarism does lend itself to a brief characterisation; for the intellectualist morality is 'eternal and immutable'. The phrase is Ralph Cudworth's, and it is Cudworth and Samuel Clarke who von Leyden cites as developing the thesis which he finds half-formed in Locke. Clarke, like Locke, is a legalist; the guiding conception in his theory is moral right and duty. Cudworth, as a Cambridge Platonist, is more concerned with the Good as distinct from the Right.[9] Their differences, however, should not obscure the points of similarity which make them both representatives of an important school of moral thought. Both hold that moral distinctions are fixed in the immutable nature of things. Far from its being the case that the moral worth of a thing is determined by the will, it is the autonomous moral worth of things which lays an obligation on the will. God's will is necessarily determined by reasons of moral goodness and rectitude, and the same reasons ought to determine the will of man.

For Cudworth, a thing is what it is because it has a certain form or nature. This is so whether the thing in question is a material object or an action. The natures which make things to be what they are are themselves independent of will:

> For though the will and power of God have an absolute infinite and unlimited command upon the existences of all created things to make them to be, or not to be at pleasure; yet when things exist, they are what they are, this or that, absolutely or relatively, not by will or arbitrary command, but by the necessity of their own nature. . . . Wherefore the natures of justice and injustice cannot be arbitrarious things, that may be applicable by will indifferently to any action or dispositions whatsoever.[10]

In much the same vein, Clarke understands moral precepts to have an objective truth analogous to the necessary truth of mathematical propositions. He maintains

> that there is *Fitness* or *Suitableness* of certain *Circumstances* to certain *Persons,* and an *Unsuitableness* of others; founded in the *nature of things,* and the *Qualifications of Persons*; antecedent to all positive appointment whatsoever; Also, that from the different relations of *different Persons one to another,* there necessarily arise a fitness or unfitness of certain *manners of behaviour* of some Persons towards others; it is as manifest, as that the Properties which flow from the Essences of different *mathematical Figures,* have different *congruities* or *incongruities* between themselves.[11]

God cannot create moral distinctions by an arbitrary fiat, for God Himself wills in accord with what is right. In Clarke's opinion, God is just as much a moral agent as man, the only difference being that God's will cannot deviate from righteousness:

> the same necessary and eternal *different Relations,* that different Things bear one to another; and the same consequent *Fitness or Unfitness* of the application of different Things or different Relations one to another; with regard to which, the Will of God always and necessarily *does* determine itself to choose to act only what is agreeable to Justice, Equity, Goodness and Truth, in order to the Welfare of the whole Universe; *ought* likewise constantly to determine the Wills of all subordinate rational Beings, to govern all their Actions by the same Rules, for the good of the Publick in their respective Stations.[12]

To the voluntarist objection (voiced, for example, by Descartes) that such an autonomous eternal and immutable morality diminishes

God's status as creator and sets constraints to His freedom, Cudworth replies:

> there is no other genuine consequence deducible from this assertion, that the essences and verities of things are independent upon the will of God, but that there is an eternal and immutable wisdom in the mind of God, and thence participated by created beings independent upon the will of God. Now the wisdom of God is as much God as the will of God . . . wisdom in itself hath the nature of a rule and measure, it being a most determinate and inflexible thing; but will being not only a blind and dark thing, as considered in itself, but also indefinite and indeterminte, hath therefore the nature of a thing regulable and measurable. Wherefore it is the perfection of will, as such, to be guided and determined by wisdom and truth.[13]

Similarly, in Clarke's opinion it follows logically from God's attributes that He must always act in accord with the objective fitness of things. As God is omniscient, omnipotent and perfectly happy, it is impossible for Him to fall into moral error or be tempted by wayward desires or superior forces. As He is perfectly good, it is impossible that He should disregard the moral worth of things and deviate from what is right. The necessity bearing upon God's will is quite compatible with His freedom of choice, for it is not a natural necessity compelling Him to do one thing rather than another. It is simply that God would not be God unless He chose according to the autonomous norms of morality.[14]

Clearly, the intellectualism of Cudworth and Clarke is in direct opposition to the second as well as the first form of voluntarism distinguished above. Words such as 'right', 'just' and 'good' apply univocally to God and to man. The view that God transcends our notions of morality inevitably collapses into the extreme view that God is amoral. As Clarke writes: 'if Justice and Goodness be not the same in God, as in our Ideas; then we mean nothing when we say that God is necessarily Just and Good. . . . Thus the *moral Attributes* of God, however they be acknowledg'd in words, yet in reality they are . . . entirely taken away'.[15] Clarke accepts that the moral precepts discernible in the nature of things are also the commands of God, for it is certain that God desires the rational part of creation to follow the same principles which of necessity determine His will.[16] Cudworth maintains that God, and indeed the civil authority, can command men to do things which are, of their own nature, morally indifferent. But a command cannot bring about an essential change in a thing; it can only make it obligatory by 'accident'. Its obligatoriness is in virtue of 'natural justice, that is, the rational or intellectual nature [which] obligeth not only to obey God, but also civil powers, that have lawful authority of commanding'.[17] Were there no natural justice there could be no grounds for obedience to any command, no matter how powerful the commander. The view that moral predicates apply univocally to God and to man also sets the intellectual theory in opposition to the third form of voluntarism which we have seen in Calvin. For Cudworth the wisdom which governs God's will is 'participated by created being'; for Clarke the moral norms to which God attends are those which are perspicuous to human reason. Neither writer, then, leaves any place for concealed reasons or hidden councils informing the will of the Almighty.

Both writers grant that the sanctions God attaches to moral precepts have an important function in that they serve to check those who might otherwise give in to temptation. Nonetheless, they insist that moral obligation arises not from any reward or punishment the agent may expect as a consequence of his action, but solely from the moral nature of the action itself. Clarke writes:

> The original *Obligation* of all, (the ambiguous use of which word as a *Term of Art,* has caused some perplexity and confusion in this matter,) is the eternal Reason of Things; That Reason, which God himself, who has no Superior to direct him, and to whose Happiness nothing can be added nor any thing diminished from it, yet constantly *obliges himself* to govern the World by.[18]

For Cudworth the view that moral obligation is founded on sanctions reveals a misunderstanding of morality:

> Did obligation to the things of natural justice . . . arise from the will and positive command of God, only by reason of punishments threatened, and rewards promised; the consequences of this would be, that no man was good and just, but only by accident, and for the sake of something else; whereas the goodness of justice or righteousness is intrinsical to the thing itself, and this is that, which obligeth, (and not any thing foreign to it) it being a different species of good from that of appetite, and private utility, which every man may dispense withal.[19]

Thus, that which is just, right or good *ought* to be pursued because it is just, right or good. Conversely, that which is unjust *ought* to be shunned because it is unjust. This analysis of moral obligation is central to ethical intellectualism and may well be considered its most important legacy.

Theological voluntarism, in whatever sense it may be understood, is an essentially theistic ethic. While intellectualism is, of course, not atheistic, it does have implications which may be termed non-theistic. Cudworth argues that his theory of intrinsic moral natures constitutes a proof of God's existence, for these ideas must inhere in an infinite and eternal mind. Clarke argues – somewhat inconsistently – that revelation is, after all, necessary for perfect moral knowledge. Yet notwithstanding their theological concerns, God is at best peripheral to the ethical systems they propound. Moral distinctions are independent of God in that He can neither create nor alter them. They inevitably determine God's will, and are accessible to unaided human reason. They carry within themselves the grounds of obligation prior to any command issuing from God or any established sanctions. It would seem, therefore, that even if God does not exist, the foundations of 'eternal and immutable morality' are secure. The non-theistic implications of ethical intellectualism are explicitly stated by Hugo Grotius: 'What we have been saying would have a degree of validity even if we should concede that which cannot be conceded without the utmost wickedness, that there is no God, or that the affairs of men are of no concern to Him'.[20] In its *de facto* separation of ethics from theology, intellectualism looks forward to the secular, humanist ethic characteristic of Enlightenment.[21]

3. Having in some measure clarified voluntarism and intellectualism as alternative ethical theories, we can now return to Locke and von Leyden's criticism of his natural law theory.

A non-theistic ethic is foreign to Locke's thinking. He makes it plain at the beginning of the *Essays* that he considers the notion of moral right and wrong unintelligible without God:

> Since God shows Himself to us as present everywhere and, as it were, forces Himself upon the eyes of men as much in the fixed course of nature now as by the frequent evidence of miracles in time past, I assume there will be no one to deny the existence of God, provided he recognizes either the necessity for some rational account of our life, or that there is a thing that deserves to be called virtue or vice. (*Essays*, p.109)

However, at least the first and third forms of voluntarism are just as uncongenial to Locke as is intellectualistic secularism. If, as the first form of voluntarism maintains, right and wrong are contingent upon the unconditioned will of God, it follows that what is right or wrong can be known only by those to whom God's will has been revealed. But much the same consequence follows when voluntarism is understood in its third form. Even though God's will is conditioned by reasons of justice, these reasons are – at least in large part – hidden from our corrupt human understanding. This being so we are to regard God's will 'as our only rule of justice'; but in this case, revelation can be the only source of moral knowledge, and, from the point of view of the creature endeavouring to know what the moral law demands, it is as if the first form of voluntarism were true. For Locke, as we have seen, what is distinctive about the law of nature is its accessibility to unaided human reason. A moral law which can be known only by divine revelation is not natural but positive: 'For whatever among men obtains the force of a law, necessarily looks to God, or nature, or man as its maker; yet whatever man has commanded or God has ordered by divine declaration, all this is positive law' (*Essays*, p.133). Nor does Locke agree with writers such as Perkins and Ames that because of the Fall our moral knowledge needs to be completed by revelation. He states repeatedly that the revealed moral law and the law of nature are identical in their content.

It appears, then, that there are elements of both voluntarism and intellectualism in Locke's theory. Von Leyden finds the shift from voluntarism towards intellectualism most prominent in *Essay VII*. Here Locke distinguishes between the unchanging law of nature and positive laws enacted to meet contingent circumstances. In contrast to the latter, the law of nature is 'a fixed and permanent rule of morals, which reason itself pronounces, and which persists, being a fact so firmly rooted in the soil of human nature' (*Essays*, p.199). Human nature being essentially the same everywhere and at all times, the law of nature must be uniform and universal:

> Since . . . all men are by nature rational, and since there is a harmony between this law and the rational nature, and this harmony can be known by the light of nature, it follows that all those who are endowed with a rational nature, i.e. all men in the world, are morally bound by this law. . . . In fact, this law does not depend on an unstable and changeable will, but on the eternal order of things. For it seems to me that certain essential features of things are immutable, and that certain duties arise out of necessity and cannot be other than they are. (ibid.)

Von Leyden sees the notion of a harmony (*convenientia*) between the law and human reason as being introduced by Locke in an attempt to arrive at a non-voluntarist, purely rational foundation for moral obligation.

But whatever Locke may say in *Essay VII*, it cannot be understood as an analysis of the concept of moral obligation. In this essay he is concerned only with the question of how far obligation extends, not with the nature of obligation itself. He is careful to keep the two topics separate. Referring to the preceding essay he remarks: 'We have already proved that his law is given as morally binding, and we must now discuss to what extent it is in fact binding' (*Essays*, p.193).

In *Essay VI* Locke's account of obligation is unequivocally voluntarist.

> Of itself and by its intrinsic force (and only so) is the divine will binding, and . . . it can be known by the light of nature, in which case it is [the] law of nature . . . since nothing else is required to impose an obligation but the authority and rightful power of one who commands and the disclosure of his will, no one can doubt that the law of nature is binding on men. (*Essays*, p.187)

Locke's argument for the universal extent of obligation has as its major premise the assumption we have already noted in his first and third arguments for the existence of the law of nature: 'all things observe a fixed law of their operations and a manner of existence appropriate to their nature' (*Essays*, p.117). As man, together with everything in the universe, is endowed by God with a function, human nature (or the way God has made man) must be suited to the fulfilment of its function. The content of the law of nature, being the rules of man's function, is therefore determined by the facts of human nature. On the supposition that human nature does not vary, all men must be subject to the same obligations (that is, bound to act according to the same rules), and this notwithstanding the diverse and even contradictory moral practices to be found amongst mankind. Thus, with respect to its content, the law of nature does not depend on 'an unstable and changeable will', but is 'firmly rooted in the soil of human nature'. There is a harmony between the content of the law of nature and human nature, but this harmony cannot establish the obligatory force of the law.

Essay VII, therefore, does not provide any support for von Leyden's interpretation. To assert that *what* men are obligated to do is determined by their nature and discoverable by their reason is not to assert, nor to imply, that the fact *that* men are obligated to do something is determined by nature or by reason. On the contrary, in Locke's account of natural law the discovery that there is a law imposing some obligation or other is logically prior to the discovery of the content of the law:

> First, in order that anyone may understand that he is bound by a law, he must know beforehand that there is a law-maker, i.e. some superior power to which he is rightly subject. Secondly, it is also necessary to know that there is some will on the part of that superior power with respect to the things to be done by us. (*Essays*, p.151)

We cannot be bound by a law before it has been properly promulgated to us. Nonetheless, it would be possible to discover that there is a divine law-maker who has willed something with respect to us, and subsequently to discover what that something is.

There is, however, an important passage in the *Essays* which does seem to endorse the intellectualist theory of obligation. This is no throwaway remark, but the characterisation of the law of nature quoted earlier: Locke declares the law to be 'the decree of the divine will . . . indicating what is and what is not in conformity with rational nature, and *for this very reason* commanding or prohibiting'. Von Leyden understands the phrase I have italicised as referring to the law's conformity with our rational nature (*Essays,* pp.56–7). Locke, then, appears to be saying that it is the reasonableness of what is commanded, and not the will of the commander, which is the source of obligation. However, the whole passage is ambiguous, both in the original Latin and in translation. The phrase may be understood equally well as referring to the divine will, and the passage be taken as a statement of the voluntarist theory of obligation.[22] In view of what Locke says elsewhere in the *Essays* this would seem the more plausible reading. The voluntarist reading receives strong support when the passage is compared with the similar, but unambiguous, statement occurring in an entry in one of Locke's Commonplace Books: 'Virtue, as in its obligation it is the will of God, discovered by natural reason, and thus has the force of a law; so in the nature of it, it is nothing else but doing of good, either to oneself or others' (King, II, p.94). Here the distinction between moral obligation and the content, or matter, of virtue is quite clear, and obligation is said to be constituted by the will of God. The entry concerning virtue is dated 1681, some twenty years after Locke wrote the *Essays,*[23] but there is no reason to believe that the thought expressed is not the same as that expressed in his early work.

Von Leyden pays insufficient attention to an important distinction Locke draws between that which binds 'effectively' and that which binds 'terminatively':

> That thing binds 'effectively' which is the prime cause of all obligation, and from which springs the formal cause of obligation, namely the will of a superior. For we are bound to something for the very reason that he, under whose rule we are, wills it. That thing binds 'terminatively', or by delimitation, which prescribes the manner and measure of an obligation and of our duty and is nothing other than the declaration of that will, and this declaration by another name we call law. We are indeed bound by Almighty God because He wills, but the declaration of His will delimits the obligation and the ground of our obedience; for we are not bound to anything except what a law-maker ... has made known and proclaimed as his will. (*Essays,* pp.185–7)

The meaning of this passage becomes clear when it is read in conjunction with the three conditions Locke stipulates as necessary for any law. As we have seen, a law is the decree of a superior will, laying down what is and what is not to be done, and binding men. The distinction in question elucidates the third of these conditions: men may be said to be bound by a law in two senses, and these correspond to two ways in which a law may be considered. First, a law considered (as to its form) is the decree of a superior will; it binds solely because it issues from a superior will. In the absence of such a will it is unintelligible to talk of anyone being bound or under an obligation; and, as it is essential to a law that it has obligatory force, this means that it is unintelligible to talk of law. The will of a superior is what sets law apart from other kinds of directives (for example, councils of prudence and pieces of advice) which do not carry obligatory force. Secondly, a law may be considered as to its content. No-one can be simply under an obligation, but must always be under an obligation to do or refrain from something. This terminative element, or content, is therefore essential in all cases of obligation. The content of a law may be said to bind in that it is what those subject to a superior will are commanded or forbidden to do; it delimits the area of their obligation. However, the content of a law cannot in itself impose an obligation. Considered in itself, the content of a given law might equally be the content of a directive which has no obligatory force. The imposition of an obligation is an act, and as such it proceeds from will.

In Locke's theory, then, the will of God is the form of the law of nature; it makes the directives of morality to be laws binding mankind. Human nature provides the necessary terminative element in the law of nature, for what God wills men to do is somehow incorporated in the way He has made them. Locke's theory of moral obligation may be summed up thus: God's will is necessary and sufficient to place men under an obligation; the facts of human nature are necessary and sufficient to delimit the obligations men are placed under. God's will and rational human nature, far from being centres for competing theories of the law of nature are complementary features of the one theory.[24]

4. Locke is correctly classified as a theological voluntarist, for he holds the moral 'ought' to depend on the will of God. Were there no God or if God did not will anything respecting human conduct the performance of some actions would still be advantageous, and the performance of others disadvantageous, to mankind. However, it could not be said that men *morally* ought to perform actions of the

first kind and refrain from those of the second kind. Thus, *moral* right and wrong could not be ascribed to such actions. Yet Locke's voluntarism does not coincide exactly with any of the three forms of voluntarism listed so far. Unlike an advocate of the first form, Locke can provide reasons why, say, murder is wrong. It is true that he does answer the question 'why ought we to refrain from murder?' in terms of the fact that God forbids murder. However, there is a similar sounding, though significantly different question: 'why is murder one of the actions we ought not to perform?' To this, a voluntarist of the first type can only answer that God forbids murder. Locke's answer is in terms of certain features of human nature. He is careful to gloss his statement that moral duties arise necessarily out of the features of human nature with the rider that 'this is not because nature or God (as I should say more correctly) could not have created man differently. Rather, the cause is that, since man has been made such as he is, equipped with reason and his other faculties and destined for this mode of life, there necessarily results from his inborn constitution some definite duties for him, which cannot be other than they are' (*Essays*, p.199). The necessity pertaining to the content of the law of nature is, then, a hypothetical and not an absolute necessity. But this does not mean that Locke is committed to the thesis that in some possible world what is vicious in this world will be morally permitted or laudable. If human beings were naturally immortal, the prohibition against murder could not be derived from the facts of human nature. This is not to say that in such a case murder would be acceptable: rather the concept of murder would have no application, for no action could count as murder. As God's will, as it is expressed in the way He has created men, is unchanging, so the content of natural law is unchanging:

> For since, according to His infinite and eternal wisdom, He has made man such that these duties of his necessarily follow from his very nature, He surely will not alter what has been made and create a new race of men, who would have another law and moral rule, seeing that natural law stands and falls together with the nature of man as it is at present. (*Essays*, p.201)

Creation is, then, not an haphazard affair, the product of divine caprice; the act of creation issues in a universe which is strictly ordered and unchanging. Locke's natural law theory also denies the third form of voluntarism, for he maintains that the moral law *qua* law of nature may be known in its entirety by unaided human reason.

Locke's account of obligation might, however, be thought to commit him to the second form of voluntarism. In the first place, there being no superior will to which God could be subject, He cannot have any obligations. As the supreme law-maker, God must be above all law and all moral right and wrong. Secondly, Locke holds that without sanctions attached to them laws are to no purpose. This suggests that God's status as a law-maker able to impose obligations upon mankind derives from His irresistible power, specifically from His power to ensure that breaches of the law He promulgates do not go unpunished. The second of these points will be considered first.

Despite the emphasis he places on sanctions attacking the law, Locke does not equate obligation with coercion. A law-maker is not a superior will simply in the sense of someone who has the power to enforce obedience, but a superior to whom others are *rightly* subject. Locke states that obligation involves a two-fold liability: a 'liability to punishment . . . arises from a failure to pay dutiful obedience, so that those who refuse to be led by reason and to own that in the matter of morals and right conduct they are subject to a superior authority may recognize that they are constrained by force and punishment to be submissive to that authority and feel the strength of Him whose will they refuse to follow' (*Essays*, p.183). The view that the obligation to obey the law arises from the punishment which follows upon disobedience confuses obligation with the naked force to which men are subject when, for example, they fall into the hands of pirates and robbers. On the contrary, in view of the primacy of the liability to pay dutiful obedience, 'all obligation binds conscience and lays a bond on the mind itself, so that not fear of punishment, but a rational apprehension of what is right, puts us under an obligation [*sed recti ratio nos obligat*], and conscience passes judgment on morals, and, if we are guilty of a crime, declares that we deserve punishment' (*Essays*, p.185). Locke is talking here of the difference in situation between a captive forced to obey a pirate and a person who owes allegiance to a ruler. Thus, the 'rational apprehension of what is right' which announces that we are under an obligation does not refer to some intrinsic quality of rectitude belonging to the content of our obligation. Rather, it refers to the right belonging to the superior to whom we are subject.

In *Essay I* Locke is careful to differentiate natural law from natural right: 'This law . . . ought to be distinguished from natural right: for right is grounded in the fact that we have the free use of a thing, whereas law is what enjoins or forbids the doing of a thing' (*Essays*, p.111). In *Essay VI* he lists three sources of this 'free use of a thing', and thus three grounds of rightful subjection 'either by natural right and the right of creation, as when all things are justly subject to that by which they have first been made and also are constantly preserved; or by the right of donation, as when God, to whom all things belong, has transferred part of His dominion to someone . . . or by the right of contract, as when someone has voluntarily surrendered himself to another and submitted himself to another's will' (*Essays*, p.185). The rightful dominion consequent upon donation or upon the making of a contract depends on the law of nature. The civil ruler has his authority from God in the sense that there is a moral precept that rulers are to be obeyed. Similarly, contract gives one man a right over another by virtue of the precept that promises are to be kept. Were it not for these moral obligations, no man could be said to possess rightful authority over another. On the other hand, God's right with respect to mankind is completely independent of law. Man's rightful subjection to God is founded in the right of creation; 'for who will deny that the clay is subject to the potter's will . . . ?' (*Essays*, p.157). The question derives from St Paul[25] but Locke is not attempting to prove a philosophical point by appeal to scriptural authority. The passage is a means of illustrating what he takes as undeniable; that God's status as Creator gives Him domination over what He creates.[26]

Locke does not say that the right of creation resides solely in the act of creation. God is said not merely to initiate our existence; our continued existence is said to depend upon God's constantly preserving us. It is this dependency of creature upon creator which Locke sees as the important aspect of the right of creation 'since we owe our body, soul, and life – whatever we are, whatever we have, and even whatever we can be – to [God] and to Him alone, it is proper that we should live according to the precepts of His will. God has created us out of nothing and, if He pleases, will reduce us again to nothing: we are, therefore, subject to Him in perfect justice and by utmost necessity' (*Essays*, p.187). In a Journal entry dated July 15th, 1678, Locke draws an analogy between the son's dependence on his father and mankind's dependence on God:

> God having given man *above other creatures of the habitable part of the universe* a knowledge of himself wch the beasts have not, he is thereby under obligations wch the beasts have not, for knowing god to be a wise agent he cannot but conclude y^{t} he has that knowledge & that faculty wch he finds in himself above other creatures given him for some use & end. If therefor he comprehend the relation between father and son & find it reasonable that his son whom he begot (only in persuance of his pleasure without thinking of his son) & nourish'd should obey & revrence him & be gratefull to him, he cannot but find it much more reasonable y^{t} he & every other man should obey and

> ever love & thank the author of their being to whom they owe all that they are. (MS f3, pp. 201–2)[27]

He returns to the theme of obligation and dependency towards the end of his career in the MS 'Ethica B':[28]

> The originall & foundation of all Law is dependency. A dependent intelligent being is under the power & direction & dominion of him on whom he depends & must be for the ends appointed him by y^t^ superior being. If man were independent he could have noe law but his own will noe end but himself. He would be a god to himself, & ye satisfaction of his own will the sole measure & end of all his actions. (MS c28, fol. 141)

This last passage recalls Locke's statements in the *Two Tracts* that, were there no law, there would be no moral right and wrong and each individual would be his own God. But a law can only impose an obligation (i.e. properly be a law) if it is promulgated by a rightful superior. God's right to promulgate the moral law is the right of creation.[29] The right of creation is, then, the keystone of Locke's legalist theory of morality, and he remains a legalist in his moral philosophy throughout his career.

Locke's notion of the right of creation serves two purposes. In the first place, it enables him to found God's dominion on something other than God's power. As God is omnipotent, human beings cannot have the power successfully to resist Him. Yet even if, *per impossibile,* they did have such power, this would not obviate God's right of creation. This right is, then, logically separate from God's power. Secondly, it provides him with an answer to the intellectualist objection against voluntarism that 'mere will' cannot impose an obligation. Locke nowhere claims that it can. The will which binds 'effectively' can only be that to which men are rightly subject. But the right asserted here is not to be sought in a standard which is independent of God: it belongs to God solely by virtue of the fact that He is the Creator of all things. Thus Locke can maintain that the divine will is 'of itself and by its intrinsic force' binding. He can consistently maintain this, because he is talking of *God's* will. Locke agrees that the moral obligations imposed by the law of nature must be founded on right, not on force. This right cannot itself depend on law, for, as Cudworth points out, not even God could enact a law establishing His own right to legislate.[30] Nor, within the terms of Locke's voluntarist theory of obligation, can it depend on something, such as Cudworth's 'natural justice' which is independent of God. This would mean that God's will is not of itself the source of obligation. The right of creation, however, is both independent of law and intrinsic to God.

While Locke does not hold moral obligation to be founded on God's naked power or mere will, there remains the other point of apparent agreement between his theory and the second form of voluntarism: as he does conceive the moral rectitude of actions to be a function of their conformity to a law willed by God, he cannot significantly assert that what God wills is right. Nevertheless, Locke does not hold God's will to be an arbitrary, completely unconditioned will. The term most frequently predicated of God in the *Essays* is 'wisdom'. In one place Locke remarks that our obligation to obey the law of nature derives 'partly from the divine wisdom of the law-maker . . . [for] it is reasonable that we should do what shall please Him who is omniscient and most wise' (*Essays*, p.183). But this remark is not followed up; Locke does not expound a non-voluntarist theory of obligation premised upon the intrinsic wisdom of what God wills. He sees God's wisdom as manifesting itself in the purposefulness of all created beings and in the ordered stability of creation as a whole. As we know God to be wise, we can be sure that the law of nature which He has promulgated is unchanging, and that its precepts apply universally.[31] Locke is not much concerned with the question of why things ultimately are as they are. The little he says on the subject in the *Essays* does have a Calvinist ring to it. All the different kinds of things in the universe are endowed by God with their own *telos*, but as to their overriding purpose 'they appear to be intended by Him for no other end than His own glory, and to this all things must be related' (*Essays*, p.157). The difference between the approach of Locke and that of intellectualists such as Cudworth and Clarke is in large part due to their differing preoccupations. The latter two writers are largely concerned with the theological question of the attributes of God. Cudworth, in particular, is intent on combating the doctrine that God's supreme sovereignty places Him beyond good and evil.[32] Locke's concerns are confined to mankind. He is attempting to explicate a moral order which governs men and justifies the institution of civil government. For Locke, God is primarily the source of this order. By His creative will He establishes its content, and by His authoritative will He guarantees it as binding on mankind.

There are remarks in Locke's later works which do appear inconsistent with the voluntarist theory of moral obligation given in the *Essays*. For example, in the *Essay Concerning Human Understanding* Locke writes: 'God himself cannot choose what is not good; the Freedom of the Almighty hinders not his being determined by what is best' (II.xxi.49). This has been understood by some commentators as an endorsement of the view that there are moral distinctions fixed in the nature of things, and that these govern God's will.[33]

However, Locke is not talking here of moral distinctions, but of goodness; and by goodness he means happiness. In Locke's view human beings necessarily strive after happiness, but God is under the necessity of actually being happy. Consequently God cannot will anything incompatible with His own happiness (II.xxi.50). Another, and more telling passage, occurs in the *Second Treatise of Government*: 'the Obligations of that Eternal Law . . . are so great, and so strong, in the case of *Promises,* that Omnipotency it self can be tyed by them. *Grants, Promises* and *Oaths* are Bonds that *hold the Almighty'* (*2nd Treatise,* §195). As God is not subject to a superior will, He cannot, on Locke's voluntarist theory, be under any moral obligations. Two interpretations of this passage seem possible. First, Locke might be indulging in a piece of rhetoric aimed at highlighting the importance of contracts; the notion of a contract is after all of central importance to his *Second Treatise.* What he says is inconsistent with his theory of moral obligation, but, as he had not published the *Essays,* this might not have bothered him. Secondly, Locke might not be ascribing a moral obligation to God, but rather making the point that it would be incompatible with God's wisdom for Him to retract a promise once made.[34] For in promising a thing, God wills that thing, and it is essential to God's wisdom that His will be immutable. Whichever interpretation is correct Locke nowhere sets forth an alternative, non-voluntarist theory of moral obligation. His account of the moral 'ought' is contained in the *Essays.*

Finally, it is important to be clear that Locke's theory of moral obligation is not a theory of moral motivation. The rectitude of an action consists in its conformity to the law of nature. Thus, to know the rectitude of an action is to acknowledge a moral obligation respecting it. However, the acknowledgement of an obligation is, according to Locke, insufficient to move the agent. He distinguishes motivation from the knowledge of moral rectitude in several places. Most notably, in a Commonplace Book entry dated 1693 he writes under the heading 'Voluntas':

> That wch has very much confounded men about the Will & its determinations has been the confounding of the notion of Moral Rectitude & giving it the name of moral good. The pleasure that a man takes in any action or expects as a consequence of it is indeed a Good in it self able & proper to move the will. But the Moral Rectitude of it considered barely in it self is not good or evill nor in any way moves the will but as pleasure & pain either accompanies the action it self or is looked on to be a consequence of it. W^ch is evident from the punishments & rewards w^ch

> god has annexed to moral rectitude or pravity as proper motives by ye will w[ch] would be needless if moral rectitude were it self good & moral pravity evil. (MS c28, fol. 114)

'Right' is the central concept in Locke's natural law doctrine, but the law could have no purchase on human conduct unless doing that which is right were in some way productive of good. 'Good' is the central concept in his moral psychology.

5. The voluntarist theory of moral obligation set forth in the *Essays* is by far the most interesting part of that work. But, as we saw in chapter 1, the claim that there is a law of nature which places obligations upon us is empty unless it can be established that reason provides us with a knowledge of the content of that law. What Locke has to say in the *Essays* concerning this knowledge leaves much to be desired. He argues that knowledge of the law is not innate to the mind of man (*Essay III*); that the law cannot be known from the general consent of men (*Essay V*); and that the private interest of the individual cannot be the basis of the law (*Essay VIII*). His positive thesis is that the law can be known by reason working with materials acquired in sense-experience (*Essay II* and *IV*).

Locke talks of the law of nature being known by the 'light of nature', but he is careful to clear this phrase of any suggestion that moral knowledge arises in some kind of direct enlightenment:

> while we assert that the light of nature points to this law, we should not wish this to be understood in the sense that some inward light is by nature implanted in man, which perpetually reminds him of his duty and leads him straight and without fail whither he has to go. . . . Rather, by saying that something can be known by the light of nature, we mean nothing else but that there is some sort of truth to the knowledge of which a man can attain by himself and without the help of another, if he makes proper use of the faculties he is endowed with by nature. (*Essays*, p. 123)

Locke excludes divine revelation as a source of knowledge of the law on the grounds that this would be a case of direct (and private) enlightenment. There are, he maintains, three other possible sources. Moral knowledge might be innate to the mind; it might be learnt from tradition; or it might have its origin in sense-experience. It is not, Locke argues, innate. Nor can it *originate* in tradition, for any tradition must be based in something other than tradition. It must, therefore, originate in sense-experience. Locke refuses to talk of reason as being itself a source of knowledge; for 'Nothing indeed is achieved by reason, that powerful faculty of arguing, unless there is first something posited and taken for granted' (*Essays*, p.125). What is posited for reason is data gathered by the senses.

Given Locke's commitment to empiricism, we would expect the derivation of the law's content to begin from an observation of men as they are. Locke does select three dispositions which he assumes to be constant features of human nature. First, men have an inclination to contemplate the works, wisdom, and power of God, and to praise Him. Secondly, all men desire to live in company with others, and this inclination for society goes beyond a self-centred desire for personal comfort; men are also admirably fitted for society by the gift of speech. Thirdly, all men have a strong instinct of self-preservation. These three natural dispositions are the basis of 'all that men owe to God, their neighbour, and themselves' (*Essays*, p.159).[35] Clearly this does not constitute a derivation of the precepts of morality. Nor does Locke claim that it does. These dispositions serve only to circumscribe the general areas of moral duty: the agent's duties to God, to others and to himself. What must be done in order to fulfil the demands of morality within these areas has still to be decided, but Locke does not go on to show how this is to be achieved. All he adds – in *Essay VIII* – is a detailed argument against the thesis that each individual's own interest is the basis from which the precepts of the law can be derived. Locke's argument against ethical egoism will be considered in chapter VII when we look at his conception of the state of nature.

The *Essays*, then, fail to solve the crucial problem of man's knowledge of the content of the law of nature. It is in the *Essay Concerning Human Understanding* that Locke turns his full attention to the problem of human knowledge. But before considering Locke's positive contribution to epistemology we will look in some detail at the negative thesis, argued both in the *Essays* and the *Essay*, that there is no innate moral knowledge. What Locke has to say on this topic clarifies his general ethical position.

III

AGAINST INNATE MORALITY

It has always been difficult to find a suitable target for the polemic against innate principles which constitutes Book I of the *Essay.*[1] Locke apparently sets out to demolish the doctrine that men are born actually knowing a number of truths, truths which are 'inscribed' or 'impressed' upon their minds by God. But where is the writer who ever maintained such a doctrine? 'And when I say *actuall* Knowledge', writes Henry More, 'I doe not mean that there is a certaine number of *Ideas* flaring and shining to the *Animadversive faculty* like so many *Torches* or *Starres* in the *Firmament* to our outward sight, or that there are any figures that take their distinct places & are legibly writ there like the *Red Letters* or *Astronomicall Characters* in an *Almanack*; but I understand thereby an active sagacity in the Soul, or quick recollection as it were, whereby some small businesse being hinted unto her she runs out presently into a more clear & larger conception.'[2] More, like many another defender of innate knowledge, is telling his readers not to take the metaphorical language of 'original inscription', etc., literally. Men are not born knowing the truths which are classified as innate; they are born with a disposition for knowledge of them. The human mind is so constituted that all men who have proper use of their reason assent to a specifiable range of propositions once these are presented (or at least 'hinted') to them in terms they understand. As Locke agrees that some propositions are self-evident he, in effect, accepts the essentials of the innatist doctrine.[3] His mistake is to take metaphorical language literally, and in so doing he directs his attack against a naive form of innatism to which no one subscribes.

Whether or not Locke does make this mistake, and whether or not the naive form of innatism is to be found in the literature of his day, are questions which need not be gone into here.[4] Whatever the answers may be, Book I of the *Essay* is not a belabouring of the empty air. For, notwithstanding that he admits self-evident propositions, Locke's arguments are also directed against innatism in its dispositional form.

1. The doctrine of innate knowledge has two aspects. Innate propositions are said to be of fundamental importance for human thought and conduct. There are two classes of propositions for which innate status is claimed: speculative principles and practical principles. Speculative principles are invariably truths of the widest generality, such as the logical law of identity. These are seen sometimes as major premises necessary in the syllogistic reasoning of the various sciences, sometimes as rules of inference in accordance with which syllogisms must be constructed. Practical principles, on the other hand, are often seen as detailed moral precepts. To take one instance, Locke's early critic, Henry Lee, compiles a list which extends from the duty of preserving one's own life to the keeping of contracts.[5] Moreover, the existence of innate practical principles is thought to be the only guarantee of an objective moral law governing all mankind. Lee argues that, in rejecting innate practical principles, Locke is forced to accept moral subjectivism and relativism. He warns that, in Locke's usage, terms such as 'Law of Nature' and 'Law of God' have changed their common meaning.

> For, if the Author of Nature has contributed nothing to our gaining the Knowledge of them in the original Constitution of our Souls and Bodies; but left us wholly in the dark, wholly at liberty to gain our Knowledge of them from *Experience* and *Conversation*; then the *Laws of Nature*, the *Laws of God*, may be words interpreted to signifie only such Rules of Action as every man voluntarily makes to himself, and shapes by the mutable Sentiments, and exemplary Practice of his own *Familiars* or *Superiors*.[6]

This charge appears in nearly all the criticisms of Book I of the *Essay*.[7] It is another contemporary, James Lowde, who gives the most succinct statement of the view that the innatist doctrine and belief in an objective moral law are inseparable: 'the Law of Nature is either the same with these naturall inscriptions, or innate notions, or the one so Founded, in the other, that they must both stand, or fall together'.[8] The doctrine of innate practical principles may, then, be seen as an attempt to provide an epistemology for the law of nature. The law *must* be known by mankind, and it *is* known because it is innate. There is a system of moral truths which men accept, simply by virtue of the make-up of the human mind.

The seventeenth-century defenders of innate knowledge were not asserting that as a matter of psychological fact there are a number of propositions which we are incapable of doubting. From this nothing would follow as to the truth of those propositions, for the inability to doubt might equally extend to false propositions. The doctrine is a piece of metaphysics. Lee writes:

> the only reason I can frame, why any Perceptions, Thoughts or Notions can be said to be *innate*, is because, according to the *present* Constitution of our Souls and Bodies, and their Relation to other parts of the Universe, there is a necessary Connexion fix'd and establish'd between some sorts of Motions or *Impressions* from external Objects, and some sort of Perceptions or Thoughts, and they may properly enough be call'd *natural* or *innate*; because by the arbitrary Constitution of the Wise Author of Nature in uniting our Souls to our Bodies, there is a *necessary* and *mutual* Communication between both, that such Motions should produce such Perceptions.[9]

The mechanistic picture is somewhat odd, but what Lee is getting at is clear anough. To say that we have an innate knowledge of something does not mean that we have always known that thing. What it does mean is that God has so constituted the human mind that, given certain external stimuli, it necessarily grasps the truth of certain propositions. Our knowledge of the propositions which are classified as innate arises because features of the constitution of the mind are, as it were, geared to features of the external world. Once these features become engaged one with another, the truth of innate propositions has an unbreakable purchase on the mind.

Historians of philosophy have generally seen the innatist thesis as a rationalist doctrine. Indeed, one of the standard text-book distinctions between the rationalists and their empiricist contemporaries is that the former maintain, and the latter deny, the existence of innate ideas.[10] Most of the writers who attack Locke on the score of his denial of innate knowledge do construe the mind's capacity to grasp innate propositions as, at least, closely related to the faculty of reason. Lowde talks of the soul having 'a natural power of finding or framing such Principles or Propositions, the Truth of Knowledge whereof no way depends upon the evidence of sense or observation'.[11] Similarly, John Milner remarks that 'of such things, as so soon as they are alledged, all Men acknowledge them to be true or good, they require no Proof or farther Discourse to be assured of the Truth or Goodness of them, we need not fear to say, that they seem to have a good Title, to be receiv'd for common Notions or Catholic Truths written in the Hearts of Men'.[12] Here innate knowledge is presented as propositional knowledge, manifesting itself in an immediate intellectual assent to the self-evident. However, an importantly different version of the thesis that there are innate practical principles appears in the three pamphlets Thomas Burnet published as *Remarks upon an Essay Concerning Humane Understanding.*

For Burnet, the practical principles of morality are innate in that they have their origin in 'natural conscience'. This is the mind's ability immediately to apprehend the moral worth of things:

> This I am sure of, that the Distinction, suppose of Gratitude and Ingratitude, Fidelity and Infidelity, Justice and Injustice, and such others, is as sudden without any Ratiocination, and as sensible and piercing, as the difference I feel from the Scent of a Rose, and of Asso-foetida. . . . it rises as quick as any of our Passions, or as Laughter at the sight of a ridiculous Accident or Object.[13]

Here the ascent the mind allegedly gives to practical principles is presented, not as an intellectual grasp of self-evident propositions, but as akin to our immediate grasp of, and reaction to, things present to the senses. Writing towards the end of the eighteenth century, the anonymous author of *Dialogues Concerning Innate Principles* assumes that Locke's opponents were, in fact, defending the existence of innate moral sentiments; they did not mean 'that the *propositions themselves* were innate, but, that *the conscious internal sentiments,* on which such moral propositions are founded are innate'.[14] The writer maintains:

> When we are told that *benevolence* is *pleasing*; that *malevolence* is *painful*; we are not convinced of these truths by reasoning, nor by forming them into propositions: but by an appeal to the innate internal affections of our souls: and if on such an appeal, we could not feel within the sentiment of benevolence, and the peculiar pleasure attending it; and that of malevolence and its concomitant pain; not all the reasoning in the world could ever make us sensible of them, or enable us to understand their nature.[15]

The theory that our apprehension of moral distinctions is analogous to our apprehension of things via the senses is not to be confused with the theory that such distinctions are founded in our feelings or sentiments. Nonetheless, both theories are united in rejecting the view that the content of morality can be made out solely by reason. We have seen that for Locke, the content of the law of nature can be made out by reason. His epistemology is, therefore, equally opposed to the non-rational and the rational version of innate morality.

2. Locke does hold the mind capable of immediately apprehending the truth of propositions. Intuition is the primary act of the understanding, in which the mind simply perceives the agreement or disagreement of two of its ideas (IV.ii.1). But, Locke argues at I.ii.

17–21, if self-evidence is taken as a sufficient mark of a proposition's having innate status, the number of innate principles will be legion, and the great bulk of them will be of no importance whatsoever. The innatist must then concede the mind to be originally stocked with a virtually unlimited supply of knowledge, most of which is useless. Although Locke ostensibly aimed it against the naive form of innatism, this point is equally effective against the dispositional form. Milner defends this form, and on his showing, it is exactly the self-evidence of propositions which gives them a title 'to be receiv'd for common Notions or Catholic Truths'.

Locke agrees that the propositions traditionally put forward as innate speculative principles are self-evident. He denies only their importance for reasoning. In the case of putative innate practical principles, however, he denies self-evidence:

> Another Reason that makes me doubt of my innate practical Principles is, That I think, *there cannot any one moral Rule be propos'd, whereof a Man may not justly demand a Reason*: which would be perfectly ridiculous and absurd, if they were innate, or so much as self-evident; which every innate Principle must needs be, and not need any Proof to ascertain its Truth, not any Reason to gain it Approbation. (I.iii.4)

Of course, the defenders of innate practical principles would simply disagree. For them, moral precepts – or at least certain fundamental moral precepts – *are* immediately given to the understanding. These principles neither need to be, nor can they be, supported with reasons.[16] For Locke, morality is not given but found out: 'the Goodness of God hath not been wanting to Men without such Original Impressions of Knowledge, or *Ideas* stamped on the Mind: since he hath furnished Man with those Faculties, which will serve for the sufficient discovery of all things requisite to the end of such a Being' (I.iv.12). In the course of arguing in the fourth of the *Essays* that the moral laws can be discovered by reason, Locke makes it plain that he is not talking of intuitive reason but of 'the discursive faculty of the mind, which advances from things known to things unknown and argues from one thing to another in a definite and fixed order of propositions' (*Essays*, p.149).

Locke's main argument against innate knowledge may be called the refutation from the absence of universal assent. Universal assent is a necessary condition for innateness. The propositions proposed as innate principles do not command universal assent, therefore, they are not innate. Universal assent is absent even in the case of self-evident speculative principles, for these are not so much as thought of, much less assented to, by children and idiots (I.ii.5). In the case of morality there is hardly a principle which has not at some time been rejected or ignored by normal adults:

> He that will carefully peruse the History of Mankind, and look abroad into the several Tribes of Men . . . will be able to satisfy himself, That there is scarce that Principle of Morality to be named, or *Rule* of *Vertue* to be thought on (those only excepted, that are absolutely necessary to hold Society together, which commonly too are neglected betwixt distinct Societies) which is not, somewhere or other, *slighted* and condemned by the general Fashion of *whole Societies* of Men, governed by practical Opinions, and Rules of living quite opposite to others. (I.iii.10)

In support of this somewhat sweeping statement Locke makes great play with travellers' tales reporting outlandish moral practices. The display of the varieties of moral practice is a familiar first move in arguments for moral relativism. There is, however, an equally familiar counter-move. Different, and even contrary, moral practices, it is argued, do not entail different or contrary moral beliefs. In some societies, let us say, it is the practice to allow one's aged parents to die in the open air. In European society such behaviour is considered morally abhorrent. Yet it may be that both societies recognise the same moral duty: that children ought to respect and care for their parents. What they differ in is the manner of fulfilling this duty; and the difference can be accounted for in terms of different factual beliefs and environmental circumstances.[17] Therefore, appearances notwithstanding, there may be very considerable agreement in the moral principles men hold.

Locke does not consider the anti-relativist argument as it is put here. Yet certain of his remarks on the innatist theory of Lord Herbert of Cherbury's *De Veritate* constitute an interesting criticism of it. Locke allows Lord Herbert's 'common notions' 'to be clear Truths, and such as, if rightly explained, a rational Creature can hardly avoid giving his assent to' (I.iii.15). But, he objects, the self-evidence of these principles is purchased at the expense of their informativeness. It is true that 'virtue is the best worship of God' and that 'men must repent of their sins', and if virtue is defined as the doing of what God commands and sin as the doing of ill actions which deserves punishment, such truths are self-evident. But then they provide no guide to conduct; for they say nothing of what kinds of actions fall under the concepts 'virtue' and 'sin':

> it will scarce seem possible, that God should engrave Principles in Mens Minds, in words of uncertain signification, such as *Vertues* and *Sins*, which amongst different Men, stand for differ-

> ent things: Nay, it cannot be supposed to be in words at all, which, being in most of these Principles very general names cannot be understood, but by knowing the particulars comprehended under them. (I.iii.19)

It is true that a difference in moral practice does not entail a difference in moral belief. However, the attempt to provide (or discover) a universal morality underlying all differences in practice is likely to result in a system of rules so vague that they cannot function as guides to conduct, as *practical* principles.

It might be thought that the refutation from the absence of universal assent is effective only against the naive form of innatism. In its dispositional form, the doctrine can accommodate the fact that some men do not assent to innate practical principles. The capacity to apprehend these principles is something which develops in the individual, and it is fully developed only in those who have the proper use of reason. Consequently, innate knowledge is not to be found in children and idiots. Furthermore, the capacity may be inhibited or perverted by education, custom, and the passions. Dispositional innatism, therefore, does not require a *universal*, but only a *widespread* assent. Innate practical principles are those accepted by all persons in whom reason functions correctly. To this Locke replies that it leaves no way of telling a genuine innate principle from one which is pretended to have such status. Once it is granted that the apprehension of innate principles can be blocked, the way is open to any group to proclaim their own opinions innate and therefore exempt from criticism: 'their Argument stands thus: The Principles which all mankind allow for true, are innate; those that Men of right Reason admit, are the Principles allowed by all mankind; we and those of our mind, are Men of reason; therefore we agreeing, our Principles are innate: which is a very pretty way of arguing, and a short cut to Infallibility' (I.iii.20).[18]

The last passage expresses the crux of Locke's objection to the whole doctrine of innate knowledge: it can be used to insulate arbitrary selected sets of beliefs against rational criticism and debate. The doctrine in its naive form does provide a hard and fast criterion whereby it can be decided whether or not a principle does have innate status. If all men were born actually knowing these truths, the question of whether a given proposition really was innate could be settled empirically. If the defender of innate knowledge maintains anything less than the naive doctrine, he is committed, so Locke argues, to confer a special status on all self-evident propositions, or to accept as sacrosanct any moral belief which can drum up sufficiently widespread support.

In his *Third Remarks,* Burnet voices the familiar charge that Locke has misrepresented the innatist doctrine: 'If by *Principles,* you understand *distinct Knowledge,* that is, distinct Idea's, and distinct Propositions; we do not hold *innate* Principles in that sense. Yet so you seem to represent them and their Idea's. . . . You exaggerate the matter, and set the question at what height you please, that you may have the fairer mark to shoot at'.[19] In a marginal note to this passage written in his copy of the *Third Remarks* Locke replies: 'Pray say plainly what is innate & imprinted & how far, & then it will be seen how far y^{u} & I disagree' (Porter, p.37).[20] Although no definite conclusion can be based on this one comment, it does suggest an answer to the puzzling question of why Locke should direct his polemic against innatism in its naive form: he may be deliberately taking what he knows to be metaphorical language literally in order to expose the hollowness of dispositional innatism. Innate principles are not 'originally inscribed' on the mind in the sense that we know them from the beginning of our existence. Nonetheless, the metaphor is apt. All that is required is some suitable stimuli in order for the mind to become conscious of the fundamental principles classified as innate. In this sense, those principles can be said to be in the mind from the beginning; given the stimuli, the 'inscriptions become legible'. For Locke, it is self-contradictory to talk of truths or ideas as being in any sense in the mind or understanding without being at the same time actually apprehended: 'For if these Words (*to be in the Understanding*) have any Propriety, they signify to be understood. So that, to be in the Understanding, and, not to be understood; to be in the Mind, and, never to be perceived, is all one, as to say, any thing is, and is not, in the Mind or Understanding' (I.ii.5).[21] But if the doctrine of innate knowledge is taken literally it is patently false. If, on the other hand, it is understood in its dispositional form, there is no means whereby innate truths can be distinguished from other truths, or indeed from falsehoods. Locke, of course, does not deny an innate capacity for the discovery of moral principles. In his marginal notes in reply to Burnet, he sums his position up thus:

> If moral Ideas or moral rules (wch are the moral principles I deny to be innate) are innate I say children must know them as well as men. If by moral principles y^{u} mean a faculty to finde out in time the moral differences of actions. Besides y^{t} this is an improper way of speaking to cal a power principles: I never denyd such a power to be innate, but y^{t} wch I denyd was y^{t} any Ideas or connection of Ideas was innate. (Porter, p.38)

In other words, unless 'innate' means literally present in the understanding at birth, the doctrine amounts to no more than the thesis that the human understanding is capable of apprehending truth. It is uninformative as to how truth is apprehended.

It was remarked earlier that the doctrine of innate practical principles may be seen as an attempt to establish an epistemology of morals. It is in fact Hooker's 'general and perpetual voice of men' given a metaphysical foundation. As it is put by William Sherlock: 'if the Soul of Man has no Inbred Knowledge, it is in vain to talk of the Light, and Voice, and Sense of Nature; if it has, then the universal Consent of Mankind can be reasonably attributed to no other Cause'.[22] Locke's objection is that this doctrine itself finally dissolves into the subjectivism and relativism it seeks to defeat. Those principles are said to be true which are acceptable to right reason. But the only criterion for the presence of right reason is the acceptance of certain principles. Locke is acutely aware of the diversity of moral beliefs amongst 'the several tribes of men'. What he demands is a decision procedure whose objectivity cannot be questioned and that will enable us to evaluate the truth of these beliefs.

3. Innate morality, even when understood in the dispositional form, appears a thoroughly antiquated piece of philosophising. However, stripped of the metaphorical language in which it is couched, the doctrine emerges as what is now more familiarly known as ethical intuitionism. There are, we have seen, two versions of innate morality, and these correspond to the rationalist and moral sense versions of intuitionism. Burnet's account of 'natural conscience' foreshadows the moral sense theory which reaches full development in the writings of Francis Hutcheson.[23]

One of the main objections brought against ethical intuitionism is exactly that which Locke brings against the appeal to right reason in innate morality: there are no agreed-upon tests for determining whether the individual's alleged capacity for immediate awareness of moral truth is being properly exercised. Hence, there is no means of resolving a clash of intuitions. In a moral dispute, the intuitionist calls upon his opponent to clear his mind of acquired prejudices and intuit the moral truth. But, if moral intuition can be inhibited by prejudice, that intuition can hardly be appealed to in deciding on which side of a dispute the prejudice lies. Although this is a difficulty for ethical intuitionism, it does not demolish the theory. Intuitionism does seem to give a correct account of the way in which we think of our moral knowledge, and this is a strong point in its favour. We very often do immediately acknowledge the moral worth and turpitude of actions. Lee challenges Locke to doubt sincerely the evil of the following:

> Expose your Children; Murder or expose to wind and weather and wild Beasts your Parents, or any Person very Aged or Sick beyond hopes of Recovery; Bury your Children alive; Geld your own Children, got on Female Captives for that purpose, &c. The Question, I ask, is, whether Human Nature, *antecedent* to Custom, Education or Law, be so form'd as to be *free* to believe such Propositions *true*, such Actions good? Or rather, whether, in the moulding of our Souls and Bodies, the Author of our Natures has not *prepossess'd* us with Inclinations to judge them *false*, and the Actions agreeable to them *evil* and *mischievous*?[24]

Lee does have a point. There would be something grotesque about entering into a *moral* debate with someone who maintained there was nothing wrong in these practices. Such a person would, we feel, show a corrupt mind.

Locke does put forward an explanation of this phenomenon of immediate moral recognition. As against Lee, he argues that the supposedly innate practical principles of morality have their genesis in the education of the child: 'such, who are careful . . . to principle Children well . . . instil into the unwary, and, as yet, unprejudiced Understanding, (for white Paper receives any Characters) those Doctrines they would have them retain and profess. These being taught them as soon as they have any apprehension; and still as they grow up, confirmed to them . . . come, by these means, to have the reputation of unquestionable, self-evident, and innate Truths' (I.iii. 22). However, even if Locke is correct in this, he has left untouched a far more substantial line of argument which has often been deployed in support of ethical intuitionism. This may be termed the argument from the autonomy of morals. According to the doctrine of the autonomy of morals, the key moral terms such as 'right', 'ought' and 'good' cannot be defined in non-moral terms; for any attempt to do so destroys their distinctive moral meaning. In consequence, a moral conclusion cannot be derived from premises, none of which contain moral terms. Given that moral discourse is thus *sui generis*, and given that moral propositions have truth-value, it follows that at least some of these moral truths must be accessible only through moral intuition.

Arguments in support of the autonomy of morals were developed in the seventeenth century, primarily in opposition to the ethical voluntarism discussed in the last chapter. The voluntarists were understood as maintaining that the moral worth of actions consists entirely in their being commanded or forbidden by some superior power such as God. Against this view it was pointed out that anyone who holds that the moral rectitude of actions is constituted by God's command is thereby precluded from significantly asserting that what God commands is right. For, on his own showing, this proposition must amount to the insignificant tautology that what God commands is what He commands. Writing at the end of the century, Shaftesbury sums up the point thus:

> whoever thinks there is a God, and pretends formally to believe that he is just and good, must suppose that there is independently such a thing as justice and injustice, truth and falsehood, right and wrong, according to which he pronounces that God is just, righteous, and true. If the mere will, decree, or law of God be said absolutely to constitute right and wrong, then are these latter words of no significancy at all.[25]

It is, of course, open to the voluntarist to accept this consequence of his theory. He may answer that as moral rightness is by definition what God commands it really is tautological that what God commands is right; the proposition is significant only as the expression of a definition.[26] Furthermore, he can argue that the voluntarist definition is the only acceptable definition of moral rightness. He may, for example, follow Descartes and maintain that the notion of a rectitude or moral worth in things which is not constituted by God's will detracts from God's omnipotence and sovereignty.

While the voluntarist might be able to counter this first point in his opponent's argument, he is in serious difficulty when it comes to moral obligation. He not only holds that rightness consists in being commanded, or willed, by God, but also that we morally ought to do what God commands. It would seem that it is always significant to ask of something which is commanded why it ought to be done, and this is so even when the commander is God. The voluntarist must accept this question when it is addressed to the command of an earthly authority. Such a command might be contrary to God's commands. Therefore, the mere fact that an action is commanded by an earthly authority does not entail that it ought to be performed. The voluntarist maintains that, when it comes to a clash between God's commands and earthly commands, the former overrule the latter. But if he maintains this, it is encumbent upon him to give an explanation of why God's commands are overruling; and obviously it is no explanation to reiterate the fact that they are God's commands. The voluntarist cannot avail himself of the answer which would be given by intellectualists such as Cudworth or Clarke, that we ought to do what God commands because His commands – unlike the commands of earthly authorities – are always right. On the voluntarist definition of right, such an answer will simply be a reiteration of the fact that they are God's commands. In face of this the voluntarist may endeavour to answer in terms of the sanctions at the back of God's commands. These are much more to be feared than earthly sanctions, and they are utterly inescapable. But against such a move it is objected that the 'ought' elicited is not a moral 'ought'; rather it is an 'ought' of prudence or self-interest. By appealing to punishments (or rewards) attendant upon actions, the voluntarist reduces morality to something which is non-moral. While the intrinsic moral rightness of an action does in some way give rise to a moral 'ought' with respect to that action, no such obligation follows from the non-moral fact that the action is commanded by God, nor from the fact that God's commands are backed by sanctions.

There are two points to be noted about the argument outlined here. In the first place, it is a general argument which can be deployed not only against ethical voluntarism, but against any theory which gives non-moral definitions of moral terms.[27] Thus, it is objected against the utilitarian who defines good as pleasure that he cannot significantly assert that pleasure is good. If he accepts this consequence, it is further objected that he can give no explanation of the moral obligation to pursue goodness. A prudential 'ought' might follow from the fact that a thing is pleasant, but the moral 'ought' is lost. Secondly, even if the argument is sound, it does not establish the truth of ethical intuitionism. Intuition is supposed to put us in touch with certain objective and immutable moral facts. The moral propositions we know by intuition are true in virtue of their expressing these facts, but this is something which has to be established quite independently of any argument in support of the autonomy of morals. For the conclusion that moral terms cannot be defined in non-moral terms is compatible with the various versions of the thesis that moral 'propositions' do not have truth-value, but are to be analysed as expressions of the agent's attitudes as to prescriptions which the agent addresses to himself. In short, it may be argued that it is impossible to give a non-moral definition of moral terms, not because our moral discourse refers to a realm of 'non-natural' moral facts, but because it does not refer to facts of any kind.

Indeed, arguments which support the autonomy of morals may be turned against ethical intuitionism, or at least against the rationalist version of that doctrine. While the advocates of rational intuitionism deny that a moral 'ought' can be derived from any non-moral fact, they take it as self-evident that such an 'ought' can be derived from certain moral facts. But it is by no means clear how a moral 'ought' can be derived from *any* facts. Clarke, for example, holds obligation to arise directly from the objective relation of moral fitness holding between things. But the conclusion '*x* ought to be done' does not follow logically from the premise '*x* is fitting'. In order for a conclusion expressing an obligation to follow, we need to add a premise to the effect that 'what is fitting ought to be done'. In other words, no statement of fact on its own can entail an 'ought' statement.

Both the rationalist and the moral sense intuitionists construe being under an obligation to do *x* in terms of having a reason to do *x*. Given this view of obligation, it may be urged against the rationalists that the fact of something being the case cannot of itself constitute a reason for acting in one way rather than another. This is not to deny that factual considerations enter into our practical deliberations and decisions, but it is maintained that facts are relevant to our decisions how to act only in so far as they are linked to our desires, wants, or needs. That is, when it comes to the practical affairs of life – including morality – it is not facts in themselves which constitute reasons for actions, but rather those facts seen in the light of the agent's attitudes and feelings. The objection against the rationalist version of intuitionism is that a purely intellectual apprehension of the moral quality of an action or of its fitness in the scheme of things cannot dispose the agent to action.[28] The moral sense version of intuitionism claims to make good this defect in ethical rationalism. The intuition of moral goodness via the postulated moral sense is not like the calm assent given to self-evident propositions. On the contrary, it is inseparably bound up with our feelings, so that we are attracted by physical beauty and repelled by deformity.[29] The advocates of the moral-sense version of intuitionism maintain the autonomy of morals, but there is a change in the notion of autonomy. The existence of an independent and immutable realm of moral values is no longer the major point of emphasis. Rather, there is a concentration on the moral agent, on his feelings and inclinations. In short, there is a move away from the doctrine of autonomous moral distinctions towards the doctrine of the autonomous moral agent, and this, as the rationalist critics of the moral sense theory saw, is a move towards subjectivism in ethics.[30]

Locke does not pay direct attention to arguments in support of the autonomy of morals, but his own moral philosophy is clearly opposed to that autonomy. For him there is no unbridgeable gap between moral and non-moral facts. Furthermore, he never wavers in his rejection of the doctrine that the agent is autonomous in that his private conscience is the arbiter of right and wrong. Most of the main points of opposition between Locke's ethics and the autonomy of morals can be discerned behind his comments on Burnet's doctrine of an innate natural conscience.

4. Burnet's first set of *Remarks* was published anonymously in 1697. The pamphlet elicited a short, ill-tempered rebuff which Locke appended to his first *Reply* to Stillingfleet. The *Second Remarks* appeared in the same year and the *Third Remarks* in 1699. Locke answered neither of these in print, but he did extensively annotate his copy of the last pamphlet.[31]

To talk of innate practical principles is, Burnet holds, to talk of natural conscience: 'a Natural Sagacity to distinguish Moral Good and Evil, or a different perception and sense of them, with a different affection of the Mind arising from it; and this so immediate as to prevent and anticipate all External Laws, and all Ratiocination'.[32] He likens the exercise of this natural sagacity to the child's perception of the different tastes of things; 'When a Child feels the difference of bitter and sweet, he knows and understands that difference in some kind of degree; for it hath its Consequences, and becomes a Principle of Action to him'.[33] Similarly, we have a knowledge of the distinction between good and evil prior to any reasoning concerning moral matters.

One of the most interesting features of Burnet's conception of conscience is his dismissal of general moral precepts. For him, conscience directly perceives good and evil in particular instances. It neither enunciates general precepts, nor does it consider particular actions in the light of such precepts. While other critics replied to Locke's challenge (at I.iii.14) to enumerate the innate practical principles with long lists of general precepts, Burnet considers these unnecessary for the moral life:

> As to the Dictates or Principles of Natural Conscience, (call them Laws of Nature, or what you please) we say, in general, that they are for the distinction of Moral Good and Evil: But the Cases are innumerable . . . wherein there may be occasion for their Exercise. The general Rule is, *Appeal with Sincerity to your Conscience* for your Direction: If that be obscur'd, perverted or sear'd, we cannot help it.[34]

He is careful to stress the autonomy of the objects of natural conscience; moral good and evil are not to be confused with other qualities which things may have;

> And when I say *Moral* Good and Evil, I mean it in contradistinction to *Natural* Good and Evil, Pleasure or Pain, Conveniences or Inconveniences, which are things of another order and character: This inward Sense . . . is simple and irrespective as to those Natural Evils or Goods, They are not its proper Objects; They may be frequently in conjunction, but not necessarily.[35]

Natural conscience does not merely discern the moral qualities of things; it also moves the agent with respect to those qualities. It is 'a Spring and Motive of our Actions . . . in reference to Moral Good and Evil: Or, which I suppose is all one, . . . a Rule or Direction to our Actions'.[36] In so far as it prompts us to morally worthy action, natural conscience resembles the regenerate conscience of the Puritan saint; Burnet, however, sees no need for divine grace and simply asserts that there is a natural conscience analogous to the mind's natural power of distinguishing the sensible qualities of things. Understandably Locke demands some evidence of its existence: 'Such an inward distinguishing sensation antecedent to all supposition of an external moral rule should be proved, till then the supposeing of it is but laying down a foundation for enthusiasme' (Porter, p.38). By enthusiasm, Locke means a pretence to personal divine revelation, though he sometimes extends the term to cover any claim to truth put forward on the grounds of personal conviction without regard to evidence or rational argument (IV.xix.5f). However, Locke's main disagreement with Burnet is not that the latter's moral epistemology leads to irrationalism and subjectivism, but that Burnet has misunderstood the nature of conscience, and that he is wrong to suppose there is a tendency towards moral goodness in human nature.

In the course of his criticism of Burnet, Locke provides a clear picture of his own conception of conscience. To Burnet's contention that natural conscience is one with what Locke calls practical principle, he responds: 'I call not conscience practical principles. Produce the place where I soe represent it. He who confounds the Judgm^{t} made with the Rule or law upon wch it is made, as the Author doth here, may perhaps talke soe' (Porter, p.38). Again he remarks: 'Conscience is not ye law of Nature, but judging by y^{t} wch is taken to be ye law . . . Conscience is the judge, not ye law' (Porter, pp.39–40). In Locke's opinion, a judgment of conscience is arrived at when the individual applies a general moral precept to his own action. The definition of conscience given in the *Essay* echoes the *Two Tracts*; it 'is nothing else, but our own Opinion or Judgment of the Moral Rectitude or Pravity of our own Actions' (I.iii.8). He goes on to say that, if conscience be cited as a proof of innate morality, it must be granted that 'contraries may be innate Principles: Since some Men, with the same bent of Conscience, prosecute what others avoid' (ibid.). He appears to see conscience as a post-facto judgment rather than one made at the moment of decision: 'Conscience dictates not but acquits or condemns upon the dictates of a superior power' (Porter, p.44). In any case, 'conscience cannot acquit or condemn us for what we doe without a law telling us it is our duty to doe or forbear'

(Porter, p.41).

Locke does not criticise Burnet only on the score that we cannot sensibly talk of a conscience which decides upon moral issues without recourse to general precepts. Burnet disregards general rules concerning the morality of kinds of actions on the grounds that the cases in which conscience is called upon to discern moral good and evil are innumerable. Indeed, on the analogy drawn between our perception of good and evil and our sense experience of the pleasant and unpleasant qualities of things, it seems that virtually all our actions will be matters of conscience: 'Though the objects be innumerable y^{t} please or displease yet sense can immediately upon the application of every one of them distinguish wch delights or wch offends. Has conscience such a discerning sense of moral good and evil in every action?' (Porter, p.44). Moral good and evil may be said to be the objects of conscience, but are they to be looked for in every action? We have seen that Locke believes that there are actions which, as they are neither prescribed nor proscribed by the law of nature, are morally neutral. This class of 'indifferent things' is of considerable importance for him as it constitutes the legitimate province of civil legislation. Burnet at least comes close to denying any such class of actions.[37]

Locke makes his own view of the scope of moral considerations plain in a letter to Denis Grenville warning him against scrupulosity. He explains that it is not the case that 'there is always some action soe incombent upon a man soe necessary to be donne preferable to all others, that if that be omitted, a man certainly failes in his duty'. On the contrary, 'God allows us in the ordinary actions of our lives a great latitude; Soe that, two or more things being proposed to be donne, neither of which crosses [a] fundamentall law. . . . I conceive tis at our choice to doe either of them'. The view that morality always demands the best action leads to moral scepticism:

> For according to this supposition the best being always to be donne, and that being but one it is almost impossible to know which is that one. There being soe many actions which may all have some peculiar and considerable goodnesse . . . and soe many nice circumstances and considerations to be weighed one against an other, before we can come to make any judgment which is best, and after all shall be in danger to be mistaken. The Comparison of those actions that stand in competition . . . being very hard to be made. And which makes the difficulty yet far greater is that a great many of those which are of moment . . . always scape us, Our short sight not penetrateing far enough into any action to be able to discover all that is comparatively

> good or bad in it: Besides that the extent of our thoughts is not able to reach all those actions which at any one time we are capable of doeing. Soe that . . . in makeing our judgment upon wrong and scanty measures we cannot secure ourselves from being in the wrong. (23 March, 1678, *Correspondence*, I, pp. 556–7)

For Locke, then, the moral life is not a perpetual striving after what is best in every situation; it is the much more prosaic business of keeping within the bounds laid down by the law of nature. There are particular occasions on which precepts of the law are obviously relevant to our conduct, and then our conduct is of moral significance. But, in Locke's opinion, 'this . . . happens seldome. At least I may confidently say it does not in the greatest part of the actions of our lives wherein I thinke god out of his infinite goodnesse considering our ignorance and frailty hath left us a great liberty' (ibid.). The precepts which make up the law of nature are the general rules which conscience is to apply to the agent's particular actions, and these precepts also serve to indicate the various circumstances in which an appeal to conscience may be called for, or a moral decision made.

In his account of conscience, Locke follows lines already familiar in Scholastic philosophy. There can be no such thing as conscience without general rules or precepts. Judgments of conscience are fallible, not only in that we may misapply general moral precepts, but also in that we may be mistaken about the true content of morality. Burnet's natural conscience is a striking departure from the Scholastic tradition. With him conscience becomes an internal moral director functioning independently of all rules. Furthermore, unless it is 'obscur'd, prevented or sear'd', conscience is an infallible director. Natural conscience does not 'meddle with generals', but then Burnet appears to see it as meddling promiscuously with all particulars.

Locke's second main criticism concerns Burnet's conception of conscience as a motive of action: 'Men have a natural tendency to what delights and from what pains them. This universal observation has established past doubt. That the soul has such a tendency to what is morally good and from what is evil has not fallen under my observation, and therefore I cannot grant it for as being' (Porter, p.38). On Burnet's account, conscience moves to action because moral goodness, once it is discerned, attracts the agent. It is said to be an innate practical principle in a sense of the latter term which Locke does admit: that is, a principle 'which upon all Occasions, excites and directs the Actions of all Men' (I.iii.12). Locke agrees that there are such principles, but they are hardly moral. The tendencies to action which are innate to human nature 'are so far from being innate

Moral Principles, that if they were left to their full swing, they would carry Men to the over-turning of all Morality. Moral Laws are set as a curb and restraint to these exorbitant Desires, which they cannot be but by Rewards and Punishments, that will overbalance the satisfaction any one shall propose to himself in the breach of the Law' (I.iii.13).

Burnet and Locke differ radically in their ethics. For Burnet moral good is the basic ethical concept; and this good cannot be defined in terms of any natural good. In his *Second Remarks* he complains that, in emphasising divine rewards and punishments as reasons for the moral life, Locke has obliterated the distinction between moral and natural good: 'How, pray you, . . . do you preserve the Distinction (that good old Distinction, which it may be you despise) of *Bonum Utile & Honestum*? In your way, either the Parts are coincident, or *Bonum Utile* is superior to *Bonum Honestum*'.[38] Locke does not take Burnet up on on this, but his own view of the distinction is set forth in a shorthand Journal entry for 16 July 1676. (This has been deciphered by von Leyden and included in his edition of the *Essays*.) In this long and important entry, Locke discusses the passions, or motive forces of action, and pleasure and pain. Pleasure and pain are the proper objects of the passions, and were they absent 'the passions would all cease, having nothing left to wind them up or set them going' (*Essays*, p.265). Happiness, which is the end of all action, consists in pleasure, and its contrary, misery, consists in pain. That which directly produces any degree of pleasure in us is in its own nature good. Locke terms the goodness of whatsoever is pleasant in itself *bonum jucundum*. But there are things which, although they are not directly productive of pleasure, are still called good. This is because they are the means whereby pleasant things can be acquired. Of these instrumental goods Locke distinguishes two kinds:

> *utile* and *honestum*, which, were they not ordained by God to procure the *jucundum* and be a means to help us to happiness . . . I do not see how they would be reckoned good at all. What good were there more in diamonds than pebbles, if they cannot procure us more of those things that are pleasant and agreeable than pebbles will? What makes temperance a good and gluttony an evil but that the one serves to procure us health and ease in this world and happiness in the other, when gluttony does quite the contrary? (*Essays*, pp.268–9)

Burnet, then, is correct in his suspicion that Locke rejects a special category of moral good which is autonomous and in itself attractive to the agent. *Bonum utile* and *bonum honestum* are distinguished only in so far as they are different means to *bonum jucundum*.

In Locke's ethics the basic moral concept is rectitude, and this is defined as conformity to law. The hedonistic analysis of good is developed further in the *Essay*, and there the notion of moral good and evil is linked with rectitude:

> Good and Evil . . . are nothing but Pleasure or Pain, or that which occasions, or procures Pleasure or Pain to us. *Morally Good and Evil* then, is only the Conformity or Disagreement of our voluntary Actions to some Law, whereby Good or Evil is drawn on us, from the Will and Power of the Law-maker; which Good and Evil, Pleasure or Pain, attending our observance, or breach of the Law, by the Decree and the Law-maker, is that we call *Reward* and *Punishment*. (II.xxviii.5)

But this is exactly the conception of moral good against which Burnet protests. In Locke's opinion, this protest arises from a failure to differentiate between good and moral rectitude. The confounding of these two is the basis of the erroneous view that there is an autonomous moral good which can of itself move the agent's will (see 'Voluntas', quoted above, pp.48–9). Both writers accept the Aristotelian conception of good as that which things aim at, or desire,[39] but what Locke denies is that there is a species of good intrinsically related to morality. Morally right actions can be called good only in the instrumental sense of the term; they are good in that they are a means to the non-moral good of pleasure or happiness.

5. On Locke's theory, what may be broadly termed a moral judgment must involve general moral precepts. Such a judgment may be a judgment of conscience, as when we either remind ourselves that the particular action we are tempted to perform is contrary to a general precept, or consider our past actions in the light of general precepts. It may be a judgment arrived at in the absence of any conflict between our inclinations and moral beliefs. We may simply recognise the applicability of a general precept to our given situation and act accordingly, as when the honest man pays his debts. It may also be a judgment passed on the conduct of others. In any case, in making a moral judgment we apply general moral precepts. Concerning those general precepts, Locke tells Grenville:

> 1° That all negative precepts are always to be obeyed.
>
> 2° That positive commands only sometimes upon occasions. But we ought to be always furnished with the habits and dispositions to those positive dutys in a readynesse against those occasions.
>
> 3° That between those two i.e. Between *Unlawfull* which are always and *necessary* quoad hic et nune which are but some-

> times there is a great latitude, and, therein we have our liberty which we may use without scrupulously thinkeing ourselves obleiged to that which in it self may be Best. (*Correspondence*, 1, p.559; cf. *Essays*, pp.193–7)

In the *Essays* Locke explains further that, although the binding force of the law of nature is universal, this does not mean that each and every precept of that law binds each and every individual. A moral precept may be general not in the sense that it applies to *all* agents, but in that it applies to *any* agent occupying a specific station in life. The moral duties of parents to their children and of rulers to their subjects are cases in point (*Essays*, p.197).

The general precepts involved in moral judgments are not to be confused with tendencies to action originally belonging to human nature. Nor are they to be thought of as imperatives. Locke is well aware of the difference between sentences expressing commands and those expressing propositions. It is only propositions which can be true or false.[40] Therefore, if the general precepts of morality are to be moral truths (and thus objects of knowledge), they must be expressed in the indicative not the imperative mood. That is, they must be propositions stating the duties laid upon mankind, and, Locke adds, 'what Duty is, cannot be understood without a Law; nor a Law be known or supposed without a Law-maker, or without Reward and Punishment' (1.iii.12). Thus, the knowledge that such and such an action is morally demanded or prohibited involves the possession of a number of interrelated concepts.[41] Reason deduces the precepts of the moral law – those truths which are distinctively moral – from non-moral facts such as the existence of God and certain truth about human nature.

A great many moral philosophers since Locke's time have accepted the doctrine of the autonomy of morals, and in consequence they have dismissed Locke's position as based upon a fallacy. Even those who have maintained that moral terms can be defined in non-moral terms and that moral conclusions can be validly derived from non-moral premises have tended to shy away from Locke's type of theological ethic. However, while it can hardly be claimed that Locke has said the last word on the nature of obligation, he can answer a number of objections which are standardly thought to be fatal to the position he advocates.

We have already seen that Locke is not open to the charge of equating the content of morality with the random dictates of an arbitrary will. Nor does he found moral obligation upon God's irresistible power, specifically His power to enforce sanctions. Locke's answer to the question why ought we to do what God commands is that, as God made us and constantly preserves us, He is a superior to whom we are rightly subject. An advocate of the autonomy of morals will, of course, object that Locke has derived a moral 'ought' from a non-moral fact. If it is part of what we mean by calling God our Maker that we ought to obey Him, the conclusion that we ought to do what God commands obviously follows. But then the argument will amount to the insignificant tautology that we ought to obey God because He is a Being whom we ought to obey. If, on the other hand, this is not part of what we mean by calling God our Maker, the conclusion that we ought to obey God does not follow from the fact that He is our Maker. Some additional premise is required before the 'ought' conclusion can be established.[42] But here it is to be noted that the question 'why ought we to do what God commands?' is ambiguous. It might be understood as a request for the reasons which will lead us to do what God commands. Or it might be understood as concerned with obligation: why does the fact that God commands us to do a certain thing place us under an obligation to do that thing? Locke addresses himself to the second question, he does not construe being under an obligation to do a thing in terms of having a reason to do it. What he derives from the facts that God exists, that He created the universe, and so on, is the further fact that Human beings have obligations. Once this fact of obligation has been established it is, for Locke, a separate question of what reasons we have for discharging our obligations.

Locke's account of moral obligation, or the moral 'ought', is thoroughly legalist. In order to be under an obligation we must be subject to a law, and this entails a law-maker. As Locke defines God's right to legislate with respect to the conduct of mankind (the right of creation) in terms of the fact that God is our Maker, for him it is true by definition that we are under an obligation to do what God commands. However, it is to be remembered that he backs up his definition by pointing out that we think it reasonable that the child ought to obey its parents. Locke is aware of other accounts which have been given of moral obligation. In the *Essay* he mentions three answers to the question why should compacts be kept:

> A Christian ... will *give* this as a *Reason*: Because God, who has the Power of eternal Life and Death, requires it of us. But if an *Hobbist* be asked why; he will answer: Because the Publick requires it, and the *Leviathan* will punish you, if you do not. And if one of the old *Heathen* Philosophers had been asked, he would have answer'd: Because it was dishonest, below the Dignity of a Man and opposite to Vertue, the highest Perfection of humane Nature, to do otherwise. (I.iii.5)

The answer expresses Locke's conception of moral obligation and is the one he supposes would be given by the Christian.

An obvious advantage of Locke's legalist account of moral obligation is that it gives a definite content to the concept of a moral 'ought' (an advantage which might also be claimed by the Hobbist). We understand perfectly well what it means to talk in the context of law of a person being 'bound' or 'under an obligation', and consequently we have no difficulty understanding an 'ought' which is explained in these legal terms. On the other hand, it is not clear what meaning is assigned to the moral 'ought' in those theories which reject a legalist conception of morality.[43] According to the intellectualist view, moral obligation derives from the 'fitness' of things or from their intrinsic 'goodness', these moral facts being apprehended by our reason. But even granted that moral facts are discovered by reason, it is difficult to see how such a discovery can generate any obligation with respect to these facts. Reason can perhaps make out rules *indicating* valuable or desirable lines of conduct, but in so doing it does not establish the distinctively moral *demand* that these rules be followed. This demand, however, is generated if these rules are considered as laws promulgated by a *de jure* authority.[44] Neither does the moral sense theory appear better placed to account for moral obligation. For one thing, the advocates of the theory have to admit that this sense and the attendant propensity towards what is apprehended as morally good can be perverted, or even effaced, in the individual agent. As Locke pointedly remarks apropos Burnet's version of the theory: 'Natural conscience supposed an innate principle suffocated by ye stupidity or vice is a pretty thing' (Porter, p.43). Aside from this, the moral sense theorist may be criticised for linking moral obligation too closely with our desires and dispositions. We think of the moral 'ought' as applying to a person irrespective of his desires. The fact that he has a strong desire to steal and is in no way disposed to pay his debts does not lead us to withdraw the relevant moral precept, or 'ought' statements in his case. This point is often put by saying that the imperatives of morality are categorical, not hypothetical.[45] But, in so far as it equates being under an obligation to do a thing with having reasons which prompt the doing of that thing, the moral sense theory would seem unable to account for the categorical nature of the moral 'ought'.[46] This difficulty does not arise if moral precepts are considered as laws.[47]

It might still be thought that Locke has failed to do justice to the moral 'ought'. He distinguishes between our having moral obligations and our having reasons for discharging those obligations. The reasons he emphasises are the rewards and punishments God has attached to the observation or neglect of the law of nature. Yet we do feel that the agent who does what is objectively right, but does it out of some non-moral consideration, such as fear of punishment or hope of reward, has not acted truly morally. He has done the right things for the wrong reason, and has not properly followed the dictate of the moral 'ought'. This is the main point in the doctrine of the autonomy of morals, and here surely that doctrine is true to our common moral consciousness. In so far as Locke ignores this aspect of the ordinary conception of moral obligation, his account is faulty. However, our belief that when the right thing is done for non-moral reasons the act is morally defective is itself vague and in need of examination, and on one interpretation of this belief, Locke can accommodate common moral consciousness.

It was mentioned earlier that in Locke's theory a moral judgment always involves general moral precepts. Thus, the agent who is trying to determine what he morally ought to do must first of all recognise the relevance of a general precept, or precepts, to his own concrete situation (for if there are no precepts relevant to his situation, no moral judgment is called for), and he will then decide what to do in the light of the precept, or precepts. Here we can distinguish a general obligation, expressed in a general precept that *x* ought to be done, and what may be termed a categorical obligation, expressed in the agent's decision that in the given situation he ought to do *x*.[48] The agent derives the conclusion 'I ought to do *x*' from the general obligation plus the fact that the obligation applies in his situation. Given that the agent acts upon this conclusion, we can say that he does what he *categorically* ought to do for a moral reason. He acts as he does because he recognises his action as a token of a type of action demanded by a general moral precept (or perhaps because he recognises the alternatives open to him as tokens or types of actions forbidden by general moral precepts).

The person who considers actions and decides what to do in the light of general moral precepts may be said to have adopted the moral point of view. Locke emphasises rewards and punishments as reasons for adopting this point of view; for it is general moral precepts which make up the content of the law of nature, and it is conformity to the law which God rewards and non-conformity which He punishes. But there is a difference between adopting the moral point of view (for whatever reason) and acting from that point of view in particular concrete situations: in the first case the precepts are accepted, in the second case they are applied. The agent who adopts the moral point of view for the non-moral reasons Locke puts forward can properly be said to act from moral reasons when he applies the general precepts he has accepted.

There are alternative points of view to the moral. There is nothing logically incoherent in a person deciding to live solely with an eye to personal pleasure, or even purely in conformity with aesthetic considerations.[49] While such persons will be indifferent to moral considerations, it is possible – and even likely – that they will sometimes perform morally right actions. Our feeling that, morally speaking, there is something amiss in a right action done for a non-moral reason may be interpreted as a recognition that the agent has adopted some point of view other than the moral. What it is that is amiss is suggested by Cudworth's remark that if 'obligation to the things of natural justice arose only by reason of punishments threatened, the consequence would be that no man was good and just, but only by accident, and for the sake of something else' (see above, p.37). An objectively right action which is performed irrespective of any moral considerations is right only by accident; the factors which decided the agent to act as he did are not those he would have considered had he adopted the moral point of view. Had these factors been different, he might equally have decided upon an action which was objectively wrong. We do not have to endorse Cudworth's view of moral obligation to accept this interpretation of our feeling about 'doing the right thing for the wrong reason'; it is equally compatible with Locke's legalist account.

Locke uncompromisingly places the end or object of moral activity outside of morality itself. We have a reason for acting morally only provided so doing will ultimately produce the non-moral good, happiness. However, this does not mean he is committed to denying what is obviously the case, that moral considerations can of themselves prompt action. All he does deny is that such a link between these considerations and action is natural, that is the expression of an innate tendency to what is morally good. On the contrary, it has to be artificially set up. One of Locke's virtues as a moral philosopher is that he separates questions of the psychology of morals from questions of the logic of morals. We will consider his moral psychology in some detail in chapter VIII. The view that virtue, or moral worth, is an end in itself is deeply entrenched in a great deal of moral philosophy, and it is maintained as a corollary that anyone deciding to take up the moral life on the grounds that it will procure him some non-moral good is *ipso facto* excluded from that life. It is worth noting that Locke is far from alone in rejecting this view. In the course of a discussion of man's final end, St Thomas Aquinas argues:

> all moral operations can be ordered to something else. This is evident from the most important instances of these actions. The

> operations of fortitude, which are concerned with warlike activities, are ordered to victory and to peace. Indeed, it would be foolish to make war merely for its own sake. Likewise, the operations of justice are ordered to the preservation of peace among men, by means of each man having his own possessions undisturbed. And the same thing is evident for all the other virtues. Therefore, man's ultimate felicity does not lie in moral operations.[50]

These are sentiments which Locke would thoroughly endorse.

Conscience in all its judgments must apply to general moral precepts. The true precepts of morality constitute the content of the law of nature. In them is expressed the moral obligations human beings are in fact under. Once a knowledge of the content of the law is established, the problem of conflicting conscientiously held beliefs will be solved. From a foundation of certain moral knowledge it will be easy to detect and rectify an erroneous conscience. The doctrine of innate morality, according to which the content of the law is immediately evident to intuition, only serves to strengthen the erroneous conscience. The law is knowable not through intuition, but through discursive reasoning; for 'moral Principles require Reasoning and Discourse, and some Exercise of the Mind, to discover the certainty of their Truth' (I.iii.I).

IV

KNOWLEDGE IN THE STATE OF MEDIOCRITY

In pursuit of the aim announced at the beginning of the *Essay* of determining the extent of human knowledge and the grounds of opinion Locke adopts what he calls the 'Historical, plain Method' (I.i.2). That is, he purports to give a theory-free description of our intellectual processes without speculation or preconceptions about the nature of the mind itself.[1] In his first *Reply* to Stillingfleet, he remarks: 'my design being, as well as I could, to copy nature, and give an account of the operations of the mind in thinking, I could look into nobody's understanding but my own, to see how it wrought' (*Works*, 4, pp.138–9). On the assumption that the operations of the mind are uniform throughout the human race, Locke's personal account will be valid for human understanding in general, and the correctness of the description set forth in the *Essay* will be checkable by each reader from his own observation. Locke's method is historical in that he traces the mind's progress from its original state, in which it is without ideas or the materials of thinking, to the stage at which language is developed as a vehicle for the public expression of thought:

> The Senses at first let in particular *Ideas*, and furnish the yet empty Cabinet: And the Mind by degrees growing familiar with some of them, they are lodged in the Memory, and Names got to them. Afterwards the Mind proceeding farther, abstracts them, and by Degrees learns the use of general Names. (I.ii.15)

The mind must have ideas in order to think, and knowledge and opinions are the products of thought. Hence, a description of the ways in which the mind works with its ideas, together with an account of their origin in experience will provide an answer to the epistemological question of the extent of human knowledge and the grounds of opinion.

The term 'idea' appears on virtually every page of the *Essay* and in a bewildering variety of contexts. Locke initially states that he uses the term to refer to 'whatsoever is the Object of the Understanding when a Man thinks . . . or whatever it is, which the Mind can be employ'd about in thinking' (I.i.8). Defined thus, an idea is apparently the intentional object of thought, or the thing as thought about as distinct from the thing existing independently of thought. However, the term is also used when Locke is talking about sense-perception. For example:

> a Snow-ball having the power to produce in us the *Ideas* of *White, Cold,* and *Round,* the Powers to produce those *Ideas* in us, as they are in the Snow-ball, I call *Qualities*; and as they are Sensations, or Perceptions, in our Understandings, I call them *Ideas*: which *Ideas,* if I speak of sometimes, as in the things themselves, I would be understood to mean those Qualities in the objects which produce them in us. (II.viii.8)

Here 'idea' does not refer to the intentional object of what would normally be called thought, but to the thing as perceived by the senses, or what may be called our percept of the thing. A further complication is introduced by Locke's stated willingness to use the term to refer to the qualities of material objects.

Locke's double use of 'idea' to refer to the objects of thought and to percepts derives from the way in which he employs the psychological concepts of thought and perception. In common with Descartes, Locke uses 'thinking' in a broad and in a narrow sense. In its broad sense the term covers mental phenomena in general, including sensation; so that to say that a person is thinking simply means that he is conscious. It occurs in this sense in Locke's extended argument against the Cartesian view that the soul always thinks (II.i.9–20). In the narrow sense, he uses the term much as we would ordinarily use it today, to denote mental activity other than sensation and especially reasoning and discursive thought. Neither does Locke use 'perception' solely in reference to sense perception. He does say that thinking should be distinguished from perceiving; for, properly speaking, the former 'signifies that sort of operation of the Mind about its *Ideas,* wherein the Mind is active . . . [while] in bare naked *Perception,* the Mind is, for the most part, only passive; and what it perceives, it cannot avoid perceiving' (II.ix.1). However, he blurs his distinction in two ways. First, even in perception the mind is said to be passive only 'for the most part'. Locke is careful to explain that impressions made by external objects on the sense organs are not themselves sufficient for sensation. It is necessary that these impressions be 'taken notice of in the Understanding. . . . *So that where-ever there is Sense,* or *Perception, there some* Idea *is actually produced, and present in the Understanding'* (II.ix.4). As this 'taking notice' which is involved in all sense-perception is an act of the mind, it qualifies as what Locke calls thinking. Secondly, 'perception' is also used to refer to purely intellectual operations and most importantly to the act of knowing. As Locke stretches the term 'thinking' to cover perception and employs 'perception' in his account of the mind's intellectual operations, it is not surprising that he should use the one term to refer both to the intentional object of thought and to what is perceived by the senses.

Locke frequently talks of ideas as 'copies', 'resemblances', 'representations', 'pictures' or 'images' of things (see, for example, II.i.15, 25; II.xi.17; II.xxix.8). This characterisation of ideas is not part of his initial definition of an idea. However, he does explicate his definition: 'since the Things, the Mind contemplates, are none of them, besides it self, present to the Understanding, 'tis necessary that something else, as a Sign or Representation of the things it considers should be present to it: And these are *Ideas*' (IV.xxi.4). The same argument is put forward in more detail in the *Second Reply* to Stillingfleet:

> Not thinking your lordship . . . persuaded, that as often as you think of your cathedral church, or of Des Cartes's vortices, that the very cathedral church at Worcester, or the motion of those vortices, itself exists in your understanding; when one of them never existed but in that one place at Worcester, and the other never existed in *rerum natura.* I conclude, your lordship has immediate objects of your mind, which are not the very things themselves existing in your understanding; which if . . . you will please to call representations . . . rather than . . . ideas, it will make no difference. (*Works,* 4, pp.390–1)

According to Thomas Reid, this line of reasoning is dictated by a cognative analogue of the physical principle that there can be no action at a distance. In thinking (including perceiving by the senses) the mind must be in contact with what it thinks about. When the things thought about are external to the mind, this cognitive contact can only be indirect. Hence the need for objects in the mind serving as representations or images of external things. It is these mental objects which the mind directly contemplates in thought; and, as the reference to Descartes' vortices shows, they are also invoked to explain how it is possible to think about the non-existent.[2]

Reid is a spokesman for what may be called the traditional view of Locke's ideas: that they are mental entities which stand as the immediate objects of mental acts and thus go proxy for things in the world. There is no doubt that Locke's ideas are mental items of some sort, and that without them there is no thinking. However, as a number of commentators have pointed out, there are remarks and phrases in the *Essay* and in other works such as the *Examination of P. Malebranche's Opinion* which suggest that he does not conceive ideas as entities existing in the mind, but rather as acts of the mind.[3] The characterisation of ideas as representations need not be inconsistent with an interpretation of them as acts. An act of thinking may be said to represent and even (in a somewhat Pickwickian sense) to picture reality in that there can be a correspondence between what we think things in the world to be and the way they in fact are.[4]

Yet the textual evidence for a 'non-entity' interpretation of Locke's ideas is equivocal. He is notoriously loose in his use of terms. In a number of passages 'perception' denotes something like the content of the perceptual act, while in other passages it denotes the act itself.[5] What he does unequivocally hold is that ideas do not exist apart from the perceptual act. He refers to memory as 'the Store-house of our *Ideas*', but he makes sure that this phrase is cleared of any implication that ideas exist in our minds without our being conscious of them:

> our *ideas* being nothing, but actual Perceptions in the Mind, which cease to be any thing, when there is no perception of them, this *laying up* of our *Ideas* in the Repository of the Memory, signifies no more but this, that the Mind has a Power, in many cases, to revive Perceptions, which it has once had, with this additional Perception annexed to them, that it has had them before. And in this Sense it is, that our *Ideas* are said to be in our Memories, when indeed, they are actually no where. (II.x.2)

This passage illustrates Locke's use of 'perception' to denote both the perceptual act and the content of the act. Nonetheless, his meaning is clear: Ideas are first produced in the perceptual situation, and when that situation no longer obtains they exist solely in virtue of being perceived in an act of remembrance. But to hold that the *esse* of ideas is *percipi* is not to hold that ideas are identical with acts of perception. The passages in which Locke does seem to equate ideas with mental acts can quite naturally be read as underlining his view that ideas have no existence apart from those acts.

In fact, Locke does not commit himself to any account of the nature of ideas. When the question is put to him by John Norris he interprets it as a request for an account of the mechanism whereby ideas are produced in the mind (even though it is abundantly clear from Norris' words that what he is after is a statement about the kind of things ideas are):[6]

> By the 'nature of ideas' . . . is meant here their causes and manner of production in the mind, *i.e.*, in what alteration of the mind this perception consists; and as to that, I answer, no man can tell. (*Remarks, Works,* 10, p.248)

Here it is important to remember that, in accord with his historical, plain method, Locke's purpose is not to put forward a theory concerning the nature of the mind and its operations, but simply to describe those operations. The key terms employed in this description are 'idea' and 'perception'. We have already mentioned that he uses the term 'perception' to denote the activity of thinking as well as sense-perception. But in describing the activity of thinking he draws upon sense perception; he holds that the 'perception of the Mind [is] most aptly explained by Words relating to the Sight' (II.xxix.2). The language in which his way of ideas is expounded is, therefore, analogical. Locke adopts what may be called a 'visual model of the mind'. That is, he supposes that the non-sensory operations of the mind, such as thinking, may be described and made intelligible in language taken over from our visual perception of things in the world.[7] It is in terms of this model that 'our *Ideas* ... are, as it were, the Pictures of Things' (II.xxix.8). As the qualifying phrase 'as it were' makes plain, Locke is not committed to the view that all ideas (or indeed any of them) are literally pictures or mental images.

Although ideas figure in the perceptual situation it would be a mistake to suppose that Locke is concerned to expound and defend a representative theory of sense-perception. He frequently uses the language of naive realism and talks of our experiencing material objects. In the few passages in which he does discuss sense-perception he adopts a causal theory which explains our perception of material objects in terms of minute particles emanating from those objects and coming into contact with our sense organs (II.viii.11–13, and *Examination,* §9). Locke can consistently hold that material objects are perceived mediately, via a causal transaction between the objects and the mind of the perceiver, and that ideas or images are involved in sense-perception without thereby committing himself to the position that what the senses perceive are always ideas in the mind.[8] But in fact a philosophical theory of sense-perception is peripheral to his main interest. In answer to Stillingfleet's complaint against his constant use of the new term 'idea' he writes:

> because treating in it [the *Essay*] of the understanding, which is nothing but the faculty of thinking, I could not well treat of that faculty of the mind . . . without considering the immediate objects of the mind in thinking, which I call ideas: and therefore ... the greatest part of my book has been taken up, in considering what these objects of the mind, in thinking are; whence they come; what use the mind makes of them . . . and what are the outward marks whereby it signifies them to others, or records

> them for its own use. And this, in short, is my way by ideas . . . which, . . . if it be new, it is but a new history of an old thing. For I think it will not be doubted, that men always perform'd the actions of thinking, reasoning, believing and knowing, just after the same manner they do now. (*Reply, Works*, 4, pp.134–5)

There is no mention of the perceptual situation in this epitome of the way of ideas. The emphasis is on the use the mind makes of ideas once they have been acquired in experience and lodged in the memory, and the term 'thinking' is used to denote intellectual rather than sensory activity.

Whether or not Locke subscribes to a representative theory of sense-perception, he does hold a representative theory of thinking. He does sometimes talk of ideas as 'pictures or images' in connection with sense-perception (for example, at II.i.25, and II.xi.17), but mostly this language occurs in connection with thinking, as distinct from sense-perception. In accordance with his visual model Locke conjectures that 'our *Ideas* do, whilst we are awake, succeed one another in our Minds at certain distances, not much unlike the Images in the inside of a Lanthorn, turned round by the Heat of a Candle' (II.xiv.9).[9] But so long as it merely has a train of ideas passing through it the mind is idling. The 'natural tendency of the Mind being towards Knowledge' (II.xxxii.6), its aim is to make use of its ideas to discover truths about things. The stage of primary importance in the mind's progress towards knowledge is its appropriation of ideas as signs of things. It is only after 'Children have, by repeated Sensations, got *Ideas* fixed in their Memories, [that] they begin, by degrees, to learn the use of Signs' (II.xi.8). When Locke talks of ideas as objects of the understanding, or what the mind is employed about in thinking, he is concerned, at least primarily, with their function as signs. He does maintain that we can acquire a knowledge of things, but this must be acquired by way of the ideas we have made into signs:

> the immediate Object of all our Reasoning and Knowledge, is nothing but Particulars. Every Man's Reasoning and Knowledge, is only about the *Ideas* existing in his own Mind, which are truly, every one of them, particular Existences: and our Knowledge and Reasoning about other Things, is only as they correspond to these our particular *Ideas*. (IV.xvii.8)

However, strictly speaking, the correspondence involved in our knowledge of things is not between our ideas and the world, but between propositions and the world. Propositions are themselves assemblages of signs.

According to Locke, 'Truth . . . in the proper import of the Word . . . signif[ies] nothing but *the joining or separating of Signs, as the*

Things signified by them, do agree or disagree one with another' (IV.v.2). He goes on to say that the '*joining* or *separating* of signs here meant is what by another name, we call Proposition. So that Truth properly belongs only to Propositions: whereof there are two sorts, *viz.* Mental and Verbal; as there are two sorts of Signs . . . viz., *Ideas* and Words' (ibid.). Locke, then, holds a correspondence theory of truth. Rather as the arrangement of elements in a picture correspond to the arrangement of elements in the thing pictured, so the assemblage of ideas constituting a true proposition corresponds to the structure of the reality the proposition is about. Falsehood is a failure of correspondence between the way the proposition is structured and the structure of reality. Locke's account of truth is complicated by the fact that he admits words as well as ideas as signs. A verbal proposition is true in virtue of there being a correspondence between the arrangement of the words in which it is formulated and the connection of the ideas those words stand for. But this truth may be 'verbal' not 'real' truth:

> that being only *verbal Truth,* wherein Terms are joined according to the agreement or disagreement of the *Ideas* they stand for, without regarding whether our *Ideas* are such, as really have, or are capable of having an Existence in Nature. But then it is they contain *real Truth,* when these signs are joined, as our *Ideas* agree; and when our *Ideas* are such, as we know are capable of having an Existence in Nature. (IV.v.8)

Locke introduces this somewhat odd distinction in order to accommodate what he calls 'fantastical' ideas, that is 'those . . . which are made up of such Collections of simple *Ideas,* as were really never united, never were found together in any Substance' (II.xxx.5). He accepts that propositions such as 'all centaurs are animals' are true. Their truth is due to the agreement between the ideas for which the word stands (IV.v.7). But because there are no centaurs, there is no reality corresponding to the proposition. Hence it is said not to contain real truth. However, most of our ideas are not fantastical, and a verbal proposition will have real truth provided it is possible to formulate a corresponding true mental proposition.

In thinking, at least the kind of thinking which is productive of knowledge, the mind joins or separates ideas and so forms propositions. According to Locke 'our Knowledge . . . all consists in Propositions' (II.xxxiii.19). This is because it is only propositions to which truth and falsity can properly be ascribed. Strictly speaking, an idea in itself is neither true nor false (II.xxxii.1). Isolated ideas are not objects of knowledge; rather they are the materials from which the objects of knowledge (propositions) are constructed.[10] They are not themselves properly thoughts, but the mental stuff we manipulate in thinking. In order to know, the mind must bring ideas together in propositions, but this is not sufficient for knowledge. In the *Elements of Natural Philosophy* Locke states that knowledge 'consists in the perception of the truth of affirmative, or negative propositions' (*Works*, 3, p.329). In the *Essay* Locke distinguishes three sorts of perception: '1. The Perception of *Ideas* in our Minds. 2. The Perception of the signification of Signs. 3. The Perception of the Connexion or Repugnancy, Agreement or Disagreement, that there is between any of our *Ideas*' (II.xxi.5). He goes on to say that all these sorts of perception are attributed to the understanding 'though it be the two latter only that use allows us to say we understand' (ibid.). In order to manipulate ideas we obviously must be possessed of them, and in order to construct propositions out of our ideas we must have appropriated them as signs. Finally, as Locke describes it in *Essay*, Book IV, knowing the truth of a proposition is a matter of perceiving a connection between ideas.

Given that knowing consists in perceiving connections between ideas, the extent of human knowledge will be determined in the first place by the ideas we have and secondly by the connection we are able to perceive between them (IV.iii.1–2). There being no innate ideas the mind in its original state is, in Locke's famous metaphor, 'white Paper, void of all Characters' (II.i.2). All ideas must be acquired in experience, of which Locke recognises two kinds: sensation and reflection. Of Reflection, Locke writes that it is a 'Source of *Ideas*, every Man has wholly in himself: And though it be not Sense, as having nothing to do with external Objects; yet it is very like it, and might properly enough be call'd internal Sense' (II.i.4). While ideas of material things derive from sensation, reflection provides us with ideas of '*Perception, Thinking, Doubting, Believing, Reasoning, Knowing, Willing,* and all the different actings of our own Minds; which we being conscious of, and observing in our selves, do from these receive into our Understandings, as distinct *Ideas*, as we do from Bodies affecting our Senses' (II.i.4).[11] There are other ideas, such as the ideas of pleasure, pain, power, existence and unity, which the mind acquires from both sensation and from reflection (II.vii).

Material things can be imaged; so it would seem that ideas given in sensation and lodged in the memory may be construed as literal mental images. Locke does seem to construe them thus when he originally makes use of the term 'idea' at the beginning of Draft A of the *Essay*: 'our senses conversant about particular objects . . . give us the simple Ideas or Images of things & thus we come to have Ideas of heat & light, hard & soft which are noe thing but the reviveing again in our mindes those imaginations which those objects when they affected our senses caused in us . . . & thus we doe when we conceive heat or light, yellow or blew sweet or bitter & c.' (§1).[12] However, perception and the other acts of the mind which are presented to reflection are not imaginable, nor can the ideas acquired from both sensation and reflection be literally images. Locke's imagist language must in these cases be understood metaphorically or analogically, and he does remark that some of our ideas 'have no sensible marks that resemble them' (IV.iii.19).

Locke works with two importantly different conceptions of reflection. Reflection is introduced as a source of ideas analogous to sensation, and the major point of analogy is that in both sensation and reflection the mind is, for the most part, passive: 'the Objects of our Senses, do . . . obtrude their particular *Ideas* upon our minds, whether we will or no: And the Operations of our minds, will not let us be without, at least some obscure Notions of them' (II.i.25). But Locke also speaks of reflection as involving an effort on the part of the mind. Mental phenomena 'make not deep Impressions enough, to leave in the Mind clear distinct lasting *Ideas,* till the Understanding turns inward upon it self, *reflects* on its own *Operations,* and makes them the Object of its own Contemplation' (II.i.8). The contemplation demanded here is obviously something more than the minimal act of taking notice necessary in 'bare naked perception'. In its passive form reflection is the same as consciousness, which Locke defines as 'the perception of what passes in a Man's own mind' (II.i.19). On his own showing active reflection is analogous not to sensation but to what may be called sensory scrutiny:

> though he that contemplates the Operations of his Mind, cannot but have plain and clear *Ideas* of them; yet unless he turn his Thoughts that way, and considers them with attention, he will no more have clear and distinct *Ideas* of all the *Operations of his Mind,* and all that may be observed therein, than he will have all the particular *ideas* of any Landscape, or of the Parts and Motions of a Clock, who will not turn his Eyes to it, and with attention heed all Parts of it. (II.i.7)

Strictly, ideas are not objects of knowledge but the materials out of which such objects may be constructed, and, although he uses the term 'idea' in this passage, Locke is clearly talking of a knowledge of the operations of the mind. The historical, plain method which he claims to adopt in the *Essay* is an exercise in active reflection or introspection.

4. In the second book of the *Essay* Locke endeavours to establish the empiricist thesis that all ideas derive from experience and in furtherance of this he sets out an elaborate taxonomy of ideas. The first distinction he draws is between simple and complex ideas. He repeatedly talks of simple ideas as the 'materials', the 'beginnings' and the 'foundation' of all our knowledge (e.g. II.i.25; II.ii.2; II.xiii.1; IV.xvii.3). One of the things he means by this is that simple ideas are the elements with which the mind operates in the production of ideas of other types (II.ii.2; II.xii.1). There are in fact two parts to Locke's thesis concerning the origin of ideas: first, that all simple ideas must be got initially in experience; second, that all ideas of other types are ultimately the product of the mind going to work on simple ideas.

Locke emphasises the passivity of the mind in the acquisition of simple ideas: 'These *simple Ideas,* when offered to the mind, *the Understanding can* no more refuse to have, nor alter, when they are imprinted, nor blot them out, and make new ones in it self, than a mirror can refuse, alter, or obliterate the Images or *Ideas,* which, the Objects set before it, do therein produce' (II.i.25). Complex ideas, on the other hand, are the products of mental activity: 'When the Understanding is once stored with these simple *Ideas,* it has the Power to repeat, compare and unite them even to an almost infinite Variety, and so can make at Pleasure new complex *Ideas'* (II.ii.2). Locke is not saying that in experience the mind is first of all presented with simples which it then proceeds to combine into complexes; so that seeing, say, a lily would be a process of perceiving its individual qualities, such as its colour, shape, and smell, one after another, and then putting these together in the complex idea of a lily. On the contrary, he holds that, at least very often, 'simple *Ideas* are observed to exist in several Combinations united together' (II.xii.1; see also II.xxiii.1 and 6; III.ix.13).[13] In distinguishing between simple and complex ideas, Locke is not concerned with the perceptual situation. The simple ideas from which complex ones are made are ideas which have been 'stored' in the understanding, that is those which can be revived by memory in the absence of the objects which first imprinted them on the mind. That a specific simple idea was originally acquired in combination with other simple ideas does not hinder its being isolated from those other ideas when it is revived in an act of remembrance. Nor does Locke use 'complex idea' to denote combinations of simple ideas produced in the passive mind during the perceptual situation. He is quite explicit that *all* complex ideas result from the mental *act* of 'combining several simple *Ideas* into one compound one' (II.xii.1).[14] The construction of complex ideas occurs after the perceptual situation when the mind goes to work on the ideas it has 'layed up'. In constructing complex ideas the mind may copy observed combinations of simple ideas, or qualities, but there is never any need for it to do so (II.xii.1). Thus, from all we can tell from the complex ideas themselves, even those which are in fact copies of patterns given to experience might be inventions of the mind. Locke's point is that it is only with respect to simple ideas that we can be sure that they are not inventions of the mind:

> it is not in the Power of the most exalted Wit, or enlarged Understanding . . . to *invent or frame one new simple* Idea in the mind, not taken in by the ways before mentioned [i.e. sensation and reflection]: nor can any force of the Understanding, *destroy* those that are there. . . . I would have any one try to fancy any Taste, which had never affected his Palate; or frame the *Idea* of a Scent, he had never smelt. (II.ii.2)

The contrast between simple ideas and the complex ideas made from them is, therefore, not a contrast between that which is in fact given and that which is made, but between that which *must* be given and that which is made.

Locke's criterion for the simplicity of ideas is clearly influenced by his visual model of the mind. A simple idea is one which 'contains it in nothing but *one uniform Appearance,* or Conception in the mind, and is not distinguishable into different *Ideas*' (II.ii.1). This description of an idea as being of 'one uniform appearance' may seem appropriate for ideas of sensible qualities. We can frame images of such qualities; for example, an image of a patch which is uniformly red. However, even this will not be simple in the required sense. For such an image must have some shape or other, and will, therefore, include the simple idea of a specific shape as well as the simple idea of a specific colour. If simple ideas are those of one uniform appearance it would seem that the question whether or not there are such ideas should be settled by observation: does introspection reveal anything in the mind which fits this description? However, Locke places far more weight on the second part of his criterion, that simple ideas are those which are 'not distinguishable into different ideas'. This suggests a conception of simple ideas as the unanalysable elements arrived at in the analysis of complex ideas. The thesis that there are such atomic elements is not based on observation, but is *a priori.* That Locke does hold on *a priori* grounds that there are simple ideas comes out in his account of definition. Briefly, words stand for ideas, and when a word stands for a complex idea it can be defined. We define a word by giving an analysis of the relevant complex idea. Locke writes: 'I will not have trouble myself, to prove that all Terms are not definable from that Progress, *in infinitum*, which it will visibly lead us into, if we should allow, that all Names could be defined. For if the Terms of one Definition, were still to be defined by another, Where at last should we stop?' (III.iv.5). Locke's throw-away argument that definition must terminate in indefinables is equally an argument that the analysis of complex ideas must terminate in unanalysable ideas. Thus, that there are simple ideas is not a contingent truth established by pointing to examples, but an *a priori* truth following from the nature of complex ideas; it is a matter of logical necessity that 'all our complex *Ideas* are ultimately resolvable into simple *Ideas*, of which they are compounded, and originally made up' (II.xxii.9). In this case the point of most importance is not that the mind makes complex ideas out of simple ideas, but that all complex ideas (no matter how the mind comes by them) are analysable into simple ideas.

As well as constructing complex ideas the mind also frames abstract, or general ideas, which may themselves be either simple or complex. There are, in Locke's account, two stages in the process of abstraction. The first consists in separating the ideas from 'circumstances of Time, and Place, and any other *Ideas*, that may determine them to this or that particular Existence' (III.iii.6); the second in the mind's decision to use the ideas thus isolated as 'Standards to rank real Existences into sorts, as they agree with these Patterns, and to *denominate* them accordingly' (II.xi.9). It is the use to which abstract ideas are put which distinguishes them from non-abstract ideas. The difference comes out clearly in Locke's account of the child's abstract idea of man:

> The *Ideas* of the Nurse, and the Mother, are well framed in the Minds; and, like Pictures of them there, represent only those Individuals. The Names they first give to them, are confined to these Individuals. . . . Afterwards, when time and a larger Acquaintance has made them observe, that there are a great many other things in the World, that in some common agreements of Shape, and several other qualities, resemble their Father and Mother, and those Persons they have been used to, they frame an *Idea*, which they find those many Particulars do partake in; and to that they give . . . the name *Man*, for Example. And *thus they come to have a general Name* and a general *Idea*. (III.iii.7).

A non-abstract idea is a sign of one, definite individual; an abstract idea is a sign of an indefinite number of individuals, the number being limited only by the condition that each exhibit the qualities selected in the abstract idea. The procedure of abstraction may be applied to ideas which are already abstract. Thus the child may use his idea of man in framing ideas of a higher level of abstractness such as the idea of animal (III.iii.8).

Locke's doctrine of abstraction has often been understood as a theory of concept formation. Although the modern term 'concept' has been given a variety of meanings, this view of the doctrine is basically correct; Locke's abstract ideas are, in certain major respects, the same as concepts.[15] The minimal criterion for a person's having a concept of, say a horse, is that he is able to recognise horses, distinguish between them and other animals, and so on. Similarly, in Locke's doctrine it is the possession of the abstract idea 'horse' which enables a person to classify particular things as horses. When we talk of a person's concept (or conception) of a thing we mean his beliefs concerning the thing's nature, or the characteristics which he takes to be essential to the thing. Locke's abstract ideas, we shall see, encapsulate essences. Finally, concepts may be logically connected or linked one to another, and knowledge of these connections is expressed in universal, logically necessary propositions. The kind of knowledge Locke terms knowledge of relation is attained when the mind perceives relations between abstract ideas. But before turning to Locke's account of knowledge, something needs to be said about three further categories in his taxonomy.

Locke classifies all complex ideas under the three headings, 'modes', 'substances' and 'relations':

> *Modes* I call such complex *Ideas,* which however compounded, contain not in them the supposition of subsisting by themselves, but are considered as Dependences on, or Affections of Substances. . . . *Ideas* of *Substances* are such combinations of simple *Ideas,* as are taken to represent distinct particular things subsisting by themselves. . . . The . . . sort of complex *Ideas* . . . we call *Relation* . . . consists in the consideration and comparing one *Idea* with another. (II.xii.4–7)

Modes themselves are classified as simple and complex. Simple modes are those 'which are only variations, or different combinations of the same simple *Idea,* without the mixture of any other, as a dozen, or score; which are nothing but the *Ideas* of so many distinct Unites added together' (II.xii.5). Mixed modes are made up of simple ideas of different kinds, as, for example, beauty, which is 'a certain composition of Colour and Figure, causing delight in the Beholder' (ibid.). Even simple modes qualify as complex ideas, for they contain more than one simple idea. According to Locke we have ideas of three sorts of substances: God, finite minds or spirits, and bodies

(II.xxvii.2). However, he pays most attention to bodies or corporeal substances, and as it occurs in the *Essay* the term 'substance' most often refers to these. Our ideas of specific substances 'are nothing else but *a Collection of a certain number of simple* Ideas, *considered as united in one thing*' (II.xxiii.14). In the case of bodies, these simples are ideas of sensible qualities together with ideas of the body's powers so far as these have been discovered by observation and experiment. Thus, our idea of gold includes the sensible qualities of yellowness and great weight together with the powers of ductility, fusibility and solubility in *aqua regia* (II.xxiii.37). Finally, the heading 'relation' covers a wide range of ideas. These are produced by the mind's act of comparing, and the '*nature . . . of Relation,* consists in the referring, or comparing two things, one to another; from which comparison, one or both comes to be denominated' (II.xxv.5).[16] Locke considers the relations of cause and effect and identity and diversity at length, but those which are of most significance in ethics are moral relations, or 'the Relation of humane Actions to a Law' (II.xxviii.17). However, the ideas of the actions which are related to a law in morality are, as we shall see, mixed modes.

5. Locke considers his originality to lie in the fact that he is the first to have 'particularly set down wherein the act of knowing precisely consisted' (*Reply, Works,* 4, p.143). Knowing he equates with being certain: 'with me, to know and be certain, is the same thing; what I know, that I am certain of; and what I am certain of, that I know. What reaches to knowledge, I think may be called certainty; and what comes short of certainty, I think cannot be called knowledge' (ibid., p.145). The certainty of knowledge is contrasted with the probability of belief and opinion: '*Probability* . . . is always conversant about Propositions, whereof we have no certainty, but only some inducements to receive them for true' (IV.xv.4). Although Locke does discuss the degrees of assent to be given to propositions in judgments of probability he really does not go beyond a list of common sense guides for judgment (IV.xvi). What in the main he aims to do is give an account of what it is to know and thereby to distinguish knowing from judgment of probability; for 'the highest Probability, amounts not to Certainty; without which, there can be no true Knowledge' (IV.iii.14).

Locke is quite clear that psychological certainty is not sufficient for knowledge. For one thing, judgments of probability may 'raise so near to *Certainty,* that they govern our Thoughts as absolutely, and influence all our Actions as fully, as the most evident demonstration' (IV.xvi.6). For Locke, when we know something we do feel convinced of its truth, but the felt conviction can be identified as knowledge only by reference to its object, that is the assemblage of ideas which makes up the proposition known. His definition of knowledge follows from his 'way of ideas'.

> Since *the Mind,* in all its Thoughts and Reasonings, hath no other immediate Object but its own *Ideas,* which it alone does or can contemplate, it is evident, that our Knowledge is only conversant about them. *Knowledge* then seems to me to be nothing but *the perception of the connexion and agreement, or disagreement and repugnancy of any of our Ideas.* (IV.i.1–2)

This definition mentions both the perception which is the mind's act of knowing and the connections of ideas which are the objects of that act. In subsequent chapters Locke discusses the act and the object separately.

Before considering Locke's discussion of the act of knowing, there are three points in the interpretation of his definition of knowledge which need to be cleared up. In the first place, Locke has usually been read as placing knowledge in the perception of connections *between* ideas; yet all that is stated in his definition is that the connections are *of* ideas. It has been argued by J.W. Yolton that, on a reading confined strictly to what Locke says, the definition allows for knowledge when the perception is of a connection between ideas and the reality they represent.[17] It is true that Locke does talk of the agreement of ideas to the reality of things (e.g. II.xxx.1 and 2). There are, however, passages in the *Essay* and in Locke's other writings which support the traditional reading. Conclusively, in the 'Abstract of the Essay', published in Le Clerc's *Bibliothèque Universelle* for 1688, Locke writes of *Essay,* Book IV: 'The first chapter shows that knowledge is nothing but the perception of the agreement or disagreement of any two ideas' (King, 2, p.275).[18] The terms of the connection perceived in the act of knowing are, then, always ideas. Secondly, the definition of knowledge covers what Locke calls 'certain knowledge', and this he distinguishes from 'real knowledge': 'Where-ever we perceive the Agreement or Disagreement of any of our *Ideas* there is certain Knowledge: and where-ever we are sure those *Ideas* agree with the reality of Things, there is certain real Knowledge' (IV.iv.18). That is, in order to attain real knowledge the mind must both perceive a connection between ideas and *be sure* that the ideas agree with reality. But, within the terms of Locke's definition, the perception alone constitutes knowing. Though at times he uses them carelessly, in Locke's philosophy the epistemic terms 'being sure' and 'assurance' are not equivalent to 'knowing' and 'knowledge'. We can *be sure* concerning the agreement of single ideas and reality, but we *know* propositions, which are assemblages of ideas. Thirdly, though Locke talks of himself as being the first to explain the nature of the *act* of knowing, he does not regard knowledge as entirely an episode in the mental life of the individual. He distinguishes between the episodic act of knowing, or 'actual Knowledge', and :'habitual Knowledge', or the knowledge we have of truths stored in our memories (IV.i.8).[19] Nevertheless, the episodic act of knowing is primary; for in order to know something in the habitual sense we must remember that we once actually perceived the connection between the relevant ideas (ibid.).

The act of knowing may be performed in three ways. Though all three yield what Locke is prepared to call certainty, the certainties are of different degrees. The first and most perfect degree of certainty is intuitive knowledge, when 'the Mind perceives the Agreement or Disagreement of two *Ideas* immediately by themselves, without the intervention of any other' (IV.ii.1). The next degree is demonstrative knowledge, in which the mind employs intervening ideas in order to reveal connections holding between the ideas initially considered. For, 'when the Mind cannot so bring its *Ideas* together, as by their immediate Comparison, and as it were Juxta-position, or application one to another, to perceive their Agreement or Disagreement, it is fain, by the Intervention of other *Ideas*... to discover the Agreement or Disagreement, which it searches' (IV.ii.2). Demonstration presupposes intuition, for the relation between the original ideas is revealed through intuition of relations between the intervening ideas. Demonstrative knowledge lacks the perfection of certainty belonging to intuitive knowledge. This is because each step in a demonstration must be held in the memory until the conclusion is reached, and, as memory is fallible, this means that we can go astray in our attempts at demonstration (IV.ii.7). The third degree Locke calls sensitive knowledge, which he defines as knowledge 'of the existence of particular external Objects, by that perception and Consciousness we have of the actual entrance of *Ideas* from them' (IV.ii.14). Sensitive knowledge '*extends as far as the present Testimony of our Senses,* employ'd about particular Objects, that do then affect them, *and no farther*' (IV.xi.9). However, Locke adds that '*by our Memory* we may be assured, that heretofore Things, that affected our Senses, have existed' (IV.xi.11).

This third degree of knowledge warrants further attention. Locke has often been accused of inconsistency in admitting sensitive knowledge. For even if my knowing, for example, that there is a book in front of me because I see it is a case of knowing the existence of a thing by the 'entrance of ideas from it', it is clearly not a case of my perceiving a connection *between* ideas. Therefore, it is not knowledge within the terms of Locke's definition.[20]

There are, however, important differences between Locke's account of intuition and demonstration on the one hand and sensitive knowledge on the other. For one thing, whereas his account of the first two is purely descriptive, he feels called upon to justify sensitive knowledge. He attempts to refute the sceptical thesis that the senses can provide no certitude that anything exists external to the mind. In the main, his reply is that, as the ideas we receive in the perceptual situation come to us irrespective of our own volition, they must be caused by something external to the mind. He adds that there is a phenomenal difference between, say the idea of a sun as it is conjured up in memory and our actual experience of the sun (IV.xi.5).[21] There is another feature of Locke's treatment of sensitive knowledge that bears directly on the question of his consistency. Though he refers to our sensory awareness of the existence of things as a degree of knowledge, the title is by way of being honorary. As A.D. Woozley has pointed out, Locke is hesitant in his use of the term 'sensitive knowledge'.[22] For example, he shows a certain reluctance about including it alongside intuition and demonstration:

> Intuition and Demonstration, are the degrees of our Knowledge; whatever comes short of one of these . . . is but Faith, or Opinion, but not Knowledge, at least in all general Truths. There is, indeed, another *Perception* of the Mind, employ'd about *the particular existence of finite Beings* without us; which going beyond bare probability, and yet not reaching perfectly to either of the foregoing degrees of certainty, passes under the name of Knowledge. (IV.ii.14)

Elsewhere he refers to sensitive knowledge as 'an assurance that *deserves the name of Knowledge*' (IV.xi.3). Now if this perception 'passes under' or even 'deserves' the name of knowledge, the implication is that it is *not* knowledge within the meaning Locke has assigned to that term. Strictly speaking, it is not knowledge but 'assurance'. If Locke does not consider sensitive knowledge to be knowledge strictly so-called, then he is not contradicting his definition of knowledge by introducing it within his general epistemology.

Having dealt with the perception which is the act of knowing Locke goes on to examine the object of knowledge. That which is known is summed up in the formula 'the connexion and agreement, or disagreement and repugnancy of any of our ideas'. These various connections are marshalled under four headings: '1. *Identity*, or *Diversity*. 2. *Relation*. 3. *Co-existence*, or *necessary connexion*. 4. *Real Existence*' (IV.i.3). As knowledge is equated with certainty and has to do exclusively with connections between ideas, it is commonly thought that these four headings include only that which can be known *a priori*. The legitimate objects of the act of knowing must be propositions which are universal and logically necessary; there can be no *a posteriori* knowledge of contingent truths. This interpretation is strengthened by the appearance of the term 'repugnancy' in Locke's definition of knowledge, for in seventeenth-century usage this may mean logical contradiction or inconsistency.[23] The notion of sensitive knowledge has been seen as an inconsistent attempt on Locke's part to accommodate a knowledge of empirical truths.[24] Even if, as has been argued, Locke's notion of sensitive knowledge is consistent with his definition of knowledge, it remains that the definition appears highly restrictive. A philosopher may, of course, have good reasons for tightening up the concept of knowledge even when such revision excludes much of what we ordinarily say we know. The problem is that Locke clearly does want to include empirical knowledge within his general scheme. He occasionally mentions a kind of empirical knowledge which he calls 'experimental knowledge':

> The Things that, as far as our Observation reaches, we constantly find to proceed regularly, we may conclude, do act by a Law set them; but yet by a Law, that we know not: whereby, though Causes work steadily, and Effects constantly flow from them, yet their *Connexions* and *Dependancies* being not discoverable in our *Ideas*, we can have but an experimental Knowledge of them. (IV.iii.29; cf. IV.vi.7)

Though sensitive and experimental knowledge are both acquired via the senses they should not be lumped together. By definition sensitive knowledge is concerned with the existence of particular things. Thus, if I assert, on the grounds of my experience, that there is a piece of gold in front of me, I am claiming sensitive knowledge. On the other hand, experimental knowledge concerns the 'secondary Qualities, Powers, and Operations' of bodies (IV.iii.29). Such knowledge will be typified by the claim, based upon observation and experiment, that the piece of gold is malleable. In other words, propositions expressing sensitive knowledge state that such and such a material object exists, propositions expressing experimental knowledge state that such and such a material object has certain properties, operates on other bodies in certain ways, and so on. It will be argued that Locke can accommodate experimental knowledge within the terms of his definition. It is an instance of knowledge of co-existence.

Locke's first and fourth heading need not detain us here. The knowledge which falls under the heading of identity, or diversity, is hardly knowledge at all, but more a prerequisite for knowledge. It consists in the mind's recognition that each of its ideas is the idea it is and is different from other ideas. Obviously, unless we could distinguish our ideas one from another we could not perceive connections between them (I.i.4).[25] 'Real existence' covers the intuitive knowledge we each have of our own existence, the demonstrative knowledge of the existence of God, and sensitive knowledge of the existence of material objects (IV.iii.21; IV.ix.2). Knowledge under the second heading consists in *'the Perception of the Relation between any two Ideas,* of what kind soever, whether Substances, Modes, or any other' (IV.i.5). This 'relative knowledge' may be acquired immediately by intuition, but Locke mostly thinks of it as yielded by demonstration. The reach of demonstration depends upon 'our Sagacity, in finding intermediate *Ideas,* that may shew the *Relations* and *Habitudes* of *Ideas* . . . [and] 'tis a hard Matter to tell, when we are at the end of such Discoveries' (IV.iii.18). He adds that he believes 'the *Ideas* of Quantity are not those alone that are capable of Demonstration and Knowledge' (ibid.).

The ideas involved in our knowledge of relation are abstract. The knowledge itself is arrived at by the contemplation of ideas and is expressed in universal propositions. It is the only general knowledge Locke recognises:

> If the *Ideas* are abstract, whose agreement or disagreement we perceive, our Knowledge is universal. For what is known of such general *Ideas,* will be true of every particular thing, in whom that Essence, *i.e.* that abstract *Idea* is to be found. . . . So that as to all general Knowledge, we must search and find it only in our own Minds, and 'tis only the examining of our own *Ideas,* that furnisheth us with that. Truths belonging to the Essences of Things, (that is, to abstract *Ideas*) are eternal, and are to be found out by the contemplation only of those Essences. (IV.iii.31; cf. IV.vi.13)

Knowledge of relation is exactly the kind of knowledge which critics have seen as the only knowledge allowed for in Locke's definition; it is *a priori* knowledge of links holding between concepts. Strictly, all demonstrative knowledge will fall under this heading; though Locke places the existence of God under the separate heading of real existence, as it is a unique case of a demonstrable existential truth.

Knowledge of relation is introduced as being concerned with ideas of any kind of things. Knowledge under the third heading is narrower in its range of ideas. It consists in the perception of 'Co-existence, or *Non-co-existence* in the same Subject; and this belongs particularly to Substances' (IV.i.6). Locke illustrates this knowledge by reference to gold and its properties:

> When we pronounce concerning *Gold*, that it is fixed, our Knowledge of this Truth amounts to no more but this, that fixedness, or a power to remain in the Fire unconsumed, is an *Idea*, that always accompanies, and is join'd with that particular sort of Yellowness, Weight, Fusibility, Malleableness, and Solubility in *Aqua Regia*, which make our complex *Idea*, signified by the word *Gold*. (ibid.).

The proposition 'gold is fixed' asserts something about the way the world is, and it would seem that Locke intends his third heading to cover *a posteriori* knowledge of the facts of the world. The difficulty is to see how he can construe such knowledge as an instance of the perception of a connection between ideas.

Here it is important to bear in mind a point noted earlier in this chapter, that Locke is prepared to use 'idea' to refer to the qualities in bodies which produce ideas (percepts) in us during the perceptual situation. This usage is quite common, especially in *Essay*, Book II (see, for example, II.xii.1; II.xxi.1; II.xxiii.1 and 6; II.xxx.6). Locke does talk of our acquiring certain knowledge of the co-existence of qualities in substances through experience. For example, at IV.iii.14, he states, 'all the Qualities that are *co-existent* in any Subject, without this dependence and evident connexion of their *Ideas* one with another, we cannot know certainly any two to *co-exist* any further, than Experience, by our Senses informs us', and at IV.xii.9, '*Experience here must teach me*, what Reasons cannot: and 'tis by trying alone, that I can certainly know, what other Qualities co-exist with those of my complex *Idea* [of gold]'. If we substitute the 'ideas' here for 'qualities' these passages read as assertions that we come to a certain knowledge of the co-existence of ideas in substances by experience. Locke's statement that he sometimes uses the term 'idea' to mean quality does not, in itself, license this substitution; for it does not entail that he sometimes uses the term 'quality' to mean idea. However, the substitution may be justified in the light of Locke's reason for using the term to mean quality.

Whatever the ambiguity of Locke's remarks on sense perception two things are evident: first, he is a realist, holding that things such as snowballs are material objects existing in the material world independently of the perceiver; second, he holds that ideas (percepts) are involved in the perceptual situation in that they are caused in us by material objects. Locke also accepts the corpuscular theory of matter. According to this theory, the snowball, as it exists in the external world, is a concatenation of atoms.[26] These atoms are possessed of the primary qualities, solidity, extension, figure, motion or rest, and number; but they are not possessed of the secondary qualities, colour, sound, taste, etc. (II.viii.9–23). When we say of a snowball that it is white, cold and round we are, Locke would agree, talking about something which exists externally to the mind. However, the secondary quality terms 'white' and 'cold' are not descriptive of the snowball as it exists in the world, for what we think of as its whiteness and coldness are really effects produced in us by the various configurations of colourless atoms. As roundness is a determinant of the determinable primary quality 'figure', it does exist in things independently of their being perceived. But when we describe a snowball as round we are not talking of the roundness of its atoms. Rather, we describe the snowball *which we immediately perceive* as round. Thus, our ordinary use even of primary quality terms is descriptive of our percepts or ideas of material objects. We might, of course, give up, or at least radically modify, our ordinary talk of snowballs being white, cold and round. Locke takes the opposite course and talks of ideas existing in material objects; and he attempts to defuse the oddness of this by instructing the reader to unpack such talk in terms of the powers of bodies to produce ideas in us. But the unpacking should go the other way too. If our quality terms as we ordinarily use them are really descriptive of ideas produced in us by the powers in material objects, our talk of observing or experiencing the existence or co-existence of qualities in such objects should be translated in terms of ideas. We are, therefore, justified in substituting 'ideas' for 'qualities' in the passages quoted above.[27]

Our knowledge consists in propositions, and in order to know the truth of an empirical proposition such as 'gold is fixed', we must formulate that proposition. Thus, ideas *qua* signs as well as ideas *qua* qualities will be involved in our knowledge of co-existence. In order to verify the proposition we must go to the perceptual situation and, in Lockean terms, note the ideas (percepts) which enter in by the senses when we perform the relevant experiment. The procedure will be the same if the proposition asserts the non-co-existence of certain qualities. On the other hand, if the proposition expressed a conceptual truth we could come to know it *a priori*, from the contemplation of our abstract ideas (concepts) of gold and fixedness. Locke does allow that the act of knowing may consist in sense perception as well as in the intellectual perception of logical links between concepts. In discussing our knowledge of the properties of bodies, he writes: 'this *co-existence* can be no farther known, than it is perceived; and it cannot be perceived but either in particular Subjects, by the observation of our Senses, or in general, by the necessary *connexion* of the *Ideas* themselves' (IV.iii.14). Our knowledge of contingent truths concerning substances is a case of the first alternative, knowing by the observation of our senses.[28]

The foregoing interpretation of Locke's knowledge of co-existence is faced with an obvious difficulty. The proposition he cites as an illustration of this knowledge looks like a universal proposition, but he is quite explicit that general knowledge can only derive from the contemplation of abstract ideas. Moreover, he tells us elsewhere that '*All Gold is fixed,* is a Proposition whose Truth we cannot be certain of, how universally soever it be believed' (IV.vi.8). Again, at IV.xvi.6, he singles out empirical generalisations about the properties of substances as examples of propositions which are only of the highest probability. However, the inconsistency here is only apparent. Locke remarks that all our knowledge is 'only of particular or *general Truths'* (IV.vi.2). It is clear that what he calls general truths can only be known *a priori,* but he is vague about what counts as a particular truth. There is a type of empirical generalisation which can, consistently with what Locke says, be accommodated within this latter area.

Locke's universal propositions respecting which we can attain certain knowledge corresponds to those Kant characterises as having strict universality. Kant contrasts these with empirical generalisations which are based upon induction from particular instances and which, therefore, can have only a comparative universality.[29] But empirical general propositions may themselves be divided according as they are generalisations about closed or about open classes of things. In the first case they are restricted generalisations; in the second case they are unrestricted. The distinction between these two types of generalisations is hard to define formally, but it is easy enough to illustrate. Thus 'all the books at present on my desk are in English' is clearly restricted, being about a definitely closed class. 'All dogs have fleas' (meaning literally each and every dog which has lived, is living or will live) is unrestricted, being about an open class. Locke does not draw this distinction, but it is arguably implicit in his epistemology.

Any observations we make in our enquiries into the co-existence of qualities in substances will be of particular things, for example individual lumps of gold. This being so, the knowledge yielded by each observation will be expressed in a singular proposition such as 'this lump of gold is fixed'. However, there is nothing in Locke's account of knowledge to preclude the conjoining of singular propositions. Each time we carry out the relevant experiment and observe the fixedness of an individual lump of gold we have actual knowledge that that lump of gold is fixed; and, as far as we can remember our observation, we have an habitual knowledge that that lump of gold is (or at least was) fixed. Given we have observed a number of different lumps of gold, we can conjoin the singular proposition which expresses our knowledge in each case, and so form a general proposition to the effect that all the pieces of gold *we have observed* are (or at least were) fixed. This will be a restricted empirical generalisation, and it will be one which the observer knows to be true. Further, assuming the pieces of gold remain available for experiment, it is a generalisation which can be verified by an exhaustive enumeration of the instances upon which it is based. Locke does have this conjoining of remembered bits of actual knowledge in mind in his description of the way the individual may come to add to his complex idea of a substance: 'For upon Trial, having found that particular piece (and all others of that Colour, Weight, and Fusibility, that I ever tried) *malleable,* that also makes now perhaps, a part of my complex *Idea,* part of my nominal Essence of *Gold*' (IV.xii.9). It is only unrestricted empirical generalisations which Locke cites as probable and therefore not properly objects of knowledge.

It will be recalled that Locke originally talks of the knowledge of 'co-existence, or necessary connexion'. Propositions asserting the necessary connection of qualities in substances have strict universality and are known *a priori.* Locke holds the human understanding to be capable of grasping the truth of a small number of such propositions. With respect to some primary qualities we know *a priori* that one cannot be found without the other; as, for example, figure presupposes extension. With respect to secondary qualities we know *a priori* that two determinants of the one determinable cannot co-exist in the one substance (IV.iii.14–15). This knowledge is, strictly speaking, knowledge of relation, which heading embraces relations between all kinds of ideas 'whether substances, modes, or any other'. What Locke denies is that we can be certain concerning the qualities observed to cluster together in particular bodies that they must so co-exist. As we cannot know this, a science of nature is impossible:

> our Knowledge concerning corporeal Substances, will be very little advanced . . . till we are made see, what Qualities and Powers of Bodies have a *necessary Connexion or Repugnancy* one with another. . . . And I doubt, whether with those Faculties we have, we shall ever be able to carry our general Knowledge (I say not particular Experience) in this part much farther. Experience is that, which is the part we must depend on. (IV.iii.16)

While Locke rejects an *a priori* science of nature, this passage shows that he includes a knowledge of substances based upon 'particular experience'.

Locke's account of knowledge under the four headings he gives is intended to make manifest the extent of knowledge. If our interpretation of the third heading is correct, the common view that his distinction between certain knowledge and probable belief coincides with the more modern distinction between *a priori* and *a posteriori* knowledge is mistaken. On the contrary, Locke's definition of knowledge allows for both *a priori,* conceptual knowledge and empirical knowledge. Propositions which are known *a priori* belong to science; those known *a posteriori* go to make up our experimental knowledge.[30] Locke says of the universal propositions which we know with certainty that they 'concern not *Existence*' (IV.ix.I). That is, they do not affirm or deny the existence of any thing, nor do they presuppose the existence of any thing. Propositions which do concern existence are those which Locke characterises vaguely as expressing particular truths. He distinguishes these two sorts of propositions according to the ways we come to know them: 'In the [latter] case, our Knowledge is the consequence of the Existence of Things producing *Ideas* in our Minds by our Senses: in the [former] Knowledge is the consequence of the *Ideas* (be they what they will) that are in our Minds producing there general certain Propositions' (IV.xi.I4). Although the 'particular' truths making up our experimental knowledge of the co-existence of qualities in substances 'concern existence', it is not a knowledge *of* existence. Here the difference between experimental and sensitive knowledge should be kept in mind. A person who asserts of a lump of gold that it is fixed is not asserting the existence of the gold to which reference is made, but rather is presupposing its existence. Knowledge of co-existence must be underpinned by sensitive knowledge. If it is to qualify as what Locke calls real knowledge we must in each case *be sure* that our experience is veridical.

6. That it is only by observation and experiment that we can come to know what qualities co-exist in various substances may seem a point too obvious for any philosopher to bother making. But Locke does not think it by any means obvious. He envisages an alternative which is, he argues, beyond the compass of human understanding:

> Had we such *Ideas* of Substances, as to know what real Constitutions produce those sensible Qualities we find in them, and how those Qualities flowed from thence, we could, by the specifick *Ideas* of their real Essences in our own Minds, more certainly find out their Properties, and discover what Qualities they had, or had not, than we can now by our Senses: and to know the Properties of *Gold,* it would be no more necessary, that *Gold*

> should exist, and that we should make Experiments upon it, than it is necessary for the knowing the Properties of a Triangle, that a Triangle should exist in any Matter, the *Idea* in our Minds would serve for the one, as well as the other. (IV.vi.11)

That is, were we able to frame abstract ideas of substances which encapsulated their essences, it would be possible to demonstrate truths concerning corporeal substances, and we could, therefore, achieve an *a priori* science of nature.

According to Locke, the word 'essence' originally meant 'the very being of any thing,, whereby it is, what it is. . . . And in this sense it is still used, when we speak of the *Essence* of particular things, without giving them any Name' (III.iii.15). But in more common usage the word is applied to the genus and species to which particular things belong. In this sense essences are constructions of the mind, 'it being evident, that Things are ranked under Names into sorts or *Species*, only as they agree to certain abstract *Ideas*, to which we have annexed those Names, the *Essences* of each *Genus*, or Sort, comes to be nothing but that abstract *Idea*, which the General, or *Sortal* . . . Name stands for' (ibid.). The essence which makes a particular thing to be what it is Locke terms a 'real essence'; the essence in accord with which we classify things he terms a 'nominal essence'.

Locke goes on to mention two rival opinions concerning 'the real Essences of corporeal Substances':

> The one is of those, who using the Word *Essence*, for they know not what, suppose a certain number of those Essences, according to which, all natural things are made, and wherein they do exactly every one of them partake, and so become of this or that *Species*. The other, and more rational Opinion, is of those, who look on all natural Things to have a real, but unknown Constitution of their insensible Parts, from which flow those sensible Qualities, which serve us to distinguish them one from another, according as we have Occasion to rank them into sorts, under common Demonstrations. (III.iii.17)

The opinion Locke rejects is the doctrine of substantial forms. As he explains it, the claim of this doctrine is that when we classify things we are guided by an intellectual apprehension of the essences or forms of these things. These essences exist independently of our classificatory activity (III.iv.9–10). What he considers the more rational opinion of essences derives from the corpuscular theory of matter mentioned earlier in connection with his use of 'idea' to mean quality. The real essences of bodies are their internal atomic structures. These are the causal bases of the sensible qualities we combine in our abstract ideas, which ideas are the standards we use in classifying particulars. Locke does not wish to dispute that particular bodies are objectively similar one to another independent of our ranking them together under the one idea:

> I would not . . . be thought . . . to deny, that Nature in the Production of Things, makes several of them alike. . . . But yet, I think, we may say, the *sorting* of them under Names, *is the Workmanship of the Understanding, taking occasion from the similitude* it observes amongst them to make abstract general *Ideas.* (III.iii.13; cf. III.vi.37; III.x.21)

His point against the doctrine of substantial forms is that, while no classificatory scheme for bodies could get off the ground unless there were observable similarities between bodies, the pigeon-holes of any such scheme are built by us. For it is the observer who selects the similarities between bodies which are relevant to their class membership.[31]

Locke's own doctrine of essences owes a great deal to the work of his friend Robert Boyle.[32] We should be clear not only what Locke rejects in the older doctrine of substantial forms, but also what he retains. Substantial forms were thought of as universals (either Platonic *universalia ante rem* or Aristotelian *universalia in re*), and as such he dismisses them entirely. Conceived thus they offend against his fundamental ontological principle that 'All Things, that exist [are] Particulars' (III.iii.1). In his view, the notion of an existent universal is self-contradictory.[33] But Locke is far from dismissing the problems the doctrine purports to solve. He is aware that the existence of substantial forms is invoked in answer to two different questions: the epistemological question of how a number of distinct particulars can be classified as being all of the one kind, and the ontological question of what makes a particular to be what it is, or have the properties it does have. His answer to the first is in terms of nominal essences, or abstract ideas. Abstract ideas have no existence outside the minds of the individuals who frame them, and as mental items they are, like everything else, particulars. They fulfil the role of universals when they are employed in classifying things. His answer to the second question is in terms of real essences, or internal corpuscular structures. As these only exist in particular bodies they are themselves particulars. So far as bodies are concerned 'nominal essence' and 'real essence' are terms belonging to different categories. But although Locke has, as it were, divided substantial forms into two categorically different essences, in accepting the notion of a real essence as making a thing to be what it is he has retained an important aspect of the original doctrine.

In framing abstract ideas of substances we are not content merely to select a few sensible qualities in accord with which we might sort particular bodies into broad classes. Our aim is to capture all the qualities of bodies and so exactly distinguish them one from another. But this we cannot achieve:

> The *complex* Ideas *Of Substances are Ectypes, Copies* . . .; but not perfect ones, not *adequate*: which is very evident to the Mind, in that it plainly perceives, that whatever Collection of simple *Ideas* it makes of any Substance that exists, it cannot be sure, that it exactly answers all that are in that Substance. (II.xxxi.13)

Our ideas would be adequate only if we were able to capture in them the real essences of substances, and Locke repeatedly asserts that these are unknowable by us:

> Our Faculties carry us no farther towards the knowledge and distinction of Substances, than a Collection of those sensible *Ideas*, which we observe in them; which however made with the greatest diligence and exactness, we are capable of, yet is more remote from the true internal Constitution, from which those Qualities flow, than . . . a Countryman's *Idea* is from the inward contrivance of that famous Clock at *Strasburg*, whereof he only sees the outward Figure and Motions. (III.vi.9)

Yet, if the real essence of a body is its internal atomic structure, there would seem to be no reason in principle why this should not be observable by us. Indeed the advances made in microscopy in Locke's day suggested the real possibility of such an extension of our observational powers.[34]

Locke does believe that if we could observe the minute constituents of bodies we may be able to come to a knowledge of their mechanical operations one upon another. Such knowledge would be akin to the watch-maker's understanding of the operations of a piece of clockwork (IV.iii.13, 15). However, he has more than this in mind when he talks of the impossibility of a science of Nature. Even were we able to observe bodies at the micro-level, this would not enable us to understand how minute particles which have only primary qualities can be the causal basis of secondary qualities: 'we can by no means conceive how any *size, figure, or motion* of any Particles, can possibly produce in us the *Idea* of any *Colour, Taste,* or *Sound* Whatsoever; there is no conceivable *connexion* betwixt the one and the other' (IV.iii.13). Although he identifies the real essences of bodies with their internal structures, what Locke demands from a real essence is that it should *make* the particular to be what it is. That is, the real essence of a body performs the function of a substantial form in that it imposes some kind of necessity on the qualities the body exhibits. Had we ideas of real essences we would be able to grasp this necessity. But observation (which is the only way we have of framing ideas of substances) could never reveal anything more than the contingent co-existence of certain secondary qualities and configurations of particulars.[35] All complex ideas other than ideas of substances are archetypes. That is they are arrangements of simple ideas made by us without regard to any patterns in nature:

> *Complex* Ideas *of Modes and Relations, are* Originals, and *Archetypes*; are not . . . made after the Pattern of any real Existence, to which the Mind intends them to be conformable. . . . These being such Collections of simple *Ideas,* that the Mind it self puts together, and such Collections that each of them contains in it precisely all that the Mind intends it should, they are Archetypes and Essences of Modes that may exist; and so are designed only for, and belong only to such Modes, as when they do exist, have an exact conformity with those complex *Ideas.* The *Ideas* therefore of Modes and Relations, cannot but be *adequate.* (II.xxxi.14)

As these ideas are archetypes, in them real and nominal essences coincide. This is something they share with simple ideas, notwithstanding that the latter are ectypes: '*essences* being thus distinguished into *Nominal and Real* we may farther observe, that *in* the Species of *simple* Ideas *and Modes,* they *are always the same*: But *in Substances, always quite different*' (III.iii.18). The two essences coincide in the case of simple ideas because, unlike our ectypal substance ideas, they lack nothing which we intend should be in them. Thus, for example, our idea of yellowness is not intended to represent anything other than the percept we have when we experience yellow things. We do not use the term 'yellow' to refer beyond the percept to, say the unobserved causal mechanism whereby it is produced in us. Similarly, our archetypal complex ideas are always adequate to the intentions with which we frame them. They are representative of things in the world only so far as those things conform to our ideas. Therefore, whatever is essential to the thing as it exists in the world must coincide with what we have made essential to our idea of the thing. There is, however, another sense in which real and nominal essence coincide in the case of archetype complex ideas. If our ideas of substances did capture real essences it would be possible for us to understand why substances are as they are, or have the properties they do have, solely by contemplating our ideas. Our archetype ideas of modes and relations do open the way for such an understanding respecting the things that fall under them. These ideas are wholly the product of the mind selecting and combining its simple ideas. Hence, we can know not only the precise number of simple ideas we intend to combine in each complex, but also understand why they have been so combined. Any mode, as it is a particular thing existing in the world, is what it is in virtue of its having the qualities or characteristics we have united in one of our archetype ideas. Therefore, in understanding the idea we understand the thing. Our understanding will be akin to that the artificer has of the things he makes. Of artificial physical objects Locke writes: 'Because an *artificial* Thing being a production of Man, which the Artificer design'd, and therefore well knows the *Idea* of, the name of it is supposed to stand for no other *Idea*, nor to import any other Essence, than what is certainly to be known, and easy enough to be apprehended (III.vi.40). The artificer understands what he makes prior to making it; for what he makes is determined by the idea or design he has in mind. Similarly, we can come to an understanding of modes and relations prior to their being instantiated.

The distinction between ectype and archetype ideas is central to Locke's defence of the reality of knowledge by the way of ideas. We have seen that for Locke the certainty attained when we perceive a connection between ideas is not the same as real knowledge. He is fully aware of the difficulty which generations of critics have seen as fatal to his whole epistemology:

> 'Tis evident, the Mind knows not Things immediately, but only by the intervention of the *Ideas* it has of them. *Our Knowledge* therefore is *real*, only so far as there is a conformity between our *Ideas* and the reality of Things. But what shall be here the Criterion? How shall the Mind, when it perceives nothing but its own *Ideas*, know that they agree with Things themselves? (IV.iv.3)

This passage has often been taken as proof that Locke subscribes to a representative theory of perception and that he is endeavouring to solve the obvious (and insoluble) problem posed by that theory.[36] However, a reading of the chapter as a whole shows Locke to be very little, if at all, concerned with sense perception or with ideas as percepts. What he wishes to establish is the conformity between abstract ideas, or concepts, and reality. He is particularly interested in defending the real truth of the universal propositions we know *a priori* from the contemplation of abstract ideas:

> Since most of those Discourses, which take up the Thoughts and engage the Disputes of those who pretend to make it their Business to enquire after Truth and Certainty, will, I presume, upon Examination be found to be *general Propositions*, and Notions in which Existence is not at all concerned. (IV.iv.8)

Mathematics, and especially geometry, provides palmary examples of such propositions. The existence or non-existence of circles, triangles, etc. in the world is irrelevant; the mathematician works with abstract ideas and makes no pretence that they copy reality. But this is not to say that the propositions of mathematics are altogether divorced from reality:

> the knowledge he [the mathematician] has of any Truths or Properties belonging to a Circle, or any other mathematical Figure, are . . . true and certain, even of real Things existing: because real Things are no farther concerned, nor intended to be meant by any such Propositions, than as Things really agree to those *Archetypes* in his Mind. (IV.iv.6)

Thus, the propositions of mathematics may be said to have real truth in a somewhat extended sense. They are not true in the strict sense of Locke's correspondence theory, that is that they correspond to an arrangement of elements actually existing in nature. However, they are true in that the ideas involved 'are such, as we know are capable of having an existence in nature' (see IV.v.8 quoted earlier).

According to Locke, 'there are two sorts of *Ideas*, that, we may be assured, agree with Things' (IV.iv.3). These are simple ideas and all complex ideas other than those of substances. Simple ideas (Locke considers only those derived from sensation) are ectypal, but we can be sure they are not forgeries with nothing in the world to back them up:

> simple *Ideas*, which since the Mind . . . can by no means make to it self, must necessarily be the product of Things operating on the Mind in a natural way. . . . From whence it follows, that *simple* Ideas *are not fictions* of our Fancies, but the natural and regular productions of Things without us, really operating upon us; and so carry with them all the conformity which is intended; or which our state requires. (IV.iv.4)

As, apart from ideas of substance, all complex ideas are archetypes there can be no question of their misrepresenting reality: 'For that which is not designed to represent any thing but it self, can never be capable of a wrong representation, nor mislead us from the true apprehension of any thing, by its dislikeness to it' (IV.iv.5). The major part of the problem, then, concerns ideas of substances. As we intend these to refer to real essences, they are all inadequate; but this does not mean they fail utterly to capture the reality of things. The only way we can be sure that they are not fantastical, or purely made-up ideas of pretended things is by observation:

> Herein . . . is founded the *reality* of our Knowledge concerning *Substances*, that all our complex *Ideas* of them must be such,

> and such only, as are made up of such simple ones, as have been discovered to co-exist in Nature. . . . Whatever simple *Ideas* have been found to co-exist in any Substance, these we may with confidence join together again, and so make abstract *Ideas* of Substances. For whatever have once had a union in Nature, may be united again. (IV.iv.12)

This solution, it should be noted, would be singularly inept if Locke were addressing himself to the problems attendant upon a representative theory of perception.

Mathematics is not the only area in which archetypal ideas are employed. Our complex moral ideas are neither inadequate ectypes nor fantastical ideas:

> *moral knowledge* is as *capable of real Certainty,* as Mathematiks. For Certainty being but the Perception of the Agreement, or Disagreement of our *Ideas*; and Demonstration nothing but the Perception of such Agreement, by the Intervention of other *Ideas* . . ., our *moral Ideas,* as well as mathematical, being *Archetypes* themselves, and so adequate, and complete *Ideas,* all the Agreement, or Disagreement, which we shall find in them, will produce real knowledge. (IV.iv.7)

Locke, then, denies the possibility of a science of nature on the grounds that there is an inevitable gap between the real essences of the things we wish to know about and the nominal essences of our ideas of those things. Conversely, he affirms the possibility of a science of morality on the grounds that in our moral ideas real and nominal essences coincide.

The coincidence of real and nominal essence in our moral ideas is a necessary condition for demonstrative real knowledge in the sphere of morality. But it is not a sufficient condition. Our ability to demonstrate truths is limited by three factors: '*First,* Want of *Ideas. Secondly,* Want of a discoverable Connexion between the *Ideas* we have. *Thirdly,* Want of tracing and examining our *Ideas*' (IV.iii.22). We are possessed of ideas of the requisite kind, but we must further be able to trace the relations between them. Locke's conception of a science of morality and the endeavours he makes to achieve it will be examined in chapters VI and VII. However, his account of moral ideas as archetypes is of interest and importance in its own right, and deserves close attention quite aside from the science of morality it suggests.

V

IDEAS, LANGUAGE AND MORAL NOTIONS

The main purpose of this chapter is to arrive at an understanding of Locke's thesis that, as our moral ideas are archetypes, in their case real and nominal essence coincide. But preliminary to this there is another topic which needs to be looked at: Locke's theory of language and word meaning. In the course of writing the *Essay* Locke came to realise that in order to fulfil his epistemological ambition of determining the 'original, certainty and extent' of knowledge it was necessary to consider the medium in which knowledge is given public expression:

> there is so close a connexion between *Ideas* and Words; and our abstract *Ideas,* and general Words, have so constant a relation one to another, that it is impossible to speak clearly and distinctly of our Knowledge, which all consists in Propositions, without considering, first, the Nature, Use, and Signification of Language. (II.xxxiii.19; cf. III.ix.21)

The distinction between real and nominal essence is introduced and expounded in Book III, the section of the *Essay* which is devoted to a discussion of language and words.

1. For Locke, language is only externally and adventitiously related to thinking. He supposes that the whole range of thought now open to us as language users would have been equally accessible had language never been invented. Language develops primarily because of our needs to communicate our thoughts one to another:

> Man, though he have great variety of Thoughts, and such, from which others, as well as himself, might receive Profit and Delight; yet they are all within his own Breast, invisible, and hidden from others, nor can of themselves be made appear. The Comfort, and Advantage of Society, not being to be had without Communication of Thoughts, it was necessary, that Man should find out some external sensible Signs, whereby those invisible *Ideas,* which his thoughts are made up of, might be made known to others. For this purpose, nothing was so fit . . . as those articulate Sounds, which . . . he found himself able to make.

> Thus we may conceive how *Words* ... come to be made use of by Men, as *the Signs of* their *Ideas*; not by any natural connexion, that there is between particular articulate Sounds and certain *Ideas*, for then there would be but one Language amongst all Men; but by a voluntary Imposition, whereby such a Word is made arbitrarily the Mark of such an *Idea*. The use then of Words, is to be sensible Marks of *Ideas*; and the *Ideas* they stand for, are their proper and immediate Signification. (III.ii.1)

In Locke's view, then, a word is first and foremost a sound which, by an arbitrary decision, has been made the public mark or sign of a private idea.[1] It is their being made the signs of ideas which endows words with meaning; for, the 'meaning of Words [is] only the *Ideas* they are made to stand for by him that uses them' (III.iv.6). The fact that the speaker has affixed words to ideas is what constitutes the difference between intelligent human discourse and the language-like, but meaningless, utterances 'Parrots, and several other Birds' can be taught to frame (III.i.1).

On the grounds of his assertion that words are the signs of, or signify, ideas Locke has commonly been interpreted as holding an ideational theory according to which the meaning of any word simply is the idea for which it stands. This interpretation, however, is in need of qualification. For one thing, the opening chapters of Book III are misleading in so far as they give the impression that Locke is embarking upon a comprehensive account of language and word meaning. His attention is directed almost entirely to what he calls general words, or terms. In the brief chapter on 'particles' he does consider propositional connectives, the copula and the word 'not'. He states explicitly that such words are not 'names of *Ideas* in the Mind', but are used 'to signify the *connexion* that the Mind gives to *Ideas, or Propositions, one with another*' (III.vii.1). Although he does not go into any detail, it seems clear that Locke would include all syncategorematic words under the heading of 'particles'. His ideational theory is, therefore, restricted in its scope; it applies only to categorematic words. Indeed it is more restricted than this; of the categorematic words, Locke really concerns himself only with nouns and adjectives. His theory is in fact a theory about general names.[2]

Given Locke's fundamental ontological principle that only particulars exist, it becomes a question of how is it possible for there to be general words, or names. It would seem that such words can only be general in virtue of standing for something which is itself general. According to Locke, words become general by being made the signs of general or abstract ideas (III.iii.6). As we saw in the previous chapter, abstract ideas are ontologically particulars; their generality resides in the fact that we use them as signs or representations of a range of particular things. Hence Locke concludes:

> That *General and Universal,* belong not to the real existence of Things; but *are the Inventions and Creatures of the Understanding . . . and concern only Signs,* whether Words, or *Ideas.* Words are general . . . when used, for Signs of general *Ideas*; and so are applicable indifferently to many particular Things; And *Ideas* are general, when they are set up, as the Representatives of many particular Things: but universality belongs not to the things themselves, which are all of them particular in their Existence, even those Words, and *Ideas,* which in their signification, are general. (III.iii.11)

Having thus accounted for the generality of words without recourse to any general natures, Locke proceeds to enquire into the 'kind of signification' general words have. Since a general word is a common name it cannot signify barely one particular thing, for then it would be a proper name. On the other hand, it cannot be said simply to signify a plurality of particulars, for then there would be no difference in use between the plural 'men' and the general word 'man'. In Locke's view there is only one other alternative:

> That then which general Words signify, is a sort of Things; and each of them does that, by being a sign of an abstract *Idea* in the mind, to which *Idea,* as Things existing are found to agree, so they come to be ranked under that name; or, which is all one, be of that sort. . . . For when we say, this is a *Man,* that a *Horse*; this *Justice,* that *Cruelty*; that a *Watch,* that a *Jack*; what do we else but rank Things under different specific Names, as agreeing to those abstract *Ideas* of which we have made those Names the signs? (III.iii.12, 13)

It is important to note that, while Locke talks here of general words being signs of ideas in the mind, he is not maintaining that whenever we use these words we are talking about ideas. In the sentences he cites the demonstrative pronouns pick out particular things in the world and the general words are used to classify these things. Locke's thesis is that we could not use general words as classificatory terms in reference to things unless we made those words stand for ideas. As Norman Kretzmann has pointed out, the main thesis of Locke's semantic theory is that *'Words in their primary or immediate Signification, stand for nothing, but the* Ideas *in the Mind of him that uses them'* (III.ii.2; cf. III.ii.1, quoted above). The qualifying phrase 'in their primary or immediate signification' clearly implies that words do have an application to things other than ideas, this secondary application being mediated by ideas. Locke is not committed to the absurd thesis that, when I say 'the dog is on the doorstep' I am not talking about public objects in the world, but about ideas in my mind.[3]

As Locke does not maintain that general words are used exclusively as signs of ideas, he can meet what is often thought to be a decisive objection against his theory of language. Locke's theory has been called the translation view of language.[4] According to this view, linguistic communication is a matter of my uttering words (articulate sounds) which I have affixed to the private ideas making up a thought in my mind, your hearing the words, and then translating them into the appropriate assemblage of ideas in your mind. It is obviously a precondition of a successful translation that the speaker and hearer affix the same words to the same ideas. If, for example, I use the world 'blue' as a sign of the same ideas for which you use the word 'yellow', your translation of my utterance containing the word 'blue' will fail to convey my thought. Locke states that speakers always assume that their words are also signs of ideas in the mind of their hearers: 'For else they should talk in vain, and could not be understood, if the Sounds they applied to one *Idea*, were such, as by the Hearer, were applied to another, which is to speak two Languages' (III.ii.4). However, on Locke's ideational theory, it appears that this assumption must be completely groundless. Given the privacy of ideas we can affix words only to our own ideas. Seemingly, then, each individual has to inspect his own stock of ideas and signify them by words of his own choice. It would be a truly remarkable coincidence if both speaker and hearer by their own 'voluntary imposition' affixed the same word to the same idea. Even if this in fact did happen, it could never be known to have happened. As the individual is acquainted only with his own ideas, he could have no reason for believing his system of word-signs to coincide with anyone else's system. Therefore, no one could have any guarantee that he understood what another person was saying. At best Locke has given an account of an essentially private language. There are powerful philosophical arguments against the possibility of such a language.[5] But even if a private language is possible, Locke has failed; for what he intends to give is an account of public language and inter-personal word meaning.

Certainly, much of Locke's text does leave him open to this objection. He insists on the privacy of ideas, and he does state that 'every Man has [an] inviolable . . . Liberty, to make Words stand for what *Ideas* he pleases' (III.ii.8). Yet later, in seeming contradiction to this, he remarks: 'Words . . . being no Man's private possession, but the common measure of Commerce and Communication, 'tis not for anyone, at pleasure, to change the Stamp they are current in; nor alter the *Ideas* they are affixed to' (III.xi.11).

The latter passage suggests that there are public rules or conventions governing the proper application of words to ideas. If Locke did hold words to be solely signs of ideas, such rules would be quite impossible. Even were it possible for the individual to set up rules in accord with which he affixed words to his own ideas, he could not teach them to others; in order to teach the rules he would have publicly to exhibit *both* the words and the ideas, and this he cannot do. In so far as we apply words to public objects, there is no problem about setting up public rules. The important point is that these rules governing the application of words to things may also serve as constraints with respect to the application of words to private ideas.

In order to affix words to our ideas we must first have acquired those ideas. They are acquired through experience, and according to Locke we can frame even abstract ideas prior to having a language (see I.ii.15). Nonetheless, as words are applied to things, we can observe those about us using words to refer to the things of which we have ideas. This being so, there are two options open to anyone affixing words to his ideas. He may exercise his 'inviolable liberty' and select words for his ideas at random, or he may attend to public linguistic usage and make words stand for his ideas according as the words are applied to the things of which he has ideas.[6] In the latter case the word–idea connections he sets up will be determined by the conventions governing word–thing connections. The presumption in linguistic communication is that both speaker and hearer have followed this second option in affixing words to their ideas. This is what Locke seems to be getting at when, after stating his thesis that words in their immediate signification stand for ideas, he goes on to say:

> Men stand not usually to examine, whether the *Idea* they, and those they discourse with have in their Minds, be the same: But think it enough, that they use the Word, as they imagine, in the common Acceptation of that Language; in which case they suppose, that the *Idea*, they make it a Sign of, is precisely the same, to which the Understanding Men of that Country apply that Name. (III.ii.4)

Clearly words could not have a *common* acceptation if each individual applied them exclusively to his private ideas. The common acceptation of words is the rules of their public use.

If what is crucial for a public language and inter-personal linguistic meaning is that words have a common acceptation, what is to be made of Locke's thesis that in their primary or immediate signification words stand for nothing but ideas in the mind of him that uses them? The answer to this question depends on the interpretation given to the term 'idea' within the context of Locke's theory of language. We have seen that, in line with his visual model of the operations of the mind, Locke does at times construe ideas as mental images, or at least as mental entities analogous to images. Certainly much that Locke says in Book III suggests that ideas are images, and critics of his ideational theory have generally taken it for granted that he does conceive them as such.[7] Many of our general words may be said to have a connection with mental images in that we apply them to objects of which we can form images. All terms which are used to refer to physical objects or their qualities have this connection, for these are things which can be presented to the senses. Locke may be interpreted as holding that the ability to call to mind mental images is an indispensable part of our ability to apply these classificatory words to things (as we have seen, abstract ideas are the basic tools we employ when we classify things). Thus, in order to obey the command to pick out the blue things from among an array of objects the individual must first of all call to mind his abstract idea of blue, that is the idea he associates with the word 'blue'. He then uses the ideas as a pattern or standard and proceeds to select particular things according as they agree with that pattern. On this account of the psychological mechanics of classifying the individual would not be able to use the word 'blue' if he did not have the abstract idea of blue for it is only by comparing particulars with the idea that he recognises them as blue and hence is licensed to *call* them blue. Here it would seem that the idea is an image.

Locke tends to think of general words simply as labels applied to or withheld from particular things. There are, of course, many other aspects to knowing the meaning of a general word than this. However, aside from this criticism, the above account of how we use general words to classify things is open to a decisive objection. On this account there are two basic moves in the classificatory procedure: first, the appropriate abstract idea is called up; second, the idea is employed as a pattern. The problem here is that the first move involves the classification of particulars. For each of the individual's ideas are particulars and from among those he must select the appropriate idea, for example the idea of gold. This preliminary exercise of the ability to classify cannot itself be explained in terms of the employment of abstract ideas. To do so would generate an infinite regress, each idea being classified by comparison with a further idea. But if we can classify particular ideas without recourse to ideas as patterns, equally we can classify particular things without recourse to such patterns. That the particular ideas are in the mind while the particular things are in the world is beside the point. Therefore, even if general words are thought of as primarily labels, Lockean ideas would appear to have no role to play.[8]

A person can have a mental image of a thing without having the ability to use the word which applies to that thing. A child, for example, may have seen lumps of gold, and hence have a memory image of gold, prior to having acquired any language. Once the child has learnt the word 'gold' he will be able to identify his image as an image of gold. He is able to so identify it because the image encapsulates the empirical characteristics in accord with which we apply the word 'gold' to things in the world. Consequently, it can be said to be an image *of gold.* However, a great many of our general words do not have a connection with mental image. Locke talks of words such as 'justice' and 'cruelty' being used in the classification of actions, but there is no set of empirical characteristics (i.e. characteristics which are imageable) such that whenever they are present the word 'justice' or the word 'cruelty' applies and whenever they are absent the words do not apply. Justice and cruelty may be manifested in an indefinite range of observable behaviour. People may, of course, associate various images with these words, but, whatever characteristics the images may encapsulate, they will not thereby be images *of* justice or cruelty.

To sum up: in case of physical objects, or what Locke calls corporeal substances, we can be said to have ideas in the sense of mental images; but our having these ideas does not explain how it is we are able to apply general words to those substances. When it comes to non-substances such as justice and cruelty, we cannot be said to have ideas *qua* mental images. *A fortiori,* our having such ideas cannot explain our ability to apply the words 'justice' and 'cruelty'. To suppose that, although we cannot literally have images of justice, cruelty, and so on, in their case we must have mental items analogous to images is to be taken in by Locke's visual model of mental activity. What then is left of Locke's thesis that words immediately stand for ideas?

Kretzmann argues that what Locke means when he speaks of one's making a word stand for, or signify, an idea is one's attaching a meaning to the word.[9] On this reading the crux of Locke's ideational theory is simply the thesis that we could not apply words to things unless those words had meaning for us. For example, a non-speaker of English who mouths the sentence 'the dog is on the door-step' has not succeeded in talking about anything; he simply does not know what he is saying (strictly he is not *saying* anything).

We have already noted that Locke holds the difference between intelligent discourse and the mere utterance of words to lie in the fact that in the first, but not in the second, case the words are marks which the speaker uses as signs of his ideas. However, in so far as ideas are the meanings speakers attach to the words they use, ideas themselves cannot be construed as either literal mental images or as items analogous to mental images. There are cases in which we may wonder whether we are faced with an intelligent use of language or a mere mouthing of words. In these cases we do not attempt the impossible task of discovering private mental items on the mind of the speaker; what we do attend to is the speaker's public use of languages. If we discover that he uses the words in the various contexts in which it is appropriate to use them and that he does not use them in inappropriate contexts we will conclude (at least in most circumstances) that his discourse is meaningful and not a repetition of something learned by rote. In fact we appeal to what Locke calls the common acceptation of words. Someone's attaching a meaning to the words he uses is his achieving a grasp of the rules governing the public use of those words. We conclude that he has achieved this on the evidence of his usage. We have seen that, even if the ideas which are the meanings of words are conceived as existing independently of language, the common acceptation of words is crucial for a public language and inter-personal linguistic meaning. The suggestion here is that, so far as they are thought of as the meanings we attach to the words we use, ideas are best conceived in terms of our grasp of the words' common acceptation; a person's having an idea of *x* will simply be his having a mastery of the use of the word '*x*'.

On this new, and admittedly non-Lockean, interpretation of ideas there will be no ideas existing in the mind independently of the existence of language.[10] Nonetheless, much of what Locke says about ideas as word meanings will still hold. A person's grasp of a bit of linguistic usage is something mental, but it is a mental capacity rather than a mental item. It is also something private in that it belongs to a particular person. However, it will still be proper to talk of several persons having the same capacity in that they are able to use words in the same way. Locke himself talks of different individuals having ideas which are 'precisely the same' (see, for example, III.ii.4, quoted above). Further, the grasp each person has of a word's common acceptation will be the meaning that word has for him, and the extent of that grasp may differ from person to person. Thus, different individuals may attach somewhat different meanings to the one word. Similarly, different individuals may make the one word stand for somewhat different ideas:

> A Child having taken notice of nothing in the Metal he hears called Gold, but the bright shining yellow colour, he applies the Word Gold only to his own *Idea* of that Colour, and nothing else; and therefore calls the same Colour in a Peacocks Tail, Gold. Another that hath better observed, adds to shining yellow, great Weight: And then the Sound Gold, when he uses it, stands for a complex *Idea* of a shining Yellow and very weighty Substance (III.ii.3)

(This passage, it should be noted, illustrates the second of the two options open to anyone affixing words to ideas.) Finally, if ideas are conceived in terms of a person's grasp of the common acceptation of words it remains true that each of us has an inviolable liberty to make words stand for whatever ideas we please. For example, having learnt how to use the words 'dog' and 'cat', there is nothing to prevent me deciding to substitute 'cat' for 'dog' in my own usage. Indeed, I may make up a word and use it in the same way as the word 'dog'is used. But in neither case am I investing a word with meaning by affixing it to a private mental item. Rather, my ability to give the word 'cat' a new meaning, or to give my new word a meaning, is parasitic upon my mastery of bits of public linguistic usage. I can only decide to use some other word in the same way (or with the same meaning) as the word 'dog' if I already have the mental capacity to follow the rules governing the use of the word 'dog'.

While Locke does have some appreciation of the importance of public linguistic usage for word meanings, he continues to think of ideas as meaningful units which are quite independent of language.[11] He does accept that we very often make use of words rather than ideas in our thinking:

> Though the examining and judging of *Ideas* by themselves, their Names being quite laid aside, be the best and surest way to clear and distinct Knowledge: yet through the prevailing custom of using Sounds for *Ideas*, I think it is very seldom practised. Every one may observe how common it is for Names to be made use of, instead of the *Ideas* themselves, even when Men think and reason within their own Breasts; especially if the *Ideas* be very complex, and made up of a great Collection of simple ones. (IV.vi.I)

But this tendency to think in words is to be deplored. Even when the high complexity of the ideas involved makes it extremely difficult to 'lay their names aside' we should endeavour to formulate our thoughts in 'mental' rather than 'verbal' propositions (IV.v.14). Nevertheless, when Locke comes to consider what he calls mixed mode ideas, he finds it very difficult to maintain any distinction between a person having an idea and their having the capacity to use the corresponding word or words.

Mixed mode ideas are archetypes, that is, in framing them we do not intend to copy patterns given in nature, but we combine simple ideas as we will. As the contents of these ideas are entirely dependent upon what we decide to combine into complexes, they 'are called *Notions*: as if they had their Original, and constant Existence, more in the Thoughts of Men, than in the reality of things' (II.xxii.2; cf. III.v.12).[12] In his discussion of mixed modes Locke has human actions primarily in mind, and especially actions of moral significance. A mode is something which is conceived of as depending for its existence on a substance. All actions qualify as modes because they have no existence apart from being performed by an agent (a substance) (III.vi.42). The actions with which Locke is concerned are *mixed* modes because in our ideas of them 'simple *Ideas* of several kinds [are] put together to make one complex one' (II.xii.5). Locke cites theft as an example, 'which being the concealed change of the possession of any thing, without the consent of the Proprietor, contains, as is visible, a combination of several *Ideas* of several kinds' (ibid.).

Mixed mode ideas are generally of a high complexity, and the principle of unity in accord with which the simple ideas combined in a mixed mode can be said to belong together is the name affixed to it:

> *Men speaking of mixed Modes, seldom* imagine or *take any other for Species of them, but such as are set out by name*: Because they being of Man's making only, in order to naming, no such *Species* are taken notice of, or supposed to be, unless a *Name* be joined to it, as the sign of a Man's having combined into one *Idea* several loose ones; and by that *Name*, giving a lasting Union to the Parts, which would otherwise cease to have any, as soon as the Mind laid by that abstract *Idea*, and ceased actually to think on it. (III.v.11; cf. II.xxii.7)

Elsewhere, in discussing the sense in which archetype ideas may be called true or false, Locke talks of the names of mixed mode ideas as standards by comparison with which an individual's ideas of justice, gratitude, glory, and so on may be judged true or false.[13] The names are taken as standards because, in the case of mixed modes, there is nothing else which can function as a standard:

> the abstract *Ideas* of mixed Modes, being Man's voluntary Combinations of such a precise Collection of simple *Ideas* . . . being made by Men alone, whereof we have no other sensible Standard, existing any where, but the Name it self, or the definition of that Name: We have nothing else to refer these our *Ideas* of mixed Modes to as a Standard . . . but the *Ideas* of those, who are

> thought to use those names in their most popular Significations. (II.xxxii.12)

So long as an idea is conceived as an image or quasi-image these remarks are hardly intelligible. However, sense can be made of them if we adopt the new interpretation of ideas suggested earlier. Then a person's idea of justice will be his grasp of the way in which the word 'injustice' is used (or the way in which equivalent words in languages other than English are used). His ideas will have unity in so far as there is a publicly established use for that word. A person will have a false idea of justice if he misuses the word, and this false idea may be corrected against the standard definition of 'justice', that definition being a reflection of the established use of the word.

Locke does realise that mixed mode terms, unlike substance terms, do not refer to things of which we can form mental images:

> When we speak of *Justice*, or *Gratitude*, we frame to our selves no Imagination of any thing existing, which we would conceive; but our Thoughts terminate in the abstract *Ideas* of those Vertues, and look not farther; as they do, when we speak of a *Horse*, or *Iron*, whose specifick *Ideas* we consider not, as barely in the Mind, but as in Things themselves, which afford the original Patterns of those *Ideas*. (III.v.12)

He also comes close to the realisation that, in the case of mixed modes, the ideas cannot be had apart from the corresponding words:

> Because there being no *Species* of [mixed modes] ordinarily taken notice of, but what have Names; and those *Species* . . . being abstract complex *Ideas* made arbitrarily by the Mind, it is convenient, if not necessary, to know the Names, before one endeavours to frame these complex *Ideas*. . . . I confess, that in the beginning of Languages, it was necessary to have the *Idea*, before one gave it the Name. . . . But this concerns not Languages made, which have generally pretty well provided for *Ideas*, which Men have frequent Occasion to have, and communicate: And in such, I ask, whether it be not the ordinary Method, that Children learn the Names of mixed Modes, before they have their *Ideas*? (III.v.15)

But, as this passage shows, Locke is inhibited by his commitment to the way of ideas. For him the primary form of discourse is mental discourse which only needs to make use of ideas, and language is nothing more than the means whereby this discourse is made public. Had we no need to communicate, language would not have been invented; and its invention makes no difference to the range of our thought. Hence, Locke supposes that all our ideas, whether ectypal ideas of substances or archetypal ideas of mixed modes, must be independent of the words which are merely the vehicles of their external expression.

2. Thus far we have concentrated on the use of general terms in the classification of particular things, in sentences such as 'this is a lump of gold'. But if I say 'gold is malleable' I am not referring to a particular lump of gold, but to gold in general. According to Locke, what I am referring to is an essence. We must have a knowledge of essences in order to apply general terms to particulars:

> For the having the Essence of any Specie, being that which makes any thing to be of that Species, and the conformity to the *Idea,* to which the name is annexed, being that which gives a right to that name, the having the Essence, and the having that Conformity, must needs be the same thing: Since to be of any Species, and to have a right to the name of that Species, is all one. As for Example, to be a *Man,* is the same thing. Again, to be a *Man,* or of the Species *Man,* and to have the Essence of a *Man,* is the same thing. (III.iii.12)

Thus, to be able to use a term such as 'man' in classifying particular things one must know the essence of man (and, if the classification is to be correct, one must know that the particulars exhibit that essence). According to the way of ideas, knowing the essence of a thing consists in having the abstract idea of that thing. The essence and the abstract idea are identical:

> since nothing can be a *Man,* or have a right to the name *Man,* but what has a conformity to the abstract *Idea* the name *Man* stands for; nor any thing be a *Man,* or have a right to be of the Species *Man,* but what has the Essence of that Species, it follows, that the abstract *Idea,* for which the name stands, and the Essence of the Species, is one and the same. (ibid.)

Following the new interpretation of ideas advocated earlier, a person's having the abstract idea of *x* will consist in his knowing how to use the term '*x*'. The abstract idea itself will be that set of characteristics which, according to the rules of linguistic usage, licenses the application of the term '*x*' to things. As the abstract idea is identical with the essence, the latter will also be the set of characteristics licensing the application of the term. On this interpretation, when I utter a sentence such as 'This is a lump of gold', I am stating that the particular thing indicated exhibits the characteristics which license the application of the word 'gold'. Similarly, if I say 'gold is malleable' I am stating that all particulars which exhibit the set of characteristics such that the word 'gold' applies to them have the characteristic of being malleable.

We saw in the previous chapter that Locke introduces the topic of essences in connection with corporeal substances, or bodies, and that his distinction between real and nominal essences is developed as an alternative to the doctrine of substantial forms. The essences which are identical with abstract ideas are nominal essences. The real essence of a body, on the other hand, is said to be that 'whereby it is what it is', and this Locke identifies with the body's internal corpuscular structure. As such, real essences exist independently of our language.[14] However, Locke maintains that whenever we use general substance terms in sentences such as 'gold is malleable' we give them a 'secret' or 'tacit' reference to these real essences:

> in the general names of Substances, whereof the nominal Essences are only known to us, when we put them into Propositions, and affirm or deny any thing about them, we do most commonly tacitly suppose, or intend, they should stand for the real Essence of a certain sort of Substances. For when a Man says *Gold is Malleable,* he means, and would insinuate something more than this, that *what I call Gold is malleable,* . . . but would have this understood, *viz.* that *Gold*; i.e. *what has the real Essence of Gold is malleable,* which amounts to thus much, that *Malleableness depends on, and is inseparable from the real Essence of Gold.* (III.x.17)

Locke agrees that 'the names of Substances would be much more useful, and Propositions made in them much more certain, where the real Essences of Substances the *Ideas* in our Minds, which those words signified' (III.x.18), but, as those real essences are unknown, the tacit reference to them in our use of substance terms constitutes an 'abuse of words'. It prompts us to believe that universal propositions predicating properties of substances express necessary truths about the nature of things. For, in Locke's opinion, if we did know the real essences of substances we would understand, say the malleability of gold, not as a brute fact but as something that followed of necessity from the nature of gold. As we know only the nominal essences of substances, we are never in a position to know the truth of such universal propositions; much less can we understand them as expressing necessary truths about the nature of things. The universal propositions we formulate about substances in fact say no more than this, that the things which exhibit the characteristics in accord with which we have decided to apply a substance term such as 'gold' have such-and-such a further characteristic. In so far as these propositions are of an unrestricted generality they are only probable, and hence not propositions which we know. If we decide to include malleability in our definition of 'gold' the proposition 'gold is malleable' will express a necessary truth; but then its truth will be determined by our linguistic conventions, and our knowledge of it will be a knowledge of words, not of things. Locke calls these propositions 'trifling' or 'verbal'.

The reference to real essences also gives rise to the false impression that one, fixed species is always being referred to whenever a given substance term is used. In talking of species of substances or applying substance terms to particular things each speaker is, and can only be, guided by the set of characteristics he takes as licensing the application of the term. But different speakers may associate the one term with somewhat different sets of characteristics; in Locke's language, they may make the one word stand for different abstract ideas or nominal essences. As, from our point of view, the boundaries of species are determined by nominal essences, 'it will follow that *each abstract* Idea, *with a name to it, makes a distinct Species*' (III.vi.38). Thus, if two speakers do use the one term in accord with different sets of characteristics they are in fact talking about different species; 'yet Men do not usually think, that therefore the Species is changed: Because they secretly in their Minds referr that name, and suppose it annexed to a real immutable Essence of a thing existing' (III.x.19). Finally, the reference to real essences leads us to use substance terms without attaching any meaning to them: 'by this tacit reference to the real Essence of that Species of Bodies, the Word *Gold* . . . comes to have no signification at all, being put for somewhat, whereof we have no *Idea* at all, and so can signify nothing at all, when the Body it self is away' (ibid.) Locke's point may be put thus: as we do not know what characteristics substances have at the level of their internal structures or real essences, these cannot serve as characteristics licensing the application of words to things. The supposition that we must apply substance terms in accord with these characteristics entails that we can never know how to use these terms.

As mixed mode ideas or notions are archetypes, in our use of mixed mode terms we do not intend any reference to unknown real essences existing in nature. Nevertheless, these terms do refer to real essences:

> *the Names of mixed Modes always signifie* (when they have any determined Signification) the real Essences of their Species. For these abstract *Ideas*, being the Workmanship of the Mind, and not referred to the real Existence of Things, there is no supposition of any thing more signified by that Name, but barely that complex *Idea*, the Mind it self has formed, which is all it would have express'd by it; and is that, on which all the proper-

> ties of the *Species* depend, and from which alone they all flow: and so in these the *real* and *nominal* Essence is the same. (III.v.4)

As mentioned earlier, when he talks of mixed modes Locke is generally thinking of human actions. It is hardly surprising that most of our mixed mode ideas should be of actions:

> For Action being the great business of Mankind, and the whole matter about which all Laws are conversant, it is no wonder, that the several Modes of Thinking and Motion, should be taken notice of, the *Idea* of them observed, and laid up in the memory, and have Names assigned to them; without which, Laws could be but ill made, or Vice and Disorder repressed. (II.xxii.10)

In the case of action terms the real essences signified clearly cannot be internal corpuscular structures. As the real and nominal essence coincide and as nominal essences are abstract ideas, these real essences must be ideas.

For Locke, then, abstract ideas framed by the mind constitute the real essences of human actions. He distinguishes three general types of human action: actions of the mind (e.g. consideration, assent); actions of the body (e.g. running, speaking); actions of mind and body together (e.g. revenge, murder) (II.xxii.10). It is the third type which engages most of his attention. Locke holds all free actions to follow from, or be caused by, acts of will (II.xxi.5). However, his theory of human freedom is quite separate from his account of actions as mixed modes. His awareness of them as *mixed* modes prevents him falling into the vulgar error of supposing that when we judge a piece of behaviour to be an action of a certain kind we are concerned solely with two factors: with a segment of the agent's private mental life and a set of his publicly observable bodily movements. On the contrary, actions are distinguished one from another according to an indefinite variety of factors; 'by their Causes, Means, Objects, Ends, Instruments, Time, Place, and other circumstances' (II.xxii, 10). Consequently, it is in general impossible to tell from what is given to the senses what action is being performed:

> the intention of the Mind, or the Relation of holy Things, which make a part of *Murther*, or *Sacrilege*, have no necessary connexion with the outward and visible Action of him that commits either: and the pulling the Trigger of the Gun, with which the Murther is committed, and is all the Action, that, perhaps, is visible, has no natural connexion with those other *Ideas*, that make up the complex one, named *Murther*. (III.ix.71)

It is the 'invisible' factors which are of major importance in determining what action is constituted by a given piece of behaviour:

> a mans holding a gun in his hand & pulling downe the triger may

> be either Rebellion Parricide. Murther. Homicide. Duty, Justice. Valor or recreation. & be thus variously diversified when all the circumstances put togeather are compard to a rule, though the simple action of holding the gun & pulling the triger may be exactly the same. (Draft A, p.85)

Locke, then, is well aware that the one piece of behaviour can, in virtue of its context, go to make up a variety of actions. Although he does not explicitly make the point, the converse of this is also true; the one kind of action may be made up by a variety of pieces of behaviour. For example, shooting is only one of the ways of committing murder.

It will be helpful to consider what Locke says about actions in the light of a distinction made by a modern philosopher between the 'form' and 'matter' of an action.[15] A report confined to the agent's observable behaviour (e.g. 'he is running', 'he is raising his arm') is very rarely a satisfactory answer to the question 'what is he doing?' or 'what action is he performing?'. Typically the questioner wants to know the significance of the behaviour, or what it amounts to. For example, running may amount to competing in a race, raising one's arm may amount to voting. The agent's behaviour is the matter of his action, and for the present it may be thought of as that which is given to the senses, that is, the agent's bodily movements. The form is that which, in the particular circumstances, and background of its occurrence, a given piece of behaviour amounts to. Thus, a person's raising his arm when a motion is put to an assembly will have the form of voting. This is not to deny that, in so far as they are not unconscious or merely reflex movements, running, raising one's arm, and so on, are quite properly referred to as actions. However, most of our action terms are not descriptive of bodily movements.

In his account of actions as mixed modes, Locke is concerned with the notions we employ when we judge a piece of behaviour to constitute a specific kind of action. Among others he cites 'theft' (II.xii.5); 'lying', 'hypocrisy', 'parricide', 'Triumph', 'wrestling', 'fencing' (II.xxii.1, 2, 4, 8, 9); 'murder', 'incest' (III.v.6); and 'adultery' (III.vi.44). For example, on Locke's definition, the form of theft is 'the concealed change of the possession of any thing, without the consent of the proprietor'. On Locke's theory of definition, a term is defined when the complex idea for which it stands is analysed into its constituent simple ideas, and the complex ideas for which these action terms stand are nominal essences. Thus, what Locke calls the nominal essence of an action is identical with what we have called its form. A piece of behaviour amounts to some kind of action or other by virtue of measuring up to a form. That is, the form of an action fulfils the ontic role Locke assigns to a real essence; it is that whereby the action is what it is. As form and nominal essence are identical, this means that in the case of actions the nominal essence functions as a real essence.

With respect to actions Locke has reinstated the opinion of real essences he is at pains to reject with respect to bodies: there are a number of essences or forms wherein particular human performances partake and so become of this or that species of action. The forms in question are not subsistent universals, but, being abstract complex ideas, they are constructs of the mind. These ideas or notions, being made by the mind without regard to any given patterns, are quite independent of actual instances of the actions of which they are notions:

> the *Ideas* of *Sacrilege*, or *Adultery*, might be framed in the Mind of Men, and have names given them; and so the Species of mixed Modes be constituted, before either of them was ever committed; and might be as well discovered of, and reasoned about, and as certain Truths discovered of them, whilst yet they had no being but in the Understanding. (III.v.5; cf. III.v.3)

Indeed, it would seem not merely that these notions *might* be framed prior to the actions being committed, but that they *must* be prior to the actions. The matter and form of an action such as adultery are complementary in the sense that, without human behaviour there would be nothing to constitute an act of adultery in the world, and without the form human behaviour could not amount to adultery. Locke does hold that our notions determine the species of actions in the world. In explaining the way in which the name gives a 'lasting union' to the simple ideas combined in a notion he writes:

> killing a Man with a Sword, or a Hatchet, are looked on as no distinct species of Action: But if the Point of the Sword first enter the Body, it passes for a distinct *Species*, where it has a distinct *Name*, as in *England* . . . it is called *Stabbing*: But in another Country, where it has not happened to be specified under a peculiar *Name*, it passes not for a distinct *Species*. (III.v.11)

As it stands, this only makes the trivial point that were our language to lack the term 'stabbing' we would not *call* any behaviour stabbing, but Locke intends something more substantial. He goes on to contrast species of actions with species of corporeal substances. So far as the latter are concerned: 'though it be the Mind that makes the nominal Essence: yet since those *Ideas*, which are combined in it, are supposed to have an Union in Nature, whether the Mind joins them or no, therefore those are looked on as distinct *Species*, without any operation of the Mind, either abstracting, or giving a *Name* to that complex *Idea'* (ibid.). In other words, while there are species of substances determined by nature, and thus quite independent of our sorting activities, the species of actions are determined solely by us.

In order to understand how it is that our notions determine species of actions it will be best to begin by considering the way our interests, purposes and concerns enter into the formation of our ideas; both those ideas which Locke classifies as ectypes and those, such as action notions, which are archetypes. It is the job of general terms to collect together particulars which are similar one to another. This is simply to say that these terms are used in classifying things. Two particular things A and B cannot be similar *tout court*; logically they must always be similar in respect of some characteristic (or set of characteristics) C. The characteristic C in virtue of which A and B are similar and are both properly called by the one general name is dictated by the purpose for which the name was introduced into our language. Locke sees us as constructing ideas of corporeal substances for the purpose of making an inventory of things existing in nature, our cataloguing principle being that particulars which are similar in respect of their sensible qualities are to be sorted under the one heading. Accordingly, our substance ideas are ectypes recording clusters of qualities which have been found to be exhibited by a number of particular bodies. That is, we apply substance terms to things in accord with the sensible qualities which co-exist in them. However, in building up our classificatory scheme for substances we are not content merely to record the few similarities which immediately strike us. Locke does not deny the existence of natural kinds of substances, but believes that 'there are certain precise Essences, according to which Nature makes all particular Things, and by which they are distinguished into Species' (III.x.21). In framing abstract ideas of substances we aim to encapsulate these ultimate similarities in the qualities of things. Unfortunately this aim can never be realised, for we cannot penetrate to the real essences of bodies. Could we do so we would understand that the qualities of bodies flow of necessity from their essences, and we would be able to tell *a priori* exactly what qualities each body must have. We could then develop a perfectly precise and whole adequate classificatory scheme, for we would have a guarantee that two bodies, which were alike at the level of their real essences or internal structures were alike in all their qualities.

As it is we must rely on the sensible qualities of bodies. Nevertheless, the more details we include within each of our substance ideas the nearer we approach our unattainable goal of a wholly adequate classificatory scheme. Thus, a complex idea of gold which combines simple ideas of qualities *a, b, c* and *d* will be more adequate than one which combines only *a* and *b,* and so on. In pursuit of a more adequate classificatory scheme we are constantly altering our ectypal substance ideas, adding to them the new qualities we discern in the substances themselves.[16] Not only does a more detailed observation of substances such as gold enlarge our idea of gold, it may also lead us to conclude that some of the particulars we originally classified as gold are not really gold. Suppose our original idea of gold combined the two qualities *a* and *b,* and suppose that our observation of particulars which qualified as gold in conformity with this idea revealed that some of them had the further qualities *c* and *d*; if we enlarge our original idea to include *c* and *d,* those particulars which exhibit only *a* and *b* will no longer qualify as gold.[17]

Locke states that the '*Essences of the Species of mixed Modes, are* not only *made* by the Mind, but made *very arbitrarily*' (III.v.3). By this he means only that in framing them we are not guided by given patterns, that is they are not ectypes. He is careful to add that they '*are not made at random,* and jumbled together without any reason at all' (III.v.7). We have seen that the reason why most mixed mode ideas are ideas of actions is because without such ideas 'laws could be but ill made, or vice and disorder repressed'. That is, Locke sees these action notions as arising from our need to regulate human conduct. This need exists because human beings are not isolated individuals having to do solely with a physical environment and standing as mere spectators of the doings of their fellows. Rather, human beings live in society and interact one with another. In consequence, what the idividual does may affect not merely the world of physical objects but also the world of human beings. Some of the effects in the latter world are looked upon as harmful and others as beneficial. Hence the need for regulations governing conduct.

Morality is, at least in large part, concerned with conduct in so far as it is productive of harm and benefit within the human world. Very roughly, those actions which are productive of harm are wrong or vicious and those which are productive of benefit are right or virtuous. It might seem, then, that the primary moral notions are the notions of right or virtue and wrong or vice, and that these gather together particular pieces of human behaviour which are similar in respect of being virtuous or being vicious. However, right and wrong are not simply characteristics which may attach to what the agent does. The notions of right and wrong belong to the highest level of moral notions and they gather together the various *species* of right and wrong actions, for example murder, theft, adultery. If I claim that what a person has done, or contemplates doing, is wrong, I must be able to specify the species of wrong action or my claim is empty; for an action can be wrong only by virtue of being an instance of a species of wrongness.[18] It is the lower level moral notions such as 'murder' and 'theft' which we employ in our everyday moral judgments and decision-making, and it is to these notions that Locke devotes most attention. Their content reflects our need to promote or discourage certain behaviour, and they gather together pieces of behaviour which amount to murder, theft, and so on. In our moral discourse we use these notions as standards against which we measure the human world.

Locke conceives all abstract ideas as standards applied in the sorting of things. We classify a particular lump of metal as gold on the grounds that the qualities it exhibits conform to those combined in our ectypal ideas of gold. Similarly, we classify what an agent does as murder on the grounds that it conforms to our archetypal notion of murder. But, as has been explained, ectypal ideas are always up for revision in the light of the new discoveries we make concerning the individual items which fall under them. Thus, in their case the things function as standards against which the ideas themselves are measured. Our moral notions are solely standards against which we measure the world; we do not measure them against the world. No matter how much information we may gather about the motives behind an individual murder, the way it was carried out, and so on, will not lead us to revise our notion of murder.

This is not to say that we can in no way develop our moral notions or change their original formulations. However, as we shall see shortly, we do this by inventing new notions which introduce new species of actions. As Locke puts it, 'in *mixed Modes* any of the *Ideas* that make the Composition of the complex one, being left out, or changed, it is allowed to be another thing, *i.e.* to be of another Species, as is plain in *Chance-medly, Man-slaughter, Murther, Parricide,* etc.' (III.x.19). These species of actions may be taken as having arisen out of the notion of homicide, but they do not enlarge our notion of homicide and make it a more adequate representation of the reality of homicide. We know perfectly well what homicide is, provided we know that it is the killing of one human being by another. The terms Locke cites name quite independent species of killing. On the other hand, where we develop an ectype idea such as 'gold', we are more adequately representing what gold is: '[he] that adds to his complex *Idea* of *Gold,* that of Fixedness or Solubility in *Aqua Regia* . . . is not thought to have changed the Species; but only to have a more perfect *Idea,* by adding another simple *Idea,* which is always in fact, joined with those others, of which his former complex

Idea consisted' (ibid.).

Locke states that in framing notions 'the Mind . . . combines several scattered independent *Ideas,* into one complex one; and by the common name it gives them, makes them the Essence of a certain Species' (III.v.6). His remark that the ideas combined in notions are scattered and independent is meant to emphasise the contrast between notions and substance ideas. The ideas making up the latter have a union in nature because they are ideas of qualities which have been found clustered together. However, it is equally true of what Locke calls 'fantastical ideas' that their constituent ideas are scattered and independent. The ideas making up the complex idea of a centaur, for instance, are never found together in nature. Locke clarified the meaning of his remark with respect to action notions by means of examples:

> For what greater connexion in Nature, has the *Idea* of a Man, than the *Idea* of a Sheep with Killing, that this is made a particular Species of Action, signified by the word *Murder,* and the other not? Or what Union is there in Nature, between the *Idea* of the Relation of a Father, with Killing than that of a Son, or Neighbour; that those are combined into one complex *Idea,* and thereby made the Essence of the distinct Species *Parricide* whilst the other make no distinct Species at all? . . . Thus the Mind in mixed Modes arbitrarily unites into complex *Ideas,* such as it finds convenient; whilst others that have altogether as much union in Nature, are left loose, and never combined into one *Idea,* because they have no need of one name. (III.v.6)

As Locke conceives ideas having a union in nature in terms of their being ideas of qualities co-existing in substances, it is strictly meaningless to talk of the idea of killing, having, or failing to have, any union with either the idea of a man or of a sheep. Nevertheless, it is clear enough what Locke is getting at: whereas we can explain why the ideas, say, of yellowness and malleability are part of our idea of gold by pointing out the recurrence of these qualities in particular lumps of gold, there is nothing observable in the world which explains why the notion of murder is confined to the killing of man and excludes the killing of other animals. The explanation of the composition of our moral notions lies not in the world but in our interests and concerns. The notion of murder develops out of our concern for the regulation of conduct affecting *human* life. That our moral notions are developed with a view to the regulation of human conduct, and not for the purpose of recording the empirical details of human behaviour, explains why they are archetypes. As archetypes they are not measured against reality, but are employed only as standards against which reality is measured; and because of this they are the sole determinants of the species to which the particular actions falling under them belong.

We decide to divide up the world of substances according to similarities in respect of sensible qualities, and this decision reflects certain interests we have in regard to that world. But the qualities co-existing in a particular body and the similarities or dissimilarities between them and the qualities co-existing in other particular bodies are independent of our interests and decisions; two lumps of gold are alike in their qualities and different from a lump of coal whether we frame the ideas or not. These similarities in respect of sensible qualities are presented to us, and, if they were not there in the world independently of us, we could not attend to them in the constructing of our abstract ideas of substances. Thus, Locke says we suppose that particular substances belong to distinct species quite apart from 'any operation of the mind' producing abstract ideas or nominal essences. Further, in the case of substances, the boundaries of species are thought of as being ultimately determined by the similarities between particulars holding at the level of their real essences. Could we penetrate to the level of these essences it is at least likely that many of the particulars we now call, for example, gold, would be differently classified. Thus these ultimate similarities stand as rivals (and superior rivals at that) to the species we draw up when we frame our abstract ideas of substances. This being the case, the question 'which species does it belong to?' is ambiguous when asked of a particular body: it might be taken as an inquiry about the abstract idea, or nominal essence, the body falls under, or it might be taken as an inquiry about its real essence. In the second sense the question is, in Locke's opinion, unanswerable; at least by creatures of our limited understanding.

When we come to our moral notions the case is quite different, for here there can be no rivals in nature for the species we draw up when we frame our notions. There are species of action such as murder, theft, and so on. All the individual pieces of behaviour which properly come under the heading of 'murder' are similar in that they conform to the notion of murder, that is the intentional killing of an innocent person with the aim of personal gain or satisfaction. But murder may be committed in an indefinite variety of ways. Hence, taken purely as phenomena in the world there is nothing to group together the pieces of behaviour which constitute murder. The shooting of a rich uncle is empirically similar to the shooting of a sheep and dissimilar to the slow poisoning of an unwanted spouse, and not even all killings of human beings count as murder. All this shows is something which must be already known to anyone capable of identifying human actions: that the action species to which an individual piece of behaviour belongs is not determined by its empirical characteristics. The question to which species a given piece of behaviour belongs is unambiguous, it is an enquiry about the notion under which the action falls. While the question is not ambiguous, this does not mean that there is always only one answer which can be given. We have other interests in human conduct besides moral interests, and moral notions are not the only action notions we have developed. The one piece of behaviour may properly be ranked under quite different notions depending on the vantage point from which it is viewed. However, these different notions are not rivals. It is not the case that, for example, the action notions which arise out of our scientific interest in human conduct are more fundamental than those arising out of our moral interest, that they more nearly approach the real essences of human actions. Rather, the differences between the various types of action notion we have developed are reflections of the different interests and concerns we have with respect to the human world.[19]

3. We saw in chapter III that for Locke making moral judgments is a matter of applying general moral precepts, these being thought of as the content of the moral law. The foregoing account of moral notions gives us a clearer picture of what it is to apply general moral precepts; it is basically a matter of classifying conduct in accord with moral notions. For example, the agent who is concerned with what he morally ought to do will want to find out whether the alternatives before him in a given situation fall under moral notions. If one of the alternatives constitutes say, theft, then it is an action coming under the general heading of vice and hence an action which ought not to be performed. Moral dilemmas arise because in some situations all the alternatives fall under moral notions which themselves come under the heading of vice. If we had not constructed moral notions for the purpose of applying them to the situation we are in, moral dilemmas could not arise. The problems which might then arise would not be moral problems, but solely practical problems of how best to achieve certain ends we have set ourselves.[20] In many situations the alternatives open to us do not fall under any moral notions. Here it is morally neutral what we do. In these situations we have, as Locke tells Grenville, a 'liberty which we may use without scrupulously thinkeing ourselves obleiged to that which in it self may be Best' (*Correspondence*, I, p.559).

On Locke's legalist conception of morality nothing can be right or wrong except in relation to a law. Consequently, he maintains that moral actions must be looked at under a 'two-fold Consideration':

> *First,* As they are in themselves each made up of such a Collection of simple *Ideas.* Thus *Drunkenness,* or *Lying,* signify such or such a Collection of simple *Ideas,* which I call mixed Modes: and in this Sense, they are . . . *positive absolute Ideas.* . . . *Secondly,* Our Actions are considered, as Good, Bad, *or* Indifferent; and in this respect, they are *Relative,* it being their Conformity to, or Disagreement with some Rule, that makes them to be regular or irregular, Good or Bad: and so, as far as they are compared with a Rule, and thereupon dominated, they come under Relation. (II.xxviii.15)

As we have described moral notions and their employment in moral judgments, to rank a piece of behaviour under such a notion is to understand it as right or wrong. Murder, for example, is a species of vice. Therefore, behaviour falling under that notion is wrong. Locke agrees that 'very frequently the positive *Idea* of the Action, and its Moral Relation, are comprehended together under one Name, and the same Word made use of, to express both the Mode or Action, and its Moral Rectitude or Obliquity' (II.xxviii.16). On the account of moral notions we have given this will *always* be the case.

However, Locke's insistence on the two-fold consideration of moral actions is not necessarily at variance with the view that in ranking an action under a moral notion we thereby consider it right or wrong. His point may be interpreted as drawing a distinction between our employment of moral notions in our everyday moral judgment and what may be termed our philosophical reflections on those notions. Our ideas of murder, theft, lying, and so on, are ideas of the wrongful taking of human life, or of property, or the wrongful utterance of falsehood. As such they are in Locke's terms, 'relative' ideas. It is analytically true that murder is wrong because 'murder' is a notion which we employ when we assess conduct from the moral point of view and because it belongs under the general moral notion, 'vice'. Thus, knowing that murder is wrong is simply knowing that the notion is used in moral judgments concerning the viciousness of conduct. Unless we do know this we will not know how to use the notion. Nevertheless, being possessed merely of the relative idea of murder as wrongful killing does not enable us to identify murders and distinguish them from killings which are not wrongful. In order to identify murders we need a 'positive' idea; for example, that murder is the intentional killing of an innocent person with the aim of personal gain or satisfaction. This description, as it makes no mention of the wrongfulness of murder, is morally neutral. As it is morally neutral it does make sense to ask whether behaviour measuring up to this description is wrong. In asking this we are not employing the notion in a moral judgment; rather, we are reflecting upon the notion itself and enquiring into its credentials as a moral notion. We are in fact doing moral philosophy. In Locke's opinion we establish the credentials of moral notions by showing that the actions they describe are enjoined or prohibited by the moral law; but the point about the two-fold consideration of moral actions holds quite aside from Locke's legalism. There is an important difference between employing a moral notion in a moral judgment and, as it were, standing back from its employment and reflecting upon the notion itself. What Locke says about the two-fold consideration of moral actions is misleading in so far as it gives the impression that *in making a moral judgment* we first of all determine that the behaviour in question falls under a notion such as murder and then judge that murder as wrong.

There is a further point concerning moral notions emerging from what Locke says about the two-fold consideration of moral actions, and this point introduces certain qualifications in what we have just said about the analyticity of propositions such as 'murder is wrong'. Locke thinks it a source of confusion that the moral rectitude or obliquity of actions should so often be incorporated in the notions we have of them. He uses the notion of stealing, or 'the taking from another what is his, without his knowledge or Allowance', to illustrate how the confusion arises. There are, he rightly points out, cases when what is done fits under this description, but is not morally wrong. For instance, 'the private taking away his Sword from a Madman, to prevent his doing Mischief, though it be properly denominated *Stealing*... yet when compared to the Law of God... it is no Sin, or Transgression, though the Name *Stealing* ordinarily carries such an intimation with it' (II.xxviii.16). It may be that in applying a moral notion such as stealing to human behaviour we are sometimes misled by the notion itself into condemning that which is morally neutral or even morally worthy; but Locke is wrong in concluding that his example shows that, in judging the morality of what is done, we should first apply a moral notion and then compare the action so identified with a moral rule. What the example does show is that the notion of stealing, like many of our moral notions, is 'open'.[21] Our moral notions reflect our concern with the benefit and harm produced by the doings of human beings, but they are tailored to paradigm cases. Thus, *generally speaking* it will be wrong to take a person's property without his allowance; but there are exceptional cases such as that of the mad-man's sword. To say of a moral notion that it is open means that we recognise circumstances in which, contrary to what is usually the case, something measuring up to the description embodied in the notion is not an instance of vice or not an instance of virtue. It might seem, then, that (at least in so far as the reference is to open moral notions) propositions such as 'murder is wrong', 'stealing is wrong' do not express analytic truths. These acts are only sometimes wrong.

It is important to take note here of the function of the predicate 'is wrong' in these propositions. It indicates the role of the notions, that they are used in picking out species of vicious behaviour. It is because the notions have this role that we want to say that the propositions are analytically true. But we saw that in order to identify murders, thefts and so on we need positive ideas, that is, morally neutral descriptions of these actions. It is *qua* positive idea that a moral notion may be open. As stealing is an open notion, when we connect the predicate 'is wrong', not with the term 'stealing', but with the relevant description we come up with a proposition which is not analytically true. Indeed, it is false; for we can think up counter-examples, behaviour which fits the description but which we are not prepared to call wrong. When faced with the openness of a moral notion such as stealing, there are three alternatives from which we can choose. First, we may emphasise the analyticity of 'stealing is wrong', and conclude that in some instances what fits the description embodied in our notion is not *really* stealing. Secondly, we may emphasise that what makes a piece of behaviour stealing just is the fact that it fits the description in our notion, and conclude that in some instances stealing is not wrong. In the case of some counter-examples we incline to the former alternative, in the case of others we incline to the latter.[22] Thirdly, we may 'close' our notion so that the behaviour we are not prepared to call wrong no longer falls under it.

As there is an indefinite number of cases in which we would want to say that what is done fits the description of stealing but is not wrong, it would be futile to attempt to close our notion by enumerating these. What we can do is frame another moral notion which will gather them all together. We might invent the notion of 'stoling' for this purpose. A suitable description of 'stoling' might be 'the taking from another what is his without his knowledge or allowance when so doing is for the protection of human beings'. Equipped with this new notion we can discriminate between the taking from another which we want to condemn as wrong and that which we want to condone. We can so discriminate because, although the notion of 'stoling' includes the description embodied in our notion of stealing, it adds something extra. Thus, by the invention of new notions we can close our original notion (though there is no guarantee that the new ones will not themselves be open).[23] We can do this, but there is no necessity that we do it. The fact of the matter is that, by and large, we find open notions perfectly adequate for the classification of behaviour from the moral point of view. The ability to recognise cases in which what is done fits the description embodied in a notion such as 'stealing' but is not wrong is an important aspect of our grasp of these notions. We are able to recognise them because we are aware of the purposes and interests reflected in our moral notions.

The invention of new notions in order to close our original ones illustrates the development of moral notions mentioned earlier. The notion of 'stoling' is not invented to accommodate some new empirical discovery we have made concerning human behaviour. We do not need to observe anyone taking a sword from a mad-man, or even believe that such a thing has been done, in order to recognise it as an action which fits our description of stealing but is not vicious. In inventing the notion of 'stoling' we added more ideas to our complex ideas of stealing, but we did not enlarge that idea and make it a more adequate representation of the phenomenon of stealing. 'Stoling' marks out an independent species of action. Locke supposes that we discover that taking the mad-man's sword is not wrong by going beyond the notion of stealing and comparing the action to a law; but, on his own account of what it is to compare an action to a law or rule, this will amount to classifying the action under a notion: 'This Rule being nothing but a Collection of several simple *Ideas*, the Conformity thereto is but so ordering the Action, that the simple *Ideas*, belonging to it, may correspond to those, which the law requires' (II.xxviii.14). Clearly we can only make this comparison if we know the law. The law cannot consist of an indefinite list of particular action descriptions such as 'taking a mad-man's sword', it must make use of a general action notion. The notion of stealing as it features in the law may be just as open as our notion; in this case a comparison with the law will obviously not help us recognise instances when something falling under our notion is not really vicious. Any appeal to the law will be helpful only if the legal notion is closed. But knowing the law involves knowing this closed notion of stealing, and hence being able to apply it directly in our moral judgments. There is not, as Locke seems to think, any call for a kind of two-stage moral judgment in which we first classify what the agent does according to our moral notions and then go on to compare it with a law.

Locke's account of notions as archetypes brings out a number of important differences between the functions of our action concepts and our substance concepts, but there are other differences which his way of ideas serves only to obscure. He refers to all abstract complex ideas (concepts) as patterns in accord with which particulars are classified. The only difference between substance ideas and notions is that, in the case of the latter, the patterns are wholly of our devising: 'in mixed Modes, at least the most considerable parts of them, which are moral Beings, we consider the original Patterns, as being in the Mind; and to those we referr for the distinguishing of particular Beings under Names' (III.v.12). While the 'pattern' metaphor is harmless enough in an account of the classification of substance according to their empirical qualities, it is highly misleading to think of the classification of actions under moral notions as similarly consisting in the application of patterns to reality.

As the ability to identify particulars falling under a specific concept is the minimal condition for the possession of that concept, anyone who has a concept of *x* will be able to recognise instances of *x* and distinguish them from instances of *y*. This is true equally of physical object concepts and of moral notions such as 'justice' and 'theft'. It is conceivable that a person might be taught to recognise instances of a substance such as gold without being taught anything else about that substance. If so, their use of the word 'gold' would extend only to its application to particular things, and their conception of gold would simply be that it is something exhibiting such and such empirical characteristics. These characteristics may be thought of as constituting a pattern in accord with which particulars are classified as gold. The minimal condition for concept possessions being fulfilled, the person does have a concept of gold. However, he has only a truncated concept, for he has no understanding of why gold should be distinguished from other substances. For him the activity of classifying has no point and is unrelated to any other activities. Our possession of notions such as 'justice', 'murder' and 'theft' is importantly different; here our fulfilment of the minimal condition for concept possession depends upon our having a mastery of the concepts which goes beyond the mere ability to identify particulars falling under them. In order to identify particular murders, thefts, and so on, we need to have grasped those actions' forms; and our grasp of the forms is inseparable from an understanding of the way of life in which those notions have a place. Thus, we cannot understand the description embodied in the notion of theft unless we know what it is for someone to be in possession of a thing, what it is for them to consent, or not consent, to someone else taking that thing, and so on. And if we cannot understand the description, clearly we are in no position to assess whether or not a given performance fits that description. Further, we need to know not only what factors count for an action falling under a specific moral notion, but also to recognise countervailing factors which count against it. For example, what the agent did is not an instance of theft if he is under the misapprehension that the thing he took is his own property. In short, we are able to employ moral notions and classify human behaviour from the moral point of view because we have an understanding of the interests and purposes behind our notions, even though our understanding of this may be vague and indefinite.

4. It might be thought that the account of moral notions given here is at odds with the general tenets of Locke's moral philosophy as these have been explained in earlier chapters. Specifically, the fact that we invent moral notions and employ them in discriminating between virtuous and vicious behaviour may appear to contradict the moral objectivism of his natural law theory. Locke is aware that his conception of the notions employed in moral discourse as archetypes constructed without recourse to any given patterns might be taken as a statement of extreme moral scepticism: 'But it will here be said, that if *moral Knowledge* be placed in the Contemplation of our own *moral Ideas,* and those, as other Modes, be of our own making, What strange Notions will there be of *Justice* and *Temperance*? What confusion of Vertues and Vices, if every one may make what *Ideas* of them he pleases?' (IV.iv.9). Locke replies that moral notions are no more the exclusive property of the individual than are mathematical notions. A person may suppose that the term 'triangle' refers to a four-sided figure, but this does not alter the fact that the term, as it has been devised by mathematicians, refers to a three-sided figure. Nor need this mistake in terminology hinder the person from understanding geometrical demonstrations of the properties of triangles, for the figure may be drawn and the proofs carried through by reference to the visual representation:

> Just the same is it in *moral* Knowledge, let a Man have the *Idea* of taking from others, without their Consent, what their honest Industry has possessed them of, and call this *Justice,* if he please. He that takes the Name here without the *Idea* put to it, will be mistaken, by joining another *Idea* of his own to that Name: But strip the *Idea* of that Name, or take it such as it is in the Speaker's Mind, and the same Thing will agree to it, as if you call'd it *Injustice.* (ibid.)

Locke is here thinking of moral notions as existing quite independently of moral language; just as a triangle may be represented and publicly shown without the use of language, so too moral notions may be set forth without the use of moral language. But this is, of course, not so. There is no way of explaining what justice or temperance is which is even vaguely analogous to the non-linguistic visual representation of geometrical figures. We find out that a person is misusing the term 'justice' not by 'stripping the idea of the name' and seeing that it is the idea we call 'injustice', but simply by seeing that his use of the term is at variance with its use in our public language. Moral notions are public property because the use of moral terms is established in our language. We have seen that, despite his talk of laying words aside and attending only to the ideas for which they stand, when it comes to moral notions Locke does appeal to the common acceptation of moral words. Public linguistic usage provides the standard in accord with which the individual may be said to have a true or false notion of justice, theft, murder, and so on.

While Locke might not be committed to the extreme subjectivist view that the various virtues and vices *are* what each individual thinks them to be, it may yet seem that he is committed to a form of subjectivism which is contrary to his natural law theory. Even given that moral notions are public property, they are still made by us. But surely the law of nature is completely objective; its content is not made by us, but discovered by us. Moreover, the view that the true content of moral notions depends upon public linguistic usage would seem to involve cultural ethical relativism. Even when two cultures do possess linguistic expressions used in, say, the condemnation of species of killing, they may well differ as to what particular actions count as wrongful killing, or murder; and the differences are likely to be greater in the case of broad notions such as justice and injustice. It would seem, therefore, that moral knowledge must go beyond a knowledge of established linguistic usage.

Here it is important to bear in mind that for Locke the content of the law of nature derives from certain features of human nature. So too do our moral notions; for these arise out of certain human needs and concerns. The content of the law of nature is objective because human nature is uniform. Equally, moral notions are objective because the needs and concerns which enter into their construction are shared by all men. In fact, the features of human nature relevant to the derivation of the law of nature are these universal needs and concerns. The law and our moral notions are, therefore, bound together. The precepts of the law are not innate to the human mind nor immediately evident to some faculty of moral intuition. They are, Locke holds, found out by discursive reasoning. The reasoning which finds them out is that which produces moral notions. We shall see that the most fruitful part of Locke's demonstration of morality is his attempt to validate our moral notions by making explicit the reasons behind them.

VI

MORALITY AND DEMONSTRATION

1. The claim that morality is capable of demonstration is by no means unique to Locke. It is also to be found, for example, in Richard Cumberland and Samuel Pufendorf, two writers who most probably had a direct influence on Locke's moral philosophy.[1] And even contemporary critics of the *Essay* such as Leibniz and John Sergeant express their approval for this aspect of Locke's thought.[2] Yet, despite the urgings of several of his friends, Locke never produced a demonstrative system of morals. In a letter to Molyneux, written some two years after the publication of the *Essay*, he shows a certain reticence when the topic is brought up: 'Though by the view I had of moral ideas, whilst I was considering that subject, I thought I saw that morality might be demonstratively made out, yet whether I am able so to make it out, is another question' (*Correspondence*, 4, p.524). Later, in *The Reasonableness of Christianity*, reticence seems to have become something like repudiation:

> it is plain, in fact, that human reason unassisted failed men in its great and proper business of morality. It never from unquestioned principles, by clear deductions, made out an entire body of the 'law of nature'. . . . He, that . . . will . . . have his rules pass for authentic directions, must show, that either he builds his doctrine upon principles of reason, self-evident in themselves; and that he deduces all the parts of it from thence, by clear and evident demonstration: or must show his commission from heaven, and that he comes with authority from God, to deliver his will and commands to the world. . . . It is true, there is a law of nature: but who is there that ever did, or undertook to give it to us all entire, as a law; no more, nor no less, than what was contained in, and had the obligation of that law? . . . Such a law of morality Jesus Christ hath given us in the New Testament; but by the latter of these ways, by revelation. (*Works*, 7, pp.140, 142, 143)

Abrams argues that, although he continues to pay lip-service to the doctrine of a natural law accessible to unaided reason, in the *Reasonableness* Locke retreats from ethical rationalism to a kind of sceptical fideism, that he comes to acknowledge 'the equal status and partial nature of every man's subjective knowledge' in the moral sphere.[3] But, however Locke's remarks in the *Reasonableness* are to be understood, he does not, even implicitly, endorse Abrams' subjective knowledge'. This 'knowledge' amounts to what, in a chapter added to the fourth edition of the *Essay* (a chapter which, from its date of publication, must express a view subsequent to the *Reasonableness*), Locke stigmatises as enthusiasm. He has particularly in mind the Sectaries' appeal to an 'inward light', but, in general, he uses the term 'enthusiasm' to refer to any feeling of conviction which is backed by nothing more than its own subjective intensity: 'they are sure, because they are sure: and their Perswasions are right, only because they are strong in them' (IV.xix.9). Far from giving epistemic status to this type of certitude, Locke is adamant that '*Reason* must be our last Judge and Guide in every Thing' (IV.xix.14).

There is, in fact, nothing in the *Reasonableness* that contradicts the rationalist approach Locke adopts elsewhere with respect to ethics. He is, by virtue of his natural law doctrine, committed to the view that the precepts of morality can be found out by unaided human reason. This finding out of the content of the law consists in the construction of moral notions. It is something that has occurred in the history of mankind. We shall see that Locke considers our common notions of virtue and vice as they feature in what he calls the law of opinion or reputation to be, by and large, an adequate reflection of the law of nature. The demonstration of morality is a task for the moral philosopher. It will consist in a derivation from certain self-evident principles of the moral notion which are already at hand. It will not reveal new moral truths concerning how we ought to act, but will establish the rational foundation of the morality we have. Locke does not reject the possibility of a demonstration of morality in the *Reasonableness*. When he talks of reason so far having failed to carry out 'its great and proper business' it is obvious that he has a science of morals in mind. But to say that reason has failed heretofore is not to say it must fail, and Locke always presents the demonstration of morality as something yet to be attained. What the *Reasonableness* emphasises is the difficulty of carrying such a demonstration through. There are good reasons why this should be emphasised here; for in the *Reasonableness* Locke is anxious to show that the Christian revelation is of importance for the moral life. Christ has announced a definitive set of moral precepts; '[there] is not, I think, any of the duties of morality, which he has not, somewhere or other, by himself and his apostles, inculcated over and over again to his followers in express terms' (*Works*, 7, pp.122). As the Messiah, Christ has all the authority needed to impose moral obligation, and this ordinary moralists, confined as they are to the suasions of reason, cannot do. Moreover, a future state of reward or punishment is an important part of what has been revealed. Previous to Christianity, philosophers had but a shadowy conception of the state of the person after death. Consequently, they concentrated on the intrinsic worth of virtue as a motive for action. This, in Locke's opinion, is a mistake; it is only the awareness of rewards and punishments which can provide a motive strong enough to prompt virtuous conduct under any circumstances (*Works*, 7, pp.148–51).

All this accords perfectly well with what Locke has maintained since the time of his early writings: that sanctions are necessary for a law to be effective and that, in so far as content is concerned, the law of nature is identical with New Testament morality. His belief in this identity comes up again in another letter to Molyneux in which the project of a science of morals is mentioned:

> As to a treatise of morals, . . . I so far incline to comply with your desires, that I every now and then lay by some materials for it, as they occasionally occur in the rovings of my mind. But when I consider, that a book of Offices, as you call it, ought not to be slightly done . . . I am in doubt whether it would be prudent, in one of my age and health . . . to see about it. Did the world want a rule, I confess there could be no work so necessary. . . . But the Gospel contains so perfect a body of Ethicks, that reason may be excused from that inquiry, since she may find man's duty clearer and easier in revelation than in herself. (*Correspondence*, 5, p.595)

This letter, dated 30 March 1696, follows the publication of the *Reasonableness*. As Locke talks of setting aside materials towards a science of morals he cannot have by that date relinquished his belief in the possibility of such a science.

2. Locke's claim that morality can be demonstrated cannot be understood and assessed unless we understand his conception of demonstration. The account of demonstration which would have been most familiar to Locke's contemporaries stems from Aristotle. Briefly, a proposition is said to be demonstrated when it is derived in accord with the rules of syllogistic inference from premises which are themselves indubitably true. The premises in a demonstrative syllogism must be indemonstrable; for if they were demonstrable their truth ought to be established by a prior demonstration. All demonstration begins from first principles or axioms. Some of these principles are restricted in scope in that they apply only to specific

areas of enquiry; for example, the principle that if equals are taken from equals the remainders are equals has application only in demonstrations concerning quantities. However, the laws of non-contradiction and excluded middle are principles which apply in all areas, for we must have a grasp of them if we are to reason at all. Of these laws Aristotle observes that they are not normally included among the premises of a demonstration syllogism, but are rather rules in accord with which we reason. On the Aristotelian account, then, a putative demonstration may be rebutted either on the grounds of truth or of formal validity. That is, it might be pointed out that at least one of the premises is false (or at least not indubitable in the sense required), or that the derivation of the conclusion from the premises violates the laws of reasoning.

Locke's conception of demonstration is explicitly opposed to Aristotle's formalism. He rejects the view that all discursive reasoning is at bottom syllogistic and denies that Aristotelian axioms provide the foundations of knowledge. In a well-known passage in the chapter 'Of Reason' in the *Essay* he remarks that 'God has not been so sparing to Men to make them barely two-legged Creatures, and left it to *Aristotle* to make them Rational. . . . He has given them a Mind that can reason without being instructed in Methods of Syllogizing: The Understanding . . . has a native Faculty to perceive the Coherence, or Incoherence of its *Ideas*' (IV.xvii.4). In his appeal to the faculty of reason against Aristotelian formal logic Locke is following Descartes, and if he did not draw his inspiration directly from Descartes' *Regulae,* he was at least well acquainted with Cartesian views through texts such as the *Port-Royal Logic.* Locke's 'native faculty of reason' is simply what Descartes calls 'natural light'.[4]

Locke agrees that any piece of correct reasoning can be reduced to one of the figures of the syllogism. However, he objects that this reduction is 'artificial'? It will, as like as not, obscure rather than reveal the connections between ideas which would be obvious to the mind in the 'natural' course of reasoning. Worse, in the hands of the intellectually disingenuous the syllogism is a positive prop for sophistry. This is its role in the disputations of the Schools, those occasions when 'Men are allowed without Shame to deny the Agreement of *Ideas,* that do manifestly agree' (IV.xvii.4). But Locke's main criticism of the syllogism is not that it can be a misleading method for the exposition of arguments, but that it can be *only* a method for the exposition of arguments: 'The Rules of *Syllogism* serve not to furnish the Mind with those intermediate *Ideas,* that may shew the connexion of remote ones. This way of reasoning discovers no new Proofs, but is the Art of marshalling, and ranging the old ones we have already. . . . So that *Syllogism* comes after Knowledge, and then a Man has little or no need of it' (IV.xvii.6). In other words, when our reasoning is restricted by the rules and figures of the syllogism it makes no progress towards new truths but merely orders what the mind already knows. Hence, syllogism '*fails our Reason in* . . . its hardest Task . . . that is *the finding out of Proofs, and making new Discoveries*' (ibid.). What Locke is after is a method which will increase knowledge, a logic of discovery.[5]

Locke's criticism of the syllogism goes hand in hand with his attack on the view that Aristotelian axioms or, as he calls them, 'maxims', are indispensable for demonstrative knowledge. His objection is the same in both cases: inasmuch as our concern is for the advancement of knowledge, the introduction of maxims is just as futile as the reduction of arguments to the figures of the syllogism. Locke agrees that the propositions cited as maxims are self-evident, but he denies that they are primary truths, either in the sense that they are those which the mind comes to know first or that all other knowledge depends upon them. In his opinion it is obvious that maxims do not serve as logical principles which must be applied in all valid reasoning: 'cannot a Country-Wench know, that having received a Shilling from one that owes her three, and a Shilling also from another that owes her three, that the remaining Debts . . . are equal . . . without she fetch the certainty of it from this Maxim, That *if you take Equals from Equals, the remainder will be Equals,* a Maxim which possibly she never heard or thought of? (IV.xii.3). The only use Locke concedes to maxims is that of a weapon against scholastic disingenuousness; they are 'of great *Use* in Disputes, *to stop the Mouths of Wranglers*' (IV.vii.11).[6]

It can hardly be disputed that formal logic is not descriptive of our normal reasoning processes, and that we can draw perfectly correct inferences and recognise propositions as expressing necessary truths without having in mind any logical principles which those inferences or propositions exemplify. But this, it may be argued, is quite beside the point; logic does not aim to describe the way we actually reason in our quest for truth, it is concerned not with discovery but with proof.[7] In his commentary on Locke's chapter 'Of Maxims', Leibniz distinguishes between the historical order in which the individual discovers various truths and the logical or, as he terms it, the natural order of the truths themselves. The former, he says, differs from individual to individual while the latter is always the same.[8] Though we can reason correctly and discover truths without recourse to logical principles, these truths can be properly proved or demonstrated only if they are taken from the subjective order of discovery and accommodated within the objective logical order; that is, only if they are derived from first principles.[9] For Leibniz the ultimate principle in the logical order of truths is the principle of identity or, what he considers to be the same thing, of non-contradiction.[10]

In Leibniz's view Locke has failed to recognise the difference between the order of discovery and the logical order of truths. In consequence his attack on formal logic is based on a misunderstanding. But here it is rather Leibniz who has misunderstood Locke. The conception of a logical order of truths depends on a conception of principles and their instances as intrinsically related. They are so related because, strictly speaking, principles are not propositions but valid formal schemata. In other words, what we have in a principle such as the principle of identity is an assemblage of variables for each of which a indefinite number of different ideas can be substituted. On this view 'lower order' propositions which differ in the ideas they contain may each embody the one principle. These propositions are different with respect to their content but the same with respect to their form. As an inference can always be expressed as a compound hypothetical proposition, there is a propositional schema corresponding to each inference. If the schema is valid so too is the inference in which it is exemplified. Hence, Leibniz holds that principles and their instances should not be opposed to one another as different truths, but the principle should be seen as that which renders the instance true.[11] The conclusion in an inference derives from a first principle in the sense that the inference conforms to the principle. The principle provides the objective guarantee of the correctness of the reasoning involved and it thereby proves the conclusion. Locke's account of reasoning and inference is totally opposed to this view of logical principles. For him principles and their instances are always extrinsically related.

After putting his rhetorical question concerning the reasoning of the country-wench Locke continues:

> I desire any one to consider . . . which is known first and clearest by most People, the particular instance, or the general Rule; and which it is gives Life and Birth to the other. These general Rules are but the comparing our more general and abstract *Ideas*, which are the Workmanship of the Mind, made, and Names given to them, for the easier dispatch in its Reasonings, and drawing into comprehensive Terms, and short Rules, its various and multiplied Observations. But Knowledge began in the Mind, and was founded on particulars. (IV.xii.3)

In Locke's opinion we reason first of all with non-abstract ideas, that is those which are signs only of one definite individual. In this he would appear to be mistaken; for we are able to identify (and hence think about) an individual thing only inasmuch as we can categorise it as a thing of some kind or other. That is, in Lockean terms, we must rank the individual under some *abstract* idea, even if one that is very broad in its scope. However, this objection does not vitally affect the point Locke is making in the above passage. Abstract ideas are of different levels of generality; the idea 'animal', for example, is more general or abstract than the idea 'man'. As Locke understands them, maxims or principles are simply propositions articulating connections between ideas of a very high degree of generality; their instances are propositions articulating the same connections between relatively less general ideas which are comprehended under the ideas involved in the maxims. For example, the proposition 'a man is a man' is an instance of the principle of identity, 'whatever is, is'; for in both propositions an idea is affirmed of itself and the highly general idea 'being' comprehends the idea 'man' (IV.vii.4). There is no room in this theory for the conception of a logical principle consisting of variables which 'stand above' ideas and for which different ideas can be substituted. Principles and their instances are equally assemblages of ideas and they are related only in virtue of the position of their respective ideas in the appropriate series of generalities. They are of use 'to stop the mouths of wranglers' because once the disputant is brought to admit a connection between the ideas in the principle he cannot get out of admitting like connection between the ideas in a proposition which is one of its instances. But this in no way means that the truth of the instance is due to the principle. The ideas articulated in the principle and those in its instance are quite distinct from one another, and for Locke this entails that the propositions express entirely separate truths.

The contrast between Locke and a defender of formal logic such as Leibniz is not simply that the one emphasises the common sense point that the business of reasoning can be carried on without recourse to logical principles, while the other emphasises the objectivity and rigour brought into our thinking through the formulation of logical proofs. Locke is concerned to give an account of the way reason attains to certainty. His inquiry is conducted in accord with the introspective historical, plain method; and, whatever the process of reasoning which leads to certainty may be, he does not question that it can be fully revealed by this method. But our intellectual processes as they are revealed to introspection always have a content, they are always thoughts about something. For Locke, if principles or maxims have any part in our reasoning they can only be propositions and as such they are assemblages of ideas. In reply to Stillingfleet, who like Leibniz argues for a formal 'way of certainty by reason' against the 'way of certainty by ideas', he remarks:

> as for principles or maxims, we shall know whether your principles and maxims are a way to certainty, when you shall please to tell us what it is, that to your lordship makes a maxim or principle, and distinguishes it from other propositions; and whether it be any thing but an immediate perception of the agreement or disagreement of the ideas, as expressed in that proposition. (*Second Reply, Works,* 4, p.389)

The propositions put forward as maxims are self-evident, but this is something they share with an infinite number of other propositions which no one would think of elevating to any special epistemic status (IV.vii.3). Locke does not deny that there is a sense in which maxims may be considered principles of reasoning. Again in reply to Stillingfleet, he says that he is at one with Aristotle in holding all correct reasoning to proceed according to the principle 'that what things agree in a third, agree among themselves'. He goes on to say:

> And if Aristotle had gone any farther to show, how we are certain, that those two things agree with a third, he would have placed that certainty in the perception of that agreement, as I have done. . . . For who can doubt that the knowledge, or being certain, that any two things agree, consists in the perception of their agreement? What else can it possibly consist in? . . . And I should wonder, if any one should allow the certainty of deduction to consist in the agreement of two things in a third, and yet should deny that the knowledge or certainty of that agreement consisted in the perception of it. (ibid., pp.383–4)

While accepting that correct reasoning conforms to this general pattern, Locke finds it quite unintelligible that such conformity should be the foundation of its correctness or certainty.

The faculty[12] of reason which Locke opposes to the artificial modes and figures of the syllogism is said to contain two natural abilities of the mind: 'Sagacity' and 'Illation or Inference'. The first of these is exercised in the finding out of intermediate ideas from which the connection between two given ideas can be derived; the second 'consists in nothing but the Perception of the connexion there is between the *Ideas,* in each step of the deduction, whereby the Mind comes to see, either the certain Agreement of Disagreement of any two *Ideas,* as in Demonstration, in which it arrives at Knowledge; or their probable connexion, on which it gives or withholds its Assent, as in Opinion' (IV.xvii.2). These two may be further analysed into four 'Degrees' of reasoning: 'the first and highest, is the discovering, and finding out of Proofs; the second, the regular and methodical Disposition of them, and laying them in a clear and fit Order, to make their Connexion and Force be plainly and easily perceived; the third is the perceiving their Connexion; and the fourth, the making a right conclusion' (IV.xvii.3). The first degree is said to be the highest presumably because it is the discovery of ideas which enter into a demonstration of a proposition as distinct from the working out of a demonstration from ideas already given. The other degrees are all manifestations of inference (illation). This account suffers somewhat from Locke's determination to place all the intellectual operations of the mind under the rubric of the way of ideas. Thus, he considers that the demonstration of certainties and the judgment of probabilities both exemplify the inferential perception of connections between ideas. However, as our present interest is in Locke on demonstration, the fact that he includes probable inference need be no more than noted.

Locke's talk of inference as a process of tracing connections between ideas gives rise to an initial difficulty in his account. In an inference we endeavour to establish something as true on the ground that it follows from something else which is true, or is at least taken to be true. For Locke, as we have seen, truth strictly can be predicated only of propositions (i.e. assemblages of ideas), not of single ideas. It would seem then that he cannot consistently describe inference as a movement from one idea to another. One way of by-passing this difficulty is suggested by Locke's cornucopian definition of 'idea' as 'whatsoever is the object of the understanding when a man thinks'. This definition might be said to allow that sometimes the objects of the understanding are not single ideas, but propositions. Such would be the case in an inference.[13] However, it is more likely that Locke's talk of the connection of ideas in an inference reflects Aristotle's influence. Aristotle developed a logic not of propositions, but of terms. Syllogistic inference depends upon a middle term which must be related to both the subject and predicated term in the conclusion. Similarly, on Locke's account a proposition is demonstrated when the ideas it contains are shown to be connected, and this is achieved by the introduction of mediate ideas which are ultimately related to the ideas in the proposition which is to be demonstrated. Hence his remark to Stillingfleet that he agrees with Aristotle's view of reasoning as exemplifying the principle that 'what things agree in a third, agree among themselves'. This Aristotelian influence is also apparent in the *Essay* when Locke does talk of inference as involving propositions: 'To infer is nothing but by virtue of one Proposition laid down as true, to draw in another as true, *i.e.* to see or suppose such a connexion of the two *Ideas,* of the inferr'd Proposition' (IV. xvii.4). Locke is careless in his account of inference, but what he says need not be read as contradicting his doctrine that ideas themselves are neither true nor false.

There is, however, a much more serious difficulty arising from Locke's account of reasoning as consisting in the tracing of connections between ideas. He purports to give a description of the way the mind attains to certainty. Accordingly, what he says about sagacity, illation and the various degrees in reasoning is descriptive of psychological phenomena. Yet, as he is interested in demonstration as the way to certain knowledge, he is concerned with it as a species of valid inference or correct reasoning. On what grounds can Locke claim that he is describing correct reasoning? He is, of course, aware that the psychological process of reasoning is not invariably valid. After the definition of what it is to infer given at IV.xvii.4, he continues: 'The Question now is to know, whether the Mind has made this Inference right or no'. His answer is that so long as the mind has proceeded 'by finding out the intermediate *Ideas,* and taking a view of the connexion of them, placed in a due order, it has proceeded rationally, and made a right Inference' (ibid.). But this amounts to the tautology that the mind infers correctly whenever it infers correctly. As explained earlier, Locke's method precludes any appeal to formal logical principles as criteria for the validity of reasoning. How, then, is he to differentiate valid from invalid inferences?

This problem would appear especially acute for Locke in view of a chapter he adds to the fourth edition of the *Essay.* Here he discusses what he calls the association of ideas. He contrasts this with the 'natural Correspondence and Connexion' some of our ideas have one with another, and which it is 'the Office and Excellency of our Reason to trace'. The association of ideas is 'another Connexion of *Ideas* wholly owing to Chance or Custom; *Ideas* that in themselves are not at all of kin, come to be so united in some Mens Minds, that 'tis very hard to separate them, they always keep in company, and the one no sooner at any time comes into the Understanding but its Associate appears with it; and if they are more than two which are thus united, the whole gang always inseparably shew themselves together' (II. xxxiii.5). The association of ideas is invoked in the first place as an explanation of acquired antipathies. Thus, for example, a man might be unable to think of (have the idea of) a particular place or person without feeling (having ideas of) pain and displeasure, because at some time he suffered pain and displeasure in that place or at the hands of that person (II.xxxiii.11–14). But, most importantly, association also infects the intellectual operations of the mind. For example, Locke suggests that it is a source of philosophical materialism; for 'Let the *Ideas* of Being and Matter be strongly joined either by Education or much Thought, whilst these are still combined in the Mind, what Notions, what Reasonings, will there be about separate Spirits?' (II.xxxii.17). The association of ideas is in fact the ape of reasoning; it 'gives Sense to *Jargon*, Demonstration to Absurdities, and Consistency to Nonsense, and is the foundation of the greatest, I had almost said, of all the Errors in the World' (II.xxxii.18).[14] The question of how Locke is to differentiate valid from invalid inferences may, then, be rephrased as a question of how he is to describe the mind's perception of a 'natural' correspondence and connection between ideas so that it is distinguishable from the mere association which unites ideas 'that in themselves are not at all of kin'.

Locke's account of the natural connections of ideas and of correct inference depends heavily upon his visual model of the mind's intellectual operations. The natural connections of ideas are those which can be 'seen' in the ideas themselves: 'In some of our *Ideas* there are certain Relations, Habitudes, and Connexions, so visibly included in the Nature of the *Ideas* themselves, that we cannot conceive them separable from them, by any Power whatsoever. And in these only, we are capable of certain and universal Knowledge' (IV.iii.29). In the earlier drafts of the *Essay*, Locke's visual account of demonstration reads almost as if he is giving a literal description rather than employing an explanatory model. In 'Draft A' we are told that,

> demonstrations . . . are as the word denotes the beare shewing of the things or proposeing them to our senses or understandings soe as to make us take notice of them as is evident in Mathematical demonstration which is but makeing use of one extension which I take for a standard & by applying it to others & perhaps them again when measured to others to see or note whether they be biger lesse or equall . . . certain knowledg or demonstration makes it self clearly appear & be perceived by the things them selves put togeather before our senses or their clear distinct Ideas put togeather & as it were lyeing before us in view in our understandings. (§27, cf. Draft B, §44)

Although this literalism is toned down to some extent in Locke's later account of demonstration, the visual element is still dominant, 'it is by vertue of the perceived Agreement of the intermediate *Idea* with the Extremes, that the Extremes are concluded to agree, and therefore each intermediate *Idea* must be such, as in the whole Chain hath a visible connexion with those two it is placed between, or else thereby, the Conclusion cannot be inferr'd or drawn in' (IV.xvii.4). As in the Draft A, the role of intermediate ideas is explicated in terms of the manipulation of a measuring device, 'the principle Act of Ratiocination is the finding the Agreement, or Disagreement of two *Ideas* one with another, by the intervention of a third. As a Man, by a Yard, Finds two Houses to be of the same length, which could not be brought together to measure their Equality by *juxta*-position' (IV.xvii.18).[15] From passages such as these it would appear that Locke considers that there is little difference of any significance between a demonstration which proceeds via the intellectual perception of connections existing between ideas in the mind and one which proceeds via the sense perception of spatial relations existing between objects in the world.

We know what it is to see congruities and incongruities between the dimensions of physical objects and what it is to determine their spatial relations by juxtaposition, or by the application of a standard measure, and there would seem to be no particular reason why this procedure of manipulating and measuring objects should not be called a demonstration of their spatial relations. We literally see that the objects placed together coincide or we literally read off their measurements from our measuring device. If for some reason we doubt the initial deliverance of our senses, the only remedy is to look again; there can be no appeal to another, more objective, more rigorous criterion for the certainty of the demonstration. Thus, to Stillingfleet's criticism that his way of ideas provides no criterion for certainty, Locke answers: 'To perceive the agreement or disagreement of two ideas, and not to perceive the agreement or disagreement of two ideas, is, I think a criterion to distinguish what a man is certain of, from what he is not certain of. Has your lordship any other or better criterion to distinguish certainty from uncertainty?' (*Second Reply, Works,* 4, p.387).[16] As it counterfeits reasoning, the association of ideas is a kind of distorting of our intellectual vision. It can be corrected (and this is the only way it can be corrected) by 'looking again' at the ideas which appear to be connected.

Yet it is surely ludicrous to suppose that the procedure involved in drawing a valid inference is analogous to the visual demonstration of spatial relations between objects. Indeed, Locke's visual account of demonstration may well be thought to constitute a *reductio ad absurdum* of his claim that 'the perceptions of the mind are most aptly explained by words relating to the sight'. There is, however, a reason why Locke should have failed to notice the inappropriateness of this visual language. He takes mathematics to be the paradigm of demonstrative knowledge. According to James Gibson, geometry was the only branch of mathematics with which Locke was thoroughly conversant. Gibson argues that the 'geometry of Euclid, with its frequent appeal to the ideal superposition of one figure upon another... coloured his whole view of mathematics and other knowledge'.[17] Whether or not this is a correct estimate of the extent of Locke's mathematical knowledge, there can be little doubt that the geometrical method of superposition is behind his talk of 'visible' connections between ideas and of 'juxtaposition' as the means of bringing these 'in view of our understandings'. Yet, even if superposition were of the essence of geometrical demonstration, it clearly could not encompass all that Locke means by demonstration. Superposition makes sense as a method of demonstration only so far as the subject matter is capable of diagrammatic representation, but we have already noted Locke's statement that some of our ideas 'have no sensible marks that resemble them, whereby we can set them down' (IV.iii.19). He is talking here specifically about moral ideas, and it is exactly in the sphere of morality that he hopes to see an expansion of demonstrative knowledge.[18] Locke's visual account of demonstration does lay him open to the charge, levelled by critics such as Leibniz and Stillingfleet, that his epistemological doctrines lead to subjectivism and scepticism. It provides no satisfactory differentiation between the natural connection of ideas supposedly traced in a valid inference and the subjective association of ideas. Talk of seeing connections in the nature of the ideas themselves is an empty metaphor; and the materialist who, according to Locke, associates the ideas of being and matter cannot be refuted if he claims to 'see' clearly their necessary connection.[19] Conversely, Locke has not established that what he considers genuine instances of perceivable necessary connections between ideas are not really explicable as random associations.

There is, however, another aspect of Locke's account of demonstration to be considered. Geometrical ideas may be given public expression in diagrams as well as words. Our moral ideas, Locke remarks, can be expressed only in words, and to these different individuals may attach different meanings. This he holds to be one of the main reasons why it is commonly thought that demonstrative certainty can be achieved only with respect to ideas of quantity:

> Diagrams drawn on Paper are Copies of the *Ideas* in the Mind, and not liable to the Uncertainty that Words carry in their Signification. An Angle, Circle, or Square, drawn in Lines, lies open to the view, and cannot be mistaken: It remains unchangeable, and may at leisure be considered, and examined, and the Demonstration be revised, and all the parts of it may be gone over more than once, without any danger of the least change in the *Ideas*. (IV.iii.19)

Here the advantage that geometrical ideas are said to possess with respect to demonstration consists not in the fact that they can be expressed as diagrams visibly exhibiting spatial properties, but that, because they can be so expressed, they are free from ambiguity and not liable to misinterpretation. There is, Locke maintains, no necessity that this advantage should be peculiar to geometry. The disadvantage of having 'no sensible marks that resemble them' which moral ideas labour under may 'in a good measure be *remedied* by Definitions, setting down that Collection of simple *Ideas,* which every Term shall stand for; and then using the Terms steadily and constantly for that precise Collection' (IV.iii.20). Locke's attempt to describe inference and demonstration in visual terms is a complete failure. What he has to say about demonstration and definition is of considerably more interest and importance.

3. As the meaning of a word is the idea for which it stands, to define a word is to reveal the relevant idea:

> *A Definition is* nothing else, but *the shewing the meaning of one Word by several other not synonymous Terms.* The meaning of Words, being only the *Ideas* they are made to stand for by him that uses them; the meaning of any Term is then shewed, or the Word is defined when by other Words, the *Idea* it is made the Sign of, and annexed to in the Mind of the Speaker, is as it were represented, or set before the view of another; and thus its Signification ascertained. (III.iv.6)

Locke lays it down that the terms in the definition must not be synonymous for the word defined, for merely to give a synonym 'is to translate, and not to define, when we change two Words of the same Signification one for another' (III.iv.9). Synonyms being disallowed, it follows that simple ideas cannot be defined, 'the several Terms of a Definition, signifying several *Ideas,* they can altogether by no means represent an *Idea,* which has no Composition at all: And therefore a Definition . . . can in the Names of simple *Ideas* have no Place. (III.iv.7). Words signifying simple ideas are to be taught to a person not by other words, but by ostension; that is, *'by presenting to his Senses that Subject, which may produce it in his Mind,* and make him actually have the *Idea,* that Word stands for' (III.xi.14).[20]

In this account of definition Locke has the speaker-hearer situation in mind. Following the suggestion of the previous chapter, we may dispense with Locke's conception of an idea as a mental item analogous to an image and say that a person's having the idea *x* consists in his having mastered the use of the relevant linguistic expression. An obvious circumstance in which a definition will be called for is when the speaker uses a word with which the hearer is unfamiliar. Thus, a person who has not previously encountered the now rather archaic term 'zopissa' will be enlightened when told that it signifies the complex 'pitch scraped off the sides of ships, and tempered with wax'. He will thereby learn how to use the word 'zopissa'. Such a definition is a report of the word's standardly accepted meaning. The speaker may also use a familiar word, but assign a special, non-standard, meaning to it. In this case, if he is to be properly understood by the hearer, he must make clear the meaning he has given to the word (e.g. 'For the purposes of this discussion by "democracy" I mean . . .'). This is known today as a stipulative definition.

While Locke recognises reportative definition as a means of enlarging a person's vocabularly and stipulative definition, he sees the function of definition as it has a place in demonstration as different to these. A person may know the meaning of a word in the sense of being able to use it correctly in ordinary discourse, yet be nonplussed if asked to state its *precise* meaning. The lack of precision or exactness in the meanings we attach to words is of little or no importance in what Locke calls their 'civil' use; 'such a communication of Thoughts and *Ideas* by Words, as may serve for the upholding common Conversation and Commerce, about the ordinary Affairs and Conveniencies of civil Life, in the Societies of Men, one amongst another' (III.ix.3). It does, however, constitute a distinct imperfection when we come to the 'philosophical' use of words, which is 'such an use of them, as may serve to convey the precise Notions of Things, and to express, in general Propositions, certain and undoubted Truths, which the Mind may rest upon, and be satisfied with, in its search after true Knowledge' (ibid.). The exactness demanded by the philosophical use of words is to be achieved by definition:

> Definition being nothing but making another understand by Words, what *Idea*, the term defined stands for, a definition is best made by enumerating those simple *Ideas* that are combined in the signification of the term Defined. (III.iii.10)

Definition, when carried through to the level of simple ideas, opens the way to demonstrative knowledge; but the task is by no means an easy one, 'it [the mind] requires pains and assiduity to examine its *Ideas*, till it resolves them into those clear and distinct simple ones, out of which they are compounded; and to see which, amongst its simple ones, have or have not a necessary connexion and dependence one upon another' (II.xiii.27). This resolution of ideas into their components is what later philosophers have called conceptual analysis, and in the seventeenth and eighteenth centuries it was known as the method of analysis.

In Locke's opinion abstract ideas or concepts are only externally related to the words in which they have their public expression, and he urges us to lay words aside as much as possible and consider only our ideas. It is true that a concept is not identical with any one word or phrase, for the one concept may be expressed by quite distinct words in different languages and even by distinct words in the one language (e.g. the Frenchman and the Englishman share the one concept which they express by the words 'mouton' and 'sheep' respectively). But this does not mean that conceptual analysis can be carried out independently of any language whatsoever. It is a contingent fact that a particular philosopher uses English words in the analysis of concepts, but it is not a contingent fact that he uses *some* words in *some* language. Even if he confines his philosophising strictly to himself, he cannot refer to concepts nor set out their analyses except by means of words.[21] We could not begin to reflect upon, say, the concept of justice unless we were familiar with the word 'justice', or its equivalent in some other language. There is, therefore, a difference between knowing the meaning of a word in the sense of being able to use it correctly, and knowing the analysis of the corresponding concept. A knowledge of the word's meaning is a prerequisite for a knowledge of the concept's analysis.

Locke is to a certain extent aware of the place of words in the analysis of concepts. In carrying out the resolution of complex ideas into their components we convert those which are obscure or confused into clear and distinct, or, as Locke prefers to say, into 'determinate' or 'determined', ideas.[22] Yet he holds that an idea taken by itself cannot be confused; for, as it is a mental item existing in the mind only in virtue of being perceived, it is exactly as it is perceived to be by the person possessing it. Confusion and obscurity enters in with the use of words:

> Now every *Idea* a Man has, being visibly what it is, and distinct from all other *Ideas* but it self, that which makes it *confused* is, when it is such, that it may as well be called by another Name, as that which it is expressed by, the difference which keeps the Things (to be ranked under those two different Names) distinct . . . being left out; and so the distinction, which was intended to be kept up by those different Names, is quite lost. (II.xxix.6)

Thus, a person who thinks of a leopard barely as a beast with spots will have a confused idea, for these characteristics are insufficient to distinguish the leopard from other spotted beasts. Again, an idea is confused when the corresponding word is used without a settled meaning; as, for example, different individuals use the word 'idolatry' to refer to a quite different thing (II.xxix.7, 9). This confusion is, Locke maintains, particularly prevalent amongst our moral terms, 'their [moral ideas] names are of . . . uncertain Signification, the precise Collection of simple *Ideas* they stand for not being . . . easily agreed on, and so the Sign, that is used for them in Communication always, and in Thinking often, does not steadily carry with it the same *Idea* (IV.iii.19). Clearly, the analysis which will dispel this confusion is not a matter of attending to some private mental item and dividing it up into its 'visible' simple parts.

What Locke says at II.xiii.27, shows that he assigns an important role to definition or analysis in demonstration. The passage, however, is ambiguous. It is unclear whether Locke conceives demonstration to be (1) the analysis of ideas followed by a second, quite distinct operation (which equally requires 'pains and assiduity') of perceiving any necessary connections there may be between the ideas arrived at by analysis; or (2) simply the analysis of ideas, this being sufficient to reveal their necessary connections. There are passages which suggest that he does understand demonstration to consist simply in analysis. He cites two instances of demonstrable moral truths:

> *Where there is no Property, there is no Injustice,* is a Proposition as certain as any Demonstration in *Euclid*: For the *Idea* of *Property,* being a right to any thing; and the *Idea* to which the Name *Injustice* is given, being the Invasion or Violation of that right; it is evident, that these *Ideas* being thus established, and these Names annexed to them, I can as certainly know this Proposition to be true, as that a Triangle has three Angles equal to two right ones. Again, *No Government allows absolute Liberty*: The *Idea* of Government being the establishment of Society upon certain Rules or Laws, which require Conformity to them; and the *Idea* of absolute Liberty being for any one to do whatever he pleases; I am as capable of being certain of the Truth of this Proposition, as of any in Mathematicks. (IV.iii.18)

The necessary truth of these two propositions follows from the definition of 'property', 'injustice', 'government' and 'absolute liberty'. Locke does no more than give these definitions; there is no hint that anything more is needed to establish the truth of the propositions. The view that Lockean demonstration is simply analysis receives further confirmation from a passage which might at first sight be taken as counting against it. Locke warns against pseudo-demonstrations which appear to increase our general knowledge of substances:

> For 'tis plain, that Names of substantial Beings, as well as others, as far as they have relative Significations affixed to them, may,

> with great Truth, be joined negatively and affirmatively in Propositions, as their relative Definitions make them fit to be so joined; and Propositions consisting of such Terms, may, with the same clearness, be deduced one from another, as those that convey the most real Truths. . . . By this method, one may make Demonstrations and undoubted Propositions in Words, and yet thereby advance not one jot in the Knowledge of the Truth of Things. (IV.viii.9)

What Locke has described here is *a priori* derivation of necessarily true propositions solely from the definition of their terms, and the procedure is said to add nothing to our real knowledge. However, it is not the method of definition or analysis which is criticised here, but its employment with respect to our ideas of substances. On the contrary, the method is explicitly endorsed; according to Locke, these 'verbal propositions' about substances 'may, with the same clearness, be deduced one from another, *as those that convey the most real truths*'. We have seen that ideas of substances are unsuitable for demonstration because in them there is a gap between real and nominal essence. The demonstration of a proposition concerning a specific substance such as gold will merely reflect the ideas we have decided to combine and refer to by the name 'gold' (i.e. the nominal essence of gold); it will not establish any certain truths about the nature of gold itself:

> *All Gold is malleable* . . . is a very certain Proposition, if *Malleableness* be a part of the complex *Idea* the word *Gold* stands for. But then here is nothing affirmed of *Gold*, but that that Sound stands for an *Idea* in which *Malleableness* is contained. . . . But if *Malleableness* makes not a part of the specifick Essence the name *Gold* stands for, 'tis plain, *All Gold is Malleable*, is not a certain Proposition. Because let the complex *Idea* of *Gold*, be made up of which soever of its other Qualities you please, *Malleableness* will not appear to depend on that complex Idea. . . . The connexion that *Malleableness* has . . . with those other Qualities, being only by the intervention of the real Constitution of its insensible parts, which . . . we know not. (IV.vi.9)

The objection that the analysis of ideas, or nominal essences, cannot yield a knowledge of things clearly does not apply in the case of those ideas in which there is a coincidence of real and nominal essence. With them an analysis of the idea will have to do with the nature of the thing, and truths arrived at by the way of analysis will count as real knowledge.

Our moral notions being instances of the coincidence of real and nominal essence, they have at least the potential to enter into demonstrations which will yield real general knowledge:

> the *Ideas* that Ethicks are conversant about, being all real Essences . . . so far as we can find their Habitudes and Relations, so far we shall be possessed of certain, real and general Truths: and I doubt not, but if a right method were taken, a great part of Morality might be made out with that clearness, that could leave, to a considering Man, no more reason to doubt, than he could have to doubt of the Truth of Propositions in Mathematicks, which have been demonstrated to him. (IV.xii.8)

As these notions are archetypes they are capable of complete and exact analysis:

> *Mixed Modes,* especially those belonging to Morality, being most of them such Combinations of *Ideas,* as the Mind puts together of its own choice . . . their Names . . . may be perfectly and exactly *defined.* For . . . Men may, if they please, exactly know the *Ideas,* that go to each Composition, and so both use these Words in a certain and undoubted Signification, and perfectly declare . . . what they stand for. (III.xi.15)

It is the possibility of exact definition or analysis which inspires Locke's hope that morality may be made a demonstrative science: 'Upon this ground it is, that I am bold to think, that *Morality is capable of Demonstration,* as well as Mathematicks: Since the precise real Essence of the Things moral Words stand for, may be perfectly known; and so the Congruity, or Incongruity of the Things themselves, be certainly discovered, in which consists perfect Knowledge' (III.xi.16). Nevertheless, there is, we shall see, more to demonstration than analysis. But before entering into an examination of this further aspect, something should be said about the kind of propositions we come to know by demonstration.

4. With the exception of the singular existential proposition 'there is a God', all the propositions known by demonstration will be general as well as certain. According to Locke there are two kinds of propositions concerning which the human understanding is capable of certainty:

> We can know . . . the Truth of two sorts of Propositions, with perfect *certainty*; the one is, of those trifling Propositions, which have a certainty in them, but 'tis but a *verbal Certainty,* but not instructive. And, secondly, we can know the Truth, and so may be *certain* in Propositions, which affirm something of another, which is a necessary consequence of its precise complex *Idea,* but not contained in it. (IV.viii.8)

Locke offers the proposition that the external angle of a triangle is bigger than either of its opposite internal angles as an example of an instructive certain proposition. He also includes under the heading of instructive propositions those which express contingent truths and which are, therefore, objects only of probable opinion not of certainty, e.g. that men are cast into sleep by opium (IV.viii.6). There are, then, three separate categories of propositions: the trifling certain which are uninformative, the instructive certain, and the instructive probable.[23] Obviously, Locke does not hold the propositions known by demonstration to have the uninformative certainty of trifling propositions. They must, therefore, belong to the second category.

Very many scholars have discovered in Locke's trifling/instructive distinction a foreshadowing of Kant's distinction between analytic and synthetic propositions (judgments), and the attendant Kantian doctrine of the synthetic *a priori*.[24] Trifling propositions have been equated with analytic propositions, and Locke's characterisation of instructive certain propositions as those 'which affirm something of another, which is a necessary consequence of its precise complex idea, but not contained in it' has been understood as picking out the propositions which Kant calls synthetic *a priori*. On this interpretation the propositions known by demonstration will be synthetic *a priori*. It would seem, therefore, that there is something more to demonstration than analysis, for, according to the standard notion of analyticity deriving from Kant, any proposition which is true solely in virtue of the analyses (definitions) of the concepts (terms) it involves is analytic. On the other hand, it may be that this interpretation of the trifling/instructive distinction is mistaken. Locke has relatively little to say about the nature of propositions which are instructive and certain, and his conception of this category has to be made out largely from his much more detailed account of the contrasting category of the trifling.

Locke's discussion of trifling propositions follows immediately after his criticism of the epistemic role assigned to maxims by the schools. There are, he says, 'Universal Propositions; that though they be certainly true, yet they add no Light to our Understandings, bring no increase to our Knowledge' (IV.viii.1). There are two main types of such trifling propositions: (1) '*Identical Propositions* . . . wherein the same Term importing the same *Idea*, is affirmed of it self'; (2) propositions in which '*a part of the complex* Idea *is predicated of the Name of the whole*; a part of the Definition of the Word defined' (IV.viii.3–4). R. S. Woolhouse has coined the term 'partially identical' to refer to trifling propositions of the second type.[25] Within this type Locke includes those 'wherein the *Genus* is predicated of the *Species*, or more comprehensive of less comprehensive Terms', and those which '*predicate any other part of the Definition of the term defined*, or . . . affirm any one of the simple *Ideas* of a complex one, of the Name of the whole complex *Idea*' (IV.viii.4–5). An example of an identical proposition would be 'a centaure is a centaure'. Partially identical propositions are those such as 'lead is a metal' (the genus predicated of the species), and 'all gold is fusible' (a part of the definition of a term affirmed of that term).[26]

Locke's account of trifling propositions is somewhat obscured by his tendency to conflate two different meanings of the term 'proposition'. At times he uses it, as most modern philosophers would use it, as a noun referring to the content of, or what is asserted in, a declarative sentence. However, it will be recalled that he says that 'Proposition consists in joining, or separating Signs' (IV.v.5; cf. 2); and this remark appears to be intended as a definition. Understood thus, 'proposition' is a noun-verbal gerund referring to the act of asserting a proposition and not to what is asserted. This failure to differentiate clearly between a proposition and its assertion makes it difficult to determine what Locke means when he says of trifling propositions that they are uninformative. Often what he appears to have in mind is a relational property of uninformativeness holding between the assertion of a proposition and persons. He states that identical propositions such as 'a vacuum is a vacuum' or 'a centaure is a cenature' can never increase our knowledge because '[they show] us nothing, but what we must certainly know before, whether such a Proposition be either made by, or proposed to us . . . since they teach us nothing but what every one, who is capable of Discourse, knows without being told' (IV.viii.2–3). Here it would seem to be the assertion of the proposition which fails to convey information, and from what Locke says it is natural enough to conclude that he identifies a proposition as trifling by the fact that its assertion (whether to oneself or to another) does not add to the stock of our true beliefs. Conversely, an instructive proposition will be identified by the fact that its assertion does add to the stock of our true beliefs. But if 'uninformativeness' is construed as a relational property holding between the assertion of propositions and persons, it can hardly be claimed that (with the possible exception of identical propositions) there are any propositions which are *always* uninformative. For whether or not the assertion of a given proposition tells a person anything will depend on that person's prior knowledge; any proposition will be informative to someone who does not already know it, and uninformative to someone who does. In other words, no proposition will be uninformative *per se*; it will always be uninformative for such and such a person at such and such a time. Similarly, there will be no proposition which is instructive *per se.* Further, Locke himself states that under certain circumstances the assertion of a partially identical proposition can tell a person something new: 'to a Man that knows the Signification of the word *Metal,* and not of the word *Lead,* it is a shorter way to explain the Signification of the word *Lead,* by saying it is a *Metal,* which at once expresses several of its simple *Ideas,* than to enumerate them one by one, telling him it is a Body very *heavy, fusible,* and *malleable'* (IV.viii.4). This concession might well be taken as tantamount to a retraction of the view he first expresses that trifling propositions cannot increase our knowledge.

Yet, notwithstanding his tendency to conflate propositions and their assertions, Locke's trifling/instructive distinction is based upon properties belonging to propositions in themselves. As the passage quoted earlier concerning the two sorts of propositions which we can know with perfect certainty indicates, the notion on which the distinction turns is that of one idea being 'part of' or 'contained in' another. A proposition is not ultimately identified as trifling by the fact that its assertion is uninformative. Rather, the uninformativeness of its assertion is consequent upon a characteristic of the proposition, that it exhibits the containment of an idea in another idea. The assertion of a trifling proposition can sometimes be informative about the meaning of a word; Locke's point is that these propositions are such that their assertion can never convey information about the things to which words refer:

> *Every* Man *is an Animal,* or living Body, is as certain a Proposition as can be; but no more conducing to the Knowledge of Things, than to say, *A Palfry is an ambling Horse,* . . . both being only about the signification of Words, and makes me know but this; That *Body, Sense,* and *Motion,* . . . *are three of those Ideas,* that I always comprehend and signify by the word *Man*; and where they are not to be found together, the name *Man* belongs not to that Thing. (IV.viii.6)

A speaker who intends to convey information about things must, of course, understand the words he uses; and, if the information is to be successfully conveyed, the hearer must attach the same meaning to those words:

> Before a Man makes any Proposition, he is supposed to understand the terms he uses in it, or else he talks like a Parrot, only . . . framing certain Sounds . . . but not, as a rational Creature, using them for signs of *Ideas,* which he has in his Mind. The Hearer also is supposed to understand the Terms as the Speaker uses them or else he talks jargon, and makes an unintelligible

> noise. And therefore he trifles with Words, who makes such a Proposition, which when it is made, contains no more than one of the Terms does, and which a man was supposed to know before: *v.g. a Triangle hath three sides,* or *Saffron is yellow.* And this is no farther tolerable, than where a Man goes to explain his Terms, to one who is supposed or declares himself not to understand him: and then *it teaches only the signification of that Word,* and the use of that Sign. (IV.viii.7)

The assertion of an identical proposition, in which the idea in the predicate position is but a repetition of that in the subject position, is never 'tolerable'. Locke stresses that we could never attain to knowledge of anything were it not for 'the Faculty we have of perceiving the same *Idea* to be the same, and of discerning it, from those which are different' (IV.viii.3). But as this recognition of the identity and diversity of our ideas is a prerequisite for all knowledge, a proposition expressing the identity of an idea with itself can never add to our knowledge; identical propositions can 'teach us nothing but what every one, *who is capable of discourse,* knows without being told'.

The chapter on trifling propositions is partly a continuation of Locke's attack on the doctrine that maxims provide the foundations of knowledge. In his opinion they are, at least for the most part, no more than identical propositions of a high level of generality. Trifling propositions of this type are analytic. Partially identical propositions may be called definitional in that asserting them is a way of getting the meaning of a word across to the hearer, as someone might teach the meaning of the word 'lead' to another, who knew the word 'metal', by saying 'lead is a metal'. This would be a reportative definition, but partially identical propositions can also feature in stipulative definitions; for they may express the meaning which the speaker assigns to a given word. Locke's second target in the chapter is what may be called concealed stipulation in propositions; that is, propositions which are put forward as expressing necessary and informative truths about things, but the truth of which depends solely upon the meanings the speaker has assigned to the terms. Locke has already cited 'all gold is malleable' as an instance of this trifling with words. This proposition is certain only if we include malleableness as part of the meaning of the word 'gold'; otherwise it is only probable. As the real essences of substances are unknown to us 'the general *Propositions* that are made *about Substances, if they are certain, are for the most part but trifling*; and if they are instructive, are uncertain, and such as we can have no knowledge of their real Truth' (IV.viii.9).

The notion of one idea being part of or contained in another suggests Locke's mental propositions. However, in his exposition of the trifling/instructive distinction he is clearly thinking mostly of verbal propositions (or perhaps the distinction between mental and verbal propositions has been tacitly dropped). With respect to partially identical propositions, then, one idea being contained in another amounts to one term being a part of the meaning of another. This may be so in two ways: either when the one term is part of the other's standardly accepted meaning; or when it is part of a meaning which has been stipulated for the other term. In both cases partially identical propositions will be analytic, their truth depending solely upon the meanings of the words, while in the second it may become apparent only after the speaker has stated the meanings he assigns to the word.

What, then, is to be made of instructive and certain propositions in which one idea is not contained in another? Are these synthetic *a priori*? They cannot be analytic in the sense that their truth follows from either the standardly accepted or from the stipulated meanings of the terms involved. However, the *analysans* arrived at by analysing a concept is something distinct from both a reportative or a stipulative definition of the concept word. The function of a reportative definition is to teach someone a new word; but anyone embarking upon the analysis of a concept must already have an understanding of the concept word. Therefore, what he is after cannot be merely a reportative definition of the word. Nor can it be equated with a stipulative definition of the word. As Locke reiterates, it is within our power to stipulate whatever meaning we like for a word. Therefore, though a person may use a word in ways which are inconsistent with the meaning he has stipulated for it, the stipulated meaning itself can be called neither correct nor incorrect. That which is offered as the analysis of a concept, on the other hand, is (like the reportative definition of a word) something which is either correct or incorrect; the philosopher is after the *true* analysis of the concept with which he is concerned. The notion of the containment of one idea in another which we have gathered from Locke's discussion of trifling propositions leaves it open that the contrasted instructive and certain propositions may be analytic in the sense that their truth follows from the analyses of the concepts involved. Of course, if there are genuine instances of the synthetic *a priori* these will fall within Locke's category of the instructive and certain. The point is, we have discovered no reason for supposing that Locke constructed this category to accommodate the synthetic *a priori*. It is misleadingly anachronistic to read his trifling/instructive distinction through Kantian spectacles. The propositions yielded by demonstration will be instructive and certain; but if there are no grounds for supposing that these need be other than analytic, it remains that demonstration may consist simply in analysis, and that the necessary connections between ideas which it reveals may be interconnections holding between them at the level of their analyses. This is the interpretation of demonstration suggested by the two moral propositions Locke cites at IV.iii.18.

It might be objected against the strategy employed here that, in concentrating on what Locke says about trifling and certain propositions, his positive characterisation of instructive and certain propositions as those 'which affirm something of another, which is a necessary consequence of its precise complex idea, but not contained in it' has been ignored. This phrase suggests that the subject idea in such a proposition has been analysed, and that the predicate idea is not a part of its analysis. So, even if Locke's account of trifling propositions captures only those which are analytic in virtue of ordinary or stipulated word meanings, the category of the instructive and certain may nevertheless exclude those which are analytic in virtue of the analyses of concepts. Further, Locke talks of necessary connections holding between simple ideas. If these are the connections demonstration reveals, the propositions yielded by demonstration cannot be analytic; as simple ideas are by definition unanalysable, they cannot be linked at the level of their analyses. It may be true that Locke develops no clear conception of the synthetic *a priori*, but what he says does commit him to a belief in propositions of this type.

In response to this criticism it is necessary to look more closely at Locke's distinction between simple and complex ideas and his closely related theory of definition. In chapter IV the claim was made that Locke's main grounds for believing in simple ideas are logical rather than psychological. It is not that he has introspected items which meet his criterion of simplicity; rather, he supposes their existence to follow from the nature of definition. If the definition of a term did not ultimately terminate in words standing for simple (i.e. indefinable or unanalysable) ideas, the process of defining it would go on *ad infinitum* (III.iv.5). As simple ideas cannot be analysed, we can only be taught to understand the words which stand for them by ostension. A definition or analysis which has been properly carried through to its furthest extent will terminate in simple ideas, and will be intelligible only to someone who has acquired those ideas in experience: 'In . . . Collections of *Ideas,* passing under one name, *Definitions, . . . may make us understand the Names* of Things, . . . provided that none of the terms of the Definition stand for any such simple *Ideas,* which he to whom the Explication is made, has never yet had in his Thoughts' (III.iv.12). In defining a word or analysing a concept we do, of course, come to a point of termination. It is also true that a person could not have learnt the meanings of all the words in his vocabulary by having them defined to him. These truths, however, do not establish Locke's conclusion that there must be indefinable terms standing for unanalysable ideas or concepts.

In order to learn the meaning of a word through its definition one has to understand the words in which that definition is expressed. Some of the words in a person's vocabulary must, therefore, have been learnt by means other than definition, for example by ostension. However it does not follow that there are *any* words which are such that they could not be taught by definitions. Which words a person learns through their definitions and which he learns by ostension might always be determined by chance circumstances having nothing to do with the words themselves. Locke's conclusion that definition or analysis must terminate in simple ideas would follow if complex ideas were understood as those which are capable of analysis, and simple ideas as those which appear in the analyses of complex ideas. But then ideas which are simple in this sense need not be unanalysable. The fact is we embark upon the analysis of an idea or concept with specific questions, problems or puzzles in view, and what we take to be its simple components will be conditioned by these. Hence, the one idea might be considered either simple or complex depending on the perspective we adopt. While there is little pedagogic point in offering an analysis of, say 'choice' in terms of 'freedom' and 'action' when 'freedom' itself has been analysed in terms of 'action' and 'choice', the possibility of an idea A, which has been analysed in terms of ideas B and C, itself appearing in the analysis of these ideas is not logically ruled out. Locke may well be correct in supposing that there are indefinable terms, but their existence is not proved by his argument from the nature of definition.[27]

The argument for simple ideas from the nature of definition is quite separate from Locke's visual conception of an idea as an item analogous to an image. Nevertheless, it is likely that this conception influenced his ready acceptance of the logical argument. In the division of an image (as in the division of the physical object of which it is an image) there does inevitably come a stage beyond which it is impossible to discern further separable parts.[28] As Woolhouse has shown, it is in many ways highly inappropriate to construe the analysis of a concept of the model of splitting an image up into its parts.[29] It is only when dealing with physical object concepts, such as the idea of gold, that Locke makes any serious attempt to follow his own prescription and analyse them into a conjoint list of the ideas he has cited as simple. Significantly these are concepts of things of which we can form images. The analyses he sketches of the moral notion 'theft' (II.xii.5), 'lie' (II.xxii.9), and 'murder' (II.xxviii.14) do not consist in such lists; and neither do the analyses of 'property', 'government', etc., which he takes as establishing the certain truth of his two moral propositions.[30] While the image model of analysis is inappropriate, it does clarify the way in which Locke thinks of one idea as part of another. Further, it is with mixed mode ideas such as moral notions that Locke hopes to attain a body of demonstrative knowledge; and the fact that in their case his practice of analysis deviates from his theory indicates a sense in which instructive and certain propositions might be said to fit his characterisation yet still follow from the analysis of the concepts involved.

An image can, as it were, stand alone. That is, we can form and have the image of, say a horse quite independently of having images of other things. This being so, the resolution of composite images into their parts can be carried out piecemeal, one image being completely resolved before attention is paid to any other. A philosopher who construes conceptual analysis on this model will, then, be committed to the view that it is an operation which can be carried out on concepts one at a time, one concept being considered in isolation from all others. In the case of images the relation 'being a part of' is asymmetrical in that if image B is a part of the whole image A, then B cannot in turn have A as one of its parts (e.g. the image of a horse's head is part of the image of a horse but not vice versa). Similarly, on this model, the relation 'being a part of the analysis of' will be asymmetrical. So the possibility of a concept B appearing in the analysis of a concept A, and A in turn appearing in the analysis of B will be ruled out. Conceptual analyses will be necessarily irreversible.

This picture of conceptual analysis does have a *prima facie* plausibility so long as we concern ourselves only with physical object concepts and are content with truncated versions of these. We saw that Locke talks of abstract ideas as patterns which we apply to the world when we classify particulars, and his talk of these as patterns is closely allied with his visual conception of ideas. A person does have a concept of, for example, gold provided he fulfils the minimal condition of being able to identify instances of that metal. If his possession of the concept amounts to no more than this his mastery of the word 'gold' will consist in his ability to attach it as a label to things. For him gold will simply be something exhibiting a certain set of empirical characteristics which he takes as licensing the application of the word 'gold'; and he will possess a concept of gold quite independently of any other physical object concepts, such as the concept of lead or of a horse. Considered at this elementary level the person's concept may be taken in isolation and analysed as a list of characteristics. Such an analysis will be irreversible, for the characteristics whereby a substance is classified as gold cannot themselves be analysed in terms of gold. It may be said that it is misleading to construe even this kind of analysis on the model of splitting up an image; for instance, the property of yellowness which is characteristic of gold is hardly analogous to a part of an image. Be this as it may, the model is thoroughly inept where the analysis of moral notions is concerned.

We saw that, unlike substance ideas, the possession of moral notions must consist in more than merely the ability to identify particular actions as falling under them. To be able to identify diverse pieces of human behaviour as all amounting to stealing or lying we have to have some grasp of the point behind such classification, and this involves our having an understanding of the way of life out of which the notions developed.[31] Therefore, a person cannot possess any moral notion in isolation; in their case the minimal condition for concept possession cannot be fulfilled apart from a complex of other concepts. When he is not trying to tailor them to his 'historical' account of the construction of all complex ideas out of simple ones originally acquired in experience, Locke shows himself aware that moral notions cannot properly be analysed into conjoint lists of characteristics making up patterns which we apply to the world. For example, in treating of justice in *Some Thoughts Concerning Education* he states that 'Children cannot well comprehend what *Injustice* is, till they understand Property, and how particular persons come by it' (§110). However, his conception of what it is for an idea to be 'part of' or 'contained in' the analysis of another is not drawn from his practice of analysis, but is conditioned by the model of splitting an image up into its parts. Consequently, when he comes to engage in the conceptual analysis of a moral notion for its own sake the result does not, on his conception of containment, reveal one idea as contained in another; nor are the ideas appearing in the analysis simple (i.e. unanalysable).

It was said earlier that the containment of one idea in another in the case of a partially identical proposition amounts to one term being part of the meaning of another, and this may be so either in virtue of the terms' standardly accepted meanings or because of the meanings which speakers may stipulate for them. Most of the partially identical propositions Locke instances involve substance ideas, and, as he treats what we have called truncated versions of these concepts, their analysis will on his showing amount to the stipulative definition of terms. Although in our use of substance terms we make a tacit (and according to Locke an illegitimate) reference to real essences, we in fact always classify particular substances according to nominal essences, or the sets of characteristics we have selected as licensing the application of substance terms. The analysis of these sortal concepts will, therefore, concern nominal and not real essences. Given that in analysing a concept we aim at something beyond a mere reportative definition of the concept word (which in this case would be a list of the characteristics standardly taken as licensing the application of the word to things), what will analysis consist in here and what will it achieve? All we can expect is that it should make our ideas clear and distinct so that our classificatory scheme more precisely delineates the differences between substances. However, on Locke's account, we achieve this not by making explicit that which is already included in our ideas or nominal essences, but by more exactly observing the qualities exhibited by the substances themselves and *adding* these to our initial nominal essences. Although in doing this we are following patterns given in nature, a statement of what we have thus come to include in a nominal essence will only express our decision to apply the concept word in accord with certain characteristics. That is, they will express stipulative definitions of the words. Propositions which are true in virtue of this type of analysis will be trifling or verbal; they will add nothing to our knowledge of the substances themselves.

Since a stipulative definition, in contrast to the analysis of a concept, is neither true nor false, what we have outlined above is not strictly an example of conceptual analysis. Genuine analysis is possible, however, with respect to archetype ideas in which real and nominal essences coincide. Locke repeatedly remarks upon the need to establish precise meanings for our moral notions:

> *Justice* is a Word in every Man's Mouth, but most commonly with a very undetermined loose signification: Which will always be so, unless a Man has in his Mind a distinct comprehension of the component parts, that complex *Idea* consists of; and if it be decompounded, must be able to resolve it still on, till he at last comes to the simple *Ideas,* that make it up: And unless this be done, a Man makes an ill use of the Word, let it be *Justice,* for example, or any other. (III.xi.9)

A stipulative definition would introduce precision into a person's use of the word 'justice'; but Locke is quite clear that the individual is not at liberty to assign any meaning he likes to the moral terms current in language. Anyone using a word such as 'justice' contrary to its common acceptation is misusing it and may be said to have a false idea of justice.[32] Yet an analysis of moral notions which is guided by the common acceptance of moral terms cannot be the whole of what Locke intends by the demonstration of morality. This procedure may bring to light conceptual links between various of our concepts, but it will not of itself explain why those concepts should be so linked.

5. Berkeley remarks that, on Locke's account, 'To demonstrate Morality it seems one need only make a Dictionary of Words & see which includes which at least. This is the greatest part & bulk of the Work'.[33] On the interpretation of Locke's conception of demonstration which has been thus far set forth this would seem a fair summary of what is involved. It is likely, however, that Berkeley intends his comment as a disparagement of Locke's project. The interesting point is that Locke himself apparently holds the analysis of moral notions to be useless as a method of arriving at worthwhile knowledge in the sphere of morality. In 'Of Ethick in General'[34] he writes:

> Who ever treats of Morality soe as to give us only the definitions of Justice & Temperance Theft & Inconstinency & tells wᶜʰ are vertues wᶜʰ are vices does only settle certaine complex Ideas of Modes with their names to them. . . . But whilst they discourse never soe acutely of temperance or Justice, but show noe law of a superior that prescribes Temperance to the observation or breach of wᶜʰ law there are rewards & punishments annexed the force of morality is lost & evaporates only into words disputes & niceties. . . . For without showing a law that commands or forbids them Morall goodness will be but an empty sound, & these Actions wᶜʰ the schools have call'd virtues or vices, may by the same authority be call'd by contrary names in an other country. (MS c28, §9; King, 2, pp. 129–30)

He goes on to contrast this treatment of morality (which teaches us 'noe more than to speake properly according to yᵉ fashion of yᵉ Country we are in') with the genuine study of the rules of right and wrong:

> there is an other sort of Morality or Rules of our actions, wᶜʰ though they may in many parts be coincident & agreeable with the former yet have a different foundation & we come to the knowledge of them a different way these notions or Standards of our actions not being Ideas of our own makeing to wᶜʰ we give names but depend upon something without us & soe not made by us but for us & these are yᵉ rules set to our actions by yᵉ declared will or laws of another who hath power to punish our aberrations. (ibid., §10, King, 2, p. 130)

It would appear from this that Locke conceives the object of real moral knowledge to be something quite separate from the notions we construct; it is a set of rules or standards which are 'not made by us but for us'.

The two main themes in 'Of Ethick in General' are, first, that morality depends upon law which in turn depends upon there being a law-maker with rightful authority over us; and, second, that actions are morally good or evil not because of any intrinsic qualities, but because of the reward or punishment (in the form of pleasure or pain) which the law-maker has annexed to their performance. The first of these themes is Locke's theory of moral obligation discussed in chapter II. The second theme has also been encountered before:

> The difference between morall & naturall good & evill is only this that we call that nāāl good & evill w[ch] by ye naturall efficiency of the thing produces pleasure or paine in us & that is morally Good or Evill w[ch] by the appointment of an Intelligent Being that has power draws pleasure or paine after it not by any nāāl consequence but by the intervention of that power. Thus drinking to Excess when it produces ye head ache or sickness is a nāāl evil but as it is a transgression of a law by w[ch] punishment is annexed to it, it is a Moral Evill. (ibid., §8; King, 2, pp.128–9)

This is another statement of the view set forth in the Commonplace Book entry 'Voluntas' and at II.xxviii.5, in the *Essay* (both quoted above, pp.48–9 and p.69). The context of Locke's apparent rejection of the examination of our moral notions as a way to moral knowledge is his criticism of philosophers such as Aristotle who merely gives an account of the various virtues and vices without founding them in God's law, and who provide no reason for the virtuous life other than the alleged intrinsic worth of virtue. To thus concentrate on what is taken to be virtuous or vicious is to begin at the wrong end:

> To establish morality upon its proper basis & such foundations as may carry an obligation with them we must first prove a law w[ch] always supposes a law maker one yt has a superiority & right to ordaine & also a power to reward & punish. ... This Soverain Law maker who has set rules & bounds to ye actions of men is god their maker. ... The next thing then to shew is that there are certain rules certain dictates w[ch] it is his will all men should conforme their actions to, & that this will of his is sufficiently promulgated & made known to all man kinde. (ibid., §12; King, 2, p.133)

The morality 'made by us' is the 'unfounded' moral doctrines of the schools; that which is 'made for us' is the content of the law. Locke, however, accepts that there is much in the former which coincides with the latter. Moreover, he says of the moral ideas which are the genuine content of the law that we come by them in the same way we come by all our other ideas, and that 'they are nothing but collections of simple ideas'. As these are complex ideas constructed from simple ideas received in experience they must at some stage have been framed by us.

Notwithstanding the passages in the *Essay* which give the impression that the demonstration of morality will take account only of our moral notions, Locke is quite clear that other concepts besides these will have to be considered:

> The *Idea* of a supreme Being, infinite in Power, Goodness, and Wisdom, whose Workmanship we are, and on whom we depend; and the *Idea* of our selves, as understanding, rational Beings . . . would, I suppose, if duly considered, and pursued, afford such Foundations of our Duty and Rules of Action, as might place *Morality amongst the Sciences capable of Demonstration*: wherein I doubt not, but from self-evident Propositions, by necessary Consequences, as incontestable as those in Mathematicks, the measures of right and wrong might be made out. (IV.iii.18)[35]

The ideas mentioned here are not moral notions nor even archetypes. Locke does not consider it a valid objection against the possibility of a demonstrative system of morality that it will involve some ideas in which there is a gap between real and nominal essence:

> For as to Substances, when concerned in moral Discourses, their divers Natures are not so much enquir'd into, as supposed; *v.g.* when we say that *Man is subject to Law*: We mean nothing by *Man,* but a corporeal rational Creature: What the real Essence or other Qualities of that Creature are in this Case, is no way considered. And therefore, whether a Child or Changeling be a *Man* in a physical Sense . . . concerns not at all the *moral Man,* as I may call him, which is this immoveable unchangeable *Idea, a corporeal rational Being.* (III.xi.16)

That is, the conception of man to be considered is that one which is appropriate to the study of morality; other conceptions (e.g. the conception of man as a physical entity) are irrelevant.

There are in fact two parts to Locke's envisaged demonstration of morality. The first concerns the existence of a moral law which imposes an obligation on all mankind. Carrying this through involves a proof of God's existence (sketched in the fourth of the *Essays* and set out in detail at IV.x, in the *Essay*), a proof that He does intend us to conform our actions to a law, and an analysis of the concept of obligation. Given the existence of the law, the second part of the demonstration is to make out its content, or determine beyond doubt the correct measures of right and wrong. Locke would consider the first of these parts to have been substantially completed in the *Essays*. It was this second to which his friend William Molyneux and others urged Locke to turn his hand. Locke never produced a finished demonstration of morality, but he does suppose that the derivation of the content of the law begins with our ordinary moral notions.

Locke distinguishes three laws against which we measure our actions in judging of their rectitude or obliquity; '1. The *Divine* Law. 2. The *Civil* Law. 3. The Law of *Opinion* or *Reputation*. . . . By the Relation they bear to the first of these, Men judge whether their Actions are Sins, or Duties; by the second, whether they be Criminal, or Innocent; and by the third, whether they be Vertues or Vices' (II.xxviii.7). The third law covers the various views current in different societies of what kinds of actions are morally right or wrong as distinct from merely legal or illegal. It is the criterion people living in society in fact employ when they judge actions from the moral point of view:

> Vertue and Vice are Names pretended, and supposed every where to stand for actions in their own nature right and wrong: And as far as they really are so applied, they so far are co-incident with the *divine Law*. . . . But yet, whatever is pretended, this is visible that these Names, *Vertue* and *Vice*, in the particular instances of their application . . . are constantly attributed only to such actions, as in each Country and Society are in reputation or discredit. . . . Thus the measure of what is every where called and esteemed *Vertue* and *Vice* is this approbation or dislike, praise or blame, which by a secret and tacit consent establishes it self in the several Societies, Tribes, and Clubs of Men in the World. (II.xxviii.10)[36]

Locke considers the objection that, in calling this criterion a law, he has forgotten his own view that a law implies a rightful authority with the power to enforce sanctions. He replies that most men pay little regard to the sanctions which back up the law of God and the positive law of the state, but generally act so as to earn the commendation and avoid the censure of their fellows (II.xxviii.12). Yet, even if moral praise and blame are thought of as rewards and punishment, the third law still appears to lack a rightful authority; and this, according to Locke, is one of the conditions which must be fulfilled by any law. The law of reputation is best understood as the moral notions we ordinarily employ when we pass judgments on conduct. It is the morality in which persons born into society are brought up and from which they derive their opinions of what is right and wrong.

Locke is emphatic that the divine law 'is the only true touchstone of *moral Rectitude*' (II.xxviii.8). His discussion of the three laws is misleading in so far as it suggests that the divine law and the law of opinion are completely distinct, and that the latter may be compared with the former much in the way that the popular estimation of what is right or wrong may be compared with the positive law stipulating what is legal or illegal. Locke does consider the divine law to be the positive morality revealed in Scripture, but he is mainly concerned with it as a law accessible to unaided human reason, i.e. as the law of nature. Despite the play he makes with the diversity of morals in his polemic against innate practical principles, he accepts the law of opinion as on the whole a trustworthy guide to the content of true morality:

> though, perhaps, by the different Temper, Education, Fashion, Maxims, or Interest of different sorts of Men it fell out, that what was thought Praiseworthy in one Place, escaped not censure in another; and so in different Societies, *Vertues* and *Vices* were changed: Yet, as to the Main, they for the most part kept the same every where . . . even those Men, whose Practice was otherwise, failed not to give their Approbation right . . . whereby even in the Corruption of Manners, the true Boundaries of the Law of Nature, which ought to be the Rule of Vertue and Vice, were pretty well preserved. (II.xxviii.11)

Here the diversity of morals is presented as a falling away from an original uniformity; it is maintained that, while in some places virtues and vices '*were* changed, they generally *kept* the same every where'. The general picture is of a once universally acknowledged moral code, genuinely embodying the law of nature, which has in the course of history partially degenerated into the variable law of opinion. The same picture is hinted at in 'On Ethick in General' where Locke takes the fact that morality has always been considered an area of inquiry distinct from either Theology, Religion or Law to be a 'plain argum[t] . . . of some discovery *still* amongst men of the law of nature, & a secret apprehension of an other rule of action w[ch] rational creatures had a concernment to conform to besides what either the priest pretended was ye immediate command of their god . . . or the Lawyer told them was the command of the government' (MS c28, §3; King, 2, p.124, italics added).

This view of the law of opinion as deriving from an original knowledge of the law of nature recalls Locke's discussion of tradition in the second of the *Essays.* While tradition cannot be considered a source of knowledge of the law of nature, it can be (and in fact often is) a source of true moral beliefs. Locke accepts that most of us acquire our moral views from tradition, for when we are children we are educated in the morality of our parents and the society into which we are born. However, it cannot be said that we thereby acquire moral knowledge: 'For what we take over from other people's talk, if we embrace it only because others have insisted that it is good, may perhaps direct our morals well enough and keep them within the bounds of dutiful action, yet it is not what reason but what men tell us' (*Essays*, p.129). To suppose that the law of nature can be properly learnt from tradition is to make it 'a matter of trust rather than of knowledge, since it would depend more on the authority of the giver of information than on the evidence of things themselves' (*Essays*, p.131). Neither can the philosopher come to an understanding of morality merely by examining what is traditionally accepted as right and wrong. For the content of traditional morality varies from place to place, whereas the content of the law of nature is unchanging and places obligations on all men. Nevertheless, the fact of traditional morality indicates the way to a genuine understanding of the law of nature. Any tradition must at some stage have had an author, someone who did not take over the content of the tradition from what others told him. In the case of morality, 'anyone who is willing to look back and trace a tradition to its very source must necessarily come to a stand somewhere and in the end recognise someone as the original author of this tradition, who either will have found the law of nature inscribed within his heart or come to know it by reasoning from the facts perceived by the senses' (ibid.). As Locke considers the doctrine that morality is innate to be untenable, it is his opinion that the moral tradition must have originated in human reasoning. The only other alternative, that it had its original in a revelation at some time vouchsafed to an individual, is rejected on the grounds that it would then reflect not the law of nature but a positive law. Granted that what we accept on trust as morally right or wrong derives from an original discovery of reason, it is possible for us to make that discovery and achieve genuine moral knowledge; '[these] ways of knowing . . . are equally open to the rest of mankind also, and there is no need of tradition as long as everyone has within himself the same basic principles of knowledge' (ibid.).

The law of opinion is a tradition which, though it has suffered distortions in various societies, still reflects its origins in an original knowledge of the law of nature. The heathen philosophers failed because they were content merely to examine and explicate the law of opinion as they found it:[37]

> these philosophers seldom deriving these rules up to their originall, nor urgeing them as the commands of the great god of

> Heaven & Earth & such as according to wch he would retribute to men after this life; the utmost inforcements they could add to them, were reputation & disgrace by those names of virtue & vice wch they endeavoured by their authority to make names of weight to their scholars and ye rest of the people. (MS c28, §4; King, 2, p.124)

Locke singles out two errors here: a mistaken theory of moral obligation and of the reasons for acting virtuously, and a failure to trace moral notions back to their originals. Moral notions are employed by all nations: 'Some measures there have been every where owned though very different some rules & boundarys to mens actions by wch they were judged to be good or bad, nor is there . . . any people amongst whome there is noe distinction between virtue & vice' (MS c28, §2; King, 2, p.123). Once moral obligation has been founded in the authority of God, the next task is to validate our moral notions by deriving them from their originals and thus clearing them of the corruptions which have been introduced since they were first framed.

Even if the law of opinion is understood as a moral tradition stemming from something other than tradition, it may be objected that there is no guarantee that original morality truly reflected the content of the law of nature. The authors of the tradition may have made mistakes which the tradition itself has only served to perpetuate. However, the validity of the source of the traditional law of opinion follows as a consequence of Locke's general natural law position. We saw in chapter 1 that Locke must reject the sceptical thesis that moral truth is unknowable. However, he is also committed to rejecting the weaker thesis that, while moral truth may be knowable, it in fact has never been known. A law of nature, the content of which is knowable yet unknown, is not a contradiction in terms, for it may be said to have been promulgated to reason in the attenuated sense that it is possible for reason to find it out. Yet a law which was knowable but in fact had never been known could not be said to be *sufficiently* promulgated; from the point of view of those whose conduct it was intended to govern it would be tantamount to an unpromulgated law, and they could not be bound by it. Were all the moral opinions current in the world reflections of an original error as to moral truth, the law of nature would never have been known. Therefore, so far as Locke conceives the law of opinion which men govern their conduct by to be a moral tradition, he must suppose it to have its origins in a knowledge of the law of nature.

6. We are now in a position to say what more there is to the demonstration of morality besides analysis. In Isaac Watt's *Logick* (a work

which shows the influence of both Locke and Descartes) analysis is described as the method which 'takes the whole Compound as it finds it, whether it be a *Species* or an *Individual*, and leads us into the Knowledge of it by resolving it into its first Principles or Parts, its generic Nature, and its special Properties; and therefore it is called the *Method of Resolution*'.[38] The other method of enquiry Watts considers is synthesis, 'which begins with the Parts and leads onward to the Knowledge of the Whole; it begins with the most simple Principles, and general Truths, and proceeds by Degrees to that which is drawn from them or compounded of them; and therefore it is called the *Method of Composition*'.[39] The two methods may appear to be in sharp contrast to each other. However, in practice they often merge so that it is difficult to distinguish them; though 'in the Sciences, when we have by Analysis found out a Truth, we use synthetic Method to explain and deliver it, and prove it to be true'.[40] Watts' description of analysis fits Locke's resolution or decomposition of complex ideas into their simple components.[41] Locke also talks of another method which from his description is equivalent to synthesis:

> General and certain Truths, are only founded in the Habitudes and Relations of abstract *Ideas*. A sagacious and methodical application of our Thoughts, for the finding out these Relations, is the only way to discover all, that can be put, with Truth and Certainty concerning them, into general Propositions. By what steps we are to proceed in these, is to be learned in the Schools of the Mathematicians, who from very plain and easy beginnings, by gentle degrees, and a continued Chain of Reasonings, proceed to the discovery and demonstration of Truths, that appear at first sight beyond humane Capacity. (IV.xii.7)

As analysis and synthesis are complementary methods, it might be supposed that Locke conceives demonstration to consist in first, the resolution of ideas into their components and second, the reconstruction of the ideas from their components in such a way as to reveal the necessary connections between them. This is correct as far as it goes, but the picture needs to be drawn in more detail.

In the *Essays* Locke remarks that 'at all times every argumentation proceeds from what is known and taken for granted, and the mind cannot discourse or reason without some truth that is given and perceived' (p.149). The discovery of the fundamental truths from which reason can proceed in a given area of inquiry is referred to in the *Conduct of the Understanding* as 'bottoming': 'To accustom ourselves, in any question proposed, to examine and find out upon what it bottoms. Most of the difficulties that come in our way, when well considered and traced, lead us to some proposition, which, known to be true, clears the doubt, and gives an easy solution of the question' (§44). The fundamental truths upon which a question bottoms are what Locke puts in the place of the trifling maxims employed in the wrangling of the Schools, 'topical and superficial arguments, of which there is store to be found on both sides . . . serve only to amuse the understanding, and entertain company without coming to the bottom of the question, the only place of rest and stability for an inquisitive mind, whose tendency is only to truth and knowledge' (ibid.). Unless the mind recognises the fundamental truths relevant to the enquiry it is engaged in, its reasoning will be productive only of error and confusion; for, 'Reason is so far from clearing the Difficulties which the building upon false foundations brings a Man into, that if he will pursue it, it entangles him the more, and engages him deeper in Perplexities' (IV.xvii.12). It was remarked earlier that we embark upon the analysis of a concept with specific questions in view; the truth, or truths, upon which the question bottoms may be seen as giving direction to the analysis.[42] These truths also provide the foundations, or 'plain and easy beginnings', for the synthetic method of reconstruction.

If we look once again at Locke's two propositions 'where there is no property, there is no injustice' and 'no government allows absolute liberty', it is obvious that these cannot be denied so long as we accept his definitions of the key terms. But Locke gives no reasons for accepting his definitions; from all that he says at IV.iii.18, they might be mere stipulations.[43] What we are presented with is, as it were, the tail-end of a demonstration, and this is all Locke there intends. Someone reflecting upon the notion of justice may discover it to include the notions of property and ownership. However, such reflection by itself does not show why justice involves property, and it is only when this is shown that the analysis of justice in which the notion of property appears can be established as the correct analysis. The method whereby an analysis is established as correct is synthesis, in which the connection of ideas revealed by analysis is derived from the relevant fundamental truths. The intermediate ideas or proofs, which are necessary for the demonstration of a proposition, and which it is the office of sagacity to find out, may in part be revealed by analysis, but this operation cannot give us the ideas which enter into the propositions on which the enquiry bottoms. Synthesis is a matter of laying out the ideas which have been discovered by the exercise of sagacity in a 'clear and fit order'; that is, of beginning from the proposition, or propositions, upon which the enquiry bottoms and proceeding, by way of whatever other propositions may be necessary, to derive the proposition put forward as a candidate for demonstration.

It should by now be quite clear why the archetypal nature of moral notions suggests to Locke the possibility of a demonstrative science of morality. As they are archetypes, moral notions may be genuinely analysed and we can know exactly what ideas go to make up each complex; as they are entirely the workmanship of the mind we are capable of understanding the principles of their construction. Moral notions are not innate; therefore, they must at some stage have been made by human beings for specific purposes and with specific interests in mind. Human nature is uniform and constant; therefore, these purposes and interests are unchanging and are shared by us all. Starting from certain fundamental truths about man we can, then, proceed to reconstruct the original making of our moral notions and thus derive the true content of the law of nature.

VII

THE ORIGINS OF MORAL NOTIONS

If it is granted that moral notions were originally constructed at some period in the history of mankind and that as first framed they did faithfully capture the content of the law of nature, it might seem that the validation of moral notions, as they now appear in the law of opinion, will be a matter of historical enquiry. Yet even if there were records of the content men originally put into a notion such as 'justice', their discovery would not serve to bottom that notion in the manner demanded by a demonstration of morality. A knowledge of the ideas men at first brought together and called by the name of justice would not in itself enable us to understand why those ideas should go together or why there should be any idea of justice. It is not because of any knowledge we may have of what has happened in the past that we are in a position to achieve this understanding, but because moral notions arise from interests and needs which are abiding features of human nature. Nonetheless, it is appropriate to couch the synthetic part of the demonstration of morality in historical terms. This, however, will not be a narrative of what in fact happened in the past but an exercise in what has been called 'conjectural or theoretical history'.[1]

1. Locke employs the method of conjectural history most obviously in the *Second Treatise of Government.* There the concept of the state of nature, or the condition men are in prior to the establishment of civil government, has a crucial role in his account of the origin and extent of political power. Although Locke does not deal directly with questions of moral epistemology in the *Second Treatise,* what he has to say about the state of nature is of considerable importance for an understanding of his moral philosophy. For, whatever ambiguities there may be in his exposition of the state of nature, it is clear that he intends the concept to encapsulate the fundamental features of human nature and of the human condition. The state of nature can, therefore, be seen as having to do not only with the origin of political authority but also with the origin of moral notions.

The state of nature is the state of men living together without civil government. As such the term does refer to an actual historical state; for Locke holds that civil authority did not come into existence with the beginning of the human race but had to be established by men.[2] The state is characterised as one of freedom and equality. Its freedom consists in the right each individual has to act as he sees fit independently of the will of any of his fellows. The equality of the state of nature is closely related to this freedom; as no man is naturally subject to the will of another in this state 'all the Power and Jurisdiction is reciprocal, no one having more than another' (*2nd Treatise,* §4). However, the freedom and equality of the state of nature does not mean that there are no restraints whatsoever on human conduct: '[It is] *a State of Liberty,* yet it is *not a State of Licence*.... The *State of Nature* has a Law of Nature to govern it, which obliges every one' (*2nd Treatise,* §6). Though human beings in the state of nature are subject to the law of nature, this is not to be looked upon as a curtailment of natural freedom but rather as a necessary condition for its proper attainment:

> For *Law,* in its true Notion, is not so much the limitation as *the direction of a free and intelligent Agent* to his proper Interest, and prescribes no farther than is for the general Good of those under that Law.... So that, however it may be mistaken, *the end of Law* is not to abolish or restrain, but *to preserve and enlarge Freedom*: For in all the states of created beings capable of Laws, *where there is no Law, there is no Freedom.* For *Liberty* is to be free from restraint and violence from others which cannot be, where there is no Law: But Freedom is not... *A Liberty for every Man to do as he lists*: (For who could be free, when every other Man's Humour might domineer over him?). (*2nd Treatise,* §57)

The freedom characteristic of the state of nature is, then, shaped by the law of nature. Similarly, natural equality depends upon the law. Locke explains that he does not suppose men to be equal one to another in all respects: age, virtue, excellence in achievements, alliances entered into, benefits given or received may all place one above another even in the state of nature (*2nd Treatise,* §54). Their equality is that of 'power and jurisdiction'. If the law of nature were not backed up by sanctions it would have no force: 'For the *Law of Nature* would, as all other Laws that concern Men in this World, be in vain, if there were no body that in the State of Nature, had a *Power to Execute* that Law, and thereby preserve the innocent and restrain offenders' (*2nd Treatise,* §57). As God has not instituted any authority competent to execute the law on earth, it follows that, prior to the establishment of civil government, 'every one has a right to punish the transgressors of that Law to such a Degree, as may hinder its

Violation' (ibid.).

The right to execute the law of nature presupposes a knowledge of the precepts of that law. In the *Second Treatise* Locke disclaims any need to enter into 'the particulars of the Law of Nature, or its *measures of punishment*', but he goes on to state that 'it is certain there is such a Law, and that too, as intelligible and plain to a rational Creature, and a Studier of that Law, as the positive Laws of the Common-wealths, nay possibly plainer' (*2nd Treatise*, §12). Elsewhere he talks of it as the law of reason (*2nd Treatise*, §§6, 57), and says of the precept against murder that it is plainly 'writ in the Hearts of all Mankind' (*2nd Treatise*, §11). On the evidence of remarks such as these several commentators have concluded that, contrary to the arguments of the *Essay*, Locke is prepared to accept the innateness, or at least self-evidence, of moral principles for the purposes of his political theory.[3] Yet even were there nothing else, the phrase 'a studier of that law' counts strongly against this interpretation. If the precepts of the law are innate or self-evident why should the individual need to study in order to know them? The single use of the innatist term 'writ in the heart' is not sufficient to prove that Locke has ignored his original thesis that the content of the law is to be worked out by discursive reason building on data acquired in experience.

If the content of the law of nature is the moral notions men originally construct, their coming to know the law will consist in their constructing these notions; and what they originally put into them will be determined by the interests and purposes the notions are intended to serve. Locke, as we have seen, identifies good and evil with pleasure and pain. As misery, which consists in pain, is the contrary of happiness, the avoidance of misery may be thought of as the negative end of action. Locke often presents the thesis that happiness and misery are the determinants of all action as a psychological truth found out by observation. Thus, in 'Of Ethick in General' he writes: 'Happynesse & misery are the two grat springs of humane actions & through the different ways we finde men soe busy in in the world they all aime at happynesse & designe to avoid misery as it appears to them in different places & shapes' (MS c28, §1; King, 2, p.122–3).[4] Elsewhere, however, he talks of happiness and misery, or pleasure and pain, not so much as causal factors setting us upon acting, but as reasons for acting in one way rather than another. If God had not so made us that a perception of pleasure was joined to several thoughts and outward sensations 'we should have no reason to preferr one Thought or Action, to another; Negligence, to Attention; or Motion, to Rest' (II.vii.3). Locke's shift from a quasi-mechanistic theory of the 'springs' of action to a hedonistic theory of reasons for action will be discussed in the next chapter. For the present the importance of the thesis that happiness is the end of action is that it indicates the purpose behind the construction of moral notions. In line with this thesis Locke defines ethics as 'the seeking out those Rules, and Measures of humane Actions, which lead to Happiness, and the Means to practice them' (IV.xxi.3). In reference to the freedom of human beings under the law of nature he remarks, 'Could they be happier without it, the *Law,* as an useless thing would of it self vanish; and that ill deserves the Name of Confinement which hedges us in only from Bogs and Precipices' (*2nd Treatise,* §57). Human happiness, therefore, provides the rationale for the construction of moral notions; under them we rank varieties of human behaviour which we find it necessary to encourage or discourage with a view to this ultimate end.

As Locke's state of nature encapsulates his view of the fundamentals of human nature, it would seem that we should turn to his account of life in this state for an understanding of what human beings need to do in order to achieve happiness. This in turn will show what properly belongs to morality, or what is the genuine content of our moral notions. Here there arises a problem, for Locke notoriously gives two seemingly conflicting descriptions of life in the state of nature. In criticism of writers who confound the state of nature with what he calls 'the state of war' Locke writes that the two 'are as far distant, as a State of Peace, Good Will, Mutual Assistance, and Preservation, and a State of Enmity, Malice, Violence, and Mutual Destruction are one from another' (*2nd Treatise,* §19). In this passage Locke is apparently taking pains to distinguish his own conception of the state of nature (and consequently his whole political theory) from the conception of philosophers such as Hobbes. However, in later passages in the *Second Treatise* this idyllic description of life in the absence of a civil power authorised to enact and enforce laws is replaced by one distinctly Hobbesian in tone. Without such an authority to appeal to '*the State of War once begun, continues,* with a right to the innocent Party, to destroy the other whenever he can' (*2nd Treatise,* §20). Nor does Locke present the state of war as a rare occurrence in the state of nature. The individual has rights and freedoms which he must relinquish upon entering civil society, yet outside civil society his enjoyment of those rights is,

> very uncertain, and constantly exposed to the Invasion of others. For all being Kings as much as he . . . and the greater part no strict Observers of Equity and Justice, the enjoyment of the property

> he has in this state is very unsafe, very unsecure. This makes him willing to quit a Condition which however free, is full of fears and continual dangers. (*2nd Treatise*, §123)

The idyllic state of nature which Locke at first describes fails to provide any reason for the move to civil society. On the Hobbesian description, the reasons are obvious: men are willing to give up the freedom they naturally have in order to avoid the state of war and ensure the preservation of themselves and their property (*2nd Treatise*, §§21, 123).[5] Obviously the state of nature cannot be both idyllic and continually fraught with fears and dangers, and if this basic concept is thus self-contradictory his political theory is vitiated at its foundations. The problem is much the same if our interest is in the state of nature as it is relevant to his moral theory. If human nature is such that the natural condition of man is idyllic there would appear to be no reason why moral notions should develop; in such circumstances happiness will already have been achieved. On the other hand, a Hobbesian state of nature suggests a Hobbesian morality in which the law of nature is nothing more than a system of rules which naturally antagonistic individuals agree to submit to out of fear and solely with the aim of self-preservation. Such a law might still be said to facilitate happiness, but only negatively in the sense that it aimed at the avoidance of misery.

Locke does hold the preservation of man to be *'the Fundamental Law of Nature'* (*2nd Treatise*, §16, cf. §11). Further, his remark in the course of his attack on innate morality that there are principles of action originally lodged in our appetites which 'if they were left to their full swing, they would carry Men to the over-turning of all Morality' (I.iii.13) is reminiscent of Hobbes.[6] On the other side, Locke remarks that 'An Hobbist, with his principle of self-preservation, whereof himself is to be judge, will not easily admit a great many plain duties of morality' ('Study' in King, I, p.191), and there is no reason to believe this statement disingenuous. And, notwithstanding the innate principles which militate against morality, Locke does hold the fundamental desire of happiness and aversion to misery to be 'Inclinations of the Appetite to good' (I.iii.3). However, the solution to the problem is not to be found in scattered remarks and comments such as these; it is necessary to look closely at what Locke has to say about the state of nature.

It is essential to Locke's concept of the state of nature that men in it are subject to the law of nature. This subjection is, of course, not something which ceases with the institution of civil government. The difference between the state of nature and civil society is that in the latter the right which each individual originally has to execute the law of nature is surrendered to an instituted political authority. Locke does not intend the idyllic passage as a description of human existence prior to political society, but as a description of what life would be like if all men constantly obeyed the law of nature.[7] To properly understand this passage we need to go back to the eighth of the *Essays on the Law of Nature,* where Locke argues against the thesis that the basic or primary precept of the law of nature is that each individual should pursue his own interest. He is concerned to refute this thesis because he sees it as a possible interpretation of his own view that the law of nature is rooted in human nature.

Locke argues in the first place that if the moral law is to be interpreted in terms of ethical egoism most of these actions we look upon as virtuous would have to be considered vices, for 'a great number of virtues, and the best of them, consist only in this: that we do good to others at our own loss' (*Essays,* p.207). Secondly, as it is impossible that every individual should in fact achieve his own interest to its fullest extent, the end aimed at by such a primary law could never be fulfilled. To the objection that ethical egoism does not require that each individual be in fact prosperous and happy, but only that they constantly endeavour to achieve this, Locke replies that such a demand means 'men are . . . by the law of nature in a state of war': 'What else indeed can human intercourse be than fraud, violence, hatred, robbery, murder, and such like, when every man not only may, but must, snatch from another by any and every means what the other in his turn is obliged to keep safe' (*Essays,* p.213). On the contrary, it is absurd to suppose that the duties men have under the law of nature are such as to engage them in constant conflict one with another. Ethical egoism cannot be true, for it rules out those other-regarding virtues, such as justice, friendship and generosity, which do promote the harmonious communal existence of mankind. Certainly, the end of the law of nature is human happiness, but the law 'willeth the Peace and *Preservation of all Mankind'* (*2nd Treatise,* §7). To achieve this general happiness it is necessary that individuals sometimes put the interests of others before their own. Even so, it is still true that obedience to the law contributes to the individual's self-interest. A morally right action, such as a repayment of a debt or the fulfilment of a promise, may be directly inexpedient for the individual; nevertheless in performing it he escapes the penalty which he would otherwise have incurred. Locke concludes that 'Utility [i.e. self-interest] is not the basis of the law or the ground of obligation, but the consequence of obedience to it' (*Essays,* p.215).

The state of nature is directly contrary to the state of war because the law of nature, to which men in that state are subject, prescribes other-regarding actions. The identification of the state of nature with the state of war arises from the error of supposing self-interest to be the basis of the law of nature. Locke may have had Hobbes in mind in the eighth of the *Essays*, but the only philosopher he mentions by name is Carneades the founder of the New Academy.[8] The idyllic passage, then, is not inconsistent with the supposedly Hobbesian passages; there is no contradiction in maintaining both that the human condition would be a state of peace and mutual assistance if human beings obeyed the law of nature and that, in the absence of a power capable of enforcing obedience, men will follow their own interests and come into conflict. Yet it seems that it is the Hobbesian passages which express Locke's view of human nature. Hobbes himself would agree that a universal conformity to the precepts of the law of nature would ensure the peace of mankind.[9] However, these passages in Locke are not nearly so close to Hobbes as some critics have imagined.

It is said that the life of the individual is uncertain and insecure in the state of nature (i.e. the pre-political state) because the greater part of men are not 'strict observers of equity and justice'. However, to say that men are not *strict* in the practice of these virtues suggests that some of the time they do pay heed to them and act accordingly; it does not mean that, in the absence of a political power to overawe them, all men constantly follow their own interests without regard for others. The state of war occurs in the state of nature, but it is not something peculiar to man's pre-political existence.[10] It comes about when one man declares 'by Word or Action, not a passionate and hasty, but a sedate settled Design, upon another Mans Life' (*2nd Treatise*, §16). In such circumstances the person who is the object of this settled design must defend himself as best he can. In the state of nature there are no positive laws and no impartial judicial authority to which an appeal may be made. Hence, he can only hope to defeat the force of his opponent by mustering a superior force of his own, and this generally means that others are drawn into the quarrel. So it is that a state of war begun in the state of nature is much more likely to continue than one begun in political society with its apparatus of positive laws and judicial decisions. The state of war may arise even between those who do have a regard for the principles of equity and justice. For in the state of nature each individual must determine what the moral law demands and execute it accordingly, and men tend to be partial when their own interests are concerned: 'For though the Law of Nature be plain and intelligible to all rational Creatures; yet Men being biassed by their Interest, as well as ignorant for want of study of it, are not apt to allow of it as a Law binding to them in the application of it to their particular Cases' (*2nd Treatise*, §124). Thus, disputes can break out concerning the moral rectitude of what has been done, and, as all men equally have the right to punish conduct which is contrary to the law of nature, 'Passion and Revenge' will be likely to lead them into a state of war (*2nd Treatise*, §125). But there are also some individuals who disregard moral considerations altogether and by their actions declare themselves 'to live by another Rule, than that of *reason* and common Equity' (*2nd Treatise*, §8). Such men put themselves into a constant state of war with respect to the rest of mankind and have to be restrained by force. Although Locke does not make it explicit, the 'other rule' is clearly the principle of self-interest. The individual who is bent upon his own interests in all dealings with his fellows will inevitably cross the interests of others and must get them into his power in order to achieve his ends. Therefore, his posture towards others will be that of a settled design against them. But Locke does not maintain that most men (much less all men) will live according to 'no other Rule, but that of Force and Violence' unless restrained by superior force (*2nd Treatise*, §16). Rather the suggestion is that such determined outlaws will be relatively uncommon even in the state of nature.

Locke differs importantly from Hobbes in that he holds men to be naturally social beings: 'God having made Man such a Creature, that, in his own Judgment, it was not good for him to be alone, put him under strong Obligations of Necessity, Convenience, and Inclination to drive him into *Society*, as well as fitted him with Understanding and Language to continue and enjoy it' (*2nd Treatise*, §77).[11] Those who maintain that ethical egoism is the only natural law governing human behaviour ignore this innate sociableness, and their opinion has 'always been opposed by the more rational part of men, in whom there was some sense of a common humanity, some concern for fellowship' (*Essays*, p.205). This does not mean that human sociableness is purely altruistic. In his long Journal entry in shorthand for 16 July 1676 Locke defines love as 'nothing but the consideration or having in the mind the idea of some thing that is able in some way of application to produce delight or pleasure in us' (*Essays*, p.265). This definition applies to the love of persons as well as the love of things. Often we love certain people because we are delighted with the good offices they do us, with their conversation and so on. This, Locke admits, is not properly love of the person. In the case of this love we care for the well-being of our friends, but only because their preservation is a necessary condition for the good things we receive from them, and if these cease our love is likely to cease also. There are, however, men of a 'nobler constitution' who take delight in the very existence and happiness of their friends or even in that of mankind in general. Nonetheless, even in these instances of noble love, the passion is 'found to take its rise and extent only from objects of pleasure and to be nothing else but having in our minds the idea of some thing that is so suited to our particular make and temper as to be fit to produce pleasure in us' (*Essays*, p.266). Locke's conception of human altruism is, therefore, quite consistent with his main thesis that the desire to obtain personal pleasure and avoid personal misery is the motive behind all our actions. However, as individuals do find other people to be sources of pleasure they will, at least very often, take account of the interests of others. For Locke the Hobbesian *homo homini lupus* doctrine is false.

As men tend to be partial to their moral judgments when their own interests are concerned, and as most of them when left completely free are not strict observers of the moral law, the state in which each individual has the executive power of the law is beset with a great number of what Locke calls 'inconveniences' (*2nd Treatise*, §90, cf. §13). Further, the fact that some men are prepared to disregard the moral law altogether and live by the rule of force and violence means that the honest man is always open to attack, an attack which he can only hope to repel by meeting force with force. These factors provide a sufficient reason for the move into civil society. In light of them men consent to give up the rights and freedom they naturally have, and submit themselves to a duly established political authority which enacts and enforces positive laws and functions as an impartial umpire in deciding controversies between individuals (*2nd Treatise*, §131; cf. §§3 and 229).

The conveniences of the state of nature are a product of the tension between man's natural sociableness and his equally natural desire for personal happiness. Were individuals completely devoid of any feeling of fellowship, the communal life which Locke envisages the state of nature to be would be impossible. On the other hand, were they completely altruistic and always ready in their actions to consider the interests of their fellows the state of nature would be in fact idyllic. This tension explains why men are not constantly obedient to the law of nature and why civil society must be instituted. Prior to this it also explains why the moral notions which are the content of the law have to be constructed.

In *Some Thoughts Concerning Education* Locke expands on his remark in the *Essay* that we are possessed of innate principles which, if unchecked, would overturn all morality. He states that 'our Natural Propensity to indulge Corporal and present Pleasures, and to avoid Pain at any rate . . . is the Root from whence spring all Vitious

Actions, and the Irregularities of Life' (*Education,* §48). Later he says that as well as loving liberty children 'love something more; and that is *Dominion*: And this is the first Original of most vicious Habits, that are ordinary and natural' (*Education,* §103; cf. §110). This Hobbesian love of dominion shows itself in the way children grow peevish and sullen when their wills are crossed and in 'their desire to have things to be theirs', or to acquire property (*Education,* §§104–5). If the individual's quest for happiness consisted solely in gaining possession of as many of the things which gave him pleasure as possible, rules which aimed at the happiness of mankind in general would appear to him an 'unnatural' restriction on his own happiness. However, the individual's quest for happiness is naturally carried on in a social context, for human nature has been made such that in a man's own judgment it is not good for him to be alone. Consequently, even from the individual's point of view, rules aimed at promoting the general happiness may be seen as resolving conflicts between his own egoistic desire for good and his desire for fellowship.

2. Knowledge of the content of the law of nature presupposes a knowledge of the existence of God, for the idea of a law necessarily involves the idea of a law-maker. In the *Essay* Locke offers a demonstration of God's existence which takes as its starting point the individual's intuitive knowledge of his own existence. As the existence of each individual has had a beginning and anything that has begun to be must have been produced by something other than itself, it follows that there must be a being which has existed from all eternity. The cause of a thing must also be the source of everything belonging to that thing, and we perceive ourselves to have various powers and knowledge. Therefore, the eternal being must be the most powerful and most knowing being. Similar reflection upon our own constitutions will lead us to deduce the other attributes which ought to be ascribed to God (IV.x.1–6).[12] In the *Essays* Locke's approach to the existence of God is somewhat different. There he presents in historical terms an account of how men came to acknowledge the existence of a creator to whom they are rightly subject. The starting point is not the individual's knowledge of his own existence, but the harmonious order which, it is evident to the senses, exists in nature. Man himself is a part of nature and he has not the power and wisdom necessary to create himself or design the order he discerns in the operation of things. Knowing this, his reason compels him to conclude that 'there exists another more powerful and wiser agent who at his will can bring us into the world, maintain us, and take us away' (*Essays,* p.153). From this it follows that God is man's rightful

superior. Further, as God is wise, it must be that He has created man for some purpose and endowed him with the attributes necessary for the fulfilment of that purpose. The argument of the *Essays* thus leads directly to the existence of the law of nature, or the rules men must follow in order to fulfil the purpose God has ordained.

In the *Essays* emphasis is placed on the notion of man as the product of God's creative activit[illegible] and this notion is also central to the argument of the *Second Tr*[illegible] 'For Men being all the Workmanship of one Omnipotent [illegible] [illegible]tely wise Maker; All the Servants of one Sovereign M[illegible] [illegible]he World by his order and about his business, they a[illegible] [illegible]hose Workmanship they are, made to last durin[illegible] [illegible] an[illegible] [illegible]rs Pleasure' (*2nd Treatise*, §6). What Locke r[illegible] [illegible]ental law of nature follows as a necessary con[illegible] [illegible]act of our being God's workmanship. As we are[illegible] [illegible] as God wills no one can have a right to prevent [illegible] [illegible]nued existence of himself or others:

> Ever one as he [illegible] [illegible]ve himself, and not to quit his Station wilf[illegible] [illegible]e reason when his own Preservation comes [illegible] [illegible]on, ought he, as much as he can, *to preserve th*[illegible] [illegible]*kind*, and may not unless it be to do Justice on [illegible] [illegible]te[illegible], take away, or impair the life, or what tends to [illegible] [illegible]ation of the life, Liberty, Health, Limb or Goods [illegible] (*2nd Treatise*, §6)

It is beca[illegible] [illegible] made us that we are His property and He has a right t[illegible] [illegible]s as He thinks fit.[13] Equally, individual human bein[illegible] [illegible] [illegible]clusive ownership rights in things by virtue of their act[illegible] [illegible]. In this man is analogous to God; for 'God makes him i[illegible] [illegible]*mage after his own Likeness*, makes him an intellectual [illegible] and so capable of *Dominion'* (*1st Treatise*, §30).

[illegible]xclusive property rights individuals have in things is founded [illegible] fact that 'every Man has a *Property* in his own *Person'* (*2nd* [illegible]*atise*, §27). It is because of this that the individual owns his [illegible]abour and consequently owns the goods he acquires by that labour: 'The *Labour* of his Body, and the *Work* of his Hands, we may say, are properly his. Whatsoever then he removes out of the State that Nature hath provided, and left it in, he hath mixed his *Labour* with, and joyned to it something that is his own, and thereby makes it his *Property'* (ibid.). The major premise in this argument may appear to contradict Locke's fundamental thesis that we are all God's property. From this thesis it follows that no individual can have property in another person, for that would be to dispossess God, but, by parity of reason, it would also seem to follow that no individual can have property in his person.

Here the analysis of the concept of a person and of personal identity given in the *Essay* is crucial.[14] Locke defines both concepts in terms of selfconsciousness: '[A person] is a thinking intelligent Being, that has reason and reflection, and can consider it self as it self, the same thinking thing in different times and places; which it does only by that consciousness, which is inseparable from thinking, and as it seems to me essential to it' (II.xxvii.9). That is, our selfhood at any given time is constituted by our reflex consciousness of our self; for '[when] we see, hear, smell, taste, feel, meditate, or will any thing, we know that we do so' (ibid.). As selfhood, or the person, at a particular time is constituted by this consciousness, so the continuation of the one person through time depends upon the sameness of consciousness:

> as far as any intelligent Being can repeat the *Idea* of any past Action with the same consciousness it had of it at first, and with the same consciousness it has of any present Action; so far it is the same *personal self*. For it is by the consciousness it has of its present Thoughts and Actions, that it is *self* to it *self* now, and so will be the same *self* as far as the same consciousness can extend to Actions past or to come. (II.xxvii.10)[15]

As the consciousness constituting the self is of action, the person is necessarily an agent. Locke includes thinking under the heading of action, and we have noted that he supposes some degree of mental activity to be involved even in the reception of ideas from the external world. However, not everything which comes under this broad conception of action is of equal importance for selfhood. For Locke '*Person* . . . is a Forensick Term appropriating Actions and their Merit; and so belongs only to intelligent Agents capable of a Law, and Happiness and Misery' (II.xxvii.26). That is, in Locke's opinion, the term has developed in language because we have an interest in the ascription of moral responsibility to individuals. What individuals are held responsible for must be something in fact done by them and it must have been done freely. It is, therefore, a consciousness of free actions which properly constitutes the person.

As we shall see in the next chapter, Locke conceives freedom as necessarily connected with understanding or rationality. Children below a certain age, idiots and madmen have not the use of reason and are, therefore, not free. This means that they are not capable of a law and cannot be held responsible for their deeds (*2nd Treatise*, §§57–60). Consequently, they do not count as persons in the forensic sense of that term. A properly free action is one which depends for its existence on an exercise of an active power we can discern within us and which Locke calls the will (II.xxi.5). In exercising this power we consider the alternatives of doing or not doing a particular action presented to our thoughts, or of continuing or ending an ongoing action we have already embarked upon, and decide one way or the other. So long as it originates in an act of will, Locke accepts the non-performance or the continuation of an action as an instance of the agent doing something. As that something would not have been done or existed except for the agent willing it, it can be said to be made by him. Therefore, by analogy with God's ownership of us, the action is the agent's property.

In willing, the agent makes a deliberate selection from alternatives open to him. Therefore he must know what he wills, and, given the action follows his willing, he must know beforehand what the action is. He has non-observational or intentional knowledge of his action, for he knows it not by virtue of finding out what it is, but because it is what he intends it to be.[16] Not every action ascribable to the agent need be one of which he has intentional knowledge. He may do *x*, but do it absent-mindedly, inadvertently, and so on. We use adverbs such as 'absent-mindedly' and 'inadvertently' to qualify our ascription of *x* to the agent because we recognise that he is not conscious of doing *x* or does not know that he does it (though he may subsequently find out about it). On the other hand, the agent may be conscious of doing *x*, but do it under compulsion, and hence unwillingly. Both when the agent is unconscious of what he is doing and when it is done unwilling the action is not made by him and consequently not owned by him. On Locke's analysis, the consciousness which constitutes the continuing self is a consciousness of owned actions:

> This personality extends it *self* beyond present Existence to what is past, only by consciousness, whereby it becomes concerned and accountable, owns and imputes to it *self* past Actions, just upon the same ground, and for the same reason, that it does the present. . . . And therefore whatever past Actions it cannot reconcile or appropriate to that present *self* by consciousness, it can be no more concerned in, then if they had never been done. (II.xxvii.26)

Thus, although the individual does not make the consciousness which is the condition of personhood, he does make that which the consciousness is of, and it is *that* consciousness which 'distinguishes himself from all other thinking things' (II.xxvii.9). In this sense the individual can be said to be the author of himself and therefore to have a property in his person.

Strictly, God's ownership of man extends to the body and the limbs and not to the rationally carried-out actions or labour of the body. This is not to say that the developed person is not subject to God's authority. We are sustained in existence by God and our rightful subjection to Him derives from this as much as from His initial act of making us. While the thesis that we are God's workmanship does not come into conflict with the notion of the individual having property in his person it may still be objected that there is a logical gap between the ownership of actions and the ownership of things acted upon. Mixing one's own labour with a thing would seem to entitle one to whatever may thereby be added to that thing but not, as Locke maintains, to the whole thing. However, in Locke's view, the individual in working upon a thing does not simply add something to it, but transforms it into a new thing. Unlike God, man cannot create *ex nihilo* but, like God, he can make something new out of pre-existing raw material. In the *Essay* an analogy is drawn between the 'Dominion of Man . . . in the great World of visible things' and the capacities of the mind respecting ideas. The mind cannot invent any new simple idea, but it can manipulate those it has received in experience and so frame new complex ideas. Similarly, man's power over things in the external world 'reaches no farther, than to compound and divide the Materials, that are made to his Hand; but can do nothing towards the making the least Particle of new Matter, or destroying one Atome of what is already in Being' (II.ii.2).[17]

The individual's property right in things is essential to his quest for happiness. His happiness, and indeed his preservation, depend upon his having an exclusive possession of various things, and if he had no right to this possession it could not be right for him to pursue happiness. Originally God gave the things of the world to mankind in common so that they may make use of them 'to the best advantage of Life, and convenience'[18] '. . . yet being given for the use of Man, there must of necessity be a means *to appropriate* them some way or other before they can be of any use, or at all beneficial to any particular Man' (*2nd Treatise*, §26). Unless there were this means, individuals would have no right to make use even of the food that nourishes them and keeps them alive, and this would be contrary to the fundamental natural law that man be preserved. Nevertheless, the original donation of the world to all mankind does set limits to private appropriation. Locke considers the objection that, if mixing one's labour with a thing constitutes one's exclusive ownership of that thing, the individual may accumulate as much property as he likes. However, God has given us the things of the earth to use and enjoy, not to waste: 'As much as any one can make use of to any advantage of life before it spoils; so much he may by his labour fix a

Property in. Whatever is beyond this, is more than his share, and belongs to others. Nothing was made by God for Man to spoil or destroy' (*2nd Treatise*, §31). This 'spoilage limitation' sets bounds to appropriation, for God gave the world 'to the use of the Industrious and Rational, (and *Labour* was to be *his Title* to it;) not to the Fancy or Covertousness of the Quarrelsom and Contentious' (*2nd Treatise*, §34). Provided there are enough goods to go round, the law of nature ensures that each individual who is prepared to labour can acquire property in things. He can thus provide for his own convenience and advantage.

That the individual's quest for personal happiness is morally legitimate may be derived from the human disposition to seek happiness. If this fundamental and universal disposition were contrary to morality the content of the law of nature could hardly be said to be 'firmly rooted in the soil of human nature'. Thus, in his Journal for 8 February 1677 Locke writes:

> if we will consider man as in this world, & that his minde & facultys were given him for any use, we must necessarily conclude it must be to procure him the happynesse wch this world is capeable of wch certainly is noe thing else but plenty of all sorts of those things wch can with most ease pleasure & variety preserve him longest in it. (MS f2. Fol.46 and in Aaron & Gibb, p.85)

However, he does not rely solely on a consideration of man's fundamental desire and the make-up of human nature to establish his view that the ultimate purpose of morality is human happiness. In an entry dated 1 August 1680 he sets out an *a priori* argument from the nature of God for this conclusion.[19] Everything which is excellent and carries no imperfection with it must make up part of our idea of God, and must be conceived as belonging to God in an infinite degree. Thus God is to be understood as a being of infinite duration, power, wisdom and goodness. Since God is 'eternall and perfect in his owne being' he cannot be thought to employ His power to improve His own condition:

> therefore all the exercise of that power must be in and upon his creatures, which cannot but be imploid for their good and benefit as much as the order and perfection of the whole can allow to each individuall in its particular ranke and station and therefore looking on god as a being infinite in goodness as well as power we cannot imagine he hath made anything with a designe that it should be miserable, but that he hath afforded it all that means of being happy that its nature and state is capable of. (MS f4, Fol.145, and in King I, pp.228–9)

It follows, then, from God's nature that He could not but intend men to be happy. Therefore, men must be able to achieve happiness and the law God has set them must aim at this end.

3. The premise that man is God's workmanship yields a number of conclusions of obvious moral significance: that the individual's life is not at the disposal of himself or his fellow men; that each individual may acquire property in the goods of the earth; and that the natural quest for happiness is morally legitimate, and in fact it is the aim of the moral law to facilitate this quest. However, Locke does not see a knowledge of these conclusions as immediately prompting men in the state of nature to the construction of moral notions. He does not conceive the state of nature as static but as developmental, involving a number of stages which human beings successively go through and which culminate in the institution of political power and civil society. At the first stage, although men are subject to the law of nature, there is no tension between their inclinations and the demands of that law.

Moral laws are, Locke states, 'set as a curb and restraint to [man's] exorbitant Desires' (I.iii.13). The desires, however, are exorbitant only when actualised in such behaviour as has a tendency to disrupt the order and harmony of the human community. In the *Second Treatise* Locke talks of an initial 'Golden Age' of humanity 'before vain Ambition, and *amor sceleratus habendi,* evil Concupiscense, had corrupted Mans minds into a Mistake of true Power and Honour' (*2nd Treatise,* §111). This age is characterised as one of 'innocence and Sincerity', and it was 'poor but vertuous' (*2nd Treatise,* §110). Locke does not suppose the innocence and virtue of the Golden Age to be due to any difference between human desires as they were then and as they are now; rather the objects of men's desires were simpler and the circumstances of life such that they found it easy to achieve them.

At this stage the family was the unit of social organisation and, the population of the earth being as yet small, nature provided more than enough of the things needed for the survival of all. The general desire for personal happiness is constant in human nature but 'Men, at first, for the most part, contented themselves with what un-assisted Nature Offered to their Necessities' (*2nd Treatise,* §45). Consequently, their way of life was simple and poor 'confineing their desires within the narrow bounds of each mans smal propertie' (*2nd Treatise,* §107). In this situation serious conflict between individuals is virtually ruled out: 'No Mans Labour could subdue, or appropriate all: nor could his Enjoyment consume more than a small part; so that it was impossible for any Man, this way, to intrench upon the right of another, or acquire, to himself, a Property, to the Prejudice of his Neighbour' (*2nd Treatise*, §36). The virtue of the Golden Age goes hand in hand with its poverty. Its decline and the subsequent development of humanity are in part due to the increase in population, but the major factor is the increased sophistication of human desires. In the Journal entry for 8 February 1677, Locke remarks 'we are in an estate the necessitys whoreof call for a constant supply of meat drinke cloathing & defence from the weather & very often physick; & our conveniences demand yet a great deale more' (MS f2, Fol.44 and in Aaron & Gibb, p.84). The Golden Age ends when men are no longer content with a mere subsistence standard of existence but set their happiness in the attainment of the conveniences of life. The pursuit of these conveniences by the individual is, of course, morally legitimate. It must, however, be regulated according to the precepts of the natural law if the general happiness of mankind is to be attained.

In the *Second Treatise* the Golden Age and the further stages of human development are decribed in completely secular terms. In this account the change from a nomadic to a settled agrarian existence and the invention of money are crucial.[20] However, in a Commonplace Book entry under the heading 'Homo ante et post lapsum' (1693), Locke virtually equates the Golden Age with the prelapsarian period of mankind, and the transition from this to the later stage of humanity is described in terms of the mythos of the Fall: 'Man was made mortal put into a possession of ye whole world, where in the full use of the creatures there was scarce room for any irregular desires but instinct & reason carried him the same way & being neither capable of covitousnesse or ambition when he had already the free use of all things he could scarce sin' (MS c28, Fol.113). As punishment for failing the test God had set them, Adam and Eve were excluded from the immortality which would otherwise have been bestowed upon them. The consciousness of their offence gave them fearful ideas of God and turned their mind from Him to the things of the world, and 'this root of all evill in them' infected their children. The curse upon the earth, which was also a consequence of their disobedience, made private possessions and labour necessary, and these 'by degrees made a distinction of conditions [and] gave ro'me for covitousnesse pride & ambition, wch by fashion & example spread the corruption wch has soe prevailed over man kind' (ibid.). As before the Fall (or during the Golden Age) instinct and reason carried man the same way, there was no need for human desires to be curbed, and consequently no call for the construction of moral notions. This may be termed the pre-moral stage of human existence, for then men conformed to the demands of the law unthinkingly.[21]

As the transition from the innocent Golden Age to the moral age takes place when the pursuit of happiness by individuals begins to generate disagreement and quarrels – or at least when the desires of individuals reach a state of sophistication such that disagreement becomes possible – it might be thought that Locke sees morality as a system of rules for the avoidance and resolution of conflict between individuals. In the course of his argument against ethical egoism he defines the basis of natural law as, 'some sort of groundwork on which all other and less evident precepts of that law are built and from which in some way they can be derived, and thus they acquire from it all their binding force in that they are in accordance with that, as it were, primary and fundamental law which is the standard and measure of all the other laws depending on it (*Essays,* p.205). The rules of morality are, therefore, derivations from a fundamental rule. Also in the *Essays* justice is mentioned as 'that chief law of nature and bond of every society' (*Essays,* p.169). Justice is not considered at any length in Locke's completed works, but it is the main moral notion considered in an unfinished paper headed 'morality' (MS c28, Fol.139–40). The manuscript is undated, but it is highly likely that it is part of the materials mentioned to Molyneux as put aside with a view to a treatise of morals.

In this paper Locke begins by defining morality as 'ye rule of mans actions for ye attaining happynesse'. The definition is justified on the grounds that, as all men constantly desire to attain happiness and avoid misery 'noe thing could be a rule or a law to them whose observation did not lead to happynesse & whose breach did [not] draw misery after it'. Given it is within God's power to continue a man's existence and capacity for pleasure and pain after death, it is at least possible that there is a future state of rewards and punishment. Locke, however, does not pursue the implications of this, but instead limits his enquiry to the means of attaining mundane happiness. He lays down two evident truths: (1) 'Man made not him self nor any other man'; (2) 'Man made not the world wch he found made at his birth'. Those yield the conclusion that no man can have an original right to any of the goods of the earth over and above the right of any other man. But so long as all things are left in common 'want rapin & force will unavoidably follow in wch state as is evident happiness cannot be had wch can not consist without plenty & security'. The notion of justice is developed as a means of preventing this condition: 'To avoid this estate compact must determin peoples rights. These compacts are to be kept or broken. If to be broken their making signifies noe thing if to be kept then Justice is established as a duty & will be the first & generall rule of our happinesse'.

However, in the world in which justice has been established it will sometimes be to the individual's advantage to break a compact and, as the end of justice, or any other moral rule, is happiness, it seems that it should be permissible for him to do so. To this objection Locke replies:

> All men being equally under one & ye same rule if it be permitted to me to break my word for my advantage it is also permitted every one else & then whatever I possesse will be subjected to the force or deceit of all the rest of men in ye world in w[ch] state it is impossible for any man to be happy unless he were both stronger & wiser than all the rest of man kinde for in such a state of rapin & force it is impossible any one man should be master of those things whose possession is necessary to his well being.

Locke, it is to be noted, is not saying that it would be irrational for me to act unjustly on occasion; my act is not likely in fact to bring about the general condition of misery which is contrary to my happiness as well as the happiness of everyone else. It would be contrary to reason only to suppose that in making an exception in favour of my own happiness I am conforming to the moral law. As the precepts of the law bind all men, if I hold an action to be lawful for me I am bound to conclude the like action performed by another to be equally lawful. In the present case if I suppose it to be morally permitted for me to renege on a compact I must suppose it be permitted for others too. But this would be to opt for a world in which the rule of force rather than the rule of justice governed human conduct, and in such a world no-one's happiness could be secured or maintained. Given the premise established earlier that the aim of morality can only be the attainment of happiness, reason cannot accept this rule of force as a moral rule. Locke states that once justice (which he terms 'the greatest & dificultest duty') is established it will not be hard to institute the other virtues 'which relate to society & soe border on Justice but yet are not comprised under direct articles of contract such as are Civility Charity Liberality'. However, except for a definition of civility, 'Morality' ends without anything being said concerning the development of these notions.

The argument of 'Morality' makes quite explicit the central position of hedonism in Locke's moral philosophy and its relation to his ethical rationalism. In the polemic against innate morality he remarks that '*there cannot any one moral Rule be propos'd, whereof a Man may not justly demand a Reason*' (I.iii.4). The reason which must be forthcoming is that the existence of the rule in some way contributes to the individual's happiness. As the alternative to the world in which the rule of justice is established is the world in which men live according to the rule of force, such a reason can be provided for justice. For under the rule of force the human condition will be such that no individual can have the security essential for even a completely selfish pursuit of happiness. This is not to deny that his acting in accord with justice will not sometimes frustrate the individual's own happiness. He has reason to acknowledge the rule of justice as a moral rule; it is a further question whether he always has reason to follow that rule.

As well as its relevance to the question of the relation between Locke's hedonism and his ethical rationalism 'Morality' is of importance for a number of other reasons. His account of the origin of justice provides the necessary underpinning for his proposition 'where there is no property, there is no injustice'; it validates the analyses he gives of the two concepts and shows that the truth of the proposition does not depend upon a mere stipulative definition of terms. Given Locke's description of the Golden Age as a period when circumstances were such 'that it was impossible for any man to acquire a property to the prejudice of his neighbour', the institution of justice – or the conscious articulation of the notion of justice – must be understood as subsequent to that age. There could be no call to initiate a rule aimed at avoiding a condition which could not possibly come about. Justice belongs to the postlapsarian phase of human existence when desires have been enlarged, and increased population has brought a scarcity of goods. What Locke has to say about the origin or justice does not conflict with the doctrine that individuals acquire property rights in things by the act of mixing their labour with them. In the *Second Treatise* this doctrine is expounded in opposition to the view that the individual's having private property depends upon 'any express Compact of all the Commoners' (II, §25; cf. §29). However, Locke is not sketching a contract theory of property in 'Morality'. The compact mentioned is necessary to determine people's rights in things not because those rights did not exist before, but because the stage at which appropriation can engender conflict between individuals has been reached.[22] 'Morality' also provides confirmation for the view that the synthetic part in Locke's demonstration of morality will be an exercise in conjectural history. It is clear both from the title of the paper and its unfinished state that Locke's intention was not simply to give an account of the origin of one moral notion in isolation from all others. Justice is said to be the general rule of our happiness and is presented as chronologically the first moral notion to be constructed. The other virtues cited are said to border on justice. Had Locke given an account of their original construction it would presumably have followed the same lines as his account of the origin of justice. That is, the notions of these virtues would have been exhibited as being constructed to meet the exigencies of the human condition as they arise in the course of man's development after the Fall.

Locke remarks in the *Essays* that no one doubts the classes of virtues and vices to be the actual law of nature (*Essays,* p.167). Assuming justice to be Locke's fundamental law, it should be possible to derive all other virtues from the notion of justice and all vices from injustice. Man might be thought to begin with the rule, or notion, of justice and then to construct other moral notions much in the way we have imagined the notion of 'stoling' to develop out of 'stealing' (see above, p.133). That is, these notions develop out of the necessity to make specific the kinds of actions which fall under the original broad notions of justice and injustice. The fundamental law is said to serve as a standard and measure with respect to the other precepts of natural law. If justice is that law, moral notions as they now appear in the law of opinion may be assessed as valid or invalid according as they turn out to be properly species of justice or injustice. A given notion will be valid so long as it satisfies two conditions: it signifies a kind of action which does properly come under the rule of justice, and it signifies that action correctly, as within the class of virtues if it is just and within the class of vices if it is unjust.

There are, however, obvious difficulties in accepting justice as the fundamental law. In the account given in 'Morality' the notion of justice develops out of the need to regulate and protect property rights. Elsewhere Locke states that '*Justice* gives every Man a Title to the product of his honest Industry, and the fair Acquisitions of his Ancestors descended to him' (*1st Treatise,* §42). But if justice and injustice concern only property they would appear far too narrow in scope to encompass all virtues and vices. The notion of theft would be validated as a vice and so would, for example, fraud, considered as a species of theft; for these actions would be violations of people's rights respecting material possessions. On the other hand, it seems that cruelty considered as violence done to the person would not count as an instance of injustice and would, therefore, not qualify as vicious. However, Locke's doctrine that each individual has a property in his own person should be kept in mind here. This property, we have seen, is logically connected with the ownership individuals can acquire in things, and Locke stipulates that in his usage the term 'property' is to be understood as meaning 'Lives, Liberties and Estates' (*2nd Treatise,* §123; cf. §87).[23] If the law of justice is conceived as having to do with property in this sense it will cover violence done to the person within its scope; the rights determined when justice is established will include the right to life and to liberty as well as the right to material possessions.

Yet there remains a problem: even when justice is interpreted in the light of this broad use of the term 'property' it would still seem not to accommodate those virtues which consist in doing positive good to others. The right to life is founded in God's ownership of man and entails the duty to preserve oneself. The right to liberty derives from the property the individual has in his person and is essentially the right to pursue one's own well-being free from interference from others. Private property in things being necessary for the fulfilment of the duty of self-preservation, the right to property derives from that duty, and the person's ownership of his labour legitimises personal appropriation from the common and determines which goods are his. As these rights belong to all men equally, it will be contrary to justice to deprive anyone of life or to damage their well-being by either depriving them of what their labour has acquired or preventing their acquisition of goods by labour. As Locke puts it: 'Reason, which is that Law [of nature], teaches all Mankind, who will but consult it, that being all equal and independent, no one ought to harm another in his Life, Health, Liberty, or Possessions' (*2nd Treatise,* §6). Understood thus, a person will fulfil the demands of justice provided he does not inhibit or molest others in their pursuit of well-being or quest for happiness. The precepts of justice will be what in a letter to Grenville Locke calls the negative precepts of the law. As these require the non-performance of various kinds of actions they can – and must – be adhered to under all circumstances (see above, p.69). In the same letter he talks of positive precepts which it is incumbent upon us to fulfil only when proper occasions arise. Locke does not give any account of these positive precepts though, 'love to god and charity to our selves and neighbours' are mentioned in passing (*Correspondence,* 1, p.556). In any case fulfilment of them is clearly more than a matter of allowing others to proceed without interference in their business of personal happiness. Further, after citing justice as that which gives the individual a title to the goods he has acquired, Locke goes on to say that similarly '*Charity* gives every Man a Title to so much out of another's Plenty, as will keep him from extream want, where he has no means to subsist otherwise' (*1st Treatise,* §42). Here charity is not presented as somehow coming under justice, but as a quite separate and independent virtue.[24] Equally, the social virtues of civility and liberty mentioned at the end of 'Morality' would appear to be independent of justice in so far as it is conceived as engendering only negative precepts. It appears that justice (at least as that notion is outlined in

'Morality') cannot serve as the fundamental law from which all other precepts may be derived and against which other moral notions may be measured.

Locke speaks of the precept that man be preserved as the fundamental law of nature. As this precept enjoins the preservation of others as well as oneself, it is distinct from the Hobbesian principle of self-preservation; and it might be thought better suited than justice for the role of a basis upon which other moral precepts can be built. If conformity to the rule of justice is to be no more than obedience to precepts forbidding harm to persons in their lives, liberties and estates, that rule may itself be construed as deriving from the rule that man be preserved. The precept of preservation will also yield charity as a positive duty, 'since 'twould always be a Sin in any Man of Estate, to let his Brother perish for want of affording him Relief out of his Plenty' (*1st Treatise,* §42). However, on Locke's conception of charity, the demands of that virtue are strictly limited; preserving others out of one's plenty means no more than preserving them, and the duty of charity is fulfilled when individuals whose labour has not sufficed to gain them the goods necessary for subsistence are kept from 'extreme want'.[25] The positive virtue of liberality cannot, therefore, be considered a further specification of the virtue of charity. Yet Locke wishes to include this virtue, and it would seem that he must build it upon some foundation other than the precept of preservation.

There is, however, one other candidate for the position of the fundamental law of nature to be found in Locke's writings. In the Journal entry for 8 February 1677, Locke mentions 'that one unquestionable morall rule doe as you would be don to' (MS f2, Fol.50, and in Aaron & Gibb, p.87). The Golden Rule also appears in his discussion of the intellectual procedure of bottoming in the *Conduct of the Understanding*: 'Our Saviour's great rule, that "we should love our neighbours as ourselves", is such a fundamental truth for the regulating human society, that, I think, by that alone, one might without difficulty determine all the cases and doubts in social morality' (*Works,* 3, pp.282–3). And in 'Of Ethick in General' he remarks, somewhat obscurely, that the objective rule of our actions set by God 'is conversant about & ultimately terminates in those simple Ideas before mentioned v.g. though shalt love thy neighbour as thy selfe' (MS c28, §11 and in King, 2, p.131). Clearly then, Locke supposes this rule to be in some way at the foundation of morality. As all individuals are intent upon gaining pleasure and avoiding pain, doing unto others as we would have them do unto us will consist in acting so as to cause them pleasure, or at least refraining from actions which will cause them pain. In the Commonplace Book entry 'Virtus' (1681) Locke sets out a utilitarian criterion of virtue and vice which may be seen as following from the hedonistic interpretation of the Golden Rule: 'Virtue . . . in the matter of it, it is nothing else, but doing of good either to oneself or others; and the contrary hereunto, vice is nothing else but doing of harm' (King, 2, p.94). This criterion, he remarks, 'if well considered, will give us better boundaries of virtue and vice than curious questions stated with the nicest destinctions' (ibid., p.95).[26]

If the Golden Rule (and the consequent criterion of virtue and vice) is to function as the fundamental law, it must be connected with the general hedonistic purpose at the back of the institution of any moral rule or the construction of any moral notion. There is, of course, no doubt that the individual will desire others to act so as to cause him pleasure, but on what grounds will he find acceptable that he should likewise do good to others? Locke endeavours to answer this question in a Commonplace Book entry 'Ethica' (1692). Once again he begins from the hedonistic thesis that a rational agent will act only with a view to obtaining pleasure. However, he does not avail himself of the 'universalisation' argument he employs in the case of justice: that if I accept it to be a law that others ought to act so as to give me pleasure I am bound to conclude that I ought to act so as to give them pleasure. He maintains that doing good to others is a source of pleasure for the agent: 'If . . . happynesse be our interest end & businesse tis evident the way to it is to love our neighbour as our self, for by that means we enlarge and secure our pleasures since then all the good we doe to them redoubles upon our selves & gives us an undecaying and uninterrupted pleasure' (MS C42. Fol.224). The pleasure Locke has in mind here is not that of receiving some benefit back from those to whom one has done good, but rather the satisfaction derived from the contemplation of one's own good deeds. However, he is forced to concede that this pleasure is not a universal fact. For those who find no satisfaction in 'acts of love and charity' the only reason for performing them is their consequences in the next life 'wherein god may put a distinction between those that did good & suffered & those who did evil and enjoyd by their different treatment there' (ibid.).

Locke's final appeal to future rewards and punishments weakens his attempt to estabish the Golden Rule as a moral principle. Given the theological framework of his ethics it follows that, *if* the rule is part of the law of nature, God will reward conformity to it and punish disobedience. But the question of whether or not it is part of the law can only be answered in terms of the pleasures and pains of this life.

That is, it must be shown that the rational agent whose major concern is personal happiness would choose to live in a world in which it was acknowledged that positive good ought to be done to others as well as to oneself.[27] Locke does provide a hedonistic justification with respect to justice, for the only alternative to justice is the dissolution of society and a condition of human existence in which no one could achieve happiness. However, the individual considering the Golden Rule is not faced with this kind of alternative. A world in which no one did positive good to others might still be just in that the negative precepts against harming others were acknowledged. In such a world the individual would be left alone to do good to himself, at least so long as he did not thereby harm others. The individual who does happen to take pleasure in the well-being of others will accept the Golden Rule as having a foundation in reason; but Locke has no answer for the rational hedonist who has no desire to perform altruistic acts of goodness, and who, therefore, opts for a world in which merely negative precepts against harming others are the only ones acknowledged. If the Golden Rule is to be founded in reason it must be shown that, quite apart from their concern or lack of concern for others, each and every individual has a reason for accepting its existence as a moral principle.

As well as the difficulty of providing a purely hedonistic reason for adopting the Golden Rule, there is another factor which militates against its acceptability as the fundamental law. Its having this status will not mean that it is a principle to be applied directly on all occasions when a moral judgment is called for. According to the description of what will count as the basis of natural law given in the *Essays,* the fundamental law will be one upon which other precepts are built and it will function as a standard against which they can be measured. On the criterion stated in 'Virtus' an action is virtuous if it contributes to human good, and vicious if it contributes to human harm. As, on Locke's account, things are good in that they are apt to cause pleasure, or at least diminish pain, and evil in that they are apt to cause pain, or at least diminish pleasure, this means that pleasure-producing actions will be denominated virtuous and pain-producing ones vicious. Moral notions appearing in the law of opinion may, therefore, be validated by determining whether the actions they signify really are productive of pleasure or pain. In its application, however, this test is not as simple as it sounds. Locke does not equate pleasure and pain with pleasant and painful bodily sensations, but is careful to include the pleasures and pains of the mind (II.xx.2). Nonetheless, he does conceive all pleasures and pains as introspectable feelings.[28] In the shorthand Journal entry for 16 July 1676, he writes: 'God has so framed the constitutions of our minds and bodies that several things are apt to produce in both of them pleasure and pain, delight and trouble, by ways that we know not, but for ends suitable to His goodness and wisdom' (*Essays*, p.265). This suggests a limited range of objects which can be identified as pleasure or pain producing. Yet what Locke emphasises in the *Essay* is not merely the subjectivity, but the relativity of pleasure and pain; what is an object of pleasure for one person often is not so for another:

> The Mind has a different relish, as well as the Palate. . . . Hence it was . . . that the Philosophers of old did in vain enquire, whether *Summum bonum* consisted in Riches, or bodily Delights, or Virtue, or Contemplation. . . . For as pleasant Tastes depend not on the things themselves, but their agreeableness to this or that particular Palate. . . . So the greatest Happiness consists, in having those things, which produce the greatest Pleasure; and in the absence of those, which cause any disturbance, any pain. Now these, to different Men, are very different things. (II.xxi.55)

'Good' and 'evil' being terms which refer to the causes of pleasure and pain, what things are good and what evil will be relative to the individual. This consequence is stated explicitly in 'Of Ethick in General': 'For good & bad being relative terms doe not denote any thing in the nature of the thing but only the relation it beares to an other in its aptnesse & tendency to produce in it pleasure or pain. And thus we see & say that w[ch] is good for one man is bad for another' (MS C28, §7 and in King, 2, p.128). In the same paper Locke remarks on the empirical fact of the diversity of morals. Apart from things absolutely necessary for the preservation of society 'all other actions . . . in some Countrys or Societys . . . are virtues in others vices & in others indifferent' (ibid., §5, and in King, 2, p.126). If actions are to count as virtues or vices according as they are productive of good or evil this situation would appear inevitable. It will not be merely a diversity of moral opinions, some of which may be true and others false, but a relativity of morals, for what is in fact virtuous or vicious in any given society will be determined by the particular relish of the members of the society expressed in the moral notions they frame. The definition of virtue and vice as the doing of good and harm respectively cannot, therefore, serve as a criterion for deciding which of two conflicting moral opinions truly reflect the content of an immutable natural law binding on all men at all times. If good and evil, in the sense of producers of felt pleasure and pain, are to be the determinants of the virtue and vice of kinds of actions there can be no such immutable law.

In the idyllic passage in the *Second Treatise* Locke describes the condition which would obtain were there universal conformity to the law of nature as 'a state of peace, good will, mutual assistance, and preservation'. The law of nature which he hopes to demonstrate is, then, not merely a system of rules aimed at preventing clashes between individuals as in their various ways they go about the quest for happiness; it is morality of love or benevolence, one which, while not requiring that the agent always does the best thing possible, does include precepts enjoining the doing of positive good to others. The problem is that the premises from which he begins lead in the direction of a morality consisting solely in precepts designed to secure the conditions under which each individual is left free to achieve happiness by his own effort. In the world in which this morality is established the individual cannot expect to receive any positive assistance from others, nor can he be expected to give it to others. For Locke, men are social beings by inclination as well as by necessity. Except for those few who forsake the law of reason and live by the rule of force, individuals are not malevolently inclined towards their fellows; but this does not entail that they have innate feelings of benevolence with respect to one another. The rational hedonist may well derive pleasure as well as profit from the company of others, but his reason in no way demands that he should have any interest in doing good to others. Given the interest he does have in the existence of society he will acknowledge rules which curb and restrain the exorbitant desires of men as an essential part of morality. If further he accepts the proposition that all men are God's workmanship he will acknowledge the duty of charity. But what he will thus far have accepted is only a minimal system of morality made up of precepts which are necessary if society and the individuals in it are to be preserved. It is a minimal morality of this kind which Locke has in mind in a Journal entry for 13 July 1678: 'If he [man] finds that god has made him & all other men in a state wherein they cannot subsist without society & has given them judgment to discern what is capable of preserving that society can he but conclude that he is obliged & y^t^ God requires him to follow those rules wch conduce to the preserving of society (MS f.3, Fol.202).[29] Even in the polemic against innate morality, where he is intent on showing the diversity of moral opinions among mankind, Locke admits that those virtues 'that are absolutely necessary to hold society together' are universally acknowledged, though he adds that these 'commonly too are neglected betwixt distinct Societies' (I.iii.10). But he is obviously concerned to find a rationally acceptable foundation for other virtues besides those essential to the existence of any society whatsoever. There can be little doubt that he sees the Golden Rule as being in some way the basis of a richer morality.[30] Yet he fails to provide a satisfactory reason for this rule, nor does he make any real attempt to derive the other precepts of morality from it. Further, the criterion of virtue and vice it suggests is inadequate as a means of deciding between conflicting moral opinions.

For Locke, of course, the New Testament expresses the true moral law. The Golden Rule is a major precept of Gospel morality and the reason why he did not produce even an outline of a demonstrative system of morals may be that he could not see how that rule was to be established as the fundamental law of nature. The argument of 'Morality' – set out as it is with definitions and axioms – is Locke's most systematic attempt to derive moral precepts from what he takes to be self-evident truths about man and the human condition. The major difficulty he runs into is indicated by the definition of civility given at the end of the paper: 'Civility is noe thing but outward expressing of good will & esteem or at least of noe contempt or hatred' (MS c28, Fol.140). The virtue is at first presented as enjoining a positive good done to others, but Locke settles for a negative precept forbidding malice. Locke's general problem is compounded by his acknowledgement (in a Journal entry for 25 January 1676) that '[there] are virtues & vices antecedent to & abstract from society, v.g. love of god. unnatural lust' (MS f1, Fol.123). If, as has been maintained here, Locke conceives the synthetic part of the demonstration of morality as an 'historical' account of the way in which the various moral notions develop in the course of man's social existence, it is difficult to see how he can accommodate these virtues and vices which are abstract from society. Or, at least, it would seem that such notions cannot be built upon the same fundamental law from which the social virtues are supposed to derive.[31]

At the end of his career Locke wrote *A Paraphrase and Notes on the Epistles of St Paul* (published posthumously in parts 1705–7). This work includes as preface an essay on the correct method of reading St Paul – and by extension all of Scripture – so as to understand the divine revelation. Briefly, the reader is advised to consider the text as a whole and approach it free from preconceptions and opinions derived from learned commentators: 'He that would understand St Paul right, must understand his terms, in the sense he uses them, and not as they are appropriated, by each man's particular philosophy, to conceptions that never entered the mind of the apostle' (*Works*, 8, p.21). Remarks such as this on the reading of Scripture may seem remote from Locke's concern with ethics. However, it is to be remembered that the crisis in the epistemology of morals he encountered at the beginning of his career (and which he tried to resolve by appealing to a rationally discernible natural law) arose from the Sectary's appeal to Scripture. The true content of morality, Locke tells us in *A Second Vindication of the Reasonableness of Christianity,* has by Christ's teaching been 'established into a legible law, so far surpassing all that philosophy and human reason attained to, or could possibly make effectual to all degrees of mankind' (*Works,* 7, p.188). The morality is legible, but it must be read aright:

> We are all men, liable to errors, and infected with them; but have this sure way to preserve ourselves, every one, from danger by them, if, laying aside sloth, carelessness, prejudice, party, and a reverence of men, we betake ourselves, in earnest, to the study of the way to salvation, in those holy writings, wherein God has revealed it from heaven, and proposed it to the world, seeking our religion, where we are sure it is in truth to be found, comparing spiritual things with spiritual things. (*Works,* 8, p.23)

We gain the rewards of heaven by the performance of our moral duties here on earth. This conclusion to his essay on the understanding of St Paul's epistles expresses his final thoughts on the problem of moral knowledge.

VIII

THE MORAL AGENT

The preceding chapters have for the most part been concerned with what may be called Locke's theory of the nature of morality; that is, with his account of moral obligation and his attempt to establish a theory of moral knowledge consentient with the principles of his general epistemology. In Locke's opinion, however, this theoretical enquiry constitutes only the first part of ethics. In a Commonplace Book entry headed 'Ethica' (1693) he writes:

> There be two parts of Ethicks the one is the rule wch men are generally in the right in though perhaps they have not deduced them as they should from their true principles. The other is the true motives to practice them & the ways to bring men to observe them & these are generally either not well known or not rightly applyd. Without this latter moral discourses are such as men hear with pleasure & approve of. The mind being generally delighted with truth especially if handsomly expressed. But all this is but the delight of speculation. Something else is required to practice, wch will never be till men are made alive to virtue & can taste it. (MS c28, Fol. 113)

Making men alive to virtue is the chief task Locke allots to the educator. As he puts it in *Some Thoughts Concerning Education*:

> 'Tis Vertue . . . direct Vertue, which is the hard and valuable Part to be aim'd at in Education. . . . All other Considerations and Accomplishments should give way and be postpon'd to this. This is the solid and substantial Good which Tutors should not only read Lectures, and talk of, but the Labour and Art of Education should furnish the Mind with, and fasten there, and never cease till the young Man had a true Relish of it, and placed his Strength, his Glory, and his Pleasure in it. (§70)

Locke's educational theory is itself founded on a psychology of human action.

1. Locke's psychology of action is set out in most detail in the much revised chapter 'Of Power' in the *Essay*, and here it is intertwined with a discussion of human freedom. For Locke it is of the

utmost importance that the moral philosopher should establish the fact of human freedom. Unless we are free we cannot be moral agents, and those who view human action as a kind of mechanical operation 'take away . . . all Moral Rules whatsoever, and leave not a possibility to believe any such, to those who cannot conceive, how any thing can be capable of a Law, that is not a free Agent: and . . . they must necessarily reject all Principles of Vertue, who cannot *put Morality and Mechanism together*; which are not very easy to be reconciled, or made consistent' (I.iii.14). Yet Locke has often been interpreted as maintaining a determinist theory of action. We are inevitably carried along in what we do by our innate desire for personal pleasure and aversion to pain, these being the causal determinants of all our action, or at least of all those which can be said to be free in the sense that we are not forced to their performance by factors external to ourselves. While Locke does to some extent subscribe to a quasi-mechanistic theory of hedonic gravitation, he also develops a quite different theory according to which genuinely free actions are explained not causally but in terms of the agent's reasons. This latter theory may be found in embryo even in his earliest discussion of freedom in Draft C; however, it comes into prominence with the revisions he introduces in the second and subsequent edition of the *Essay*.

Locke conceives power as two-fold: active power, or the capacity to bring about change, and passive power, or the capacity to receive change. Sensation furnishes us with a clear and distinct idea of passive power, for we constantly observe the sensible qualities of the things about us to undergo change. As we cannot conceive that there is a change in anything without there being something to bring it about, observation of bodies in the world does suggest the idea of active power.[1] Yet the idea thus obtained is obscure. All action, Locke maintains, consists either in thinking or motion, or a combination of these, and our observation of bodies is confined to their motion. We see one billiard-ball strike another and so communicate its motion, but the motion in both these bodies is a passion rather than an action; we never see the actual production or initiation of motion (II.xxi.4). For a clear and distinct idea of active power we must turn to reflection: 'we find in our selves a *Power* to begin or forbear, continue or end several actions of our minds, and motions of our Bodies, barely by a thought or preference of the mind ordering, or as it were commanding the doing or not doing such or such a particular action. This *Power* . . . is that which we call the *Will*' (II.xxi.5). The will, then, is the mind's power to produce actions. Locke includes under the term 'action', the forbearance as well as the performance of an action, for the agent may be said equally to act when he consciously refrains from doing something proposed to him as when he actually does it (II.xxi.28).

Locke begins the discussion of human freedom by clarifying the key concepts involved. Reflection informs us that our power to initiate, continue or put an end to actions is limited in extent, and thence 'arise the *Ideas* of *Liberty* and *Necessity*' (II.xxi.7). Liberty is opposed to necessity and the former should not be confused with volition:

> *Volition* . . . is an Act of the Mind knowingly exerting that Dominion it takes it self to have over any part of the Man, by imploying it in, or withholding it from any particular Action. . . . *Liberty*, on the other side, is the power a Man has to do or forbear doing any particular Action, according as its doing or forbearance has the actual preference in the Mind, which is the same thing as to say, according as he himself *wills* it. (II.xxi.15)

Locke also differentiates between the agent's liberty, or freedom in his actions, and his voluntary actions. In illustration of the difference he cites the case of a man who awakes to find himself locked in a room with a friend he had been longing to see. As the man in this situation prefers to remain in the room rather than go out, his staying there is, Locke maintains, a voluntary act, it is something he does willingly. Yet the man cannot be said to act freely, for, as he was asleep when conveyed into the room he had no alternative but to enter it, and as the door is now locked he has no alternative but to remain. Therefore, '*Voluntary . . . is not opposed to Necessary; but to Involuntary.* For a Man may preferr what he can do, to what he cannot do; the State he is in, to its absence or change, though Necessity has made it in it self unalterable' (II.xxi.11). Nonetheless, though volition is not sufficent to constitute freedom, it is essential to freedom, for all involuntary acts are necessary. For example, no one would consider a man a free agent when by a convulsive movement of his arm he strikes himself or his friend, or when his bodily movements are a manifestation of St Vitus Dance. Such behaviour is quite unthinking and just as much under necessity as are the mechanical movements of inanimate bodies: '*Liberty* cannot be, where there is no Thought, no Volition, no Will; but there may be Thought, there may be Will, there may be Volition, where there is no *Liberty*' (II.xxi.8).[2] Nor is it only convulsive bodily movements which come under the heading of necessity; Locke accepts that there are occasions when 'a boisterous Passion hurries our Thoughts, as a Hurricane does our Bodies, without leaving us the liberty of thinking on other things, which we would rather chuse', and then we cannot be said to act as free agents, or exercise the power of liberty (II.xxi.12). In Locke's usage, an action is voluntary provided it is in accord with the agent's will or preference, but it manifests the agent's freedom only when circumstances are such that there are genuinely open alternatives between which he may settle his preferences.

As both the will, or the capacity for acts of volition, and freedom, or liberty, are powers it is a category mistake to ascribe freedom (or the lack of it) to the will; hence the traditional question of the freedom of the will is unintelligible: 'For who is it that sees not, that *Powers* belong only to *Agents*, and *are Attributes only of Substances, and not of Powers* themselves? So that this way of putting the Question, *viz.* whether the *Will be free*, is in effect to ask, whether the *Will* be a Substance, an Agent, or at least to suppose it' (II.xxi.16). The debate over free will derives from a conception of the will as a special faculty existing within the person. But, Locke points out, if we postulate a faculty, or agent, which does our willing for us we should equally be prepared to accept faculties for all the other actions we perform and 'make a speaking *Faculty*, and a walking *Faculty*, and a dancing *Faculty*, by which those Actions are produced' (II.xxi.17).[3]

Just as one power cannot be intelligibly ascribed to another, so also one cannot be said to operate upon another. Thus, it is improper to talk of the will operating on the agent's power of understanding, or *vice versa*. This is not to say that our thoughts have nothing to do with our will:

> this or that actual Thought may be the occasion of Volition, or exercising the power a Man has to chuse; or the actual choice of the Mind, the cause of actual thinking on this or that thing: As the actual singing of such a Tune, may be the occasion of dancing such a Dance, and the actual dancing of such a Dance, the occasion of singing such a Tune. But in all these, it is not one *power* that operates on another: But it is the Mind that operates, and exerts these Powers; it is the Man that does the Action, it is the Agent that has power, or is able to do. (II.xxi.19)

However, the link between thinking and willing is stronger than this suggests. It is not merely that only thinking beings are capable of willing and that their acts of will may be occasioned by some of their thoughts; as what is willed is always the doing or forbearing of some action proposed to thought, willing must always be occasioned by thought. Locke brings out the connections between the understanding and the will in a paper titled 'Judging-Election-Resolution':

> Judging is a bare action of the understanding, whereby a man, several objects being proposed to him, takes one of them to be

> best for him. . . . Election . . . is, when a man judging any thing to be best for him, ceases to consider, examine, and inquire any farther concerning that matter; for, till a man comes to this, he has not chosen, the matter still remains with him under deliberation, and not determined. Here, then, comes in the will, and makes Election voluntary, by stopping in the mind any farther inquiry and examination. (King, 2, p.106)[4]

Locke uses words such as 'ordering', 'directing', 'choosing', 'preferring' and 'volition' to refer to the act of willing, but he points out that these do not exactly capture what it is to will. For example, a man may consider flying and walking and settle his preference on the former, but it could hardly be said that he wills to fly (II.xxi.15). In order properly to will, the agent must not only consider alternatives and settle his preference on one, he must at the time believe there to be some alternative open to him other than the action he chooses or prefers (even if it is only the alternative of not performing that action).

Locke's insistence on the element of deliberation and the belief in alternatives in the act of willing sharpens the distinction he wants to draw between the power of willing and the power of freedom. It is clear that the agent may will, and so perform, a specific action in the mistaken belief that there were other alternatives open to him; or he may will an action only to find that its performance is not open to him. In neither case does the agent act freely, and in the latter case he may be said to be balked in carrying through what he wills. Locke has in mind occasions when we are so balked in one of the accounts he gives of necessity:

> Where-ever Thought is wholly wanting, or the power to act or forbear according to the direction of Thought, there *Necessity* takes place. This in an Agent capable of Volition, when the beginning or continuation of any Action is contrary to that preference of his Mind, is called *Compulsion*; when the hind'ring or stopping any Action is contrary to his Volition, it is called *Restraint*. (II.xxi.13)

However, if compulsion and restraint is taken as definitive of necessity, a free action cannot be simply one in which the agent does not act under necessity. The man in the room with his friend may settle his preference on remaining in the mistaken belief that the door is unlocked and he could leave. In this case he will have willed to remain; and he cannot be said to be under compulsion or restraint, for by definition these involve a person's being forced to behave in a manner *contrary to the preference of his mind.*

Elsewhere Locke does give an account of necessity, or lack of freedom, which rules out the possibility of the man's remaining in the room being a free action: 'Where-ever any performance or forbearance are not equally in a Man's power; where-ever doing or not doing, will not equally follow upon the preference of his mind directing it, there he is not *Free*, though perhaps the Action may be voluntary' (II.xxi.8). Thus, the agent can be said to act freely only when the circumstances are such that had his preference been otherwise, he would have acted otherwise. On the other side, notwithstanding the care he takes to distinguish between a voluntary and a free action, Locke tends to conflate the power of willing and the power of freedom. Thus, the initial definition of the will as a power to produce actions barely by a preference of the mind given at II.xxi.5, is very nearly identical with the definition of liberty given at II.xxi.15. This is not due merely to carelessness on Locke's part; it reflects an ambiguity in his notion of willing. He conceives an act of willing as the causal antecedent of actions which cannot be explained either as convulsive bodily movements or as the result of factors which compelled the agent. Now if this act is conceived as the cause which brings a particular action about, it must be combined with the power of freedom; for were the agent not free to do what he willed that action would not be brought about. But he also thinks of willing as a process of deliberation and decision making preceding an action or the attempt to act. Understood thus, the agent may will yet not be free to bring the willed action about; and, as the action is not performed, his willing is, of course, not the cause of his performing it. More will be said about this ambiguity below.

According to Locke the question of whether the will is free is unintelligible; however, the question of whether a man is free can be asked. He answers in the affirmative:

> if I can, by a thought, directing the motion of my Finger, make it move, when it was at rest, or *vice versa*, 'tis evident, that in respect of that, I am free: and if I can, by a like thought of my Mind, preferring one to the other, produce either words, or silence, I am at liberty to speak, or hold my peace: and *as far as this Power reaches, of acting, or not acting, by the determination of his own Thought preferring either, so far is a Man free.* (II.xxi.21)

That we can on very many occasions thus initiate actions or forebear their performance is evident to experience; and that the agent should be able to do what he wills is, Locke concludes, all the human freedom that can be demanded. However, he goes on to discuss two further questions which he says philosophers have seen as relevant to the debate concerning freedom: 'whether a man be free to will', and 'whether he be free to will which of the alternatives open to him he pleases'.

Locke initially answers the first of these questions in the negative: '*Willing* or *Volition* being an Action, and Freedom consisting in a power of acting, or not acting, *a Man in respect of willing, or the Act of Volition, when any Action in his power is once proposed to his Thoughts, as presently to be done, cannot be free'* (II.xxi.23). The main argument for this conclusion is as follows: It is 'unavoidable' that an action, the performance or non-performance of which depends upon the agent's will, be either performed or not performed, or, in Locke's words, it must either 'exist or not exist'. As the existence of such an action depends upon the agent's willing its performance and its non-existence upon his willing its non-performance, it is therefore 'absolutely necessary' that he will the one or the other. To will something is to prefer it to the other open alternatives; hence, Locke concludes:

> it is unavoidably necessary to prefer the doing, or forbearance, of an Action in a Man's power, which is once so proposed to his thoughts; a Man must necessarily *will* the one, or the other of them, upon which preference, or volition, the action, or its forbearance, certainly follows, and is truly voluntary: But the act of volition, or preferring one of the two, being that which he cannot avoid, a Man in respect of that act of *willing,* is under a necessity, and so cannot be free. (ibid.)

However, if this conclusion is to be treated as anything other than a tautology it cannot be said to follow from Locke's premises. The 'unavoidability' and 'absolute necessity' to which he refers both amount to logical necessity. The first premise is the logical truth that any action the performance or non-performance of which is willed by the agent is an action which is either performed or not performed, and this is just a special case of the broader logical truth that any action is either performed or not performed. The second premise is also a logical truth: that any action which is performed because its performance is willed or not performed because its non-performance is willed is an action with respect to which either its performance or non-performance has been willed. The most that can be validly derived from these premises concerning any action once proposed to the agent's thoughts is that *if* he in fact performs that action and its being performed is due to his so willing then he has so willed, and similarly if he does not perform that action and its being not performed is due to his so willing then he has so willed. This is a necessary (and obviously trivial) truth. Locke, however, sees the argument as establishing the substantive claim that whenever an action is proposed to the agent as within his power it must, as a matter of psychological necessity, elicit a separate act of willing either its performance or non-performace.

Locke's argument fails to establish his conclusion. Moreover, the conclusion would appear to be false. Certainly when an action is proposed to him the agent may perform an act of will in that he considers the alternatives of doing or not doing it and settles his preference upon one or the other. But there is clearly another possibility; he may think of an action as within his power without settling his preference either way. There are actions concerning which we do not deliberate even though we are aware that it is open to us either to perform or not perform them. These actions we simply do or do not do. As it is logically necessary that any action proposed to the agent must either be performed or not performed, Locke's conclusion will follow if preferring to do a proposed action is construed as actually doing it and preferring to forbear it is construed as actually forbearing it. But then the *act* of preferring or willing drops out of sight; it is no longer a separate act at the back of the agent's public behaviour, but just his doing or forbearing various actions within his power.

Locke's tendency to conflate the power of willing and the power of freedom has already been noted. If freedom or liberty is conceived as the power to do or forbear a particular action it would seem that we are free whenever these two alternatives are open to us. On this conception of freedom a great proportion of our everyday actions may be called free; for in most of our conscious activity we do have alternatives open to us in that we are not forced to do what we do. However, Locke assumes that whenever we are free in this sense our doing or forbearing an action issues from an antecedent act of will:

> considering the vast number of voluntary Actions, that succeed one another every moment that we are awake, in the course of our Lives, there are but few of them that are thought on or proposed to the *Will*, 'till the time they are to be done: And in all such Actions . . . the Mind in respect of *willing* has not a power to act, or not to act . . . it cannot avoid some determination concerning them, let the Consideration be as short, the Thought as quick, as it will, it either leaves the Man in the state he was before thinking, or changes it; continues the Action, or puts an end to it. Whereby it is manifest, that it orders and directs one in preferences to, or with neglect of the other, and thereby either the continuation, or change becomes unavoidably voluntary. (II.xxi.24)

The 'voluntary actions, that succeed one another every moment we are awake' are apparently those which we do willingly. However, when Locke talks at the end of the passage of actions becoming 'unavoidably voluntary' he means that they are preceded by acts of will (i.e. at least some deliberation culminating in a preference to do one thing rather than another), and he supposes that whenever we act willingly our actions must be voluntary in this sense. But, even on Locke's own account of voluntary action, there seems no reason why all voluntary actions should be preceded by acts of will. The man locked in the room might be so delighted to see his friend that he does not, even for an instant, think of the alternative of leaving; yet in this case it is surely still true to say that he prefers to stay, and, this is all that Locke stipulates as necessary to render the act voluntary. Such voluntary actions which are not preceded by acts of will may still be said to be done freely provided there are alternatives open to the agent, in which case there will be freedom in respect of action without an exercise of the power of volition.

Locke's supposition that all that the agent does when he is not under necessity must issue from an act of will, derives from his general conception of power. We postulate powers in substances in order to account for the changes we observe in them. When a change in a substance is wrought by something external to it the substance itself manifests only a passive power, or an aptness to undergo that change. On the other hand, when a substance initiates change either in itself or in other things its doing so manifests active power. Thus, in the case of a human action such as walking if the person's ceasing to stand still and beginning to walk is a change which is forced upon him he manifests only a passive power, but if his walking is something he initiates it springs from an exercise of the active power which Locke calls the will. Locke realises that forbearing to perform a given action can be said to be something a person does. Therefore, when conditions are such that this forbearance is not forced upon the person it must also be explained in terms of an exercise of his will. This explains Locke's over-hasty conclusion that we are under a necessity to perform an act of will whenever an action within our power is proposed to us. The existence or non-existence of any such action must be caused by something. As the cause is not some force acting upon the agent and either compelling or restraining him, it can only be his act of will; even though Locke has to admit that in most cases the alleged act is virtually simultaneous with the performance or forbearance of the action.

Locke's answer to the second question of whether a man is free to will either of the alternatives before him is also in the negative or, to be more exact, he dismisses the question as absurd:

> to ask, whether a Man be at liberty to will either Motion, or Rest; Speaking, or Silence; which he pleases, is to ask, whether a Man can *will*, what he *wills*; or be pleased with what he is pleased with. . . . they, who can make a Question of it, must suppose one Will to determine the Acts of another, and another to determine that; and so on *in infinitum*. (II.xxi.5)

The infinite regress argument deployed here depends upon the assumption that if the agent's willing *A* rather than *B* is to be free it must be preceded by a further act of willing to will *A*. The regress is both infinite and vicious; for this second act can be free only if it is itself preceded by a still further act, and if the series of acts of will had a beginning in one which was not free (i.e. not preceded by an act of will) its lack of freedom would vitiate the freedom of all the others. This argument is a familiar move in the determinist critique of libertarianism, the determinist point being that, whereas we can be said to will to do *A*, our willing it is causally conditioned. The libertarian, however, may reply that the assumption upon which the argument rests is unwarranted; our acts of will are free in that they are not preceded by anything, but are themselves the first cause of what we do.[5] The standard determinist counter-move is that if the act of will is uncaused it is not free but a random or chance act, its randomness being passed on to the action willed. Locke's position is somewhat different. The infinite regress he envisages is not so much one of causal determinants but of reasons. From Draft C onwards his main thesis is that the agent's liberty with respect to which alternative he wills would be an imperfection in that it would make his choice arbitrary and hence irrational. The revisions made in the chapter 'Of Power' are all aimed at clarifying his view that properly free actions are those which are grounded in rational decisions.

2. In the first edition of the *Essay* Locke's thesis is that what the agent wills, or the direction he gives to his actions, is constantly determined by his apprehension of what is apt to produce the most pleasure and the least pain for him. As each individual's happiness consists in pleasure and the absence of pain, happiness is said to be the general determinant of the will. On Locke's hedonistic doctrine of good and evil this means that *'the greater Good is that alone which determines the Will'* (II.xxi.29, 1st ed.).[6] When the object of our will is the good or evil immediately attendant upon a given action we cannot be mistaken about our greater good: 'For as to present Happiness and Misery, when that alone comes in consideration, and the consequences are quite removed, *a Man never chuses amiss*; he knows what best pleases him, and that, he actually prefers.

Things in their present enjoyment are what they seem; the apparent and real good are, in this case, always the same' (I.xxi.58). As the pleasures and pains attendant upon an action in many cases are not confined to the action itself, it is possible for us to go astray in what we will. We will amiss whenever we disregard or fail to recognise the future pleasures and pains consequent upon an action. In these cases, '*Things* come to be *represented* to our desires *under deceitful appearances . . . by the Judgment* pronouncing wrongly concerning them' (II.xxi.61).

In the second edition Locke shifts from an emphasis on the intellectual apprehension of good as the motive determining the will to what might be taken as an account of the non-intellectual roots of action:

> *what is it that determines the Will in regard to our Actions?* And that upon second thoughts I am apt to imagine is not, as is generally supposed, the greater good in view: But some (and for the most part the most pressing) *uneasiness* a Man is at present under. This is that which successively determines the *Will,* and sets us upon those Actions, we perform. (II.xxi.31)[7]

He gives two reasons for his modified account of what moves the will. In the first place, it is evident that individuals do often acknowledge their greatest happiness to lie in one direction yet voluntarily act in a contrary direction. Locke cites the example of the drunkard destroying his health (II.xxi.35), and of those who by their mode of life risk the loss of the eternal joys of heaven (II.xxi.44). Hence, something more than the mind's apprehension of good is required to determine the will. Secondly, theoretical considerations show that the merely intellectual apprehension of an absent good cannot move the will; for, 'tis against the nature of things, that what is absent should operate, where it is not' (II.xxi.37). The idea of an absent good can, of course, be brought before the mind, but it can have no efficacy with respect to action unless accompanied by an uneasiness in the agent; 'Till then the *Idea* in the mind of whatever good, is there only like other *Ideas,* the object of bare unactive speculation; but operates not on the will, nor sets us on work' (ibid.).

Locke's conception of uneasiness is, to say the least of it, shadowy. At times it is presented as an introspectively identifiable item of our mental life, as when he writes, 'it seems to me evident, that the will, or power of setting us upon one action in preference to all others, is determin'd in us, by *uneasiness*: and whether this be not so, I desire every one to observe in himself' (II.xxi.38). If, as the word suggests, Locke thinks of uneasiness as some sort of violent feeling it is obvious to experience that it is not operative in all our voluntary actions.[8] At other times, however, he appears to more or less equate uneasiness with desire; for every voluntary action is said to be determined by 'the uneasiness of desire, fixed on some absent good, either negative, as idolency to one in pain; or positive, as enjoyment of pleasure' (II.xxi.33). Yet he has explained earlier that in some circumstances we may will something which is contrary to what we desire (II.xxi.30). Again he uses 'uneasiness' as a blanket term covering a variety of mental states of the agent; for example, aversion, fear, anger, envy, shame (II.xxi.39); hunger, heat, cold, weariness, the desire for honour, power, or riches (II.xxi.45). In fact Locke's uneasiness is best understood as the state the agent is in whenever he recognises some factor as vitiating his happiness. It is because our general aim in our actions is always our own happiness that uneasiness is able to determine the will; whatever states may be grouped under that term, they are all incompatible with our happiness:

> whilst we are under any *uneasiness,* we cannot apprehend our selves happy, or in the way to it. Pain and *uneasiness* being . . . inconsistent with happiness; spoiling the relish, even of those good things which we have. . . . And therefore that, which of course determines the choice of our *will* to the next action, will always be the removing of pain . . . as the first and necessary step towards happiness. (II.xxi.36)

We experience uneasiness, then, not when we simply judge that the possession of some absent good would make us happier, but when our consciousness of the lack of that good makes us unhappy. Of course, there may be times when the agent is content with his present situation, and therefore does not suffer any uneasiness. At these times he will continue in whatever course of action he happens to be following; 'The motive, for continuing in the same State of Action, is only the present satisfaction in it' (II.xxi.29). Strictly speaking, what uneasiness brings about is a change in the direction of the will.

As at any one time there may be a number of different factors vitiating our happiness, so we may suffer a number of uneasinesses simultaneously. Of these sundry uneasinesses it is the 'most pressing', 'the most important and urgent' which determine the will (II.xxi.31, 40). Thus far Locke's introduction of the notion of uneasiness serves to emphasise the determinism nascent in his denial that the agent can be free to will which alternative he pleases. Indeed, the doctrine that the will is determined by the most pressing uneasinesses would appear to differ little, if at all, from the mechanistic doctrine he declares to be inconsistent with the existence of morality. But while the notion of uneasiness strengthens the determinist thread in Locke's theory of action at the same time it helps him clarify his conception of what it is for the agent to act freely.

According to the dominant doctrine of freedom in the first edition of the *Essay*, the agent acts freely provided the alternative of doing or forbearing a proposed action is open to him, or within his power, and his doing or forbearing it is something he wills. However, the direction in which he wills, or the choice he makes, is itself determined; so that, while it is true to say of the agent that he could have done otherwise than he in fact did if he had chosen to, it is not true to say that he could have chosen otherwise. Locke grants that the agent is not free when what he does springs from 'a boisterous Passion' or (as he adds in the 2nd ed.) 'an impetuous *uneasiness*' such as love or anger (II.xxi.12, 53). But if the will is always determined by the most pressing or most urgent uneasiness experienced by the agent, it would seem that, even when the uneasiness is not of such intensity as to be called boisterous or impetuous, this must still negate freedom in action. However, Locke introduces a further feature in his theory of action, and with it a new conception of human freedom.

The further feature is the mind's capacity to stand back from what happens to be the most pressing uneasiness of the moment and examine whether the action prompted by that uneasiness really is conducive to the true happiness of the agent:

> There being in us a great many *uneasinesses* always solliciting, and ready to determine the *will*, it is natural ... that the greatest, and most pressing should determine the *will* to the next action; and so it does for the most part, but not always. For the mind having in most cases, as is evident in Experience, a power to *suspend* the execution and satisfaction of any of its desires, and so all, one after another, is at liberty to consider the objects of them; examine them on all sides, and weigh them with others. In this lies the liberty Man has; and from the not using of it right comes all that variety of mistakes, errors, and faults which we run into, in the conduct of our lives, and our endeavours after happiness; whilst we precipitate the determination of our *wills*, and engage too soon before due *Examination*. (II.xxi.47)

The difference between an impetuous uneasiness and those normally experienced is that the former is of such an intensity that the agent cannot suspend its execution and estimate the worth of the action it prompts; whilst in its grip 'we are not Masters enough of our own Minds to consider thoroughly, and examine fairly' (II.xxi.53). That in most cases we are able to stand back from the uneasiness pressing upon us does not mean that uneasiness ceases to have a role in the production of our actions. Locke holds that it is uneasiness which initiates the action the agent selects after a due examination: 'For when he has once chosen it, and thereby it is become a part of his Happiness, it raises desire, and that proportionably gives him *uneasiness,* which determines his *will,* and sets him at work in pursuit of his choice on all occasions that offer' (II.xxi.56). But then uneasiness is a state which the agent has, as it were, induced in himself; it is his desire for the object which he has decided best suits with his idea of happiness.

Locke does talk of men being under a necessity to suspend and examine the uneasiness which press upon them, but he does not mean that they are causally necessitated in this:

> the inclination, and tendency of their nature to happiness is an obligation, and motive to them, to take care not to mistake, or miss it; and so necessarily puts them upon caution, deliberation, and wariness, in the direction of their particular actions, which are the means to obtain it. Whatever necessity determines to the pursuit of real Bliss, the same necessity, with the same force establishes *suspence, deliberation,* and scrutiny of each successive desire, whether the satisfaction of it, does not interfere with our true happiness, and mislead us from it. (II.xxi.52)

The word 'obligation' is the clue to Locke's meaning. We are under a necessity to suspend our desires and deliberate with respect to them, not in the sense that we must do so, but in the sense that we ought to do so. The suspension and examination of our desires, Locke goes on to say, is something 'we are able to do; and when we have done it, we have done our duty' (ibid.).

The new view that freedom consists in the ability to suspend the causal sequence in which the most pressing uneasiness of the moment determines what the agent does leads Locke to qualify his original thesis that we cannot be free to will or not will with respect to a proposed action:

> Liberty 'tis plain consists in a Power to do, or not to do; to do, or forbear doing as we *will.* . . . But this seeming to comprehend only the actions of a Man consecutive to volition, it is farther enquired, whether he be at Liberty to *will,* or no? and to this it has been answered, that in most cases a Man is not at Liberty to forbear the act of volition; he must exert an act of his *will,* whereby the action proposed, is made to exist, or not to exist. But yet there is a case wherein a Man is at Liberty in respect of *willing,* and that is the chusing of a remote Good as an end to be pursued. Here a Man may suspend the act of his choice from being determined for or against the thing proposed, till he has examined, whether it be really of a nature in it self and consequences to make him happy, or no. (II.xxi.56, 5th ed.)[9]

Locke's position here is complex and may appear contradictory. He states that in *most* cases (not as he formerly thought in all cases) we are not at liberty to forbear the act of volition once the action is proposed; yet at II.xxi.47, he states that in *most* cases we do have the power to suspect the promptings of uneasiness and examine the alternatives before us, that is to forbear the act of volition. Here again it is important to keep in mind the ambiguity in Locke's notion of what it is to will. He introduces the will as that which explains actions in which the agent is neither compelled or restrained; such actions issue from the active power of the agent's will. Considered thus, the act of will tends to merge with the agent's performance or non-performance of the proposed action, and what he does might just as well be said to issue directly from the most pressing uneasiness. On the other hand, on the conception of an act of will as involving deliberation, the power to suspend the natural causation of uneasiness will be a necessary condition of this act. We are robbed of this power only when the most pressing uneasiness amounts to a boisterous passion. But having the power is not the same thing as exercising it. In most of the voluntary actions which succeed one another during our waking lives we do not deliberate, and, what is more, we have no occasion to deliberate. The suspension of action which allows for deliberation is called for only when the action proposed is one which may be contrary to the agent's overall and long-term goal of personal happiness. If the proposed action arouses no uneasiness in the agent so that he simply continues in the course of action he was upon, or if it does arouse uneasiness and he immediately changes his course of action so as to be rid of that uneasiness, he can be said to do what he does without deliberating about it. In these cases the agent may be said to be free in the sense that he is not forced (either by external circumstances or internal passions) to act in one way rather than another. His action being free in this sense, he can also be said to retain the power to stand back and deliberate. However, if there is no question of the non-performance (as in the first case) or the performance (as in the second case) of that action having consequences contrary to the agent's happiness there is no occasion to exercise that power; the agent simply has nothing to deliberate about.

An obvious circumstance in which deliberation may be called for is when the proposed action is of moral significance. Locke holds a mechanistic view of human action to be inimical to morality because it leaves no room for moral responsibility, and hence none for rewards and punishment. The power of suspending our uneasinesses and examining the alternatives (the reality of which power he takes to be evident to experience) is his answer to mechanism:

> And here we may see how it comes to pass, that a Man may justly incur punishment, though it be certain that in all the particular actions that he *wills,* he does, and necessarily does will that, which he then judges to be good. For though his *will* be always determined by that, which is judg'd good by his Understanding, yet it excuses him not: Because by a too hasty choice of his own making, he has imposed on himself wrong measures of good and evil. (II.xxi.56, 5th ed.)[10]

Were it the case that we could not but act in accord with the most pressing uneasiness of the moment, human action would be mechanically determined. However, we can form a general picture of what constitutes our happiness and we can judge whether or not a particular action will promote that happiness. Even when the agent ignores the long-term goal of happiness and immediately follows the prompting of uneasiness he is still free; for he might have exerted the power to check the determination of uneasinesss and have acted in accord with his judgment of the long term good and evil of the alternatives before him. This power is 'the hinge on which turns the *liberty* of intellectual Beings in their constant endeavours after, and a steady prosecution of true felicity' (II.xxi.52).

When it comes to particular actions the agent's freedom is a matter of degree:

> The stronger ties, we have, to an unalterable pursuit of happiness in general . . . the more are we free from any necessary determination of our *will* to any particular action, and from a necessary compliance with our desire, set upon any particular, and then appearing preferable good, till we have duly examin'd, whether it has a tendency to, or be inconsistent with our real happiness. (II.xxi.51)

At the bottom end of the scale are occasions when the agent follows his infallible knowledge of which action will give him the most immediate pleasure or the least immediate pain. Such actions may shade into those in which some boisterous passion renders deliberation impossible. But Locke warns against the excuse that when we knowingly do wrong it is because our passions are too strong for our moral judgment: 'Nor let any one say, he cannot govern his Passions, nor hinder them from breaking out, and carrying him into action; for what he can do before a Prince, or a great Man, he can do alone, or in the presence of God, if he will' (II.xxi.53). We are, therefore, most free when we choose to do that which we know to be morally right in the teeth of our inclination to do the opposite.

Although Locke continues to talk of uneasiness as determining the will even on those occasions when we stand back and deliberate on whether the proposed actions accord with our true happiness, the tenor of his later doctrine is that properly free actions spring, not from some occurrent feeling of the agent, but from reason. Uneasiness, considered as a feeling causing us to act in one way rather than another, needs to be checked by reason if we are to attain our ultimate happiness:

> Without Liberty the Understanding would be to no purpose: And without Understanding, Liberty (if it could be) would signify nothing. If a Man sees, what would do him good or harm, what would make him happy or miserable, without being able to move himself one step towards or from it, what is he the better for seeing? And he that is at liberty to ramble in perfect darkness, what is his liberty better than if he were driven up and down, as a bubble by the force of the wind? (II.xxi.67)

The universal desire for happiness is not a kind of gravitational force determining all our actions, but rather a general aim, or project, which provides a structure for our practical reasoning. If a given action within the agent's power will contribute to his general happiness in the sense that it will in the long term, at least, procure him a greater balance of pleasure than of pain, he has a reason for performing it; if the contrary is the case he has a reason for not performing it. On the other hand, without this constant desire for happiness, rational deliberation and choice would be impossible, for no reason could be given for our doing one thing rather than another. Locke insists that it is a perfection of our nature rather than a restraint or diminution of freedom that we should be determined 'to desire will, and act according to the last result of a fair *Examination*' (II.xxi.47). The supposition that we are able to choose an alternative contrary to this result makes freedom an imperfection:

> A perfect Indifferency in the Mind, not determinable by its last judgment of the Good or Evil, that is thought to attend its Choice, would be so far from being an advantage and excellency of any intellectual Nature, that it would be as great an imperfection, as the want of Indifferency to act, or not to act, till determined by the *Will*, would be an imperfection on the other side. (II.xxi.48. Cf. 1st ed., 30)

Such a freedom of indifferency would be an imperfection because it would divorce 'free' action from the understanding or reason:

> If to break loose from the conduct of Reason, and to want that restraint of Examination and Judgment, which keeps us from chusing or doing the worse, be *Liberty*, true Liberty, mad Men and Fools are the only Freemen. . . . The constant desire of Happiness, and the constraint it puts upon us to act for it, no

> Body, I think, accounts an abridgement of *Liberty*, or at least an abridgement of *Liberty* to be complain'd of. (II.xxi.50. Cf. 1st ed., 33)

It should be noted that Locke states only that the mind is *determinable* by its last judgment of good and evil, not that it is constantly so *determined*.[11] He is not committed to denying the possibility of irrational action. It is when we act as rational agents that we are not at liberty to will (in the sense of initiate) either of the alternatives open to us in a particular situation; if the reasons in favour of the first alternative outweigh those in favour of the second we cannot but elect to do the first rather than the second: 'the very end of our Freedom [is] that we might attain the good we chuse. And therefore every Man is put under a necessity by his constitution, as an intelligent Being, to be determined in *willing* by his own Thought and Judgment, what is best for him to do' (II.xxi.48, 5th ed.). Rational deliberation concerning a proposed action must come to an end somewhere. In Locke's view, it properly comes to an end when the agent has an understanding of what truly constitutes his happiness and when he has correctly estimated the relevance of the proposed action with respect to that happiness.

Locke's account of rational action may be termed a hedonistic theory of reasons for actions. It is, however, quite distinct from egoistic hedonism as a psychological theory offering a causal explanation of action. There is no inconsistency in rejecting egoistic hedonism as a psychological theory yet holding that the only adequate reason an agent can be given for performing an action is that it will in some way redound to his own happiness.[12] Locke does suppose that in all cases we must be moved to action by some psychological mechanism. Thus, as we have seen, he maintains that even when after due deliberation the agent has decided upon a course of action it is uneasiness which 'sets him at work in pursuit of his choice'. However, the concept of uneasiness is too broad and vague to be of much service in a causal explanation of human action.[13] Locke acknowledges that both the forbearance and the performance of a proposed action count as instances of the agent acting. He might, therefore, have concluded that action is not something human beings need to be spurred into, but rather that a person is always doing something even though what he is doing is sometimes best specified in terms of what he is refraining from.[14] On this picture the question is not so much what causes or initiates our action as what guides us in our acting. Being guided to act in a certain way is a matter of following rules; it is not a matter of being caused to act by some antecedent condition or occurrences.[15] Locke sees actions deliberately embarked upon subsequent to the suspension of pressing uneasiness as being determined by the guidance of reason.

> That in this state of Ignorance we short-sighted Creatures might not mistake true felicity, we are endowed with a power to suspend any particular desire, and keep it from determining the *will,* and engaging us in action. This is *standing still,* where we are not sufficiently assured of the way: Examination is *consulting a guide.* The determination of the *will* upon enquiry is *following the direction of that Guide*: And he that has a power to act, or not to act according as such determination directs, is a *free Agent.* (II.xxi.50)

According to Locke's second thoughts on the subject of human freedom, it is not sufficient for a free action that it springs from the agent's power of will, for the exercise of that power may itself be causally determined by what happens to be the most pressing uneasiness of the moment. To be properly free an action must be informed by the agent's judgment concerning the best thing to be done in the circumstances.[16] In many of our actions it may be that we do simply follow the determination of uneasiness; nevertheless, we are free agents so long as we retain the power to suspend this determination: we are free to act freely.

3. Locke's major concern in his discussion of freedom and the will is to accommodate moral responsibility and especially our responsibility for wrong-doing. Morally wrong actions derive from a kind of error; 'the Foundation of Vice [lies] in wrong Measures of Good' (IV.xx.16). We can be held responsible for such actions because the error is due to a failure to exert our power of suspending the uneasiness or desires pressing upon us and carry through an examination of the good or evil of the alternatives before us. The foundation of virtuous conduct, on the other hand, lies in this power of suspending the immediate satisfaction of our desires prior to the judgment of reason: 'the great Principle and Foundation of all Vertue and Worth, is placed in this, That a Man is able to *deny himself* his own Desires, cross his own Inclinations, and purely follow what Reason directs as best, tho' the Appetite lean the other way' (*Education,* §33). According to Locke's theory of reasons for actions, the only reason a person can be given for acting in one way rather than another is that the recommended action will in the end promote his own happiness. It is, therefore, incumbent upon Locke to show that the virtuous life is a reasonable choice notwithstanding, as he says in the *Essays,* that a great number of the virtues consist in our doing good to others at our own loss.

The task of proving the reasonableness of the virtuous life for the individual is distinct from that of founding the content of the moral law on reason. Given that it is rational to accept a world in which, for example, the rule of justice is established in preference to one without justice, it follows that we are all under a moral obligation to act justly; but, on Locke's account of obligation, there remains the question of the reason the agent has to conform to the rule when injustice is more profitable for him. In the case of the negative precepts of the law we will very often at least lack positive reasons for disobedience. Only those who live by the rule of force and prosecute a settled design against their fellows actually make it their interest to invade the property of others. Nevertheless, even those who do have some concern for fellowship are likely on occasion to find conformity to these precepts contrary to their advantage, and then they will be possessed of reasons for disobedience. Although he has difficulty in providing them with a rational foundation, Locke clearly regards actions and action dispositions which fall under notions such as liberality and civility as making for the general happiness of mankind, and therefore as good. Altruistic actions in general may be characterised as ones in which the agent strives to promote the interest or pleasure of someone other than himself. It would seem that the agent can be given no positive reason for performing such actions, and on those occasions when they can only be performed at his own loss he has a positive reason against them.

Locke's argument for the reasonableness of virtue turns on the possibility of rewards and punishments in the next life. The bare possibility that a life of virtue will earn reward, and a life of vice punishment, after death constitutes an overwhelming reason for living in accord with the moral law:

> The Rewards and Punishments of another Life, which the Almighty has established, as the Enforcements of his Law, are of weight enough to determine the Choice, against whatever Pleasure or Pain this Life can shew, when the eternal State is considered but in its bare possibility, which no Body can make any doubt of. . . . This is evidently so, though the vertuous Life here had nothing but Pain, and the vicious continual pleasure: which yet is for the most part quite otherwise. . . . But when infinite Happiness is put in one Scale, against infinite Misery in the other; if the worst, that comes to the pious Man, if he mistakes, be the best that the wicked can attain to, if he be in the right, Who can without madness run the venture? . . . Whereas on the other side, the sober Man ventures nothing against infinite Happiness to be got, if his Expectation comes to pass. If the good

> Man be in the right, he is eternally happy; if he mistakes, he is not miserable, he feels nothing. On the other side, if the wicked be in the right, he is not happy; if he mistakes, he is infinitely miserable. (II.xxi.70)

Locke's whole argument bears a striking resemblance to Pascal's famous 'wager' argument for belief in God. And, like Pascal, what he is arguing for is not simply the reasonableness of accepting a belief, but of adopting a specific way of life.[17]

Locke distinguishes between the life lived in accord with self-interest and the life lived in accord with the moral point of view in the eighth of the *Essays,* where he argues that the individual's own interest cannot be the basis of the law of nature. His argument for the reasonableness of virtue may be considered a defence of the latter against the former. Were there no chance of divine reward or punishment, it *would* be unreasonableness to act virtuously when such action contravened our private happiness.[18] In other words, it would be unreasonable to adopt the moral point of view and consider the virtue or vice of actions when we deliberate on what we ought to do:

> For if there be no Prospect beyond the Grave, the inference is certainly right, *Let us eat and drink,* let us enjoy what we delight in, *for to morrow we shall die.* This, I think, may serve to shew us the Reason, why, though all Men's desires tend to Happiness, yet they are not moved by the same Object. Men may chuse different things, and yet all chuse right, supposing them only like a Company of poor Insects, whereof some are Bees, delighted with Flowers, and their sweetness; others, Beetles, delighted with other kinds of Viands; which having enjoyed for a season, they should cease to be, and exist no more for ever. (II.xxi.55)

Given the fact of a future state of rewards and punishment it obviously will be in each person's self-interest to live virtuously. Even if the existence of such a state is not something which can be known with certainty, the bare possibility of eternal misery being consequent upon a refusal to adopt the moral point of view is sufficient to determine our judgment in favour of virtue. That it is reasonable to suppose the life of virtue to be in the agent's ultimate self-interest does not mean that there is really no distinction between it and a life lived in accord with self-interest. As argued in chapter III, the fact that a person adopts the moral point of view in the first place out of considerations of self-interest does not obviate the difference between his deciding what to do from that point of view and his deciding in the light of self-interest. In the particular situation he will take into consideration the virtue or vice of the alternatives before him, and these considerations will determine his judgment. From the point of view of self-interest, on the other hand, the virtue or vice of the alternatives is irrelevant. A self-interested person may in a given situation do what morality requires, but this will only be because in that situation the demands of morality happen to coincide with the demands of self-interest.

The heavenly reward of virtue is important in Locke's moral philosophy for another reason: it provides the final aim of all human existence. Because the tastes of individuals differ widely, and consequently they look upon quite different objects as making up their happiness, there is no *summum bonum* to be pursued upon earth. It is the joys of heaven alone which can constitute a proper object of desire for each and every individual: 'For that being intended for a State of Happiness, it must certainly be agreeable to every one's wish and desire: Could we suppose their relishes as different there as they are here, yet the Manna in Heaven will suite every one's Palate' (II.xxi.65). However, it is not simply because the reward of heaven is so constituted as to suit everyone's taste that it is the ultimate good. The heavenly state of happiness transcends any conception we can form from our earthly experience of pleasure; it is, as St Paul tells us, 'what *Eye hath not seen, Ear hath not heard, nor hath it entered into the Heart of Man to conceive*' (II.xxi.41, quoting I. Cor. 2:9). Nevertheless it is just this state which we are all – however obscurely – seeking. In his Journal for 26 September 1675, Locke reflects upon the fact that none of the objects which men pursue and place their happiness in are free from the charge of being ultimately unsatisfying to those who seek them. This is because 'in all those things there is really a deficiency, a dark side which whoever has the skill to shew cannot faile to produce contemp or dislike of it'. He goes on to say:

> We are so remote from true and satisfying happynesse in this world that we know not wherein it consists but yet soe much we apprehend it that we are sure it is beyond what all those imperfect things can afford us since it is said that noe body yet hath attempted to write against it to defend it, or give mankinde any disgust of it, everyone being by the strong impressions he findes on his owne mind convinced that happynesse is a state that hath noe imperfection nor liable to any exception.
> (MS, f.1, Fol.445–7)[19]

Locke in fact works with two conceptions of happiness. There is the imperfect happiness of individuals in this world, and this consists in the possession of those things which happen to give them pleasure and the absence of those things which happen to give them pain; but there is also the transcendent perfect happiness of heaven. The latter is completely beyond our mundane experience, but we have an inkling of it in so far as we recognise the inherent defectiveness of all earthly pleasure.

Locke's ethic is teleological in a double sense. The end of the law of nature is to facilitate the general happiness of mankind in this world. Locke does not make the mistake of supposing that obedience to the law must therefore promote each agent's personal happiness in this world. In his argument for the reasonableness of the virtuous life he tends to place most emphasis on the possibility of eternal misery being a consequence of vice. On the positive side what makes the virtuous life a proper object of choice for the individual is the belief that such a life in this world is the indispensable means to perfect happiness in the world to come. Locke's conception of the double end of human existence is well expressed in his Journal entry for 8 February 1677. After remarking that we must conclude man's faculties to have been given him so that he might procure the happiness which this world can provide, he goes on:

> It being . . . possible & at least probable that there is an other life where we shall give an account of our past actions in this to the grat god of heaven & earth here comes in another and the main grat concernment of mankinde & that is to know what those actions are that he is to doe what those are he is to avoid what that law is he is to live by here and shall be judg by hereafter. (MS, f.2, Fol.49–50, and in Aaron & Gibb, pp.85–8)

The knowledge necessary for encompassing the 'main great concernment' of each and every individual cannot be divorced from that necessary for the general well-being of mankind in this world, for the law according to which each individual will be judged hereafter is the law of the temporal and imperfect happiness of mankind.

4. Anyone convinced by Locke's argument for the reasonableness of virtue will coolly judge the life of virtue to be better than the life of vice or of pure self-interest. However, Locke has argued that such a cool judgment about the goodness of a course of action or of an object cannot of itself move the agent to act; unless it is accompanied by, or at least leads to, a state of uneasiness or desire in the agent, the intellectual acknowledgement that the virtuous life is the only means to attain the perfect happiness of heaven will not prompt him to act virtuously. Furthermore, it can hardly be denied that some human beings, at least, act out of a regard for virtue without ever having considered the rewards which may accrue to them or the punishments they may avoid. On Locke's theory such a spontaneous adoption of the life of virtue would appear quite inexplicable.

As we have seen, Locke holds that, as well as having the power to suspend the immediate operation of uneasiness, the mind is able to generate uneasiness with respect to that which, after a due examination, it has judged to be good: 'by a due consideration and examining any good proposed, it is in our power, to raise our desires, in a due proportion to the value of that good, whereby in its turn, and place, it may come to work upon the *will*, and be pursued' (II.xxi.46). Whatever objections may be raised against his conception of uneasiness as some sort of feeling which spurs the agent into action, Locke is surely correct in his main point: there is a difference between judging a thing to be desirable or worthwhile and actually desiring or wanting that thing. The primitive sign of a person's wanting something is his trying to get it, and we certainly can both believe it to be in our power to get a thing and sincerely acknowledge its desirability without trying to get it. Moreover, we can, by a consideration of the thing we have judged to be desirable, bring ourselves to want that thing. According to Locke we ought to cultivate a desire for what we have judged to be desirable:

> the forbearance of a too hasty compliance with our desires, the moderation and restraint of our Passions, so that our Understandings may be *free* to examine, and reason unbiassed gives its judgment, being that, whereon a right direction of our conduct to true Happiness depends; 'tis in this we should employ our chief care and endeavours. . . . and not permit an allow'd or supposed possible great and weighty good to slip out of our thoughts . . . till, by a due consideration of its true worth, we have formed appetites in our Minds suitable to it, and made ourselves uneasie in the want of it, or in the fear of losing it. (II.xxi.53)

The individual who coolly understands the eternal bliss of heaven to be his greatest good can, then, bring himself to want that good.

As the one is not intrinsically pleasant and the other not intrinsically painful, virtue and vice are not good and evil in themselves. They are, however, good and evil in a secondary sense: 'not only present Pleasure and Pain, but that also which is apt by its efficacy, or consequences, to bring it upon us at a distance, is a proper Object of our desires, and apt to move a Creature, that has foresight; therefore *things* also *that draw after them Pleasure and Pain, are considered as Good and Evil*' (II.xxi.61). Thus, someone who really does desire heaven and believes the virtuous life to be the only means of attaining it will come to a genuine desire to act virtuously and avoid vice.

This account of judgment leading to a deliberate cultivation of a desire for the thing judged to be good still leaves in obscurity the phenomenon we have termed the spontaneous adoption of virtue, that is, the pursuit of virtue for its own sake and not because it has been judged good as a means to something else. How a virtuous life of this kind is possible is explained in *Some Thoughts Concerning Education.* Locke maintains that the rational adult has the ability to train himself to desire virtue as a secondary good. He also believes that the child can be trained to regard virtue as a good in itself.

Locke talks of the young child in the care of the educator as 'white Paper, or Wax, to be moulded and fashioned as one pleases' (*Education,* §216).[20] The 'white paper' metaphor echoes the *Essay,* where it expresses the absence of any intellectual content in the mind's original make-up. In the context of his theory of education it expresses Locke's belief that human nature has no innate moral tendencies, either towards moral good or moral evil. He rejects the orthodox interpretation of the doctrine of original sin according to which human beings are born with a definite bias towards evil.[21] The innate principles of action which would, if unrestrained, lead to the overturning of all virtue are not in themselves manifestations of moral corruption. Locke does say that it is the business of the educator to 'root out and destroy' the child's 'Natural Propensity to indulge Corporal and Present Pleasure, and to avoid Pain at any rate' (*Education,* §48), but this does not mean he regards such a principle of action as evil.

First and foremost the child must be taught self-denial:

> the Principle of all Vertue and Excellency lies in a Power of denying our selves the Satisfaction of our own Desires, where Reason does not authorize them. This Power is to be got and improved by Custom, made easy and familiar by an *early* Practice. . . . I would advise, that, contrary to the ordinary way, Children should be used to submit their Desires, and go without their Longings, even *from their very Cradles.* (*Education,* §38)[22]

However, were the child brought to deny the natural tendency to grasp present pleasure and avoid present pain out of a fear of corporal punishment the aim of education would be lost. The discipline of the rod only reinforces the root cause of vice, for then the child only foregoes the pleasure of immediate indulgence so as to escape a greater pain: 'The Child submits and dissembles Obedience, whilst the Fear of the Rod hangs over him; but when that is removed, and . . . he can promise himself Impunity, he gives the greater Scope to his natural Inclination; which by this way is not at all altered, but on the contrary heightened and increased in him; and after such restraint, breaks out usually with the more Violence' (*Education,* §50). Or if such chastisement does cure the child of his natural tendency towards the indulgence of his passions, this is at the expense of producing 'a *low spirited moap'd* Creature' who will probably prove 'an useless thing to himself and others' (*Education*, §51, cf. §46). The child is to be brought to practise genuine self-denial not by means of what is usually thought of as punishment, but chiefly by means of approval and disapproval. Children are, Locke maintains, at a very early age 'sensible of *Praise* and Commendation. They find a Pleasure in being esteemed, and valued, especially by their Parents, and those whom they depend on' (*Education*, §57). It is only when shame is associated with wrong doing that the child will come to deny himself pleasures which the desires of the moment prompt him to pursue. This sense of esteem or shame is to be made 'sink in the deeper, and be of more Weight' (*Education*, §58) by bestowing agreeable things on the child when he acts virtuously and disagreeable things when he acts viciously. However, these things are not to be presented as particular rewards and punishments for particular actions, but as good or evil rightly attending upon the performance of virtuous or vicious acts:

> In this way the Objects of their own Desires are made assisting to Vertue; when a settled Experience from the beginning teaches Children, that the Things they delight in belong to, and are to be enjoyed by those only, who are in a State of Reputation. If by these Means you can come once to shame them out of their Faults, (for besides that, I would willingly have no Punishment) and make them in Love with the Pleasure of being well thought on, you may turn them as you please, and they will be in Love with all the ways of Vertue. (ibid.)

That is, the child will think of virtue and vice, not merely as forms of conduct which as a matter of fact elicit commendation and blame from those about him, but as forms of conduct which merit, or deserve, commendation and blame.

The child's love of the ways of virtue will not only be manifest in a ready obedience to the negative precepts of the law. In the *Education* Locke is especially concerned with the inculcation of the altruistic virtues whereby positive good is done to others. As the desire of having things in our possession and under our dominion is the root of all evil it 'should be early and carefully weeded out, and the contrary Quality of a Readiness to impart to others, implanted' (*Education*, §110). Similarly, 'the Principles of good Nature and Kindness', the outward expression of which is civility, are to be made habitual in the child 'by Credit and Commendation, and the good Things accompanying the State' (*Education*, §67).[23] Though the educator is to reinforce these virtues by 'good things', Locke's aim is not the person who practises liberality and civility as a means, but one who values such conduct for its own sake. Tangible rewards are the educators means of moulding this type of character: 'Children having made it easie to themselves to part with what they have, good Nature may be settled in them into an Habit, and they may take Pleasure, and pique themselves in being *Kind, Liberal* and *Civil* to others (*Education*, §110).

The individual whose character has been thus shaped by education does have a reason for practising even the altruistic virtues, namely that he takes pleasure in so acting. Though Locke recognises pleasures of the mind as well as of the body, he conceives pleasure as a kind of sensation or feeling caused in us by various things; like pain it is a simple idea which accompanies our experiences of things (II.xx.1). In our quest for happiness it is the experience of this sensation which we are after. Here Locke is mistaken; very few pleasures can be assimilated to sensations caused by things.[24] If pleasure was separate from and only causally related to the objects which give us pleasure, then it would be possible to identify and attend to the pleasure derived from, say, the performance of a Mozart symphony quite independently of our experience of hearing the music (just as we can attend to the sensation of toothache independently of the tooth which causes it). The notion of taking pleasure in something is closely connected with the notion of liking or enjoying it; and we like things because of specific qualities and characteristics which they possess, not because of some introspective sensation they produce in us. Our liking for a given thing is not determined solely by its characteristics but also by our tastes; and Locke is, of course, correct in maintaining that individuals differ widely in their tastes. But a person's tastes are not fixed innately, they can be developed and refined (as well as deadened and perverted), and their development is not a matter of setting up new causal relations between his mind and things. Generally speaking, we want or desire the things we like, and thus a person's tastes and behavioural dispositions are related. The doctrine put forward in the *Education* is that the individual can be taught to want to be virtuous and so to act virtuously.

Had Locke followed up his insight into the malleability (as distinct from the diversity) of human desires he may have produced a more satisfactory psychology of action. As it is the fact of malleability poses a problem for Locke's general moral theory. On his definition ethics is the science which seeks the rules and measures of human actions which lead to happiness, and happiness is construed as pleasure. Each individual has an infallible knowledge of the immediate pleasure he derives from a thing and, therefore, cannot be mistaken about what makes him happy at a given time, or what is good for him at that time. He can be mistaken about what constitutes his true happiness only in that he settles for a lesser source of pleasure in preference to a greater. The grading of sources of pleasure (and hence of goods) is up to the individual; for the man who in fact derives more pleasure from wine than from sound health, the bottle is the greater good (II.xxi.54). With the realisation that a person's tastes can be developed the question arises in which directions should they be developed, or in what objects should the person be taught to take pleasure. The presupposition here is that it is better to take pleasure in some things rather than others. As the development of one's taste is a matter of 'learning new pleasures' this question cannot be answered by an enquiry into the individual's grading of sources of pleasure. It demands rather an investigation into the characteristics of various possible objects of pleasure and desire. If it is accepted that it is better to take pleasure in some things rather than others, such an enquiry will be necessary prior to embarking upon the task Locke assigns to ethics; for it is only then that we can decide what pleasures should constitute happiness for a person.

This love of virtue brought about by the educator's manipulation of the innate capacity for shame and the desire to be well thought of is the nearest Locke gets to the adoption of the virtuous life for its own sake. The ultimate reason we all have for opting for virtue is that in doing so we escape the risk of eternal misery and may attain perfect happiness. However, Locke believes that the majority of those who follow what they believe to be the ways of virtue do so, not from considerations of divine rewards and punishment, but because their conduct is endorsed by the 'law of opinion or reputation'. As put in the fragment 'Philanthropoy [sic] or The Christian Philosophers' (1675):

> Mankinde is supported in y[e] ways of Vertue or Vice by the Society he is of & y[e] Conversation he keeps: Example & Fashion being y[e] great Governours of this World. The 1st Question, every man ought to aske in all things he doth, or undertakes; is, how is this acceptable to God? But the first Question most men aske, is, how will this rend. [recommend?] me to my Company, and those, whose esteeme I value? He yt askes neither of these Questions, is a Melancholy Rogue; & all ways of the most dangerous & worst of men. (MS c27, Fol.30[c])

It might be objected that what is involved here is not the love of virtue but rather the love of the commendation and esteem of others, virtue being adopted and valued only as a means. However, the pleasure we take in the esteem of others does not simply derive from our knowledge that as a matter of fact they do think well of us, but from our belief that our conduct is such as to merit their esteem.

Similarly, we do not suffer the pain of shame when others think badly of us for an action we do not believe to be shameful. In Locke's scheme the child is brought up to see the life of virtue, not as something which will inevitably be accompanied by the esteem of others, but as something which deserves such esteem. The agent in whom this view has been inculcated will act virtuously even in circumstances in which commendation is not forthcoming. In a list of the various things which constitute happiness Locke includes both 'reputation' and 'doing good'. The former is the actual enjoyment of the good opinion of others, but the latter is distinct from this as it can be enjoyed quite independently of others: 'For I finde the well cooked meat I eat to day does now noe more delight me. . . . The purfumes I smelt yesterday now noe more affect me with any pleasure. But the good turne I did yesterday a year seven year since continues still to please & delight me as often as I reflect on it' ('Thus I thinke', MS c28 Fol. 143). The educator by cultivating and manipulating the child's sense of esteem and shame brings him to take pleasure in doing good. The end product of a properly carried out education is a person who, because he sees virtue as something worthy of esteem, centres his self-esteem upon virtue and consequently needs to be virtuous.

It was argued in chapter 1 that the principles we apply in our judgment of conscience have a purchase on our conduct because we hold them as moral convictions and feel guilty or uneasy when we act against them. For Locke, a person's conscience, or moral convictions, is a product of education. We are not possessed of an innate moral sense which distinguishes right from wrong and prompts us to follow the ways of virtue; we must be taught to relish virtue. In Locke's scheme moral education achieves the end which Perkins and Ames maintain can be achieved only by divine grace: it makes the person an agent who fulfils the demands of morality not through fear but willingly. Just as (in Perkins' words) the conscience regenerated by grace 'doth by certaine sweete motions stirre men forward' to obedience to the moral law, so the properly educated individual takes pleasure in virtue. If moral education is to be successful it must be correct in its cognative content; the principles instilled must truly reflect the moral law. The discovery of the true measures of virtue and vice belongs to the first, theoretical part of ethics. The task of the second, practical part is to produce the moral agent in whom 'Constance, Reason, & Pleasure goe togeather' (MS c28, Fol. 113).

CONCLUSION: LOCKE'S MORAL PHILOSOPHY

Professor Aaron writes of Locke that '[it] is in vain that we search in his pages for a consistent ethical theory'.[1] The main theme of the present study is a denial of this conclusion. Though he continues to believe it to be within the compass of human understanding, Locke does not furnish a demonstrative system of morals; and for this reason his theory may be said to be incomplete. However, incompleteness is not the same as inconsistency. The views concerning morality he does expound do not betray 'an inner contradiction in his thoughts'.[2]

Specifically, Locke's hedonism is not, as is frequently claimed, at odds with his ethical rationalism. The *Essays* (and particuarly *Essay* VIII) has been seen as an anti-hedonistic work. Yet even here there is a hint of the later doctrine that the whole purpose of morality is the achievement of human happiness, and that if mankind could be happier without it the moral law would vanish: 'the observance of this law [of nature] gives rise to peace, harmonious relations, friendship, freedom from punishment, security, possession of our property, and – to sum it all up in one word – happiness (faelicitas)' (*Essays*, p.215). Admittedly, this statement is not made in Locke's own voice; he imagines it being put forward as grounds for the thesis he opposes: that the basis of natural law is 'each man's own interest'. However, he does not deny the premise, only that the egoistic conclusion can be validly derived from it. It is, Locke points out, necessary to distinguish between an action which of itself is profitable for the agent and one which is useful because it is in accordance with a moral precept. For example, keeping a promise may in itself be to the agent's disadvantage, nevertheless, because the precept that promises ought to be kept is supported by sanctions, the act will be of utility for him, in the negative sense that he thereby averts the penalty due to promise breaking, a penalty which would not exist were it not for the precept. Nonetheless, the rational individual will acknowledge that, even though the observance of it is at times to his disadvantage, the existence of this precept does facilitate the general happiness. A world in which it was not acknowledged that promises ought to be kept would lack the social stability and security which is a prerequisite for the successful pursuit of personal happiness.[3] Locke does not fall into the error of supposing that obedience to moral rules which makes for the general happiness must on each occasion contribute to the happiness of the individual agent. In working out the content of the law of nature reason does begin from the premise that each individual seeks personal happiness. However, as human beings neither in fact live in isolation one from another nor desire to do so, and as the precepts of morality are conceived as binding on all men, reason decides upon the virtue or vice of kinds of actions in light of their relevance to the general conditions which make possible or advance the achievement of happiness.

Locke's rationalism would be inconsistent with hedonism if the former entailed that the virtue or vice of actions is discerned by a rational intuition of their intrinsic moral qualities. But the rationalist version of ethical intuitionism is rejected by Locke in his polemic against innate morality; it is discursive reason working with data given in experience which finds out what the moral law demands. Again, there would be an inherent contradiction in Locke's thought if his hedonism entailed the act-utilitarian principle that in each particular set of circumstances the morally right action is the one which, in those circumstances, is likely to produce the greatest amount of happiness or pleasure. On this principle moral rules and notions are, at most, of secondary importance, for it is easy enough to think of circumstances in which the performance of an act falling under the notion of, say, murder, would in fact promote more happiness than unhappiness.[4] Act-utilitarianism, then, leaves no room for the negative moral precepts which are absolute in the sense that they are to be obeyed under all circumstances; these will be only rules of thumb which may be ignored in particular cases. For Locke, the morality of a particular act is always determined by the virtue of viciousness of the type of action of which it is a token. Moreover, the act-utilitarian principle would itself appear to be absolute. That is, it demands that we always act so as to produce the most happiness. If this demand is taken seriously, there can be no class of indifferent, or morally neutral, actions; for anything we do might be assessed according to the happiness it brings about. Locke insists that there is such a class of actions. The view that there are areas of human behaviour which lie outside the spheres of morality and religion is crucial both to his authoritian argument in the *Two Tracts* and to his later defence of toleration. As interpreted here, act-utilitarianism manifests the error – which Locke ascribes to Grenville – that it is always morally incumbent upon us to do the best thing.

The definition of virtue as the doing of good and of vice as the doing of harm, which Locke puts forward in the Commonplace Book entry 'Virtus', might be understood as a kind of rule-utilitarian principle to be applied, not to particular acts, but to moral precepts or notions. It may be agreed that virtue and vice have to do with human good and harm, but the crucial question is what is to count as constituting good and harm in concrete situations. On Locke's hedonistic account of good and evil things which are good for one individual may be neutral or even evil for someone else. The only absolute and universal source of pleasure he acknowledges is the reward stored up in heaven; but, whilst we can be sure that this good is such as to suit everyone's palate, its nature is beyond our earthly comprehension. It is, therefore, at least difficult to see how these definitions can be employed as criteria for the virtue and vice of kinds of actions or as a principle for deciding between conflicting moral precepts or opinions. Nonetheless, it is possible to derive what may be called a negative utilitarian principle from Locke's hedonistic account. Let it be granted that the objects of pleasure and pain differ from person to person, there will still be actions which hinder or prevent anybody's quest for happiness, no matter what the objects of their pleasure may be. Actions against a person's life, or which confine their liberty so that they cannot keep, or acquire, the things they desire will fall into this category. Such actions will always be productive of evil, at least in that they lessen the individual's pleasure. Hence, on Locke's definition of vice, they must be accounted vicious. Yet we have seen that Locke wants to accommodate virtues which enjoin us to do more than merely refrain from harming others. His relativism respecting the causes of pleasure and pain means that he lacks a satisfactory utilitarian test for these positive virtues.

Later philosophers who were avowedly utilitarian in their moral theories learnt a great deal from Locke.[5] Yet, notwithstanding the emphasis he places on happiness as the end of morality, Locke himself cannot be properly categorised as a utilitarian. His ethic is a natural law theory of morality. Many critics, from Henry Lee on, have objected that, although he makes free use of the phrase 'law of nature', Locke's philosophy is contrary to the natural law doctrine. Some of the misconceptions which have given rise to this criticism have already been dealt with. Locke does not find the content of morality in the arbitrary will of God. The view of him as a theological voluntarist is due to a failure to distinguish between his account of moral obligation and his moral epistemology. Were there no God there could be no moral law; but the content of the law is discoverable by reason working with the facts of human nature, or, more broadly, the circumstances of the human condition. Nor is Locke a cultural moral relativist, holding right and wrong to be determined by the variable law of opinion. Generally speaking, the individual is educated in the morality of the society into which he is born, and therefore the moral notions he acquires are those current in that society. Though Locke maintains (what is surely an obvious truth) that individuals first learn to distinguish right from wrong in this way, he insists that the true touchstone of moral rectitude is the unvarying divine law standing behind the law of opinion. The fact that he does not finally settle upon a rationally founded law from which all other precepts of morality can be derived is hardly evidence that he does settle for ethical relativism. There are, however, other grounds for the view that Locke departs from the classical natural law tradition, for that tradition is usually understood to involve a metaphysical world picture which he certainly does reject in large part.

In the third of his arguments for the existence of the law of nature in the *Essays* Locke characterises law as 'that which prescribes to every thing the form and manner and measure of working'; and we have seen that this is a paraphrase of Richard Hooker's definition of law. The setting of this definition is the basically Aristotelian world picture of Christian humanism; a picture brilliantly painted in Book I of the *Laws of Ecclesiastical Polity.* Hooker's exposition of the law-governed universe is dominated by two concepts: final causality and order. Each particular thing, be it a purely physical object or a living organism, has a form, or fixed nature, by virtue of which it is an instance of a specific kind of thing, and in accordance with which it operates in a specific manner. The form a thing has, and thus the law of its operation, is due to God's creative act, an act which is not arbitrary, but ruled by the eternal law which God has freely adopted. The various laws governing creation are, therefore, all aspects of the one eternal law. The causality involved in the operation of a thing is construed, in light of the Aristotelian distinction between actuality and potentiality, as primarily the working of appetite, or desire. With the exception of God, who is what He is completely and eternally, all things exist partly in actuality and partly in potentiality. What each thing desires and strives for is the full actualisation of its potentiality. This actualisation is its final cause, or end, for the sake of which it moves or acts. The distinction between actuality and potentiality and the conception of final causality which it involves is best illustrated by a consideration of the way in which we still ordinarily think of organic bodies. An acorn is actually an acorn, but it has the potential to grow into an oak. Growing into oaks is not just something acorns regularly happen to do: it lies in the nature of acorns to do so. Yet although the oak stands as the actualisation of the potentiality latent in the acorn, it may still be said that there is something lacking of the full actualisation of that potentiality. A mature oak is subject to decay and, even though decay occurs naturally, decay is still a falling away from the proper nature of the oak. Further, a given oak may be a good or bad specimen of its kind. Thus, the stunted or gnarled tree has not achieved all that existed potentially in the acorn. It is, therefore, the constantly held perfection of form which things strive after. This being so, the distinction between actuality and potentiality is equally applicable in the realm of purely physical bodies. Although these do not grow, they do operate more or less perfectly in accord with their natures; stones fall and in doing so seek their proper place, the planets revolve in tune with the appropriate geometry of planetary motion, and so on.

This aspiration after perfection of form is the dynamic of the whole universe, and, as there can be no perfection which does not proceed from the perfection of God himself, all things, in a sense, desire to be like God. This desire manifests itself throughout creation in two main ways: first, in endeavouring to continue in existence, a thing attempts to imitate God in the eternity of His being; secondly, in endeavouring to operate in conformity with the laws of its nature, it attempts to imitate God in the immutability and precision with which He follows the eternal law. This is not to say that things operate in isolation one from another. The universe has the same kind of unity as a work of art, for every single thing in it not only strives after its own perfection but has a contribution to make to the perfection of other things.

The pattern of interconnected ends which constitutes the order of the physical world is intended for the benefit of man as he is the peak of sublunary creation. Were the laws governing the operations of what Hooker calls natural agents to be suspended even for a short time, the result would be chaos, and man would be ruined. In contrast to natural agents, which strive to perfect their natures unconsciously or only instinctively, man is able intellectually to apprehend his own nature and voluntarily obey the law appropriate to it. As it is the possession of reason which distinguishes man from the inanimate or the merely sentient part of creation, the end of his nature is rational action. Hooker holds the distinctively human element in this end to be knowledge (ultimately the knowledge of God) and growth in the exercise of virtue. Men, being voluntary agents, are capable of transgressing the law. Transgression is a kind of error; for, as all rational actions are performed under the aspect of the good, it consists either in the agent preferring an apparent to a real good or a lesser good to a greater. Such error is as much an inlet to chaos as would be the contravention of those laws which natural agents follow of necessity; the order of human society is part of the universal order and the moral law of nature governing men is one aspect of the eternal law governing all things.

Even when it is recognised that Locke is not a voluntarist with respect to the content of morality, the concept of moral law he works with might still be thought to differ significantly from the classical natural law conception. For him it is essential to any law that it should be the decree of a superior will. On Hooker's definition of law, on the other hand, the term would appear to refer to a principle of development inherent in the nature of the thing. The law, therefore, exists in virtue of the existence of the thing, independently of any act of a superior will. While some natural law theorists, such as Grotius, were prepared to hazard the hypothesis that there would be a law of nature even if there were no God, most Christian writers within the tradition did trace the binding force of the law to God's will. Locke's theory emphasises the will of a superior or 'that which binds effectively', but this is not a significant departure from the classical view as it is to be found in philosophers such as Aquinas and Hooker.[6] He certainly could not be considered a natural law theorist if he maintained that the content of morality was alien to human nature and imposed by God upon man, but quite clearly he does not hold this view.

A rather more formidable objection against the interpretation of Locke as a philosopher of natural law derives from what he has to say about substantial forms. Although he is prepared to accept that things have real essences from which their qualities somehow flow, he holds those essences – except in the case of things we construct ourselves – to be beyond our understanding. Yet it would seem essential to the natural law doctrine sketched above that we do have an understanding of the form or real essence of human nature. Without this understanding we could hardly know the law which governs the proper development of man, and this law, in Hooker's words, 'comprehendeth all those things which men by the light of their natural understanding evidently know, or leastwise may know, to be beseeming or unbeseeming, virtuous or vicious, good or evil for them to do'.[7] Further, as the end towards which a thing strives is the perfection of its form, in the natural law doctrine the concepts of form and of final causation are interconnected. Locke accepts the corpuscular theory according to which the real essences of bodies are configurations of atoms in motion. While these atomic structures may be said to fulfil the ontological function of forms in that they make bodies to be what they are, the qualities and operations of those bodies will be explained in terms of efficient, not final, causes. We cannot comprehend the way in which the motion of atoms produces ideas of secondary qualities in the observer, but the explanations of natural phenomena which we can achieve have no use for the notion of things striving to attain an end. The mechanical artifact rather than the living organism provides the explanatory model.[8]

The corpuscular theory favoured explanation in terms of efficient causes, but not all its exponents denied a place to final causes. Robert Boyle is most probably Locke's major source for the theory and he defends scientific enquiry into final causes. There is, Boyle points out, an ambiguity in the notion of a thing working for an end: the end in question may be something the thing either *seeks* to realise or something it *serves* to realise. Strictly speaking, it is only beings capable of knowing ends and forming intentions to achieve them who can seek to realise something. Even if the thesis that inanimate beings are possessed of a special kind of knowledge in accord with which they seek their own ends is intelligible, it offends against the methodological principle that entities are not to be multiplied beyond necessity. Nonetheless, such things can still be said to have ends in the sense that they may be instruments serving purposes formulated by intelligent beings. As God is creator of the universe, it is reasonable to suppose that everything in it fulfils purposes which He intends. In opposition to Descartes, Boyle argues that it is possible for us to know something of these purposes and thus to understand the mechanical operations of things in terms of their final causes, or the functions they have been assigned by God.[9] The belief that the universe is an ordered system is central to Locke's third argument for the existence of the law of nature in the *Essays*; there he talks of God assigning men some work to do and designing human nature so that it is suitable for that work (*Essays*, p.117). Later he states that 'since man is neither made without design nor endowed to no purpose with these faculties which both can and must be employed, his function appears to be that which nature has prepared him to perform' (*Essays*, p.157). Thus, while Locke does not explicitly reject the Aristotelian world picture in this early work, his position is at least compatible with Boyle's view of final causes.

What has been called the 'mechanisation of the world picture' does not entail the banishment of teleological explanation; but it does lead to a revision of the concept of final causation, and it may be questioned that the revised concept can be utilised in a natural law ethic. For Hooker and other writers in the natural law tradition, virtuous conduct promotes the perfection of man's form. Their theory may, therefore, be termed an ethic of self-realisation. On the other hand, it may be said that the conception of man as having an end, in the sense of a function or purpose in the general scheme of things, degrades human beings to the status of instruments, and, even when the function is thought to be assigned by God, this view cannot yield a satisfactory account of morality.[10] There are places in the *Essays* where Locke's language might suggest such a view, but he cannot be said to be committed to it even in that work. He does not conceive God making men as a watchmaker constructs a watch. In his view the main characteristic of human nature relevant to moral philosophy is that all men strive after happiness, and he argues that God could not have made man for any purpose other than that they should be happy. In the case of human beings, therefore, God's purpose and the intentions men formulate and endeavour to carry through coincide.[11]

Locke departs furthest from the classical natural law tradition in his treatment of good and evil. In that tradition goodness is whatever contributes to the perfecting of a thing's form, and consequently the good for a thing is dictated by its form. The good for man is, therefore, something objective and it is sought by all men in virtue of their shared human nature. Men may be mistaken in their judgments about the goodness of things, but their real happiness consists in the attainment of what is truly good for them or proper to their nature. According to Locke's theory, men constantly seek to attain those things which give them pleasure and avoid those which give them pain. It is with respect to pleasure and pain that things are denominated good and evil. As the causes of pleasure and pain are relative to the individual, there is no objective and universal content to human happiness. Even the joy of heaven cannot be considered man's *summum bonum* in the sense that it perfects human nature. Rather, Locke conceives the reward in the next life to be such that it will be a source of pleasure without any admixture of pain for all men, no matter how diverse their tastes. Though a person's tastes can be moulded by education, the question of whether or not a given thing is a source of pleasure must finally be decided by the individual.

Yet even Locke's subjectivist and relativist account of good and evil may be seen as arising out of an endeavour to defend the traditional natural law ethic. We have seen that the existence of the law of nature can be maintained only if it can be shown how men come to know its content. The problem with deriving this content from a knowledge of the good proper to man is that there is no general agreement as to what that good may be. Hooker in fact falls back on the 'general and perpetual voice of men' as a guide to moral truth and accepts intuitionism as an account of our knowledge of, at least, the first principles of natural law.[12] Locke dismisses these attempts to solve the epistemological problem, and he has good grounds for dismissing them. One point of agreement among the theorists of natural law was that man's happiness consisted in the attainment of his proper good. Locke takes as the fundamental and evident truth about human nature the proposition that all men seek happiness, and he tries to give the concept of happiness content by defining it in terms of pleasure and the absence of pain. But it is also evident that individuals take their pleasures in different ways and find them in different objects. Thus, if what is good constitutes human happiness, there is no such thing as the good for men as such: 'Hence it was . . . that the Philosophers of old did in vain enquire, whether *Summum bonum* consisted in Riches, or bodily Delights, or Virtue, or Contemplation: And they might have as reasonably disputed, whether the best Relish were to be found in Apples, Plumbs, or Nuts; and have divided themselves into Sects upon it' (II.xxi.55). At times Locke presents the proposition that men seek happiness as an empirical truth and he incorporates it in a quasi-mechanistic theory according to which happiness and misery are 'the two great springs of human actions'. However, in his final account of human freedom it is of most importance as the basic of a theory of reasons for actions. The law of nature is the object of reason both in the sense that its existence and content can be discerned by reason and in that men have reasons for accepting its dictates. Accepting the dictates of the law is not the same as obeying them, and from the point of view of the individual, obedience is reasonable *at all times* because the law is backed up by sanctions. But this is not inconsistent with the fact that, in his attempts to derive the universal content of the law, Locke remains true to his hedonism and proceeds from considerations of human happiness. Certainly, these attempts are hampered by his relativism respecting pleasure and pain, and in the end he can provide a rational foundation for only a minimal content of the law of nature; but in this he is no worse off than other natural law theorists. The critics' claim that in Locke's published works the phrase 'the law of nature' is nothing more than a *façon de parler* is without justification.

NOTES

Introduction

1. Marginal note in Tyrrell's copy of the *Essay* in the British Museum Library.

2. See von Leyden's introduction to the *Essays*, p.69.

3. cf. Locke's unfinished paper 'De Arte Medica': 'True knowledge grew first in the world by experience and rational operations, and, had this method been continued, and all men's thoughts been employed to add their own trials to the observations of others, no question physic, as well as many other arts, had been in a far better condition than now it is; but proud man, not content with that knowledge he was capable of and was useful to him, would needs penetrate into the hidden causes of things, lay down principles and establish maxims to himself about the operations of nature, and then vainly expect that nature or in truth God himself, should proceed according to those laws his maxims had prescribed him' (H. R. Fox Bourne, *The Life of John Locke*, vol.I, pp.224-5).

4. Locke is far from being alone in preaching the narrowness and unimportance of speculative knowledge compared with practical moral knowledge. Perhaps the best known expression of this attitude is the advice to Adam which Milton puts into the mouth of Raphael (*Paradise Lost*, Bk.VII, esp. 167-78). But it is also found amongst philosophers; for example, in Pierre Gassendi and Pierre Nicole, two writers with whose thought Locke was well acquainted. See Gassendi's 'Lettre sur le livre de Lord Edouard Herbert', trans. Bernard Rochet, in *Actes du Congrès du Tricentenaire de Pierre Gassendi*; and Nicole's essay 'Of the Weakness of Man', in *Discourses: Translated from Nicole's* Essays *by John Locke*, ed. Thomas Hancock. Locke's notion of human existence as a state of mediocrity may owe something to Pascal's *Pensées*.

5. Locke's contemporary critics tended to see the *Essay* as promoting a general scepticism. John Sergeant is an exception in realising that it is metaphysical knowledge which Locke singles out for attack: 'I am a little apprehensive, from some Words in his Introduction, expressing his Dis-like that Men *let loose their Thoughts into the vast Ocean of Being*; and his Conceit that this brings Men to *Doubts* and *Scepticism*, that he has taken a Prejudice against METAPHYSICS; whose proper Object is, those Notions of the Thing which abstracts from *Matter* and Motion, and concern *Being* only' (*Solid Philosophy Asserted*, p.114).

6. On the notion of 'scientia' see the article by W. A. Wallace in *The Catholic Encyclopedia.*

Chapter 1. *Conscience and Moral Knowledge*

1. *John Locke: Two Tracts on Government*, edited with an introduction, notes and translation by Philip Abrams (Cambridge 1967). For the date and circumstances of composition see Abrams' introduction, pp.10-17.

2. This controversy and the details of Locke's involvement in it are discussed in Abrams' introduction, esp. pp.17-25 and ch.II.

3. In his appeal to consequences, Locke reiterates the main theme of the Anglican case against toleration. See G. R. Cragg, *From Puritanism to the Age of Reason,* ch.IX.

4. As Locke himself maintains in *A Letter Concerning Toleration.*

5. cf. J. D. Mabbott, *John Locke,* pp.173-4.

6. See especially the 'Preface to the Reader' of the *First Tract* and the opening paragraphs of the *Second Tract.*

7. *A Discourse of Conscience* in *William Perkins, 1558-1602,* p.6. Ames defines conscience as 'a *practicall* judgment, by which, that which a man knoweth is particularly applyed to that which is either good or evill to him, to the end it may be a rule within him to direct his will' (*Conscience with the . . . Cases Thereof,* Bk.I, p.2).

8. See Gilbert Ryle, 'Conscience and Moral Convictions', in *Analysis,* vol.7 (1940). Ames would appear to have the same point in mind when he remarks that 'Conscience being referred to *judgment,* is distinguished from the bare apprehension of truth. For Conscience doth alwaies suppose an assent that is firme and setled' (*Conscience with the . . . Cases Thereof,* Bk.I, pp.1-2).

9. See Ryle, 'Conscience and Moral Convictions'. The case of conscientious objection should be distinguished from 'academic' moral disagreement. The appeal to conscience is appropriate only when pressure is exerted to bring us to go against our moral convictions. When the truth or wisdom of our moral convictions is merely questioned, the appeal to conscience is more than is called for. In this case the appropriate response is a reasoned defence of our convictions.

10. *Discourse of Conscience,* p.32.

11. ibid., p.65.

12. On the Puritan conception of a new order to be established by the elect in this world and the clash with the Anglican 'old order', see David Little, *Religion, Order, and Law,* Pt.II. See also A. S. P. Woodhouse, *Puritanism and Liberty,* Introduction, section III.

13. According to Perkins 'unfallible certentie of pardon of sinne and life everlasting is the propertie of everie renued conscience' (*Discourse of Conscience,* p.61). Similarly Ames holds that 'A Conscience purged from dead works both necessarily bring with it a certaine knowledge of grace' (*Conscience with the . . . Cases Thereof,* Bk.II, p.10).

14. Anglican complaints against the appeal to conscience in justification of civil strife are common in the literature of the day. Jeremy Taylor, for example, writes that 'Nothing is more usual, than to pretend conscience to all the actions of men which are public and whose nature cannot be concealed. If arms be taken up in a violent war, enquire of both sides why they engage on that part respectively, they answer, because of their conscience. Ask a schismatic why he refuses to join in the communion of the Church; he tells you, it is against his conscience. And the disobedient refuse to submit to laws; and they also in such cases pretend conscience. . . . And so suspicion, and jealousy, and disobedience, and rebellion, are become conscience' (*Ductor Dubitantium,* Bk.I, ch.i, Rule 3, 1). Cf. John Selden, *Table Talk,* 'Conscience'.

15. cf. Bagshaw: 'many more *Absurd,* and more *Destructive* and *Fatal Consequences* attend the Doctrine of *Imposition,* than the Doctrine of *Christian Liberty*. . . . The first Inconvenience is, the Impossibility to fix a point where the Imposer will stop. For do but once grant, that the *Magistrate* hath power to Impose, and then we lie at his mercy, how farre he will go' (*The Great Question,* p.10).

16. For divisions of law along other lines see Aquinas, *Summa Theologiae,* 1a 2ae, 91, 1; Hooker, *Laws of Ecclesiastical Polity,* I, iii, 1, xvi, 7; Hobbes, *Leviathan,* II, 26. Locke's division is closest to that given by Robert Sanderson in *De Obligatione*

Conscientiae, v, ii. Locke, as Abrams points out, draws heavily upon Sanderson's work throughout the Latin tract.

17. See *Romans,* XIV. Much of the argument for toleration revolves around this passage and in the *Two Tracts* Locke does his best to minimise the 'fraternal law'.

18. *Conscience with the . . . Cases Thereof,* Bk.I, p.4.

19. As Ames puts it, 'This *Synteresis* differs onely in respect of apprehension from the Law of Nature, or from that Law of God, which is naturally written in the hearts of al men; for the law is the obiect, and *Synteresis* is the obiect apprehended, or the apprehension of the obiect' (*Conscience with the . . . Cases Thereof,* Bk.I, p.5).

20. cf. Perkins: 'the Scriptures of the olde and new testament . . . containe in themselves sufficient direction for all actions. As for the law of nature though it affoarde indeede some direction; yet it is corrupt, imperfect, uncerten: and whatsoever is right and good therein, is contained in the written word of God' (*Discourse of Conscience,* p.42).

21. cf. Milton: 'Every believer has a right to interpret the Scripture for himself, inasmuch as he has the Spirit for his guide, and the mind of Christ is in him; nay, the expositions of the public interpreter can be of no use to him, except so far as they are confirmed by his own conscience' (*De Doctrina Christiana,* in *Works,* vol.XVI, p.265).

22. cf. Hobbes: 'It is either *science* or *opinion* which we commonly mean by the word *conscience*: for men say that such and such a thing is true in or upon their conscience; which they *never* do when they think it *doubtful,* and therefore they *know,* or *think* they know it to be true. But men, when they say things upon their conscience, are not therefore presumed certainly to know the truth of what they say; it remaineth then, that the word is used by them that have an *opinion, not* only of the *truth* of the thing, *but* also of their *knowledge* of it, to which the *truth* of the proposition is consequent. *Conscience* I therefore define to be *opinion of evidence*' (*Human Nature,* ch.6, in *English Works,* vol.IV, pp.29-30).

23. In the *First Tract* Locke defines 'imposing on conscience' as 'the pressing of doctrines or laws upon the belief or practice of men as of divine original, as necessary to salvation and in themselves obliging the conscience, when indeed they are no other but the ordinances of men and the products of their authority' (*1st Tract,* p.139).

24. It is small wonder that Bagshaw considered this distinction as it appears in the Anglican case against toleration to be 'meerly coyned to serve a turn, without the least Foundation, either in *Scripture* or *Reason*' (*The Second Part of the Great Question,* pp.13-14).

25. *Ecclesiastical Polity,* I.viii.3 and 11.

26. See *Summa Theologiae,* 1a 2ae, 19, 5-6.

27. Concerning the sceptic's need to assume the existence of objective standards of truth, see W. von Leyden, *Seventeenth Century Metaphysics,* pp.75f.

28. *Summa Theologiae,* 1a 2ae, 90, 4.

29. The *Essay Concerning Toleration* exists in four drafts, one of which is published in Fox Bourne's *Life of John Locke,* vol.I, pp.174-94.

30. For a comparison of Locke's early and later views on toleration and government, see Abrams' introduction to the *Two Tracts,* ch.IV, and J. W. Gough's introduction to the *Epistola de Tolerantia,* esp. pp.4-12.

Chapter 2. *Law and Obligation*

1. *John Locke: Essays on the Law of Nature,* translated and edited by W. von Leyden (Oxford 1954). For the probable date of composition see von Leyden's introduction, pp.10f.

2. See *Nicomachean Ethics,* I, 7.14, 1098^{a} and V, 7.1, 1134^{b}18.

3. cf. Hooker: 'That which doth assign unto each thing the kind, that which doth moderate the force and power, that which doth appoint the form and measure, of working, the same we term a Law' (*Ecclesiastical Polity*, I.ii.I). Locke quotes Hooker's definition, with an acknowledgment of the source, in the *Two Tracts*. See *2nd Tract*, p.221.

4. Mill's 'Nature' was first published in 1874 in his *Three Essays on Religion.*

5. Some commentators, notably Leo Strauss (*Natural Right and History*) and Richard H. Cox (*Locke on War and Peace*) have read Locke as a crypto-Hobbist. Their interpretation is founded on the hypothesis that Locke carefully conceals his genuine, unpalatable doctrine behind a fair show of language. That is, that he systematically says what he does not mean. The evidence for the concealment hypothesis is, to say the least, meagre. For a criticism see J. W. Yolton, 'Locke on the Law of Nature' in *Philosophical Review*, 67 (1958); Hans Aarsleff, 'Some Observations on Recent Locke Scholarship' in *John Locke – Problems and Perspectives*, ed. Yolton. On the evidence of Locke's text we can be confident that, in so far as he is a voluntarist, his voluntarism is theological in character.

6. *Works*, ed. Haldane and Ross, vol.II. pp.250-1. For a discussion of Descartes' voluntarism, see Emile Bréhier, 'The Creation of the Eternal Truths in Descartes' System', in *Descartes*, ed. Doney.

7. *The Questions Concerning Liberty, Necessity and Chance*, in *English Works*, ed. Molesworth, vol.v, p.146.

8. *Institutes of the Christian Religion*, I.xvii.2. For a general survey of the Calvinist–Puritan doctrine of God and the ambiguity of utterances concerning His will, see Perry Miller, *The New England Mind – the seventeenth century*, pp.10-21.

9. Cudworth (1617-88) published his massive, albeit unfinished, *True Intellectual System of the Universe* in 1678. His similarly unfinished *Treatise Concerning Eternal and Immutable Morality* appeared posthumously in 1731 and much of his work still remains in manuscript. Nevertheless Cudworth's ideas were in the seventeenth-century air, for he writes as a representative of the Cambridge Platonist school and was moreover a popular university teacher. Clarke (1675-1729) was Boyle Lecturer in 1704 and again in 1705, the two series of lectures being published as *A Demonstration of the Being and Attributes of God* and *A Discourse Concerning the Unchangeable Obligations of Natural Religion.* His moral philosophy is most fully developed in the latter work. For the differences between Cudworth and Clarke, see J. A. Passmore, *Ralph Cudworth*, pp.100-3. See also James Martineau, *Types of Ethical Theory*, vol.II, pp.425-74, and A. N. Prior, *Logic and the Basis of Ethics*, esp. chs II and III.

10. *Eternal and Immutable Morality*, I.ii.2.

11. *Unchangeable Obligations of Natural Religion* (1st ed.) p.47.

12. ibid., p.5.

13. *Eternal and Immutable Morality*, I.iii.7.

14. See *Being and Attributes of God* (1st ed.) pp.243f. *Unchangeable Obligations of Natural Religion*, pp.61f.

15. *Unchangeable Obligations of Natural Religion*, pp.33-4.

16. See ibid., pp.144f.

17. *Eternal and Immutable Morality*, I.ii.4.

18. *Unchangeable Obligations of Natural Religion*, pp.69-70.

19. *True Intellectual System*, vol.III, p.512.

20. *De Jure Belli ac Pacis*, Prolegomena, sect.II. Grotius was not the first natural law theorist to voice this sentiment. On Grotius' 'impious hypothesis', see M. B. Crowe, *The Changing Profile of Natural Law*, pp.223-8.

21. See J. A. Passmore, *Ralph Cudworth*, ch.VII.

22. cf. John W. Lenz, 'Locke's Essays on the Law of Nature', in *Philosophy and Phenomenological Research*, pp.110-11.

23. King misdates this paper at 1661. His mistake is corrected by Abrams' introduction to the *Two Tracts*, p.9.

24. cf. Lenz, 'Locke's essays on the law of nature', pp.106-7. Locke's distinction is derived from Robert Sanderson's *De Obligatione Conscientiae*, V, 5.

25. See *Romans*, IX, 20-1.

26. In the note to *Romans*, IX, 20 in his *Paraphrase and Notes on the Epistles of St Paul* Locke argues that the Apostles' words should not be understood as referring to God's dealings with individual persons, and so supporting the Calvinist doctrine of absolute reprobation. Rather, they refer to God's providential handling of nations with respect to their temporal welfare. See *Works*, vol.VII, pp.341-2.

27. In contrast to the interpretation given here, von Leyden reads this passage as an expression of an intellectualist theory of obligation. See 'John Locke and Natural Law', in *Philosophy*, vol.31 (1956).

28. In R. I. Aaron's opinion 'Ethica B' is one of the first drafts for a projected work on a necessary system of morals, a work which Locke turned his attention to after publishing *An Essay Concerning Human Understanding*. See his *John Locke*, 3rd ed., p.256, n.1.

29. The notion of God's right of creation as the ultimate source of moral obligation is not peculiar to Locke. It appears, for example, in Calvin's *Institutes*, II.ii.2. Locke's elder contemporary John Wilkins writes that, beside the right of dominion dependent upon conquest, purchase, or compact, 'there is another ground of subjection, which men cannot pretend to, namely, the *Giving of Being* to a thing. And this must needs, above all other claims be the greatest imaginable right, for the government and disposal of that thing, according to the pleasure of him that made it' (*Principles and Duties of Natural Religion*, 5th ed., pp.148-9). But Locke differs from these writers in emphasising that human beings are dependent on God not only in the sense that He gave them being, but also in that He constantly preserves them.

30. See *Eternal and Immutable Morality*, I.ii.3.

31. Locke wisely avoids the thorny problem of the moral status of God's particular commands to individuals or groups. However, in the course of his argument that the binding force of the law of nature is perpetual and universal he does consider the permission God gave the Israelites to despoil the Egyptians of their property (*Exodus*, xii, 35f). This, Locke argues, is not an example of the suspension of a natural law precept, for God owns all things and it is perfectly in accord with the law that He give His property to whom He will (*Essay*, pp.201-3).

32. See *Eternal and Immutable Morality*, I.i.5.

33. See, for example, von Leyden's introduction to the *Essays*, p.58, n.6.

34. cf. Hooker: 'The law whereby He worketh is eternal, and therefore can have no show or colour of mutability: for which cause, a part of that law being opened in the promises which God hath made (because his promises are nothing else but declarations what God will do for the good of man) touching those promises the Apostle hath witnessed, that God may as possibly 'deny himself' and not be God, as fail to perform them' (*Ecclesiastical Polity* I.ii.6).

35. cf. Aquinas, *Summa Theologiae*, Ia IIae, q.94, art.2.

Chapter 3.
Against Innate Morality

1. Locke argues against the doctrine of innate moral knowledge both in the third of the *Essays on the Law of Nature* and in the first book of *An Essay Concerning Human Under-*

standing. As the arguments contained in the former are repeated and expanded in the latter, we will concentrate on the *Essay.*

2. *An Antidote against Atheisme,* I.V.

3. cf. John Norris: *Cursory Reflections . . . upon an Essay Concerning Human Understanding,* pp.4-5. Henry Lee considers the debate over innate principles 'altogether needless; and that, if the Question was stated in *common* Words, this Author's [Locke's] Sentiments wou'd not appear so widely different from others, who speak Sense on this Subject' (*Anti-Scepticism,* p.4).

4. The distinction between a naive and a dispositional form of the doctrine of innate knowledge is drawn by J. W. Yolton in *John Locke and the Way of Ideas,* ch.II, sect.I. However, Yolton's description of the naive doctrine (p.29) does not completely fit the doctrine Locke is explicitly attacking. Locke insists that the individual be born with an awareness of innate truths. Yolton allows the naive innatist to claim that the truths are not known till the individual reaches intellectual maturity. Yolton's chapter is, nonetheless, an invaluable account of contemporary criticism of Book I of the *Essay.*

5. *Anti-Scepticism,* p.11.

6. *Anti-Scepticism,* Preface (p.4).

7. cf. Thomas Becconsall: *The Grounds and Foundation of Natural Religion,* p.46; John Milner: *An Account of Mr Locke's Religion,* p.50; William Sherlock: *A discourse Concerning the Happiness of Good Men* (5th ed.), pp.99-100.

8. *Moral Essays,* p.50. The advocates of innate morality also drew support from St Paul's saying that the Gentiles who have not the revealed law nevertheless have by nature 'a law written in their hearts' (*Romans,* II, 14-15). See, for example, Thomas Burnet: *Third Remarks upon an Essay Concerning Humane Understanding,* p.13, and Leibniz: *New Essays Concerning Human Understanding,* Preface, p.43.

9. *Anti-Scepticism,* p.6.

10. Locke is often said to attack the doctrine of innate ideas. However, his aim is to disprove innate propositions, which are the objects of knowledge. That there are no innate ideas is a further argument against the existence of such propositions. For, were there any such, they would be made up of ideas; 'if the *Ideas* be not innate, there was a time, when the Mind was without those Principles; and then, they will not be innate, but be derived from some other Original' (I.vi.I).

11. *A Discourse Concerning the Nature of Man,* p.53.

12. *An Account of Mr Locke's Religion,* p.177.

13. [First] *Remarks,* p.5.

14. *Dialogues,* p.8.

15. ibid., p.11.

16. cf. Lee: 'It's true, there may be occasion to *explain* the Sense of the words of a *practical* Proposition . . . but there needs no Argument to convince any unprejudic'd Person of the Fitness of *observing* it, after he knows the sense of the words' (*Anti-Scepticism,* p.16).

17. cf. W. Hudson: *Ethical Intuitionism,* pp.52-3.

18. cf. Hobbes: '[The] common measure, some say, is *right reason. . .* But commonly they that call for right reason to decide any controversy, do mean their own' (*De Corpore Politico,* Pt.II, ch.10, in *English Works,* Vol.IV, p.225).

19. *Third Remarks,* pp.6-7.

20. Locke's copy of Burnet's *Third Remarks* is in the Yale University Library. I quote throughout from Noah Porter's 'Marginalia Locke-a-na' in the *New England and Yale Review,* vol.7 (1887). Porter's transscriptions have been corrected against the Locke holograph.

21. Sherlock bases much of his defence of innate knowledge on the rejection of Locke's view that to be in the mind is to be perceived: 'The first Question between us, is, Whether any Notion or Idea can be in the Mind, which the Mind does not

actually perceive. That this may be is plain in Fact; for no Man actually perceives any Thing, but what he actually thinks of; yet every Man, every Day he lives, has a thousand Things in his Mind, which he does not actually think of, and so many Ideas he has in his Mind, which he does not perceive. . . . But the second State of the Question is, Whether we can say, that any Ideas are in our Minds, which we did never perceive? I ask, Why not, if they may be there and not perceiv'd? Why may not a Child have such Ideas as he never did perceive, as well as a Man have Ideas which he has no actual Perception of?' (*A Discourse*, p.85).

22. *Discourse Concerning the Happiness of Good Men*, p.100. Hooker, however, rejects innate knowledge. See *Laws of Ecclesiastical Polity*, I.vi.I.

23. The term 'moral sense' seems to have been introduced into ethics by Lord Shaftesbury. See 'An inquiry concerning virtue or merit', in *Characteristics of Men, Manners, Opinions, Times*, ed. Robertson, vol.I, p.262. Shaftesbury is also prepared to call the principles of morality innate ideas. See 'The moralists', in *Characteristics*, vol.II, p.135.

24. *Anti-Scepticism*, p.12.

25. 'An inquiry concerning virtue or merit', in *Characteristics*, vol.I, p.264. Cf. the passage quoted from Clarke in ch.II above, p.36.

26. The definition will be a real definition, that is one which does not simply report the way in which the word 'right' is used, but which purports to give the essential characteristics of rightness.

27. The voluntarist attempts to define moral rightness in terms of God's will is an instance of what G. E. Moore has famously christened the naturalistic fallacy. See *Principia Ethica, passim*. For a history of arguments against this alleged fallacy prior to Moore, see A. N. Prior's *Logic and the Basis of Ethics*.

28. Francis Hutcheson, for example, argues that, in so far as reason is understood as the capacity for finding out truths, it has nothing to do with action: 'Whatever *attribute* can be ascribed to a *generous kind Action*, the *contrary Attribute* may as truly be ascribed to a *selfish cruel Action*: Both Propositions are equally *true*, and the two contrary Actions, the Objects of the two *Truths* are equally *conformable* to their several Truths, with that sort of *Conformity* which is between a Truth and its Object. This Conformity then cannot make a Difference among Actions, or recommend one more than another either to *Election* or *Approbation*, since any Man may make as many Truths about Villainy, as about Heroism, by ascribing to it *contrary Attributes*' (*Illustrations on the Moral Sense*, pp.213-14).

29. cf. Hutcheson: 'as the Author of *Nature* has determin'd us to receive, by our *external Senses*, pleasant or disagreeable Ideas of Objects, according as they are useful or hurtful to our Bodies; and to receive from *uniform Objects* the Pleasures of *Beauty* and *Harmony*, to excite us to the Pursuit of Knowledge, and to reward us for it . . . so he has given us a Moral Sense, to direct our Actions, and to give us still *nobler Pleasures*' (*An Inquiry into the Original of our Ideas of Beauty and Virtue*, Treatise II, Sec.I, VIII).

30. See, for example, John Balguy's criticism of Hutcheson in *The Foundations of Moral Goodness* (Selby-Bigge: *British Moralists*, §528). Cf. Hume's remark to Hutcheson: 'I wish from my Heart, I coud avoid concluding, that since Morality, according to your Opinion as well as mine, is determin'd merely by Sentiment, it regards only human Nature & human Life. . . . If Morality were determin'd by Reason, that is the same to all rational Beings: But nothing but Experience can assure us, that the Sentiments are the same' (*Letters of David Hume*, ed. Greig, vol.I, p.40).

31. As well as criticising the ethics of the *Essay*, Burnet also takes up

Locke's remark that God may have endowed matter with the power of thought (IV.iii.6). In his marginal annotations Locke replies to both criticisms, but pays most attention to Burnet's arguments against his ethical views.

32. *Third Remarks*, pp.7-8.

33. ibid., p.7.

34. ibid., p.15.

35. ibid., p.8.

36. ibid., p.9.

37. Puritanism also is typically suspicious of the category of indifferent things. Hooker, for example, accuses his Puritan opponents of holding 'that one only law, the Scripture, must be the rule to direct in all things, even so far as to the "taking up of a rush or straw"' (*Ecclesiastical Polity*, II.i.2). The Puritan attack on the notion of indifferent things is discussed by Herschel Baker in *The Wars of Truth*, pp.226-9.

38. *Second Remarks*, p.25.

39. 'Every art and every inquiry, and similarly every action and pursuit, is thought to aim at some good; and for this reason the good has rightly been declared to be that at which all things aim' (*Nicomachean Ethics*, I, 1094a 3). This definition is taken over by Aquinas and enters into Scholasticism in general. See, for example, *Summa Theologiae*, Ia. Q5, Art.1.

40. Burnet, who is indifferent whether natural conscience be called '*knowledge*, or *Sense*, or *Instinct*', finds it odd that Locke should deny that the dictates of conscience can be truths unless they are formulated as propositions. To this Locke replies: 'As odd as it is, it is true, yt there is noe truth or falshood but in a verbal or mental proposition' (Porter, p.41).

41. Locke considers this a further argument against innate morality. For if the supposed innate practical principles are to be innately understood as duties, a whole range of ideas must be postulated as innate (I.iii.12).

42. cf. A. N. Prior: *Logic and the Basis of Ethics*, pp.27-8.

43. G. E. M. Anscombe has argued that, in abstracting the moral 'ought' from its setting in a law conception of ethics, modern moral philosophy has deprived the term of any content and reduced it to 'a word of mere mesmeric force'. See 'Modern moral philosophy', in *Philosophy*, 33 (1958).

44. cf. von Leyden's remarks on the intellectualist account of moral obligation in *Essays*, p.53.

45. Thus, we withdraw the hypothetical imperative 'If you want to catch the last train you ought to leave now' when our guest denies any desire to catch the train. But we do not withdraw the moral (categorical) imperative 'You ought to return the silverware you have just pocketed' when our guest denies any desire to do so. The distinction derives mainly from Kant's *Groundwork of the Metaphysic of Morals*.

46. It would seem to be a consequence of Hutcheson's moral sense theory that if we were bereft of the requisite moral sentiments, we could not be under any moral obligations. In Balguy's view, this consequence shows the falsity of Hutcheson's theory: 'Let it be supposed, that we had been formed destitute of natural Affection; and more particularly, that we found in our Hearts no kind Instinct towards our Benefactors: Would Gratitude, upon this Supposition, have been absolutely out of our Power? Might we not nevertheless, by the Help of Reason and Reflection, discover ourselves to be under Obligations, and that we ought to return good Offices or Thanks, according to our Abilities?' (*Foundations*, in Selby-Bigge: *British Moralists*, §S30).

47. In one of his letters to Hutcheson, Gilbert Burnet writes: 'Obligation is a Word of a *Latin* Original, signifying *the Action of Binding*; which therefore, in a *Moral Sense*, . . . must impart the *Binding* An Intellectual Agent by some Law; which can be no other than that of *Reason*' (*Letters between the Late Mr. Gilbert Burnet, and Mr. Hutchinson*, p.63). However, as the term 'law' in 'law of reason' must be understood meta-

phorically, so his rationalist analysis of obligation is metaphorical.

48. The terms 'general obligation' and 'categorical obligation' are borrowed from Prior's *Logic and the Basis of Ethics*, p.41.

49. For an account of an amoral life lived from what may be called an aesthetic point of view see J-K. Huysmans' novel *À Rebours*.

50. *Summa Contra Gentiles*, III, 34. What to Aquinas is foolishness is not even a stumbling-block to an eighteenth-century rationalist such as Richard Price. Talking of the happiness to be enjoyed by the blessed in heaven, he writes: 'the very reward expected is itself virtue; the highest degrees of moral improvement; a near resemblance to God; opportunities for the most extensive beneficence, and admission into a state into which nothing that defileth can enter, and the love and hope of which imply the love of goodness' (*A Review of the Principal Questions in Morals*, ed. Raphael, p.195).

Chapter 4. *Knowledge in the State of Mediocrity*

1. Locke's method in the *Essay* derives from the empiric practice in medicine which he learnt from Thomas Sydenham. In a letter to Thomas Molyneux, 20 January 1693, Locke remarks: 'general theories . . . are for the most part but a sort of waking dreams, with which when men have warm'd their own heads, they pass into unquestionable truths, and then the ignorant world must be set right by them. Tho' this be . . . beginning at the wrong end, when men lay the foundation in their own phansies, and then endeavour to sute the phaenomena of diseases, and the cure of them, to those phansies. I wonder that, after the pattern Dr. Sydenham has set them of a better way, men should return again to that romance way of physick. . . . What we know of the works of nature, especially in the constitution of health, and the operations of our own bodies, is only by the sensible effects. . . . So that there is nothing left for a physician to do, but to observe well, and so by analogy argue to like cases, and thence make to himself rules of practice' (*Correspondence*, 4, pp.628-9). See also Locke's paper 'De Arte Medica', in Bourne, *The Life of John Locke*, vol.I, pp.222-7.

2. Reid's discussion of Locke's ideas is contained in his *Essays on the Intellectual Powers of Man*, II, ix. He writes: 'Philosophers, ancient and modern, have maintained that the operations of the mind, like the tools of an artificer, can only be employed upon objects that are present in the mind. . . . Therefore, objects that are distant in time and place must have a representative in the mind . . . some image or picture of them, which is the object that the mind contemplates. This representative image was, in the old philosophy, called a *species* or *phantasm*. Since the time of Des Cartes, it has more commonly been called an *idea*' (*The Works of Thomas Reid*, ed. Sir William Hamilton, vol.I, p.227).

3. For recent arguments for the interpretation of Locke's ideas as mental acts rather than mental entities, see Douglas Greenlee: 'Locke's idea of "idea"', and 'Idea and object in the essay', both in *Locke on Human Understanding*, ed. I. C. Tipton; A. D. Woozley's Introduction to the Fontana edition of the *Essay*; J. W. Yolton: *Locke on the Compass of Human Understanding*, Ch.5. See also, Yolton: 'On being present to the mind: a sketch for the history of an idea', in *Dialogue* 14 (1975), and 'Ideas and knowledge in seventeenth-century philosophy', in *Journal of the History of Ideas* 13 (1975). This 'unorthodox' interpretation is not entirely a product of modern scholarship. A useful summary of earlier views on the nature of Locke's ideas is given by Justus Buchler in 'Act and object in Locke', in *The Philosophical Review* 46 (1937).

4. cf. Woozley's introduction to the *Essay*, p.33.

5. Locke's ambiguous use of the term 'perception' has been noted by Gunnar Aspelin in '"Idea" and "Perception" in Locke's *Essay*', in *Theoria* 33 (1967).

6. See Norris' *Cursory Reflections upon a Book call'd, An Essay Concerning Human Understanding*, pp.3-4. The term 'idea' was common currency among the Cartesians, from whom Locke takes it over. In the *Port Royal-Logic*, Arnauld remarks that '*idea* is amongst the number of those words which are so clear that they cannot be explained by others, since there is none more clear and simple than themselves' (Pt.I, ch.i). See further, Robert McRae, '"Idea" as a philosophical term in the seventeenth century', in *Journal of the History of Ideas* 26 (1965).

7. See Alexander Fraser, 'Visualization as a chief source of the psychology of Hobbes, Locke, Berkeley and Hume', in *American Journal of Psychology* 4 (1892).

8. In the *Examination of P. Malebranche's Opinion*, §51, Locke puts what appears to be the standard objection against a representative theory of perception. That he does so has been seen by Woozley as strong textual evidence that he cannot himself accept the theory (Introduction to the *Essay*, p.27). But Locke is arguing against Malebranche's 'opinion of seeing all things in God', not against the type of representative theory critics have discerned in the *Essay*. See H. E. Matthews, 'Locke, Malebranche and the Representative Theory', in *The Locke Newsletter*, no.2 (1971).

9. The device Locke is thinking of in this passage has been described by Samuel Alexander in 'Locke's Lantern', in *Mind* 38 (1929).

10. That we cannot know or be certain concerning isolated ideas is further stressed in the *Reply* to Stillingfleet: 'Nor is it one idea by itself, that . . . makes us certain; but certainty consists in the perceived agreement or disagreement . . . of distinct ideas, as they stand in the proposition whose truth or falsehood we would be certain of' (*Works*, 4, p.60).

11. Locke adds that when he talks of reflection as the source of our ideas of the 'operations' of the mind he is using this term 'in a large sense, as comprehending not barely the Actions of the Mind about its *Ideas*, but some sort of Passions arising sometimes from them, such as the satisfaction or uneasiness arising from any thought' (II.i.4).

12. The phrase 'ideas or images of things' recurs in the corresponding passage in Draft B (§18), but in Draft C it is replaced by 'Ideas or representations of things', and in the published *Essay* this becomes 'distinct *Perceptions* of things' (II.i.3).

13. Indeed, it is arguably Locke's opinion that simple ideas are never given singularly; for he writes of the simple idea of '*Unity*, or One' that 'every Object our Senses are employed about; every *Idea* in our Understandings; every Thought of our Minds brings this *Idea* along with it' (II.xvi.1). Cf. P. A. Schouls, 'The Cartesian Method of Locke's *Essay Concerning Human Understanding*', in *Canadian Journal of Philosophy* 4 (1975).

14. There is one passage in the *Essay* in which Locke does use the term 'complex idea' to refer to a *given* combination of ideas, as distinct from a combination of ideas constructed by the mind: ' though they [brutes] take in, and retain together several Combinations of simple *Ideas*, as possibly the Shape, Smell, and Voice of his Master, makes up the complex *Idea* a Dog has of him; or rather are so many distinct Marks whereby he knows him: yet, I *do not* think they do of themselves ever compound them, and *make complex* Ideas' (II.xi.7). However, as Schouls (op. cit.) points out, the passage may be read as providing grounds for the conclusion that Locke does *not* intend 'complex idea' to refer to given combinations of ideas. For, immediately after referring to the dog's complex idea he corrects himself. What

the dog has is not strictly speaking a complex idea of his master, but 'rather . . . so many distinct Marks whereby he knows him'.

15. The abstractionist doctrine of concept formation (which did not originate with Locke) has come in for a good deal of well deserved criticism in recent years. See, for example, P. T. Geach, *Mental Acts*, chs 6-10.

16. Locke was never sure how to classify relations. Although at II.xii.7, they are included as a species of complex idea, he opens that chapter by distinguishing between the mind's act of 'combining several simple *Ideas* into one compound one', and its act of 'setting them by one another, so as to take a view of them at once, without uniting them into one'. The first act is said to be the way 'all Complex *Ideas* are made'; the second to be the way by which the mind 'gets its *Ideas* of Relations' (II.xii.1). In *Essay*, Book III, relations are grouped together with mixed modes and treated more or less as a species of modes (e.g. III.v.16; III.x.33). See further, Aaron, *John Locke*, pp.179-81.

17. See *Locke and the Compass of Human Understanding*, pp.110-11.

18. For other passages which count against Yolton's interpretation, see A. D. Woozley, 'Some remarks on Locke's account of knowledge', in *The Locke Newsletter*, 3 (1972), and Ruth Mattern, 'Locke: "Our knowledge which all consists in propositions"', in the *Canadian Journal of Philosophy*, 8 (1978). Mattern cites the passage from Locke's 'Abstract'.

19. Locke recognises memory as a crucial factor in all of the mind's intellectual operations: 'It is of so great moment, that where it is wanting, all the rest of our Faculties are in a great measure useless: And we in our Thoughts, Reasonings, and Knowledge, could not proceed beyond present Objects' (II.x.8).

20. See R. I. Aaron, *John Locke*, p.238; James Gibson, *Locke's Theory of Knowledge and its Historical Relations*, p.176; J. D. Mabbott, *John Locke*, pp.90-1; D. J. O'Connor, *John Locke*, p.163.

21. Locke also combats dream scepticism. To the contention that what we suppose to be the external world may be 'but the series and deluding appearances of a long Dream', he replies: (1) If the sceptic does suppose that life is a long dream he cannot really question that our senses put us in touch with an external reality, but only dream that he questions it. (2) There is no doubt that some of the things we think of as external objects can be sources of pain to us; and this, as it concerns our happiness or misery, is all we need to know (IV.xi.8).

22. See 'Some remarks on Locke's account of knowledge'.

23. See Yolton's introduction to the Everyman edition of the *Essay*, p.xx, n.1.

24. R. I. Aaron sees Locke as developing two quite separate theories of knowledge: 'He opens Book IV of the *Essay* with a theory of knowledge applicable . . . merely to knowledge of relations between abstract ideas, a universal, hypothetical, and highly abstract knowledge, best typified in mathematics. Another theory becomes necessary for knowledge of particular existences. Consequently, Locke's whole account of knowledge is far from consistent, for he does not even try to remove this dualism or to relate the two theories' *John Locke*, p.246.

25. Locke's account of the knowledge of identity, or diversity, is markedly influenced by his visual model of the mind. He writes: 'A Man infallibly knows, as soon as ever he has them in his Mind that the *Ideas* he calls *White* and *Round*, are the very *Ideas* they are, and that they are not other *Ideas* which he calls *Red* or *Square*' (IV.i.4). Clearly, what Locke has in mind is our immediate sensory recognition of the sameness or difference of particular material objects.

26. Locke does not claim the corpuscular theory of matter to be

certainly true. He accepts it only as the hypothesis which goes 'farthest in an intelligible Explication of the Qualities of Bodies; and I fear that Weakness of humane Understanding is scarce able to substitute another' (IV.iii.16).

27. In outlining a causal theory of perception with respect to primary qualities, Locke writes, 'since the Extension, Figure, Number, and Motion of Bodies of an observable bigness, may be perceived at a distance *by* the sight, 'tis evident some singly imperceptible Bodies must come from them to the Eyes, and thereby convey to the Brain some *Motion,* which produces these *Ideas,* which we have of them in us' (II.viii.12). At times, however, he appears to equate secondary qualities with the 'sensible qualities' of bodies (e.g. II.viii.14 and 23). This suggests that he holds the primary qualities of bodies never to be the objects of our senses. He does point out in the *Elements of Natural Philosophy* that, strictly speaking, we do not *see* the primary quality of figure or shape: 'Besides colour, we are supposed to see figure: but, in truth, that which we perceive when we see figure, as perceivable by sight, is nothing but the termination of colour' (*Works,* 3, p.325).

28. cf. IV.xii.12: 'In the Knowledge of Bodies, we must be content to glean, what we can, from particular Experiments: since we cannot from a Discovery of their real Essences, grasp at a time whole Sheaves; and in bundles, comprehend the Nature and Properties of whole Species together. Where our Enquiry is concerning Coexistence, or Repugnancy to co-exist, which by Contemplation of our *Ideas,* we cannot discover; there Experience, Observation, and natural History, must give us by our Senses, and by retail, an insight into corporeal Substances. The Knowledge of Bodies we must get by our Senses, warily employed in taking notice of their Qualities, and Operations on one another'.

29. See *Critique of Pure Reason,* B4. (trans. Kemp Smith, pp.43-4).

30. Locke's Journal entry for 26 June 1681 begins, 'There are two sorts of knowledg in the world generall and particular founded upon two different principles, i.e. true Ideas and matter of fact or history' (Aaron and Gibb, p.116). At IV.vi.7, in the *Essay* he briefly contrasts experimental and universal knowledge.

31. cf. Locke's letter to William Molyneux, 20 January 1693: 'This I do say, that there are real constitutions in things from whence those simple ideas flow, which we observ'd combined in them. And this I farther say, that there are real distinctions and differences in those real constitutions one from another; whereby they are distinguished one from another, whether we think of them or name them or no. But that that whereby we distinguish and rank particular substances into sorts or genera and species, are not those real essences or internal constitutions, but such combinations of simple ideas as we observe in them' (*Correspondence,* 4, p.626).

32. See especially Boyle's *The Origin of Forms and Qualities According to the Corpuscular Philosophy,* first published in 1666. Locke's debt to Boyle is examined at length by Bill Barger in *Locke on Substance.*

33. cf. Locke's *Second Reply* to Stillingfleet: 'the difficulty to me is, to conceive an universal nature, or universal any thing, to exist; which would be, in my mind, to make an universal a particular: which, to me, is impossible' (*Works,* 4, p.166).

34. cf. II.xxiii.11: 'Had we Senses acute enough to discern the minute particles of Bodies, and the real Constitution on which their sensible Qualities depend, I doubt not but they would produce quite different *Ideas* in us; and that which is now the yellow Colour of Gold, would then disappear, and instead of it we should see an admirable Texture of parts of a certain Size and Figure. This Microscopes plainly discover to us'.

35. There is a further reason why the real essence of a body which makes it what it is is unknowable by us. Though we consider each particular body to be 'an entire thing by it self, having all its Qualities in it self, and independent of other Things', bodies are in fact 'Retainers to other parts of Nature' for most of the qualities they exhibit (IV.vi.11). Knowledge of the real essence of one substance, then, is likely to involve knowledge of the physical world as a whole. Locke most probably takes this point from Boyle. See *The Origin of Forms and Qualities,* in *Works,* ed. Birch, (1744) vol.2, p.464.

36. Aaron, for example, maintains that Locke's way of ideas makes it impossible for him to provide any criterion for the agreement of ideas with things (*John Locke,* p.238). For a different reading see Kathy Squadrito: 'The Essay 4.4.3', in *The Locke Newsletter,* no.9, (1978).

Chapter 5. *Ideas, Language and Moral Notions*

1. Locke also mentions a second, private use of words: men use them 'to record their own Thoughts for the Assistance of their own Memory' (III.ii.2). But his main interest is in words as vehicles of communication.

2. See Norman Kretzmann: 'The main thesis of Locke's semantic theory'.

3. cf. Kretzmann, 'The main thesis of Locke's semantic theory' *passim.*

4. See Jonathan Bennett: *Locke, Berkeley, Hume: Central Themes,* p.1.

5. The classic argument against the possibility of a private language is to be found in Wittgenstein's *Philosophical Investigation,* pt.I, §§243-80. There are, however, almost as many different interpretations of Wittgenstein's argument as there are commentators upon it. For a comparison of the linguistic theories of Wittgenstein and Locke, see Godfrey Vesey: 'Locke and Wittgenstein on language and reality', in *Contemporary British Philosophy,* 4th series.

6. Locke recognises these two options: 'when they [children] have got the skill to apply the Organs of Speech to the framing of articulate Sounds, they begin to make *Use of Words,* to signify their *Ideas* to others: These verbal Signs they sometimes borrow from others, and sometimes make themselves, as one may observe among the new and unusual Names Children often give to things in their first use of Language' (II.xi.8).

7. See, for example, William P. Alston: *Philosophy of Language,* pp.24-5.

8. The objection set out here applies equally to complex ideas thought of as images. For a more detailed criticism, see Jonathan Bennett, *Locke, Berkeley, Hume,* pp.11-20.

9. See Kretzmann, 'The main thesis of Locke's semantic theory', p.132.

10. In John Horne Tooke's opinion Locke is mistaken in supposing that he is giving an account of ideas existing independently of language. On the contrary, 'the *whole* of Mr. Locke's Essay [is] a philosophical account of the *first* sort of abbreviations in Language [i.e. terms]'. See, *The Diversions of Purley,* pt.I, ch.ii.

11. Ian Hacking has argued that Locke is not concerned to develop what modern philosophers call a theory of meaning. Rather, he is interested in the theory of signification, and this is quite different to a theory of linguistic meaning. See Hacking: *Why does Language Matter to Philosophy?,* ch.v. However, *pace* Hacking, Locke does use the word 'mean' as well as the word 'signify', and he states quite explicitly that the *meaning* of words is the ideas they are made to stand for.

12. Locke defends his use of the word 'idea' and his distinction between notions and ideas in his *Reply* to Stillingfleet: 'For that notion will not so well stand for every immediate object of the mind in thinking, as idea does, I have . . . somewhere given a reason in my book; by showing that

the term notion is more peculiarly appropriated to a certain sort of those objects, which I call mixed modes: and, I think, it would not sound altogether so well, to say the notion of red, and the notion of a horse, as the idea of red, and the idea of a horse' (*Works*, 4, p.133).

13. As we have seen, it is only propositions and not ideas which are strictly true or false. When in ordinary discourse we term an idea true or false there is, Locke maintains, 'still some secret or tacit Proposition, which is the Foundation of that Denomination' (II.xxxii.1).

14. Locke does say that 'essence', even when used in the sense of the real constitution existing within a thing, '*relates to a Sort*, and supposes a *Species*: For being that real Constitution, on which the Properties depend, it necessarily supposes a sort of Things, Properties belonging only to *Species*, and not to Individuals'. He continues, 'there is no individual parcel of Matter, to which any ... Qualities are so annexed, as to be *essential* to it, or unseparable from it ... take away the consideration of its being ranked under the name of some abstract *Idea*, and then there is nothing necessary to it, nothing inseparable from it' (III.vi.6). Locke is not, as it might seem, retracting his thesis that an individual body has a real essence which makes it what it is. Rather, he is underlining the difference between essence *qua* internal constitution and *qua* sortal concept. A property, say, yellowness, is essential to (the sort of thing) gold solely because we have included it in our abstract idea of gold. Hence, we can say of an individual identified as a lump of gold that it *must* be yellow. As, by hypothesis, its yellowness is causally dependent upon its internal constitution, we can also say that it *must* have the real essence (which is unknown to us) which causes yellowness. It is because our talk of essential properties is thus dependent on our having framed abstract ideas that we cannot talk of anything as essential to, or necessarily belonging to, a bare unnamed particular body. The body itself exists as it is quite independent of any of our ideas. Suppose that it is yellow, yellowness cannot be said to be essential to it; but then neither can the internal constitution or real essence, upon which the sensible property of yellowness depends, be essential to it.

15. The distinction between 'form' and 'matter' applied here (as well as much else in this chapter) has been taken from Julius Kovesi's *Moral Notions*.

16. Thus Locke writes that 'it is not enough, for the avoiding Inconveniences in Discourses and Arguings about natural Bodies and substantial Things, to have learned ... the common but confused ... *Idea*, to which each Word is applied ... but we must, by acquainting our selves with the History of that sort of Things, rectify and settle our complex *Idea*, belonging to each specifick Name. ... It were therefore to be wished, That Men, versed in physical Enquiries, and acquainted with the several sorts of natural Bodies, would set down those simple *Ideas*, wherein they observe the Individuals of each sort constantly to agree' (III.xi.24-5). In Locke's view, the compilation of natural histories to a large extent takes the place of the unattainable science of body. See Yolton: *Locke and the Compass of Human Understanding*, pp.72-5.

17. As Locke puts it: 'Should there be a Body found, having all the other Qualities of Gold, except Malleableness, 'twould, no doubt, be made a question whether it were Gold or no. ... This could be determined only by that abstract *Idea*, to which every one annexed the name *Gold*: so that it would be true Gold to him ... who included not Malleableness in his nominal Essence ...; and on the other side, it would not be true Gold ... to him, who included Malleableness in his specific *Idea*' (III.vi.35).

18. Some 'lower level' moral notions are much broader than

others. Thus we get a far vaguer picture of what was actually done when we are told that a person committed an act of cruelty or ingratitude than when we are told that he committed a murder or theft. An action falling under a broad notion such as 'cruelty', may be further specifiable in terms of a narrower notion. The material element in an act of cruelty might, for example, be murder. But there is no necessity that what falls under a broad moral notion should also fall under a narrow one. The point made here is that, if an action really is right or wrong, good or bad, it must fall under some notion which itself falls under the highest level notions of right, wrong, good and bad. These latter notions, it is worth noting, are not exclusively moral notions.

19. We may, of course, have a variety of different interests with respect to the substances we find in the world, and hence classify them from different points of view. From a practical point of view, for example, we can develop a classificatory scheme according to which particular substances are grouped together as they are similar in respect of the use we can make of them. Such a scheme will divide the world of substances quite differently to one based on similarity in respect of sensible qualities; for things which are quite dissimilar in appearance may still have the one use. However, the ideas which constitute the pigeon-holes in this scheme will be archetypes. The use a thing has for us is not something belonging to it quite independently of us. In finding a use for a substance we are not copying anything in the world, but measuring the substance against a standard we have thought up.

20. cf. Kovesi: *Moral Notions,* pp.111-12.

21. On the 'openness' of moral notions, see Kovesi: *Moral Notions,* ch.IV.

22. In the case of taking the madman's sword we would probably be prepared if pressed to say that, given the circumstances, it was not really stealing. On the other hand, we would probably rate the taking of a crucial document from the enemy in time of war as stealing but not wrongful stealing.

23. cf. Kovesi's account of the notion 'savingdeceit' in *Moral Notions,* p.106f.

Chapter 6.
Morality and Demonstration

1. Pufendorf devotes Bk.I, ch.ii of *De Jure Naturae et Gentium* to a defence of the view that morality can be set forth in a demonstrative system. Locke warmly recommends Pufendorf's work in his educational writings. See *Concerning Education* §186 and *Concerning Reason and Study,* in *The Educational Writings of John Locke,* ed. Axtell, pp.294, 400. For Locke's possible debt to Cumberland's *De Legibus Naturae,* see James Gibson's 'Locke's theory of mathematical knowledge and of a possible science of ethics', in *Mind* 5 (1896). Locke's claim itself influenced Jean Barbeyrec's lengthy account of the history of moral philosophy prefixed to his translation of Pufendorf's *De Jure.*

2. cf. Leibniz, 'On Locke's Essay on Human Understanding' in *New Essays Concerning Human Understanding and Other Writings,* tr. Langley, p.17; and Sergeant, *Solid Philosophy Asserted,* pp.406-7.

3. Introduction to the *Two Tracts,* p.48.

4. See J. A. Passmore, 'Descartes, the British empiricists, and formal logic', in *The Philosophical Review* 62.

5. Similarly Descartes attacks formal logic on the grounds that an argument in syllogistic form can only tell us what we already know: 'Dialecticians are unable to devise any syllogism which has a true conclusion, unless they have first secured the material out of which to construct it, that is unless they have already ascertained the very truth which is

deduced in that syllogism. Whence it is clear that from a formula of this kind they can gather nothing that is new, and hence the ordinary Dialectic is quite valueless for those who desire to investigate the truth of things' (*Rules for the Direction of the Mind,* Rule x, *Works,* tr. Haldane & Ross, vol.1, p.32).

6. According to Locke, the source of the erroneous belief that maxims are the indispensable foundations of knowledge is the practice of scholastic disputation: 'The Schools have made Disputation the Touchstone of Mens Abilities, and the *Criterion* of Knowledge, adjug'd Victory to him that kept the field.... But because by this means there was like to be no Decision between skilful Combatants ... certain general Propositions, most of them indeed self-evident, were introduced into the Schools, which ... were look'd on as general Measures of Truth, and serv'd instead of Principles ... beyond which there was no going.... And thus these *Maxims* getting the name of *Principles* ... were by mistake taken to be the Originals and Sources, from whence all Knowledge began, and the Foundations whereon the Sciences were built' (IV.vii.11).

7. Thus Archbishop Whately (with whom the revived study of logic began in England) maintains that Locke and those who have followed him in criticising traditional logic have completely misunderstood the nature of the science: 'For Logic, which is, as it were, the Grammar of Reasoning, does not bring forward the regular Syllogism as a distinct mode of argumentation, designed to be *substituted* for any other mode; but as the form to which *all* correct reasoning may be ultimately reduced: and which, consequently, serves the purpose (when we are employing Logic as an *art*) of a test to try the validity of any argument' (*Elements of Logic,* 9th ed., p.8).

8. See *New Essays,* IV.vii.9 (Langley, p.470). The issue between Leibniz and Locke over the role of maxims is discussed in detail by Margaret Wilson in 'Leibniz and Locke on "First Truths"', in *Journal of the History of Ideas* 28 (1967).

9. See *New Essays,* IV.xii.6 (Langley, p.523): 'what [Locke has] said regarding the connection of ideas as the true source of truths needs explication. If you are willing to content yourself with the confused sight of this connection, you weaken the exactness of demonstration.... Yet if you wish this connection of ideas to be distinctly seen and expressed, you will be obliged to recur to definitions and identical axioms.'

10. As Leibniz states his position in 'On Locke's Essay on Human Understanding': 'nothing should be taken as first principles but experiences and the axiom of identity or (what is the same thing) contradiction, which is primitive, since otherwise there would be no difference between truth and falsehood; and all investigation would cease at once, if to say yes or no were a matter of indifference' (Langley, pp.13-14).

11. See *New Essays,* IV.vii.10 (Langley, p.471).

12. Locke talks of reason as a faculty in order to distinguish his use of the term from other uses (IV.xvii.1). But he has earlier been careful to state that in his usage the word 'faculty' does not signify any kind of distinct entity acting in its own right. A faculty is simply an ability or power to act (II.xxi.17). Human beings do not reason because they are possessed of something which is itself able to reason; they themselves have the ability to reason.

13. cf. R. I. Aaron, *John Locke,* p.225. Aaron remarks that in Locke's usage 'to perceive an agreement [between ideas] may mean perceiving a relation within propositions or, again, it may mean perceiving a relation, namely, implication between propositions'. Aaron makes no attempt to explain or justify this double usage.

14. In a letter to Molyneux (26 April 1695) Locke mentions his

additional chapter on the association of ideas as treating of a phenomenon 'which has not, that I know, been hitherto consider'd' (*Correspondence,* 5, p.353). But as A. C. Fraser points out, the association of ideas as described by Locke had been recognised by a succession of writers from Aristotle onwards, and most especially by Hobbes. See Fraser's edition of the *Essay,* note 1 to II.xxxiii.

15. It has been argued by Leon Roth in *Descartes' Discourse on Method,* ch.VII, that there is a radical difference between the account of demonstration found in the drafts and that published in the *Essay.* In the drafts demonstration is said to establish truth not by proof but by intuition (Draft A, §27; Draft B, §44). According to Roth, the published account of demonstration as a chain of intuitions involving mediate ideas is the fruit of Locke's study of Descartes, a study which postdates the writings of Drafts A and B. But, while it is certainly true that the 'chain conception' is much more exactly stated in the *Essay,* the view that demonstration involves the introduction of mediate ideas is present, at least in embryo, in 'Draft A'. For this is surely the point of Locke's remark about the employment of a standard measure in mathematical demonstration. When Locke characterises demonstration as intuitive rather than by proof, he is not, as Roth supposes, equating it with immediate intuition; he is denying that demonstration is a matter of formal proof. This denial is, of course, completely in accord with the doctrine of the *Essay.*

16. cf. *Essay,* IV.xiii.2: 'as far as Men's Senses are conversant about external Objects, the Mind cannot but receive those *Ideas,* which are presented by them, and be informed of the Existence of Things without: and so far as Men's Thoughts converse with their own determined *Ideas,* they cannot but, in some measure, observe the Agreement, and Disagreement that is to be found amongst some of them, . . . and if they have Names for those *Ideas* . . . they must needs be assured of the Truth of those Propositions, which express that Agreement, or Disagreement, they perceive in them, and be undoubtedly convinced of those Truths. For what a Man sees, he cannot but see; and what he perceives, he cannot but know that he perceives'.

17. 'Locke's Theory of Mathematical Knowledge and of Possible Science of Ethics', in *Mind* 5 (1896), p.39.

18. In Drafts A and B Locke does restrict demonstration to the sphere of mathematics: 'we [know] by demonstration noething but the equality or inequality of quantitys compard & their several proportions. . . . And this is the knowledge we have of the truth or falsehood of propositions wherein magnitudes or numbers are predicated one of another which can be noe otherwise but as biger or lesse or equall. & also of all other things that are measureable by number or extension, as motion, time weight &c.' (Draft A, §12; cf. Draft B, §§44-6).

19. Indeed, if the truth or falsity of materialism is to be determined by some kind of seeing in the mind's eye, a materialist like Hobbes might be thought to have the better case: 'though men may put together words of contradictory signification, as *Spirit,* and *Incorporeall*; yet they can never have the imagination of any thing answering to them' (*Leviathan,* I, xii).

20. Locke puts forward his own theory of definition as an improvement on the scholastic method of defining *per genus et differentia.* See III.iii.10.

21. See R. S. Woolhouse, *Locke's Philosophy of Science and Knowledge,* p.12.

22. '*By* determinate, *when applied to a* simple Idea, *I mean that simple appearance, which the Mind has in its view, or perceives in it self, when that Idea is said to be in it: By* determined, *when applied to a* complex

Idea, *I mean such an one as consists of a determinate number of certain simple or less complex Ideas, joyn'd in such a proportion and situation as the Mind has before its view, and sees in it self when that Idea is present in it, or should be present in it, when a Man gives a name to it. I say* should *be: because it is not every one, nor perhaps any one, who is so careful of his Language, as to use no Word, till he views in his Mind the precise* determined *Idea, which he resolves to make it the sign of'* (Preface to the Reader, p.13). This passage was added to the fourth edition of the *Essay.* In the body of the work Locke frequently uses the term 'clear and distinct idea'.

23. Woolhouse (*Locke's Philosophy of Science,* p.16) maintains that in acknowledging that there are universal propositions which are both instructive and certain, Locke departs from the position he adopts in Draft A: 'all Universall propositions that are certain are only verball or words applyd to our owne Ideas & not instructive: & vice-versa all universall propositions that are instructive (i.e. informe us any thing about the nature qualitys & operations of things existing without us) are all uncertain' (§27). However, as the passage in parenthesis shows, by 'propositions that are instructive' Locke means those which say something about substances in the world. In the *Essay* such universal propositions (at least if they are of an unrestricted generality) are still considered, for the most part, to be uncertain. Further, in the same draft Locke states that 'Mathematicall universall propositions are both true & instructive because as those Ideas are in our mindes soe are the things without us' (§30).

24. See, for example, James Gibson, *Locke's Theory of Knowledge,* pp. 135-6; Thomas Webb, *The Intellectualism of Locke,* ch.VI; Woolhouse, *Locke's Philosophy of Science and Knowledge,* esp. ch.I. See also, A. C. Ewing, *A Short Commentary on Kant's Critique of Pure Reason,* p.18, n.1. Kant himself finds a hint of his own distinction in Locke, see *Prolegomena to any Future Metaphysic,* §3. This 'standard' interpretation of Locke's trifling/instructive distinction has recently been attacked by Sybil Wolfram; 'On the Mistake of Identifying Locke's Trifling-Instructive Distinction with the Analytic-Synthetic Distinction', in *The Locke Newsletter* no.9 (1978). See also Robert G. Meyers, 'Locke, Analyticity and Trifling Propositions', and Wolfram, 'Locke's Trifling-Instructive Distinction – A Reply' (to Meyers), both in *The Locke Newsletter,* no.10 (1979) and no.11 (1980) respectively.

25. Woolhouse, *Locke's Philosophy of Science,* p.3.

26. Locke considers the predication of a genus term of a species which falls under it to be but a shorthand way of indicating several of the simple ideas contained in the complex idea the species term stands for. See III.iii.9-10.

27. cf. Woolhouse, *Locke's Philosophy of Science,* pp.52-6.

28. Compare Berkeley's argument against the mathematician's notion of an infinitely divisible finite extension: 'Every particular finite extension, which may possibly be the object of our thought, is an *idea* existing only in the mind, and consequently each part thereof must be perceived. If therefore I cannot perceive innumerable parts in any finite extension that I consider, it is certain they are not contained in it: but it is evident, that I cannot distinguish innumerable parts in any particular line, surface, or solid, which I either perceive by sense, or figure to my self in my mind: wherefore I conclude they are not contained in it. Nothing can be plainer to me, than that the extensions I have in view are no other than my own ideas, and it is no less plain, that I cannot resolve any one of my ideas into an infinite number of other ideas, that is, that they are not infinitely divisible' (*Principles of Human Knowledge,* §124).

29. Woolhouse, *Locke's Philosophy of Science*, pp.38-45; 52-6.

30. Locke does, at least in the case of the notions of lying and murder, attempt to present his analysis in terms of a list of simple ideas. The notions of a lie, for example, is said to be 'made of these simple *Ideas*: 1. Articulate Sounds. 2. Certain *Ideas* in the Mind of the Speaker. 3. Those words the signs of those *Ideas*. 4. Those signs put together by affirmation or negation, otherwise than the *Ideas* they stand for, are in the mind of the Speaker'. He goes on to remark that this list 'is enough to shew, that it [the complex idea] is made up of simple *Ideas*: And it could not but be an offensive tediousness to my Reader, to trouble him with a more minute enumeration of every particular simple *Idea*, that goes to this complex one' (II.xxii.9). The fact that no-one could be brought to understand what lying is by being given this list is enough to show its inadequacy as an analysis of the notion; and 'more minute enumeration' of simple ideas along the same lines could hardly do other than compound the confusion.

31. In illustration of the way in which our moral notions may be incomprehensible to those whose way of life is entirely different, it is instructive to recall the problems Gulliver encounters when he tries to explain the comparatively straightforward notion of lying to the naturally virtuous Houynhnm. See Jonathan Swift, *Gulliver's Travels*, pt.IV, ch.IV.

32. Henry Lee remarks that on Locke's showing 'the Reason why Morality may be demonstrated, is because every one making his Ideas of Virtues and Vices, according to his Fancy, he will be upon as sure Grounds as if he demonstrated, because no body will be able to judge but himself, whether his Ideas be right or wrong, and consequently he can never be confuted' (*Anti-Scepticism*, p.235). As Locke does explicitly maintain that the individual may misuse moral terms and have incorrect notions of justice, etc., this criticism is completely unjustified.

33. *Philosophical Commentaries*, 690 (ed. Luce, p.245). Cf. Locke's statement that *'to enumerate all the mixed Modes*, which have been settled, with Names to them ... would be to make a Dictionary of the greatest part of the Words made use of in Divinity, Ethicks, Law, and Politicks, and several other Sciences' (II.xxii.12). Berkeley also remarks, presumably with the two propositions at IV.iii.18 in mind, that 'Locke's instances of Demonstration in Morality are according to his own Rule trifling Propositions', *Commentaries*, 691.

34. Von Leyden conjectures that 'Of Ethick in General' was written while Locke was living in exile in Holland, that is, between September 1683 and February 1689 (*Essays*, p.69). However, the criticism of definition or analysis as a means to genuine moral knowledge is already to be found, in much the same words, in Draft A, dating from 1671. Compare Draft A, §25, and 'Of Ethick in General' §24.

35. cf. Locke's Journal entry for 26 June 1681: 'he that has a true Idea of god of himself as his creature or the relation he stands in to god and his fellow creatures and of Justice goodness law happynesse &c. is capable of knowing morall things or have a demonstrative certainty in them ... I doe not say that presently he hath thereby that certain knowledge ... he may believe others that tell him soe but know it not till he hath imploid his thoughts on it and seen the connection and agreement of those Ideas and soe made to himself the demonstration i.e. upon examination seen it to be soe' (Aaron & Gibb, pp.116-17).

36. Many of Locke's contemporary critics seized on passages such as this as evidence that he was committed to moral relativism. In a footnote to II.xxviii.11, added to the second edition of the *Essay* and addressed specifically to the criticisms of James Lowde, Locke states 'I was there, not

laying down moral Rules, but shewing the original and nature of moral *Ideas*, and enumerating the Rules Men make use of in moral Relations, whether those Rules were true or false: and pursuant thereunto I tell, what has everywhere that denomination, which in the language of that place answers to *Vertue* and *Vice* in ours, which *alters not the nature of things*, though Men generally do judge of, and denominate their actions according to the esteem and fashion of the Place or Sect they are of'. See also, Locke's letter to James Tyrrell, 4 August 1690 (*Correspondence*, 4, pp.110-13).

37. In the first edition of the *Essay* Locke refers to the third law as the 'philosophical law', 'not because Philosophers make it, but because they have most busied themselves to enquire after it, and talk about it' (II. xxviii.10). He might have in mind Aristotle's view that moral philosophy cannot attain to demonstrative certainty, but must be content to draw its findings from an investigation of opinions held by 'the wise and the many'. See *Nicomachean Ethics*, I, 3-4.

38. *Logick: or, the Right Use of Reason in the Enquiry after Truth*, pt.4, ch.i, 11th ed., 1755, pp.314-15.

39. ibid., p.314.

40. ibid., p.316.

41. At III.xi.9, Locke uses the term 'analysis' to refer to this procedure.

42. The 'fundamental truth' that all our ideas originate in experience may be seen as giving direction to Locke's analysis of ideas such as 'number' and 'infinity' in Book Two of the *Essay*.

43. cf. Aaron, *John Locke*, p.262.

Chapter 7. *The Origins of Moral Notions*

1. cf. Hans Aarsleff: 'The state of nature and the nature of man', in *John Locke, Problems and Perspectives*, ed. Yolton, p.104.

2. One of the major theses of the *Second Treatise* is 'That all Men are naturally in that State [of Nature], and remain so, till by their own Consents they make themselves Members of some Politick Society' (§15).

3. See, for example, Peter Laslett: Introduction to *Two Treatises of Government*, pp.94-5 and C. E. Vaughan: *Studies in the History of Political Philosophy before and after Rousseau*, vol.1, p.163. See also Morton White: 'Original sin, natural law, and politics' in the *Partisan Review*, 23 (1956). White sees Locke as contradicting the doctrine of the *Essay* not in that he makes the law of nature innate, but in that he holds its precepts to be self-evident.

4. cf. Locke's marginal annotation to Burnet's *Third Remarks*: 'Men have a natural tendency to what delights and from what pains them. This universal observation has established past doubt' (Porter, p.38).

5. cf. *A Letter Concerning Toleration*: 'the pravity of mankind being such, that they had rather injuriously prey upon the fruits of other men's labours than take pains to provide for themselves; the necessity of preserving men in the possession of what honest industry has already acquired, and also of preserving their liberty and strength, whereby they may acquire what they farther want, obliges men to enter into society with one another; that by mutual assistance and joint force they may secure unto each other their properties, in the things that contribute to the comfort and happiness of this life' (*Works*, 6, p.42).

6. cf. *Leviathan*, pt.II, ch.xvii: 'For the Lawes of Nature . . . of themselves, without the terrour of some Power, to cause them to be observed, are contrary to our naturall Passions, that carry us to Partiality, Pride, Revenge, and the like'.

7. cf. Richard Ashcraft: 'Locke's state of nature: historical fact or moral fiction?' in *The American Political Science Review*, 62 (1968).

8. Locke does add that 'there have been a number of people ever since who have assented to this doctrine very eagerly' (*Essays*, p.205).

9. According to Hobbes 'the first, and Fundamentall Law of Nature . . . is, *to seek Peace, and follow it*' (*Leviathan*, pt.1, ch.xiv).

10. '*Want of a common Judge with Authority, puts all Men in a State of Nature: Force without Right, upon a Man's Person, makes a State of War,* both where there is, and is not, a common Judge' (*2nd Treatise*, §19).

11. cf. *Essay*, p.157: '[Man] feels himself not only to be impelled by life's experience and pressing needs to procure and preserve a life in society with other men, but also urged to enter into society by a certain propensity of nature and to be prepared for the maintenance of society by the gift of speech and through the intercourse of language'. Contrast Hobbes: 'men have no pleasure, (but on the contrary a great deale of griefe) in keeping company, where there is no power able to overawe them all' (*Leviathan*, pt.1, ch.xiii).

12. Locke goes on to argue that the first cause cannot be material. His proof of God's existence owes a great deal to Cudworth's *True Intellectual System*. See the Journal entry for 18 February 1682 in Aaron & Gibb, p.118.

13. In the *First Treatise* Locke argues at length against the thesis that parents have authority over their children because they make them and give them life. On the contrary, God is the only one who can be truly said to make a human being: '[His] Fatherhood is such an one as utterly excludes all pretence of Title in Earthly Parents; for he is *King* because he is indeed Maker of us all, which no Parents can pretend to be of their Children' (§53).

14. My own account of Locke's concept of property in one's own person is heavily indebted to James Tully's brilliant exposition in his *A Discourse on Property*, pp.104-10.

15. Locke's account of personal identity in terms of sameness of consciousness is put forward as an alternative to an account in terms of the sameness of substance whether material or immaterial. See II.xxvii.16, etc.

16. Locke gives an instance of such intentional knowledge at IV.xi.7: 'Thus I see, whilst I write this, I can change the Appearance of the Paper; and by designing the Letters, tell before-hand what new *Idea* it shall exhibit the very next moment, barely by drawing my Pen over it'. Cf. Tully, *A Discourse on Property*, p.108.

17. cf. *Second Treatise*, §46: 'of those good things which Nature hath provided in common, every one . . . had a Property in all that he could affect with his Labour: all that his Industry could extend to, to alter from the State Nature had put it in, was his'. See also Tully, *A Discourse on Property*, pp.116-17 and A. W. Sparkes, 'Trust and teleology: Locke's politics and his doctrine of creation', in the *Canadian Journal of Philosophy* 3 (1973).

18. Locke's doctrine of common ownership is argued in opposition to Sir Robert Filmer's doctrine that by 'Donation of God, Adam was made sole Proprietor of the whole earth' (*1st Treatise*, §41). See also *Second Treatise*, §1.

19. This entry was brought to my attention by Dr John Anglim.

20. On Locke's Golden Age and subsequent stages in the state of nature, see John Anglim: 'On Locke's state of nature', in *Political Studies*, 26 (1978), and Richard Ashcraft: 'Locke's state of Nature: historical fact or moral fiction?', in *The American Political Science Review*, 62 (1968).

21. Prior to the Fall man knew not 'ye difference between good & evill' (MS c.28, Fol.113).

22. The transition from the first stage of property rights to the stage at which they are settled by compacts is described in the *Second Treatise*, §45: '*Labour*, in the Beginning, *gave a Right of Property*, where-ever any one was pleased to imploy it, upon what was common . . . and though afterwards, in some parts of the

World, (where the Increase of People and Stock, with the *Use of Money*) had made Land scarce . . . the several *Communities* settled the Bounds of their distinct Territories, and by Laws within themselves, regulated the Properties of the private Men of their Society, and so, *by Compact* and Agreement, *settled the Property* which Labour and Industry began'.

23. cf. *Second Treatise*, §173: 'By *Property* I must be understood here, as in other places, to mean that Property which Man have in their Persons as well as Goods'.

24. cf. *Second Treatise*, §5 where Locke mentions 'the Judicious Hooker's' 'great Maxims of *Justice* and *Charity*'.

25. For a chilling picture of what Locke takes to be the demands of charity with respect to paupers see his scheme for poor relief submitted to the Board of Trade during the session of 1697. The document is quoted in full in Fox Bourne's *Life*, vol.II, pp.377-91, and its tone may be gathered from Locke's remark that to the 'belly-full of bread' with which children in working schools are to be daily provided 'may be also added, without any trouble, in cold weather, if it be thought needful, a little warm water-gruel; for the same fire that warms the room may be made use of to boil a pot of it'.

26. In 'Virtus' justice is mentioned only as one among other virtues such as temperance and mercy the bounds of which are determined by 'the good or Evil, they are like to produce'.

27. It should be noted that Locke adopts the positive formulation of the Golden Rule. Compare Hobbes who favours the negative formulation, *'Do not that to another, which thou wouldest not have done to thy selfe'* (*Leviathan*, pt.I, ch.xv).

28. The modes of pleasure and pain are simple and 'the way of knowing them is, as of the simple *Ideas* of the Senses, only by Experience. For to define them by the Presence of Good or Evil, is no otherwise to make them known to us, than by making us reflect on what we feel in our selves, upon the several and various Operations of Good and Evil upon our Minds, as they are differently applied to, or considered by us' (II.xx.I).

29. cf. 'Of Ethick in General': 'it cannot be supposed yt any men should assocate togeather & unite in the same Comunity & at ye same time allow yt for Comendable i.e. count it a virtue nay not discountenance & treat such actions as blameable i.e. count them vices wch tend to ye dissolution of yt society in wch they were united' (MS c.28, §5, and in King, 2, p.126).

30. cf. Ethica (1692): 'Love all the world as you doe your childe or self and make this universal and how much short will it make the earth of heaven' (MS c.42, Fol.224).

31. In the *First Treatise* Locke glances in the direction of a sexual morality derived from the law of nature: 'Adultery, Incest and Sodomy . . . are . . . Sins, which I suppose, have their Principle Aggravation from this, that they cross the main intention of Nature, which willeth the increase of Mankind, and the continuation of the Species in the highest perfection, and the distinction of Families, with the Security of the Marriage Bed, as necessary thereunto' (§59). One difficulty here is that on Locke's first premise a deliberately chosen life of celibacy would also appear condemned as vicious.

Chapter 8. *The Moral Agent*

1. Locke throughout accepts the causal principle 'that what ever had a beginning had a cause without its self that gave it a beginning i.e. made it be' as a truth of which we have certain knowledge. See Draft A, §16; Draft B, §140, *Essay*, IV.x.3.

2. It is because we do not ascribe thought to material objects that we do not ascribe freedom to them either: 'A Tennis-ball, whether in motion by the stroke of a Racket, or lying still at rest, is not by any one taken to be a *free Agent*. If we enquire into the Reason, we shall find it is,

because we conceive not a Tennis-ball to think, and consequently not to have any Volition, or preference of Motion to rest, or *vice versa*; and therefore has not *Liberty*, is not a free Agent; but all its both Motion and Rest, come under our *Idea* of *Necessary*, and are so call'd' (II.xxi.9).

3. Locke is often credited with being the first philosopher to attack the faculty theory of the will. However, J. A. Passmore has shown that Ralph Cudworth, at least, precedes him in this, and it is likely that Locke's own criticism derives from Cudworth. See Passmore's *Ralph Cudworth*, pp.93-5.

4. cf. the definition given in Locke's Journal entry for 13 July 1676: 'Willing *voluntas* i.e. wherein the minde doth after consideration or at least some thought begin continue change or stop some action which it finds in its power soe to doe' (Aaron & Gibb, p.80).

5. cf. A. C. Fraser's footnote 3 to *Essay*, II.xxi.26 (vol.2, p.328).

6. cf. Hooker's definition of willing: 'To choose is to will one thing before another. And to will is to bend our souls to the having or doing of that which they see to be good' (*Ecclesiastical Polity*, I.vii.2). Locke quotes this definition in a Journal entry (which King dates 26 June 1681) and follows it by a definition of his own which parallels that in his entry for 13 July 1676 (MS f.5, Fol.84-5. See King, I, p.228).

7. In a letter to Molyneux (15 July 1693) Locke remarks that it was 'by observing only the mistake of one word (viz. having put things for actions . . .) I got into a new view of things, which, if I mistake not, will satsifie you, and give a clearer account of humane freedom than hitherto I have done' (*Correspondence*, 4, p.700). The mistake to which Locke refers occurs in his discussion of whether we are free to will or not will. At II.xxi.25 and 28 of the first edition, he poses the question in terms of whether we are free to will or not will any 'thing' once it is proposed to our thoughts as in our power. In later editions these passages are rewritten replacing the word 'thing' by 'action'. But Locke does not elaborate, and it is by no means clear why he supposes his original use of 'thing' to be a mistake nor how his noticing it gave rise to the modifications in his view of freedom. However, this and a subsequent letter to Molyneux (*Correspondence*, 4, p.722) include useful summaries of his new conception of freedom.

8. See Berkeley's pointed criticism: 'Uneasiness precedes not every Volition This evident by experience' (*Philosophical Commentaries*, 628, ed. Luce, p.221).

9. In Draft C and the first four editions of the *Essay* Locke included an infinite regress argument in support of his view that the agent cannot be free to will or not will once an action is proposed to him: 'to make a Man free in this sense, there must be another antecedent *Will*, to determine the Acts of this *Will*, and another to determine that, and so *ad infinitum*: for where-ever one stops, the Actions of the last Will cannot be free: Nor is any Being, as far as I can comprehend Beings above me, capable of such a freedom of Will, that it can forebear to *Will, i.e.* to preferr the being, or not being of any thing in its power, which it has once considered as such' (II.xxi.23, 1st ed.). Presumably this argument is deleted because Locke has come to realise that the suspension of uneasiness is something we do freely without an antecedent act of willing to do it, and that our doing it does involve our neither willing nor not willing a proposed action.

10. At IV.xvii.4, Locke shows how the proposition 'Men can determine themselves' can be demonstrated given the truth of the proposition 'Men shall be punished in another world'.

11. Locke uses the world 'determinable' in the corresponding passage in Draft C and the first edition of the *Essay*.

12. Bishop Butler may be cited as an example of a philosopher who rejects egoistic hedonism as a psychological theory while accepting a basically hedonistic theory of reasons for actions. In the sermon 'Upon the Love of our Neighbour' he brings forward decisive objects against egoistic hedonism as a general theory of action. Nonetheless, he concludes with an assertion of the hedonistic theory of reasons. See *Butler's Fifteen Sermons*, ed. W. R. Matthews, pp.168, 181-2.

13. Jean le Clerc, for example, was puzzled by Locke's assertion that uneasiness initiates all our actions: 'On pourroit seulement demander si ce plaisir, ou cette *easiness* . . . est toûjours de telle nature que malgré cela l'esprit ne puisse se determiner du côté opposé. . . . Au moins il me semble qu' en mille choses je puis fair, ou non, et que je ne me détermine que parce que je le veux, sans trouver plus de plaisir d'un côté que d'une autre' (*Correspondence*, 5, p.104). In reply Locke distinguishes between the successive uneasiness which for the most part determine our will, but which we might resist; the violent uneasiness which we cannot resist; and completely indifferent actions, such as putting on a right or left shoe first, in which the motive of uneasiness appears to be absent. Yet he goes on to explain that uneasiness enters in even with respect to these unimportant actions. For they are mixed up with the significant actions of our lives in which 'the minde is determined by some sensible uneasinesse'; and consequently in them we are prompted to do one thing rather than another by the mind's general 'desire and necessity of dispatch, that it may not be hindered in the pursuit of what is judgd of more moment by a lingring suspence between equall and indifferent things . . . and in these the uneasiness of delay is sufficient to determin and give the preference to one it matters not which side' (*Correspondence*, 5, pp.159-60). But here surely the concept of uneasiness is spread so thin as to become very nearly empty of content.

14. cf. Richard Norman, *Reasons for Actions*, p.78. However, Norman points out that it would be a mistake to suppose this the only correct way of looking at all human action. It is merely a corrective to the opposite view that all actions are a case of the agent being detached by some force from his normal state of inaction.

15. The fact that we explain those human actions in which we think of the agent as acting freely in terms of his reasons rather than in terms of antecedent causes is not itself sufficient to refute the determinist thesis. It might be argued that even when reasons can be given for what a person does there is always also a causal explanation which is, in some sense, more fundamental.

16. Locke states that 'The great Excellency and Use of the Judgment, is to observe Right, and take a true estimate of the force and weight of each Probability; and then casting them up all right together, chuse that side, which has the over-balance' (IV.xvii.16).

17. See Pascal's *Pensées*, trans. A. J. Kailsheimer, §418, pp.149-53. As Locke had a copy of the *Pensées* in his library it is likely that his argument is borrowed directly from Pascal.

18. cf. 'Of Ethick in General': 'rewards & punishm:ts are the good and evill whereby superiors enforce the observance of their laws it being impossible to set any other motive or restraint to ye actions of a free understanding agent but the consideration of good or evill that is pleasure or pain yt will follow from it' (MS c28, §8; and in King, 2, p.129).

19. The same sentiment is expressed of 'Ethica B': 'Happynesse is a continuation of content without any molestation. Very imperfect in this world noe body happy here. certain. May be perfect in an other world possible. probable' (MS c28, Fol.141).

20. Similarly, at the beginning of the *Education* Locke writes: 'I think I may say, that of all the Men we meet

with, Nine Parts of Ten are what they are, Good or Evil, useful or not, by their Education. 'Tis that which makes the great Difference in Mankind' (§1). Again, in the *Conduct of the Understanding,* he emphasises that 'the difference, so observable in men's understandings and parts, does not arise so much from natural faculties as acquired habits' (*Works,* 3, p.215).

21. In Locke's opinion the consequence of Adam's fall for his posterity is only bodily death. His main reason for rejecting the doctrine that the first transgression has rendered us all liable to eternal punishment and placed us under the necessity of sinning is that it would be contrary to God's justice and goodness so to condemn His creatures for a fault they had not actually committed. See *The Reasonableness of Christianity,* in *Works,* 7, pp.4-10. See also the Commonplace Book entries 'queres concerning y[e] Imputation of Adams Sin to his Posterity', 1692 (Commonplace Book in the Library of Arthur A. Houghton, Jr.), and 'Homo ante et post lapsum' 1693 (MS c28, Fol.113).

22. This power of denying ourselves the satisfaction of our desires is one with the power to suspend uneasiness which Locke sees as essential to human freedom. The power is itself innate, but we need to be brought to exercise it. As Locke puts it in the *Conduct,* 'We are born with faculties and powers capable of almost anything . . . but it is only the exercise of those powers which gives us ability and skill in any thing, and leads us towards perfection' (*Works,* 3, p.213). See also Locke's remark in the *Second Treatise*: 'we are *born Free,* as we are born Rational; not that we have actually the Exercise of either: Age that brings one, brings with it the other too' (§61).

23. According to Lady Masham, Locke thought civility 'not only the great ornament of life, and that that gave lustre and gloss to all our actions, but looked upon it as a Christian duty that deserved to be more inculcated as such than it generally was'. Quoted in Fox Bourne's *Life,* Vol.II, p.533.

24. On the mistake of assimilating pleasures to feelings or sensations, see Gilbert Ryle's 'Pleasure' in *Dilemmas,* pp.54-67.

Conclusion.
Locke's Moral Philosophy

1. *John Locke,* pp.266-7.

2. ibid., p.254.

3. In fact in such a world the institution of promising could not exist, for it is internal to the notion of some utterance being a promise that the utterer intends to place himself under an obligation to perform what is promised. Locke has at least some appreciation of the fact that the rule 'promises ought to be kept' is logically part of what it is for there to be promises. See his remark in 'Morality' that if the compacts men enter into are to be broken then 'their making signifies noething'.

4. cf. Bishop Butler: 'some of great and distinguished merit have, I think, expressed themselves in a manner which may occasion some danger to careless readers, of imagining the whole of virtue to consist in singly aiming, according to the best of their judgment, at promoting the happiness of mankind in the present state; and the whole of vice in doing what they foresee, or might foresee, is likely to produce an overbalance of unhappiness in it; – than which mistakes none can be conceived more terrible. For it is certain, that some of the most shocking instances, of injustice, adultery, murder, perjury, and even of persecution, may, in many supposable cases, not have the appearance of being likely to produce an overbalance of misery in the present state; perhaps sometimes may have the contrary appearance'. Dissertation II, 'Of the Nature of Virtue', appended to *The Analogy of Religion.*

5. cf. A. P. Brogan: 'John Locke and utilitarianism', in *Ethics* 69 (1959).

6. Hooker refuses to confine the term 'law' to 'a rule of working which

superior authority imposeth', but includes under it 'any kind of rule or canon, whereby actions are framed' (*Ecclesiastical Polity*, I.iii.1). Nevertheless, he holds that all things other than God work according to a law 'whereof some superior, unto whom they are subject, is author' (ibid., I.ii.2). See further note 256 to Otto Gierke's *Political Theories of the Middle Age*, trans. Maitland, pp.172-4.

7. *Ecclesiastical Polity*, I.vii.9. John Wild considers Locke's scepticism concerning knowledge of real essences to be evidence that he cannot be included within the natural law tradition. See *Plato's Modern Enemies and the Theory of Natural Law*, pp.128-9.

8. Hooker says of form as it belongs to inanimate creatures that it 'is a thing proportionable unto the soul in living creatures' (*Ecclesiastical Polity*, I.iii.4, footnote). Compare Locke's likening of the unknown internal constitution of material substances to 'the inward contrivance of that famous Clock at *Strasburg*' (III.vi.9).

9. See Boyle's *Disquisition about the Final Causes of Natural Things* (1688). Descartes denies the explanatory value of final causes on the grounds that the ends which God intends things to serve are beyond our comprehension. See *The Principles of Philosophy*, I, xxviii; also *Meditation IV*, and *Reply to Objection V*, in Haldane and Ross, vol.I, pp.230-1; p.173; vol.II, p.223.

10. cf. K. E. M. Baier: *The Meaning of Life*, pp.18f.

11. Locke often likens the relation between God and men to that between a father and his children. For example, at II.xxi.53, he writes: 'God, ,who knows our frailty, pities our weakness, and requires of us no more than we are able to do, and sees what was, and what was not in our power, will judge as a kind and merciful Father'. It is worth noting that not all of Locke's readers endorse this amiable sentiment. In one copy of the *Essay* in the National Library of Scotland, the above passage is annotated with the terse comment, 'God made Mr. Locke, now Mr. Locke makes God'.

12. The principles are '[such] things as soon as they are alleged, all men acknowledge to be good; they require no proof or further discourse to be assured of their goodness' (*Ecclesiastical Polity*, I.viii.5).

BIBLIOGRAPHY

Aaron, Richard I. *John Locke*. 3rd ed. Oxford 1973.

Aarsleff, Hans. 'Some observations on recent Locke scholarship' in *John Locke – Problems and Perspectives*. Ed. J. W. Yolton. Cambridge 1969.

—— 'The state of nature and the nature of man' in *John Locke – Problems and Perspectives*. Ed. J. W. Yolton. Cambridge 1969.

Alexander, Samuel. 'Locke's lantern'. *Mind 38* (1929) 271.

Alston, William P. *Philosophy of Language*. Englewood Cliffs, N.J. 1964.

Ames, William. *Conscience with the Power and Cases Thereof*. [London?] 1639.

Anglim, John. 'On Locke's state of nature'. *Political Studies* 26 (1978) 78-90.

Anscombe, G. E. M. 'Modern moral philosophy'. *Philosophy* 33 (1958) 1-19.

Aquinas, St Thomas. *Summa Contra Gentiles*. Trans. Vernon J. Bourke. Notre Dame 1975.

—— *Summa Theologiae*, vol.2 (1a 2-11). *Existence and Nature of God*. Trans. Timothy McDermott. London 1963.

—— *Summa Theologiae*, vol.18 (1a 2ae 18-21). *Principles of Morality*. Trans. Thomas Gilby. London 1965.

—— *Summa Theologiae*, vol.28 (1a 2ae 90-97). *Law and Political Theory*. Trans. Thomas Gilby. London 1966.

Aristotle. *Nicomachean Ethics*. Trans. Sir David Ross. Oxford 1966.

Arnauld, Antoine. *The Art of Thinking. (Port Royal Logic)*. Trans. James Dickoff and Patricia James. Indianapolis 1964.

Ashcraft, Richard. 'Locke's state of nature: historical fact or moral fiction?'. *The American Political Science Review* 62 (1968) 906-7.

Aspelin, Gunnar. '"Idea" and "Perception" in Locke's Essay'. *Theoria* 33 (1967) 278-83.

Bagshaw, Edward. *The Great Question Concerning Things Indifferent in Religious Worship*, 3rd ed. London 1660.

—— *The Second Part of the Great Question Concerning Things Indifferent in Religious Worship*. London 1661.

Baier, K. E. M. *The Meaning of Life*. Inaugural Lecture delivered at Canberra University College, 1957. Canberra 1957.

Baker, Herschel. *The Wars of Truth: Studies in the decay of Christian Humanism in the earlier seventeenth century*. Cambridge, Mass. 1952.

Balguy, John. *The Foundations of Moral Goodness*, in *British Moralists*. Ed. L. A. Selby-Bigge. Vol.2. Oxford 1897.

Barbeyrac, Jean. *An Historical and Critical Account of the Science of Morality*, in *The Law of Nature and Nations*, by Samuel Pufendorf. Ed. Jean Barbeyrac, trans. Basil Kennett. London 1729.

Barger, Bill. *Locke on Substance.* Manhattan Beach, California 1976.

Becconsall, Thomas. *The Grounds and Foundation of Natural Religion, Discovered in the Principal Branches of it, in Opposition to the Prevailing Notions of the Modern Scepticks and Latitudinarians.* London 1698.

Bennett, Jonathan. *Locke, Berkeley, Hume: Central Themes.* Oxford 1971.

Berkeley, George. *Philosophical Commentaries.* Ed. A. A. Luce. London 1944.

—— *The Principles of Human Knowledge.* Ed. T. E. Jessop. London 1945.

Bourne, H. R. Fox. *The Life of John Locke.* 2 vols. New York 1876.

Boyle, Robert. *A Disquisition about the Final Causes of Natural Things,* in *The Works of the Honourable Robert Boyle.* Ed. Thomas Birch. Vol.5. London 1772.

—— *The Origin of Forms and Qualities according to the Corpuscular Philosophy,* in *Works,* vol.3. London 1772.

Bréhier, Emile. 'The creation of the eternal truths in Descartes' system', in *Descartes: A Collection of Critical Essays.* Ed. Willis Doney. London 1968.

Brogan, A. P. 'John Locke and utilitarianism'. *Ethics 69* (1959) 79-93.

Buchler, Justus. 'Act and object in Locke', *The Philosophical Review 46* (1937) 528-35.

[Burnet, Thomas] *Remarks upon an Essay Concerning Humane Understanding: in a Letter Addres'd to the Author.* London 1697.

—— *Second Remarks upon an Essay Concerning Humane Understanding: in a Letter Addres'd to the Author.* London 1697.

—— *Third Remarks upon an Essay Concerning Humane Understanding: in a Letter Addres'd to the Author.* London 1699.

Butler, Joseph. *Fifteen Sermons Preached at the Rolls Chapel,* and *A Dissertation upon the Nature of Virtue.* Ed. W. R. Matthews. London 1964.

Calvin, John. *Institutes of the Christian Religion.* Trans. Henry Beveridge. 2 vols. London 1962.

Clarke, Samuel. *A Demonstration of the Being and Attributes of God: More Particularly in Answer to Mr. Hobbes, Spinoza, and their Followers.* London 1705.

—— *A Discourse Concerning the Unchangeable Obligations of Natural Religion, and the Truth and Certainty of the Christian Revelation.* London 1706.

Cox, Richard H. *Locke on War and Peace.* Oxford 1960.

Cragg, G. R. *From Puritanism to the Age of Reason.* Cambridge 1950.

Crowe, Michael Bertram. *The Changing Profile of the Natural Law.* The Hague 1972.

Cudworth, Ralph. *The True Intellectual System of the Universe,* and *A Treatise concerning Eternal and Immutable Morality.* Ed. John Harrison. 3 vols. London 1845.

Cumberland, Richard. *A Treatise of the Laws of Nature (De Legibus Naturae).* Trans. John Maxwell. London 1727.

Descartes, René. *The Philosophical Works.* Trans. Elizabeth S. Haldane and G. R. T. Ross. 2 vols. Cambridge 1967.

Dialogues Concerning Innate Principles. Containing an Examination of Mr. Locke's Doctrine on that Subject. [Anon.] London 1779.

Ewing, A. C. *A Short Commentary on Kant's Critique of Pure Reason.* London 1961.

Fraser, Alexander. 'Visualization as a chief source of the psychology of Hobbes, Locke, Berkeley and Hume'. *American Journal of Psychology* 4 (1892) 230-47.

Gassendi, Pierre. *Lettre sur le Livre de Lord Edouard Herbert, Anglais, De La Verite.* Trans. Bernard Rochet, in *Actes du Congrès du Tricentenaire de Pierre Gassendi.* Paris 1957.

Geach, Peter. *Mental Acts: Their Content and Their Objects.* London 1971.

Gibson, James. *Locke's Theory of Knowledge and its Historical Relations.* Cambridge 1917.

—— 'Locke's theory of mathematical knowledge and of a possible science of ethics'. *Mind* 5 (1896) 38-59.

Gierke, Otto. *Political Theories of the Middle Age.* Trans. F. W. Maitland. Cambridge 1951.

Greenlee, Douglas. 'Locke's idea of "idea"', *Theoria* 33 (1957) 98-106.

—— 'Idea and object in the *Essay*', in *Locke on Human Understanding.* Ed. I. C. Tipton. Oxford 1977.

Grotius, Hugo. *The Law of War and Peace (De Jure Belli ac Pacis Libri Tres).* Trans. Francis W. Kelsey. Oxford 1925.

Hacking, Ian. *Why does Language Matter to Philosophy?* Cambridge 1975.

Hobbes, Thomas. *Leviathan,* in *The English Works of Thomas Hobbes.* Ed. Sir William Molesworth. Vol.3. London 1839.

—— *De Corpore Politico, or The Elements of Law,* in *English Works,* vol.4. London 1840.

—— *Human Nature, or The Fundamental Elements of Policy,* in *English Works,* vol.4. London 1840.

—— *The Questions Concerning Liberty, Necessity and Chance,* in *English Works,* vol.5. London 1841.

Hooker, Richard. *Of the Laws of Ecclesiastical Polity.* 2 vols. Everyman Library. London 1907.

Hudson, W. D. *Ethical Intuitionism.* London 1967.

Hume, David. *Letters of David Hume.* Ed. J. Y. T. Greig. 2 vols. Oxford 1969.

Hutcheson, Francis. *An Essay on the Nature and Conduct of the Passions and Affections. With Illustrations on the Moral Sense.* London 1728.

—— *An Inquiry into the Original of our Ideas of Beauty and Virtue.* London 1735.

—— *Letters between the Late Mr. Gilbert Burnet, and Mr. Hutcheson.* London 1735.

Huysmans, J-K. *Against Nature (À Rebours).* Trans. Robert Baldick. Penguin Books, Harmondsworth 1959.

Kant, Immanuel. *Critique of Pure Reason.* Trans. Norman Kemp-Smith. London 1968.

—— *Groundwork of the Metaphysics of Morals.* Trans. H. J. Paton. London 1962.

—— *Prolegomena to any Future Metaphysics.* Trans. Peter G. Lucas. Manchester 1953.

King, Peter, Lord. *The Life of John Locke, with extracts from his correspondence, Journals, and Common-Place Books.* 2 vols. London 1830.

Kovesi, Julius. *Moral Notions.* London 1967.

Kretzmann, Norman. 'The main thesis of Locke's semantic theory', *Philosophical Review* 77 (1968) 175-96.

Lee, Henry. *Anti-Scepticism: or, Notes upon each Chapter of Mr. Locke's Essay Concerning Humane Understanding.* London 1702.

Leibniz, Gottfried. *New Essays Concerning Human Understanding, together with some of his shorter pieces.* Trans. A. G. Langley. Chicago 1949.

Lenz, John W. 'Locke's essays on the law of nature'. *Philosophy and Phenomenological Research* 17 (1956-7) 105-13.

Little, David. *Religion, Order, and Law: A Study in Pre-Revolutionary England.* Oxford 1970.

Locke, John. *The Lovelace Collection of the papers of John Locke in the Bodleian Library.* Oxford.

—— *The Correspondence of John Locke.* Ed. E. S. de Beer. 8 vols. Oxford 1976- .

—— *Discourses: Translated from Nicole's Essays by John Locke.* Ed. Thomas Hancock. London 1828.

—— *The Educational Writings.* Ed. James Axtell. Cambridge 1968.

—— *Epistola de Tolerantia.* Ed. Raymond Klibansky, trans. J. W. Gough. Oxford 1968.

—— *An Early Draft of Locke's Essay together with Excerpts from his Journals.* (Draft A). Eds R. I. Aaron and Jocelyn Gibb. Oxford 1936.

—— *Draft A of Locke's essay Concerning Human Understanding.* Ed. Peter H. Nidditch. University of Sheffield 1980.

—— *An Essay Concerning the Understanding, Knowledge, Opinion and Assent.* (Draft B). Ed. Benjamin Rand. Cambridge, Mass. 1931.

—— *An Essay Concerning humane understanding in fouer books.* 1685. (Draft C). Xerox of the MS in the Pierpont Morgan Library, New York.

—— *An Essay Concerning Human Understanding.* Ed. A. C. Fraser. 2 vols. New York 1959.

—— *An Essay Concerning Human Understanding.* Ed. Peter H. Nidditch. Oxford 1975.

—— *Essays on the Law of Nature, together with transcripts of Locke's shorthand in his Journal for 1676.* Ed. W. von Leyden. Oxford 1965.

—— *Two Tracts on Government.* Ed. Philip Abrams. Cambridge 1967.

—— *Two Treatises of Government.* Ed. Peter Laslett. Cambridge 1963.

—— *The Works of John Locke.* 10 vols. London 1823.

Lowde, James. *A Discourse Concerning the Nature of Man, Both in his Natural and Political Capacity, Both as he is a Rational Creature, and Member of a Civil Society.* London 1694.

—— *Moral Essays; Wherein some of Mr. Locke's and Monsir Malbranch's Opinions are briefly examin'd.* London 1699.

Mabbott, J. D. *John Locke.* London 1973.

McRae, Robert. '"Idea" as a philosophical term in the seventeenth century'. *Journal of the History of Ideas* 26 (1965) 175-90.

Martineau, James. *Types of Ethical Theory.* 2 vols. Oxford 1889.

Mattern, Ruth Marie. 'Locke: "Our Knowledge which all consists in propositions"'. *Canadian Journal of Philosophy* 8 (1978) 677-95.

Matthews, H. E. 'Locke, Malebranche and the Representative Theory'. *The Locke Newsletter*, no.2 (1971).

Meyers, Robert G. 'Locke, analyticity and trifling propositions'. *The Locke Newsletter*, no.10 (1979).

Mill, John Stuart. *Three Essays on Religion.* London 1904.

Miller, Perry. *The New England Mind: the Seventeenth Century.* Cambridge, Mass. 1967.

[Milner, John] *An Account of Mr. Locke's Religion, Out of his Own Writings, and in his Own Words.* London 1700.

Milton, John. *De Doctrina Christiana.* Trans. Charles R. Sumner, in *The Works of John Milton*, vols.15-16. New York 1934.

—— *Paradise Lost.* Birmingham 1759.

Moore, G. E. *Principia Ethica.* Cambridge 1903.

More, Henry. *An Antidote against Atheisme*, in *Philosophical Writings of Henry More.* Ed. Flora Isabel Mackinnon. Oxford 1925.

Norman, Richard. *Reasons for Actions.* Oxford 1971.

Norris, John. *Cursory Reflections upon a Book Call'd An Essay Concerning Human Understanding. In a Letter to a Friend.* London 1690. The Augustan Reprint Society, no.93. Los Angeles 1961.

O'Connor, D. J. *John Locke.* Penguin Books, Harmondsworth 1952.

Pascal, Blaise. *Pensées.* Trans. A. J. Kailsheimer. Penguin Books, Harmondsworth 1966.

Passmore, John A. 'Descartes, the British empiricists, and formal logic'. *The Philosophical Review* 62 (1953) 545-53.

—— *Ralph Cudworth: an interpretation.* Cambridge 1951.

Perkins, William. *A Discourse of Conscience*, in *William Perkins: 1558-1602, English Puritanist.* Ed. Thomas F. Merrill. Nieuwkoop 1966.

Porter, Noah. 'Marginalia *Locke*-a-na'. *New Englander and Yale Review* 7 (1887) 33-49.

Price, Richard. *A Review of the Principal Questions in Morals.* Ed. D. D. Raphael. Oxford 1974.

Prior, Arthur N. *Logic and the Basis of Ethics.* Oxford 1961.

Pufendorf, Samuel. *Of the Law of Nature and Nations (De Jure Naturae et Gentium).* Trans. Basil Kennett, with the Notes of Jean Barbeyrac. London 1729.

Reid, Thomas. *Essays on the Intellectual Powers of Man*, in *The Works of Thomas Reid.* Ed. Sir William Hamilton. Vol.1. Edinburgh 1872.

Roth, Leon. *Descartes' Discourse on Method.* Oxford 1937.

Ryle, Gilbert. 'Conscience and moral convictions'. *Analysis* 7 (1940) 31-9.

—— 'Pleasure', in *Dilemmas.* Cambridge 1960.

Sanderson, Robert. *De Obligatione Conscientiae*, with English notes, including an abridged translation by William Whewell. Cambridge 1879.

Schouls, P. A. 'The Cartesian method of Locke's *Essay Concerning Human Understanding*'. *Canadian Journal of Philosophy* 4 (1975) 579-601.

Selden, John. *Table Talk.* Ed. S. W. Singer. London 1847.

[Sergeant, John] *Solid Philosophy asserted, against the Fancies of the Ideists: or, the Method to Science Farther Illustrated. With Reflexions on Mr. Locke's Essay concerning Human Understanding.* London 1697.

Shaftesbury, Anthony Ashley Cooper, third Earl. *Characteristics of Men, Manners, Opinions, Times.* Ed. John M. Robertson. 2 vols. London 1900.

Sherlock, William. *A Discourse Concerning the Happiness of Good Men, and the Punishment of the Wicked, in the Next World.* 5th ed. London 1735.

Sparkes, A. W. 'Trust and teleology: Locke's politics and his doctrine of creation'. *Canadian Journal of Philosophy 3* (1973) 263-73.

Squadrito, Kathy. 'The Essay 4.4.3'. *The Locke Newsletter*, no.9 (1978).

Strauss, Leo. *Natural Right and History.* Chicago 1965.

Swift, Jonathan. *Gulliver's Travels.* Oxford 1959.

Taylor, Jeremy. *Ductor Dubitantium, or the Rule of Conscience*, in *The Whole Works of Jeremy Taylor*, vol.3. London 1835.

Tipton, I. C. (ed.) *Locke on Human Understanding.* Oxford 1977.

Tooke, John Horne. *The Diversions of Purley.* London 1860.

Tully, James. *A Discourse on Property: John Locke and his Adversaries.* Cambridge 1980.

Vaughan, C. E. *Studies in the History of Political Philosophy before and after Rousseau.* Ed. A. G. Little. 2 vols. New York 1960.

Vesey, Godfrey. 'Locke and Wittgenstein on language and reality'. *Contemporary British Philosophy: 4th Series.* Ed. H. D. Lewis. London 1976.

Von Leyden, W. 'John Locke and natural law'. *Philosophy 31* (1956) 23-35.

—— *Seventeenth Century Metaphysics.* London 1971.

Wallace, W. A. 'Scientia', article in *The Catholic Encyclopedia.* Vol.12. New York 1967.

Watt, Isaac. *Logick: or, The Right Use of Reason in the Enquiry after Truth.* 11th ed. London 1755.

Webb, Thomas E. *The Intellectualism of Locke: An Essay.* Dublin 1857.

Whately, Richard. *Elements of Logic.* 9th ed. London 1851.

White, Morton. 'Original sin, natural law, and politics'. *Partisan Review 23* (1956) 218-36.

Wild, John. *Plato's Modern Enemies and the Theory of Natural Law.* Chicago 1953.

Wilkins, John. *Of the Principles and Duties of Natural Religion.* 5th ed. London 1704.

Wilson, Margaret D. 'Leibniz and Locke on "First Truths"'. *Journal of the History of Ideas 28* (1967) 347-66.

Wittgenstein, Ludwig. *Philosophical Investigations.* Trans. G. E. M. Anscombe. Oxford 1963.

Wolfram, Sybil. 'On the mistake of identifying Locke's trifling-instructive distinction with the analytic-synthetic distinction'. *The Locke Newsletter*, no.9 (1978).

—— 'Locke's Trifling-Instructive Distinction – A Reply'. *The Locke Newsletter*, no.11 (1980).

Woodhouse, A. S. P. *Puritanism and Liberty.* 2nd ed. London 1974.

Woolhouse, R. S. *Locke's Philosophy of Science and Knowledge.* Oxford 1971.

Woozley, A. D. Introduction to the Fontana Library abridgement of Locke's *Essay.* London 1968.

Woozley, Anthony D. 'Some remarks on Locke's account of knowledge'. *The Locke Newsletter*, no.3 (1972).

Yolton, John W. Introduction to the Everyman edition of Locke's *Essay*. London 1961.

—— *John Locke and the Way of Ideas*. Oxford 1956.

—— *Locke and the Compass of Human Understanding*. Cambridge 1970.

—— 'Locke on the law of nature'. *Philosophical Review* 67 (1958) 477-98.

—— 'On being present to the mind: a sketch for the history of an idea'. *Dialogue 14* (1975) 373-88.

—— 'Ideas and knowledge in seventeenth-century philosophy'. *Journal of the History of Philosophy 13* (1975) 145-65.

—— (ed.) *John Locke: Problems and Perspectives*. Cambridge 1969.

INDEX